Curiosities of Art and Nature

The new annotated and illustrated edition of Martin Martin's classic

A Description of the Western Islands of Scotland

The Islands Book Trust, launched in 2002, is based in the Ness district of the island of Lewis in the Outer Hebrides. The Trustees, half of whom are residents of Ness, aim to make a substantial contribution to the islands by promoting appreciation and use of the large collections in Ness now available to the public, developing links with the Northern Isles and other Nordic areas, continuing programmes of talks and visits, and producing further publications on related subjects. The Trust issues a quarterly newsletter.

Duntulm c1815
(From: William Daniel: A Voyage round the North and North-West Coast of Scotland)

Curiosities of Art and Nature

The new annotated and illustrated edition of Martin Martin's classic

A Description of the Western Islands of Scotland

Edited by Michael Robson

Published by **The Islands Book Trust**
10 Callicvol
Port of Ness
Isle of Lewis
HS2 0XA

2003

Printed and bound by Kelso Graphics, The Knowes, Kelso, Scottish Borders TD5 7BH.
Telephone: (01573) 223214 • Fax: (10573) 229944

ISBN 0 9546238 1 9

This book was published with the support of the following:

Heritage Lottery Fund

Contents

Page

Acknowledgements

The task of editing has been made much easier, and even possible, by numerous people, for whose help we are extremely thankful. We are especially grateful to:

Argyll and Bute Library Service, John Ballantyne, Mary Beith, British Library, Maureen Byers, Mary Carmichael, Andrew Currie, Heather Dewar, Camille Dressler, Edinburgh University Library (Special Collections), Alison Fraser, Ian Fraser, Jack Gibson, Leiden University, Donald and Margaret McCusbig, John Angus McCusbig, Jonathan Macdonald, Maggie Macdonald, Iain Maciver, Angela Macleod, Donald MacRury, William Macsporran, Angus John Macvicar, John Marsden, John Moore, Donald Morrison, Donnie Morrison, National Archives of Scotland, National Library of Scotland, Orkney Library and Archive, Owners of MS Collections (incl. Macdonald Papers at Clan Donald Centre, Macleod Muniments at Dunvegan Castle), Royal Society Library, Brian Smith, Margaret Storrie, Western Isles Library Service, Peter Youngson; other authors of the many books, from Martin himself onwards, about the Hebrides and the Northern Isles.

Without the assistance of Annabel Mackenzie the book would never have been prepared for publication in 2003, and without people, too many to name, over the years it would never have been possible even to attempt a new edition.

List of Illustrations

Note on the Illustrations

The older illustrations are intended to suggest the scene and how it was understood in Martin's lifetime, while the photographs provide a modern view of some of the things he wrote about three centuries ago.

Foreword

Martin Martin's book on the Western Islands of Scotland, whose tercentenary we celebrate this year, is a most remarkable work. It is the first detailed account of the islands, which as the author notes in his Preface were in 1703 'but little known, or considered, not only by Strangers, but even by those under the same Government and Climate.' Moreover, unlike most of the accounts which followed, Martin was a native of the islands and a Gaelic speaker. He was therefore in a unique position to describe the early customs and beliefs of the islanders from the inside.

His book was one of the main triggers for the 'discovery' of the islands by the outside world in the succeeding two centuries. Indeed, we know from James Boswell that Dr Johnson carried a copy of Martin with him during his famous tour in 1773, and that despite Johnson's criticisms of the book it played an important part in his decision to visit the islands.

But Martin's book was emphatically not like many of the dozens which followed. While concerned to cover the natural history as well as the human history of the islands, Martin did not describe the scenery – an aspect which became a major theme of the Romantic movement's view of the Hebrides. It is not a guide book, and does not mention some of the features such as Fingal's Cave which later were established as highlights on the itineraries of future travellers.

Instead, Martin aimed to present a first hand account of a little known area in a spirit of scientific observation and with a view to improving the circumstances of those who lived there. Of course, he had his prejudices. There are many references to 'pagan and Papist superstitions' which he believed were 'ridiculous' and an obstacle to progress. He believed that agriculture should be improved and that the Government should encourage a fishing trade to the economic benefit of the islanders.

Even though Martin talked about the many 'Curiosities of Art and Nature' which he encountered, he did not do so in the romantic way which characterised many later accounts of the Hebrides. He spoke of the 'Natural Beauty' which many islanders demonstrated, and of 'the successful Practice of the Islanders in the preservation of their Health', but he was not sentimental. His observations were always precise and grounded in fact.

It cannot be denied, as Johnson uncharitably pointed out, that Martin Martin's book has defects. It is not clearly structured, and contains a hotch-potch of loosely related material covering the natural world, customs and religion, antiquities and monuments, diseases and cures, and suggestions for economic development. It moves from island to island in an unpredictable manner, missing out some, and including others such as Orkney and Shetland which might appear to be outwith the geographical scope of the title. It shows every sign of having been put together hurriedly.

But for all that, it is a veritable goldmine of information, and by far our most detailed early account of the islands. It forms a natural choice for the first publication of The Islands Book Trust, based in the island of Lewis, which aims to promote historical knowledge and comparative research of Scottish islands in their wider Celtic and Nordic setting. The Trust also aims to bring together islanders and outside experts to discuss historical themes in the belief that both can learn from each other and that the literary and historical heritage of the islands is a most valuable resource for current and future economic, social, and community development.

This new edition marks the 300th anniversary of Martin's book. It contains a digital image reproduction of the original 1703 edition, together with extensive new notes, an introduction, and illustrations. I hope it will be of interest to local people living in the islands and to those outside for whom the Scottish islands exercise such a strong and continuing fascination.

JOHN RANDALL
CHAIRMAN, THE ISLANDS BOOK TRUST
October, 2003

Introduction

Martin Martin was a native of north Skye. From records at Leiden University it appears that he was born in 1669 but it is not known where and how he received his earlier education. His family background and ancestry also remain something of a mystery.

There is a widely held belief that he was a member of a Martin family living on lands called Bealach in the upper or northern part of the Trotternish district. The area of these lands is clearly shown on Matthew Stobie's plan (1764) of the Macdonald of Sleat possessions in Trotternish and within its boundaries were included both Duntulm Castle and the hills to the east.[1] In itself the name *Bealach*, which is the usual Gaelic word for a hill pass, may seem rather inappropriate when applied to a farm so close to the sea, but the location of the house or houses was near the narrow way through below inland cliffs, a kind of pass, necessarily taken by travellers approaching from the south (see frontispiece). In 1824 a house called 'Bellach' stood not far from the ruins of Duntulm Castle on the east side of the road which by then ran round the whole 'wing' of Trotternish, and this may have been the ancient site of the 'Ballach' shown on the Blaeu map of Skye.[2]

In 1718 the lands of Duntulm and two 'Ballachs' were in the possession of Mr Alexander Nicolson, tacksman; and in the same year the two pennylands of Cleat were held by 'Martine Martine'. Cleat is not on the Stobie plan but is presumably represented by the hill and loch called Cleat about 2 miles west-north-west of Staffin and may have been absorbed into the lands of Flodigarry. This Martin Martin was not the author but probably his nephew. On 15 April 1732 Sir Alexander Macdonald of Sleat granted to 'Marten Marten late of Cleat' a tack of 'the ten penny lands of Duntulm and upper and lower ballochs with houses biggings yards tofts crofts mosses muirs meadows grassings Shealings' and so on, all in the parish of St Mary (Kilmuir) in Trotternish. This tack, which of course explains the 'two Ballachs', was to last for 16 years and Marten was permitted to keep an 'inn house' in Duntulm and to 'sell liquour at the kirk of St Mary'. Other conventional conditions covered a rent of 240 merks and the required payment of dues and services at the 'Miln of Kilmaluack.'[3]

The firm identification of 'Marten Marten late of Cleat' poses some difficulties as other Macdonald estate tacks of Trotternish lands indicate that there may have been others of the same name at the same time. That he was Martin Martin's nephew seems probable because a Martin Martin, eldest son to the deceased John Martin of 'Flodigary', certainly was. In April 1732 John's son Martin received a tack of the seven pennylands of Flodigarry and the 'Isle of Altivick', later called Flodigarry Island, and of the six pennylands of 'Clachglass', all of which he already held. But was John's son the same as the Martin Martin who in 1734 received a share of Valtos and the Martin Martin who then also became one of the two tacksmen of the pennylands of Elishader and Mealt? All these lands were broadly in the same district and portions of them at least could have been held by one man. That there were other, possibly related, Martin families in the area seems likely.[4]

It may be, then, that the Martin Martin who entered the lands of Duntulm and Bealach in 1732 was the first of the name there and therefore the person who gave rise to the tradition that Martin Martin, author, was of the Bealach Martins, which in a sense he would have been if the new tacksman of 1732 was indeed his nephew. The references to possibly several Martin Martins, alive in the author Martin's own lifetime, are certainly of some importance, and it is to this period that traditional information and stories recorded in the later 19th century by Alexander Carmichael may relate. In one story there is a reference to 'an taigh Mhartuin Mhoir a Bhealaich', the house of big Martin of Bealach, which could be a suitable name for a man who possessed the lands of several farms. This story, about 'Martuin a Bhealaich' and his marriage to a daughter of Macleod of Raasay, mentions him at another point by the name of 'Martin Macillemhartuinn (Martin Martin)'.

Carmichael also wrote down a song which he accompanied with an explanatory tale:

'This song was composed by a woman known as Beasa Mhor, Big Bess, to Martain Martain – better known as Martuin a Bhealaich – Martain of Bealach. Big Bess was a remarkably handsome woman. She was dairymaid to Martain till he married when she left.

'When Martain died from the bursting of a blood vessel Big Bess came and tapped at the window where the body lay. They allowed her in and she fell upon the bosom of the dead man and kissed him again and again with her arms round him, drinking the blood oozing from his mouth and smearing her breast over the region of the heart with the clotted blood. She never washed this off again.

'Some of those present were for sending her away but Martain's wife forbade them and said that such devotion could only come from God and not from man. After a little the woman withdrew as silently as she entered.'

The timeless, almost superstitious elements in this story, such as the drinking of the blood of a dear one, mean that it is not possible to relate it to any particular Martin, nor necessarily to Martins at all, but clearly it, and the previous references, preserve some impression of a significant figure of the past, possibly a Martin, caught up in tradition. This figure could as well be the Martin Martin of 1732 as one of his distant ancestors, and a sentence in a late 19th century paper on Kilmuir and its placenames is no more precise: 'A century and a half ago the Duntulm Bealach was tenanted by Mairtainn a Bhealaich, a descendant of whose family was the late Field Marshall Sir Donald Martin Stewart.' However, the uncertainty of the author Martin Martin's supposed connection with a Bealach family is apparent too in another comment in the same paper: 'A part of the present farm [Bealach?] beside the castle belonged to the family doctor of the chief [Macdonald of Sleat] while at Kilmaluag two miles to the North-East was Tigh-na-h'Airde, the residence of the tutor of the Macdonalds.'[5]

Whatever traditions there may have been, little was known about Martin Martin in the early 1880s when the Napier Commission investigating the conditions of crofters took an interest in his book. According to William Mackenzie Martin's *Description of the Western Islands* was 'so valuable in information and details that Lord Napier's Committee got it reprinted for the use of the Commission'. An editorial note to the publication (1884) shows that its author was then almost as much a mystery as his background still is:

'With the exception of a few outstanding particulars, little is known regarding the author ... Martin Martin appears to have been a native of the Hebrides, and well connected. He finished his education at the Edinburgh University, taking the degree of Master of Arts in the year 1681, and thereafter had apparently spent some time in foreign travel. Ultimately he resided in Skye, and is supposed to have held some post in connection with the estates of a section of the Macleod family. If this was the case, one would suppose that he may in addition have been a small proprietor himself, or in some other way be a person of means and position, as he styles himself "Gentleman," and likewise must have expended a great amount of time and money in the investigations and journeyings he made among his native islands.'

The editor believed that Martin must have visited all the islands in person. Even less was known, he added, about Martin's 'after years'.[6]

It is remarkable, therefore, that only twenty years later a much fuller account of the Martin family appeared. It formed a section of the third volume of *The Clan Donald*, published in 1904. Here it was stated that the Martins of Skye had their 'principal residence' at 'Bealloch' and that 'for many generations' they were 'men of considerable importance and high standing in the social life of the Isle of Skye'. Said to be 'of education and culture' at a period 'when there were few such in the Western Isles', the Martins were supposed to be associated through marriage and appointments with the Macdonalds of Sleat, whose family papers apparently showed that estate management was sometimes in Martin hands.

A Martin pedigree then followed, in the course of which it appeared that Martin Martin was the third son of a Donald Martin who served the Macdonalds as chamberlain of Trotternish and who married Mary, daughter of Alexander, brother to Sir Donald Macdonald of Sleat. All that was said of the eldest son, also Donald, was that he fought at the battle of Killiecrankie and that he married a daughter of Macdonald of Cuidrach, a short distance south of Uig in Trotternish. That Donald was in fact a minister in North Uist who refused 'to conform to Presbyterianism' and 'quietly deserted his charge' to become tacksman of Skudiburgh near Uig seems inconsistent with his participating at Killiecrankie, and this may not be the only uncertainty in the *Clan Donald* family tree. The second son, John, was said to have fought in the same battle, to have received a tack of Flodigarry (which he certainly did), and to have become factor for the Trotternish district of the Macdonald estate.[7]

The historical value of the *Clan Donald* Martin section is questionable. The authors provide no precise sources for their information, and there seem to be no relevant documents among the surviving Macdonald papers at Armadale other than the tacks already mentioned. Yet their material appears to have been accepted as they presented it by, for instance, William Mackenzie whose *Skye: Iochdar-Trotternish and District* came out in 1930, and to have become established among later generations of Martins and elsewhere.

No definite link has been discovered by the present editor between Martin Martin and the lands of Bealach, nor is it known whether there were indeed Martins of Bealach in his day. Apart from conclusions drawn from Martin's own career and writings there seems to be nothing to substantiate the claim that he was of a particularly distinguished family, nor any information which would throw more light on the good early education from which he must obviously have benefited. He could have been the son of a minister. Nevertheless, in view of the certainty that his elder brother John was tacksman of Flodigarry and that the eldest brother was called Donald, it is more than likely that the family did belong to northern Skye and possible that *The Clan Donald* authors had good reason for associating it, in some way, with Bealach.

*

Martin is supposed to have graduated from Edinburgh University on 7 January 1681 but, rather curiously, was admitted to the use of the University library on 7 November 1683. Certainly a Martin Martin did graduate in 1681 but if the Leiden record of his age is correct then it would seem at least unlikely that he would have graduated at the age of 12 and there is therefore the possibility that another Martin Martin is involved somewhere, either at Edinburgh or at Leiden! The Edinburgh records may therefore or may not be the earliest records of him.[8] Thereafter the main and almost the only source of biographical information for over a dozen years is a series of discharges and receipts and a few other small documents containing reference to him or bearing his signature.

As 'governour to the Laird of Mcdonal younger' Mr Martin Martin was a witness to a deed signed at 'Armidell' (Armadale) in the Sleat district of Skye on 30 March 1686. This deed was discovered in 1931 by George M Fraser, solicitor in Portree and factor for the Macdonald estates in Skye, who had been 'arranging some old MacDonald Charter chest papers', and it was printed in the 1934 edition of Martin's work. The document is now in the Macdonald archive at Armadale.[9]

Though Martin may have been 'governour' at Armadale for some time there seems to be no reason to suppose that he was appointed immediately upon graduation, although his possible presence in Edinburgh in 1683 could be put down to his having accompanied the young Macdonald laird to that city as he did the young Macleod a few years later. Given the marriage links between the Macdonalds of Sleat and the Macleods of Dunvegan it was probably quite easy for him to take up a similar post with the latter family, and this had happened by early summer 1686:

'I Mr Martin Martin Governour to the Laird of McLeoid younger grants me to have receaved from John McLeoid of dunvegan the sowme of one hundred merks scots mony in part of payment of the fee due to me for my attendance to his forsaid sonn from Whitsunday eightie sex to Whitsonday nixt to come quherof I grant the receipt and herby discharges the forsaids of the abovewrittin sowme as Witness my hand Dunvegan the eighteenth day of august on[e] thousand Sex hundred eightie sex years'.[10]

When he signed the next receipt, on 20 October 1686, Martin and his charge were in Edinburgh, where they had lodging for which at first £6 sterling per quarter was paid to 'our Landslord'. This remained the usual form of subsequent receipts over the next few years, including that of 30 August 1692 when Martin acknowledged payment of 116 merks and 16 pence 'for the use of Mrs Isabell McLeod'. Occasionally other transactions were Martin's responsibility, as when shoes for the young laird and 'your man' were purchased by Martin from John Fithie, cordiner (shoemaker) in Potterrow, Edinburgh. For some of the time at least John Brown, janitor of 'the Colledge of Edinburgh', was their landlord. In October1687 he was paid £20 sterling for six months board 'to the young Laird of MacLeod with his governour and servant at my house' from 29 June to the end of the year, and a further £10 was paid to him on 21 February 1688, when it transpired that the servant was called 'Neill Makleod'.[11]

In addition to his duties as governor Martin, being someone who could write, acted as a witness or drew up receipts on behalf of other parties. His name appeared too in accounts of money spent on the young laird, and even when reference to him as governor ceased after 1692 his connection with the Macleods was not entirely broken off. At Dunvegan he was succeeded as 'governor' to the new young laird by 'Mr Neill Beaton' who was there by July 1699 and in 1701 was also a 'student in theologie' at Edinburgh. Contact with the Macdonalds of Sleat was either renewed in the 1690s or, more probably, had never been interrupted.[12]

While in Edinburgh Martin would have had opportunity to extend his social acquaintance and perhaps it was then that he met with Sir Robert Sibbald, busy collecting material for an intended description of Scotland covering, in two volumes, ancient traditions, topography, history and natural history. If they did meet at that time Sibbald must have recognised in Martin as a young educated Skyeman a potentially valuable researcher and contributor, while for his part Martin could equally well have enjoyed entry into a new world of learned people, 'virtuosoes' as they were sometimes called, made possible through the connections and influence of Sibbald. It seems to have been Sibbald, who for instance introduced Martin to contact with the Royal Society in London and recommended that he communicate with the secretary, Hans Sloane, and submit articles to the Society's *Philosophical Transactions.* Over the next few years all these new and stimulating lines of interest were successfully pursued. It may be that following communication in person or by letter with such men as Sibbald and Sloane, both of them medical doctors, Martin first had the idea of becoming a doctor himself; and it was certainly because of their own scientific activities that he undertook journeys of exploration through the Hebridean islands, gathered together all sorts of objects and pieces of information, and learned that what he discovered could make the subject of possibly more than one publication.

It has become fashionable to date Martin's researches for his *Description of the Western Islands of Scotland* to 1695, although Erskine Beveridge thought that he must have 'begun to gather materials' for his book before 1680 since in describing Benbecula he wrote that the island belonged to 'Ranal Mackdonald of Benbecula' who, according to *The Clan Donald* (Vol.III p.279), died in 1679.[13] Though rather too young to have begun deliberate collection in the 1670s he may have made visits to one or two of the islands early in the 1695 summer, or even in the course of the two previous years, but at the end of June he travelled to the continent. On 17 August 1695 he had been in London only two days, having come 'by the Pacquet from Holland quher I stayed since the beginning of July'. Any correspondence could, he said, reach him 'at Mans Coffee house', and this address presumably remained valid until October when he left for the north. By mid December he was back at Dunvegan and had assembled perhaps his first attempt at Royal Society recognition:

'Be pleas'd to deliver the Inclosed remarks to the Viscount Tarbat and if he [be already?] at London send them to him by the first post. I have dir[ected] another Copy of them to Dr Slaen being pronounced Dr Slo'n, one of the greatest Virtuosoes of the royall Society. My Lord will be satisfied to have these remarks and those that I will send herafter especially since I am to acquant Dr Slo'n and the president Sir Robert Southwell that my Lord obleidged me to send all my observations to the Royall Society, for my Lord will do me the favour to Writ in my favour to the President quhen I go to London. I had no time to discourse him upon this subject at Edinburgh.'[14]

Soon an expedition was being planned for early in 1696, as Martin indicated in a letter from Dunvegan to John Mackenzie of Delvine:

'The Impression of your former kyndnes is yet recent with me, tho near the ultima Thule, I do not forget my friends tho never so remot. The badness of the season and the accident befallen my leg, Conspired to retard my progress, quhich I must Contract within a lesser Compass then was first proposed. I'm resolved Shortlie for the long Isle ..'[15]

Evidently the visit to the 'Long Island', by which was meant the whole of the Outer Hebrides, took place in May or June, or both, after which Martin returned to Dunvegan and wrote again to Delvine on 25 June:

'If this place did afford any thing Worthy your observation I would not omit to acquaint you. The Course of my travels has not much enriched the Curiosity of the virtuosi. I am Latelie Come from the Long Island quher there is not one minister to preach – I am uncertain as to the parson of Harries, this puts a fair oportunity for the Popish priests Who will not lose time at such a juncture a short space might dispose the Comon people for poperie or Atheism, the Contempt of Baptism, and Sponsors or Gossops as they call them here inclines them the more to poperie for they will have there Children Christned tho by a Layman. The Privateers have ruined the trade of these comes by our Coasts. Sr Donald is yet at Uist I have no account of his Sumonds but that they were execut and left at the Kyle.'[16]

Though Martin does not say how he made the voyage to the Long Island it is clear that his visit was a fairly brief one and that some risk existed of being assailed at sea by 'Privateers'. He also reveals that as a definite presbyterian he had no sympathy for 'poperie' and was even suspicious of the episcopalian John Campbell, 'parson of Harries', with whom he was to go to St Kilda a year later.

Martin returned to Edinburgh and wrote to Dr David Gregory, of the Royal Society and professor of astronomy at Oxford, on 1 August:

'Before I came from London October last a Friend of yours advised me to wait upon Mr Charleton, who promised to consider me above the Common rate, if I should bring him any Curiosities from our Western Islands, which I did not omit in the Course of my short Travels in Skie Harries South and North Uist and some Isles. Dr Gordon thereafter, made my acquaintance with Dr. Sloane, who expects great things from our Western isles. I promised to inform him of any natural observation I could learn, and now understanding by Dr. Gordon that you are one of the Royal Society, I rather addressing my self to them by you, than any other, being perswaded of your inclination to further my design, as of your influence on them, please to peruse the within written specimen of Curiosities, with an Essay of Observations for the Royal Society; you will be pleased to communicate to Dr. Sloane, and such as you think fit at London or Oxford. If he with your self will influence the Royal Society to ratify what you determine for my future encouragement, to prosecute a further Enquiry into the Natural History of all the Western Isles of Scotland, If this Essay be satisfying, it will engage them to give me the encouragement that is necessary for such an Undertaking Pray be carefull, not to deliver any observation that may deserve a Censure ..'[17]

This letter towards the end shows that Martin was looking for Royal Society financial support for the much larger project which he planned and which was to result in his *Description of the Western Islands*. It mainly related, however, to those 'remarks' which he had prepared the year before and perhaps to any addition or alteration made following his Long Island visit; and it was copied as 'A letter from Mr [Martin] Martin to Dr Gregory concerning his Observations in the North of Scotland'. A further letter from Martin to Dr Hans Sloane, the secretary of the Royal Society, in September 1696 made similar points:

'I Writ to you December last a few Observations and having had no retourn I presume to give this second trouble, being encouradged by your own Comands; having travell'd a few of our Western Isles I have made a small Collection of such Curiosities as these afford. Be pleased to receave here inclosed a Coppy of this Specimen, as also of the Naturall observations, according to your Injunction, And after perusall, If this Essay please you, Comunicat the same to Mr Charleton (for whom I design a share of the Curiosities) and to such of the R. Society as are in the City, as may determine the rest to give me the necessary encouradgment for a forder and more criticall enquiry into the Naturall history of these already viewed, and all the rest [of] the western Isles of Scotland, this I am able to performe with greater Adwantage then any other in regard of the Languadge and my Interest in those of the first rate in these places. I depend upon you in this and if your leasure permitt let me have your Advice I Wrot to Dr Gregory to this effect but Cannot be speedy in regard of his absence from London ..'[18]

As in the letter to Gregory Martin was giving notice of his wish to write that much more extensive and 'more criticall' account of the islands, which he expected would be of great interest to the Royal Society and for which he hoped to receive 'the necessary encouradgment', i.e. money, to cover at least some of his costs. He also stated for the first time the advantages he enjoyed in being a Gaelic speaker and in having a close acquaintance with 'those of the first rate', meaning apparently the Macdonald of Sleat and Macleod of Dunvegan and Harris families of Skye with their social connections in the Hebrides and elsewhere. There was a great deal still to be done in order to complete the larger project. So far he had visited only 'a few of our Western Isles', by which might be meant his native isle of Skye, Uist, Harris and 'some isles', possibly one or two small ones off Harris such as Berneray and Taransay. He had to find a means of travelling to other places, to cultivate Society support and, if possible, to secure the 'encouragement' he needed.

The 'Essay' was published in the Royal Society's Philosophical Transactions, under the title of *Several Observations in the North Islands of Scotland*, in October 1697, a year after the letter to Sloane, which was written from Edinburgh at a time when Martin was 'to be found at Alexander Hendersons Taylor in the Canongate'.

At the beginning of 1697 Martin was back in Skye, at Duntulm, and at some point thereafter at Armadale. In the summer he made a visit lasting about three weeks to St Kilda, and possibly to other islands. By the beginning of August he had returned to Armadale where he wrote to let Dr Sloane know what he had been doing:

'I have travelled several western Isles from these I am now retourned hither. I have been in the remote and remarkable St Kilda quhich differs as much from the rest as it is distant from them Providence having distinguished them in many things both as to ther naturals as well as Morals from the rest of mankind, to whom they be said to be antipods in several respects. In these I have pursuant to my undertaking Collected one hundred natural Curiosities and near the like number of natural observations. I resolve to be at Edinbrough the 18 Instant at quhich time and place your Advice will determine me as to my Journey to London Please to let me understand if the Royal Society will accept of and Consider my pains in purchasing the Curiosities, and accordingly I shall steer my course.'[19]

Still seeking financial aid and perhaps feeling that he was not going to be given a simple grant to help him on his way Martin was evidently trying to achieve the same end by selling his collection of 'curiosities' to the Society, but, in Edinburgh again at the end of September, he had apparently been disappointed. Another letter to Sloane was due:

'I received yours of the tenth Instant for quhich I retourn you many thanks. It has been my misfortun, not my fault, that your former letters should have miscarried, and though I Cannot recall my lost time and labour, I am very sensible of your discretion in delivering your sentiment of the Royall S. There is no bussiness calls me to London at present since this project has vanished into air, I am determined to retire for the Country once in October, before quhich time I leave A Coppy of the description of St Kilda to be given you and quhatever Corner of the world Contains me I shall endeavour on all occasions to approve myself Sr. Your most humble servant.'[20]

In spite of his declaration about the 'Country' Martin was in London in late November, intending to stay until mid February, lodging with 'Mistris Peeps next door to the Grossers' in Coventry Street, and no doubt pushing forward the publication of his description of St Kilda. In the meantime Dr Charles Preston, superintendent of the Edinburgh Physic Garden and none too well acquainted with the islands, wrote to Sloane in October 1697 on the subject of Martin's forthcoming work:

'I have met frequently with Dr Sibbald and Mr Martin who informs me he has Lately travelled thorough some of the western Isles as Scay [Skye], Lewis hareys, hirta and St Kilda and has made severall curious observations of the natural products of those Isles but more particularly of St Kilda ..'

Martin, he said, was 'about to give a Description of those Isles their manner of goverment, Customs and what curious observations he has made there' to the Society and the world, sending it to London to have it printed. Preston was presumably referring to the description of St Kilda only, filling what Martin called '5 Sheets of paper' and, because St Kilda was the greatest curiosity of all, serving perhaps as the ultimate attempt upon the Society's funds.[21]

Sibbald and Martin were all this time in touch over the curiosities and descriptions which Martin could now provide of an almost unknown part of Britain. In an 'Essay relating to the Natural History of Scotland' Sibbald made frequent reference to Martin's account of St Kilda, which, if he was writing towards the close of 1697, he could have read ahead of publication the following year. That the two men had contact in person is evident from Sibbald's 'Essay': 'Mr Martin showed me a piece of Rock Talk, with a gritty stone adhering to it like the Emerile'; 'Mr Martin showed me some pieces of White Corall taken up about the West Isles of Scotland, some at 20, some at 30, some at one Fathom deep'. Much indeed of Sibbald's natural history account was derived directly from Martin, and, upon reading Preston's letter to Sloane of 16 November 1697, this is not surprising:

'Mr Martin has carryed all his Curiosities along with him [to London], that he Collected in the Western Isles, as the Skins of fowls, Minerals, Coral, Talk, Nitre, Ambergriece, Shells etc. and I beleive he will make you the first Complement, I wish there may be some way fallen upon to give him Encouragement for he Spares no pains in Collecting things.'[22]

Martin's St Kilda book, dedicated to the president of the Royal Society, was published in 1698. Most of his time in St Kilda was taken up with his and John Campbell's examination of Roderick, called by Martin the 'impostor', and this and his hunt for curiosities seem to have been the main purposes of his visit. While both protestant religious motives and natural history enquiry may have spurred him to undertake his hazardous journey in an open boat hired locally in Harris or Pabbay, Martin was surely responding to the continued scientific requirements of both Sir Robert Sibbald and of the Royal Society, though perhaps he and Campbell were also on a mission for some church authority, synod or presbytery, to deal with Roderick. From Martin's point of view Roderick's reported behaviour could have struck him as one of the most interesting curiosities St Kilda at that time had to offer.

Apart from the publication one of the most significant events of 1698 was a meeting with the mapmaker, John Adair, who was busy, as Charles Preston put it in a letter to Dr Sloane, 'Surveying this Country'. Adair had responded to Sibbald's research queries issued in 1682 and had produced his own set of similar questions in 1694. Outside the members of the Royal Society and Sibbald in particular Adair was probably one of the very few other persons to whom Martin provided information. An act of 15 June 1686 'In Favours of John Adair, Geographer, for Surveying the Kingdom of Scotland, and Navigating the Coasts and Isles thereof' made provision that the sheriff of each Scottish county would 'Appoint one or two knowing men, in each Paroch, to go alongst with the said *John Adair*, when he is actually Surveying the same' to give him local information as required. It is likely that Martin was eventually to be one such 'knowing' man.[23]

In the same letter, undated but certainly of 1698, Preston told Sloane that Adair had given 'an Account of the Roman Wall, and the inscriptions found there', and was soon to be off on a larger adventure: 'He sets out for the Western Isles, a few days hence, 5 or 6 Months Voyage. The Publick hath allowed £500 to Defray his Charges, he carries 20 men along with him, one skilled in Botany. I wish Mr. Martin had been of the number. I doubt not we shall Account of Several Curiosities from those parts.' As it turned out Martin was one of the number. At the end of the year Adair himself wrote: 'Last May having provided a vessel, and other things needfull, I sailed from Leith to the Orkneys, and thence by farro-head to the Lewes, where I Spent some time, and was in Harris, Uist, Rum, Canna, and many other western Islands, in all which I made the Necessary Observations for the main designe, and likewise met with Several Things worthy Notice.' Martin could hardly have travelled to distant Orkney and perhaps to Shetland if he had not been with Adair and without such a visit would probably not have included them in his book. He might not have found it easy otherwise to go to Rum and Canna and to return to Lewis, Harris and Uist. It must be supposed therefore that he left Leith with Adair in May 1698, by which time his book on St Kilda had appeared in print as Preston had said in his letter: 'I hear Mr. Martins Book of St.Kilda is published.'[24]

Relations between Adair and Martin may have been reasonably good at the start of the voyage but after five months things had changed. Moving over to the mainland coast in September 'when sailing in those Seas becomes dangerous' Adair continued south for the sixth month. On 13 October Preston wrote to Sloane: 'As for Mr Adair he is not yet returned from his voyage to the western Isles, but he is expected here by end of this month.' In the same letter Preston added: 'Mr Martin went in company, so that I doubt not they will return fraughted with a Large cargoe of natural curiosities.' In the event the expedition seems to have lasted into early November, the ship having been driven ashore three times and delayed by storms and rain, and then Adair, always in financial difficulties through lack of sufficient funding support, had to face up to the consequences of his expenditure on the voyage. He had spent £875 on equipment and £457 on the actual venture. The latter sum had to cover payment to Thomas Whyte, master of the ship *Mary* of Leith, the hire of a pinnace, the services of two pilots from Leith and Stornoway, and the wages of a surgeon. In order to meet these expenses he had to borrow, and one result was that some of those who participated in what has been called 'a major scientific expedition' did not get properly paid. It appears that Martin was one of those who did not receive what he had been promised.[25]

A further letter from Preston to Sloane was also undated but was apparently written around mid November 1698:

'Mr Adair returned from his voyage some dayes agoe he has gone thorow many of the north and western Islands, he has collected what natural curiosities did fall in his way as fowles, fishes shells plants some of a prodigious bigness some Kind of those beans thrown in upon the Isles of Orkney, plants as the arga Cheophrasti and Chamepericlymeny grow there plentifully: odd Kind of stones coralls, a Kind of Magnet. the ship is not yet come about but is daily expected so that I cannot give any particular account untill it arrive but I think it not amiss you write to him a Letter and I doubt he will give an account of what he met with in his voyage … Mr Martin who was with Mr Adair some pairt of the voyage is also arrived, but I have had no time to discourse him.'[26]

Martin was surely of considerable use to Adair in the Hebrides at least, as a Gaelic speaker and interpreter and provider of placenames. He could have advised on directions, warned of some dangers, and suggested inlets in which to take shelter. Whatever practical help he may have been the journey allowed him to see or visit islands not previously known to him and to gather information for the book he had in mind. But what return was there for his services? At the end of December 1698 when Martin was back on shore Sir Robert Sibbald wrote to Hans Sloane:

'I must recommend to your favour the Bearer my friend Master Martine, who hath been at great paines in making a description of the Isle of Sky – (the biggest of our West isles) and some other of the isles. It heth him coast much paines and expense, and John Adair instead of rewarding him as he promised, heth treated him scurvily. I shall intrest you to employ your friends to get him some incouradgement and reward from the Court. He was borne in the Isle of Sky, was Governour to the Chieffs of the Clans in these isles and heth that interest and favour with them, they will doe for him what they will doe for no other, their Language is his Mother Language, and he is well acquainted with their Maners and customes and is the person here most capable to Serve the Royall Society in the accounts of what relateth to the description of these Isles.'[27]

Using what in many ways were old and familiar arguments combined with Martin's own description of the advantages he possessed as a collector and researcher in the isles, Sibbald had rather more success than Martin's pleas for encouragement and offer to sell curiosities to the Society. In mid March 1699 Sloane launched an appeal which looked for financial aid by subscription:

'Whereas Mr Martin Martin is acquanted with the language and has travelled over many of the Hebrides or western Isles of Scotland to Inform himself of the naturall productions as well as Moral History of them, we the underwritten believing him well qualified to promote naturall history and gett accounts of usefull things do each of us for himself and not one for another promise to give him towards his encouragement the sums severally by us underwritten he furnishing us with the samples of such curiosities as he finds and usefull remarks he makes in his travels, the half of which several sums to be given in hand the other half at the delivery of such curiosities and remarks as he shall discover

'I do subscribe on the Conditions above mentioned two guineas, Whereof I have now given him one. Hans Sloane.[28]

Whether Sloane's example was enough to stir many others to contribute is unknown but the approach was certainly intended to make up for Adair's 'scurvy' treatment of Martin and perhaps a recognition of the failure by the Royal Society to reward previous efforts in curiosity collecting. It also provided an 'encouragement' to enable Martin to continue his work and to plan a publication which would contain all those 'remarks' which Sloane looked for. Acceptance by such distinguished authorities as Sibbald and the Society must at last have had its effect upon 'the Court' or the government since only two weeks later, at the end of March 1699, the Exchequer granted Martin £25 'in consideration of the charges and pains he has been at in accompanying John Adair for taking of the north-west seas and islands, and prosecuting the natural history of the same'.[29]

The 'further Enquiry' Martin had mentioned to Dr Gregory three years earlier could now be pursued with greater determination, and some urgency was necessary. In his November 1698 letter Charles Preston had also said of Adair that 'he seems resolved to give a short history of his voyage apairt from his other work and to publish it very suddainly'; and in his own letter of 20 December 1698 John Adair had written of his wish to return to the Hebrides in 1699: 'I am resolved to be there early next Spring, and use all means to get the Survey of the West Isles finished, and so soon as possibly [possible?] published ..' There was therefore a risk of a competition, in which Adair might prove to be the first to produce a book about what the two men, in their different ways, had discovered in the islands.[30]

*

In the course of the next year Martin must have concentrated on preparing his *Description*, trying to complete it as soon as possible, although this did not prevent him from further collecting, and he may even have found time to visit one or two more islands. He probably also wrote the general accounts of 'Ancient and Modern Customs', 'Second Sight', and a 'Fishing Trade'. On 16 January 1700 he sent to Sloane another instalment of 'curiosities', with a letter 'Containing Some Strange Observations in some of the Western Isles of Scotland' and particularly mentioning second sight:

'If you had been endued with that rare faculty of the Second Sight, you could no more avoid Seeing of me frequently, than the Islanders do in the same Case; For in the whole Course of my late Travells when any thing that was remarkable fell under my Observations, I presently directed my thought towards your Society. Our Isles afford a Greater variety of Natural as well [as] Moral Observations, than I expected; of both these I have amazed [i.e.amassed] a considerable number, and this Disposes me to Employ the next Summer in making a more exact Survey of them than hitherto. If your Virtuosi would contribute to carry on the undertaking, I will Travel upon the Terms of your first proposal, or to be more particular, I am willing to procure the various Specimens produced in Skie, which is above 100 miles in Circumference, and to Deliver a Copy of its Description to each Subscriber, upon my return. But if they please to have the

Lewis which is above 200 miles in Circumference, I am ready to undertake it: and if a Suitable Encouragement were allowed, I could oblidge for both these Isles, when your Convenience allows your advice is expected ..'[31]

The 'Strange Observations' included a tenant's house in what Martin called 'the Parish Cariness' [i.e.Carinish] in North Uist where no cock would crow, and a calf with eight feet at 'Skeriness' in Skye. There were also two instances of second sight, one of them relating to Martin himself. These 'Observations', together with the latter part of the letter suggest that Martin was almost thinking he might be a kind of professional collector of oddities on behalf of the Society.

Whether or not he received further Society support Martin could well have spent part of the summer of 1700 refreshing his memory of some islands or visiting new ones. But as usual he was short of money and now turned once more to the family in which he had once been employed. On 20 June 1700, in fulfilment of their 'aprobatione' in July 1699 and with the consent of Norman Macleod of Macleod, 'John McLeod of Tallaskir Rory McLeod of Hammire and Alexander McLeod of Grisernish' sent an order to Mr Alexander Macleod, advocate, in Edinburgh, desiring 'that upon sight of these you pay as much as you think fitt at this time' from 'the Fyftie pound sterling mony Left to .. Mr Martine by the late Laird of MakLeod for honorous Causes in his latter will' to 'Mr Martine Martine outt of the first of MakLeod's rents and place the same in his accompts'. And on 9 October 1701 Martin did receive 560 merks (£372.6s.8d scots or just over £31 sterling) out of the £50, a sum which he must have greatly appreciated at a time when his book was nearing completion. He was in London at the end of November 1701 when he wrote, presumably to Mr Alexander Macleod:

'My Natural history will be ready in manuscript by the end of December, and after a calcul[ation] of the charges for publishing of the same, it is no less than 41 lib. [£41] without quhich it Can turn to no account, therfor I am forc'd to trouble you with the present state of my caice, and Intreat you may be pleas'd to advance the 340 merks remaining of the 900 [£50 sterling] and after receipt therof a part of the charges must be upon credit. Please to deliver this summ to Captin Neil McLeod who will transmit it here, and his receipt for the same will be of equal force with that of mine. This with my humble duty to McLeod and Mr John McKenzie is all ..'

Payment was prompt and Captain Neil, in the Foot Guards, acknowledged receipt of the 340 merks on 15 December.[32]

If indeed the manuscript was ready by the end of 1701 another eighteen months passed before the printer was finished with it. On 26 June 1703 Martin told Mackenzie of Delvine that 'my book is to be compleat ten days hence', but there seems to have been a little delay which he reported to Dr Sloane in July:

'The printer has disappointed me of the book which will not be finished before tomorrow,. Please to receave the Inclosed Title, the contents of which you know pretty well; If those at your meeting give in their crown a piece to any you please to name, Ile provide the books as soon as they are bound, for I do not bind any before they are bespoke..'[33]

Some members of the Society put in their crowns immediately for on 29 July a package was sent to Sloane: 'The Bearer my freind has in my absence taken the 20 books to be disposed as you think fit among your meeting.' Martin himself was going to Windsor, to look for a sum of £60 which he expected.[34]

So the *Description of the Western Islands of* Scotland was finished and issued ahead of Adair, who was in any case held up by lack of funds, but Martin's work certainly looks as though it was written or printed in a hurry. Four years afterwards the Royal Society published one other article by Martin, in volume 25 of its Philosophical Transactions. This volume is thought to be dated 1706-1707, and the article, covering Martin's final 'curiosity', was written in March 1707. Its title was:

'A Relation of a Deaf and Dumb Person, who recover'd his Speech and Hearing after a Violent Fever: With some other Medicinal and Chirurgical Observations. By Mr. Martin Martin.'

The person in question was Daniel Fraser from near Inverness, whose ability to hear and speak came not as a recovery but for the first time when he was perhaps in his twenties. Martin's comment on his speech is of interest as relating to other remarks he made on the subject in his book:

'he is understood now tolerably well, tho he yet retains the *Highland* Accent, as *Highlanders* do who are advanc'd to his Years before they learn the *English* Tongue: he can speak no *Irish*, for it was in the *Low Lands* of *Scotland* that he first heard and spoke.'

Added to the end of this little tale were several preventatives, recipes and treatments, one relating to Skye and the neighbouring mainland, the rest unlocated. And so far as is known this brought Martin's literary career to a conclusion.

*

Very little is known about the rest of Martin's life.

Following the appearance of his book in the late summer of 1703 he returned to Skye. In December that year a Martin Martin described himself as 'servitor to Sir Donald McDonald of Sleatt', but this was probably a different man who, in acknowledging receipt of 50 merks from '[Mrs?] Donald McLeoid in glenelg', signed his name at 'Moungostot' [Monkstad or Mougstot in Kilmuir] in an unfamiliar hand as 'Martien martien'. However the receipt serves as a reminder that the Martins of north Skye were closely linked to the Macdonald estate, and letters through most of 1704 and in 1706 from Martin to Mackenzie of Delvine and others, often dealing with his brother John's financial affairs, were all sent from Duntulm or Armadale. But Martin's own finances were not entirely satisfactory. In April 1703, before his book was published, he wrote from London to tell John Mackenzie that 'the Earle of Cromarty was so kind as to procure me the Queens letter to the Treasury to advance 60 lib in consideration of my charges, and as an additional favour his Lordship dispensed with the ordinary dues on this occasion'. Unfortunately there were difficulties in getting hold of the money. He wanted Mackenzie to remind the Earl 'of his promise to recommend my precept to the Lords Comissioners of the Treasury ... and this will be the finishing strooke to the whole. If the precept is not answered, my expectation from my patron Falls by consequence since my book Cannot otherwise be published in regard of the rogues I have to deal with'. In June Martin wrote to Mr James Mackenzie 'to present my order for the 60 lib to the Treasury, and let it have its fate, for I am not to make a publick acknowledgement of what I am not like to obtain'. He thought of addressing the Queen again, but decided to wait to see what Mr James achieved. At the end of the year he was despairing of receiving his £60 'any other way than by your means', and was looking for any help he or John Mackenzie could find, and it was not until 13 March 1707 that he was at last able to write to Mackenzie to thank him for the money – 'you have purchas'd me out of the fire'.[35]

There were other concerns to think about although they were not yet causing much trouble. When at Armadale in July 1704 Martin wrote that 'health is a blessing most enjoyed by those who use the means to preserve it; and is that which I never once wanted when allowed to go my own pace'. It was perhaps in London or on the continent that he was not allowed to go at his own pace and that his health did suffer, whereas in Skye and the islands he seems to have flourished, at least for a while.[36]

Still short of funds Martin apparently took up tutoring and being a 'governor' again in 1704. He referred then to 'His young Squire' who was 'a wholesome lively boy, of a more delicat complexion than the generality in this place, being very tractable, and of a good capacity'. This boy was probably a Macdonald, perhaps Donald, son of Sir Donald known as 'Domhnull a Chogaidh', Donald of the War, who had been Martin's charge in the mid 1680s.[37]

In the spring of 1707 and cheered up by the receipt of his money Martin was still in Skye but left for the south in late April, and thereafter spent most of his remaining years in London or on visits abroad. By now he seems to have determined to become a doctor of medicine. He was also again a 'governor', this time to John Mackenzie of Delvine's son, whom he took with him to Holland in 1708 when he evidently visited Leiden. On 5 September 1708 Martin wrote from 'Hague' to Mackenzie: 'Since my return from the Spa, Your Son and I have been together both in Country and Leyden near five weeks time', and in February 1709, when at Leiden again, he comforted the father with the news that his son 'is free from wine women, and gaming to which last he is altogether a Stranger'. Moreover the son attended to his studies very carefully. They were back in London in May 1710 having left Holland sooner than expected, and then Martin, who had apparently graduated at Leiden as a doctor by October that year, lived in the city apart from occasional visits to the country, possibly for health reasons, and again to the continent. There has been disagreement as to whether he actually practised as a doctor.[38]

In September 1716 Martin was in Paris, staying with 'Monsieur Gregoir visa vis La Comedie rue St Germain'. He was in touch with Hans Sloane, hoping perhaps that he might again be asked to find some 'curiosities':

'Since my travels have not afforded Matter for your Instruction, I was obliged to disobey your Commands by my silence. I presume now before returning to acquant you with my resolution of leaving this place within three weeks, and if you think me Capable of serving you here you may freely Command.

'I intend to travel again as soon as an opportunity offers.'[39]

But an opportunity did not arise and there is something rather forlorn about Martin's letter as if he had lost his way somehow. On 27 November he told Mackenzie of Delvine that he had been back in London a month and had been confined to his room 'by a violent Asthma'. His brother John had long been owed money by Sir Donald Macdonald who was in financial and other difficulties after the 1715 Jacobite rising and, in Martin's view, had not 'pursued the true Method for obtaining his pardon'. There were therefore good health and money reasons for staying in his lodging rather than going off on travels, and correspondence could be addressed: 'For Doctor Martin, to the cair of Mr Cross at the Smyrna Coffee house Pel Mel. London.'[40]

Communications from Martin to Mackenzie in 1717 were all sent from London, and the last one that year, of 19 December, contained the message: 'I am but lately recovered from a shortness of breath that held me a months time.' Again, towards the end of February 1718 when he was in Kensington, he wrote: 'I have been taken ill of an Asthma these three months last past, and have been very near dying last week, but now am past all danger, and think to return to London once next week.' He was not however clear of danger and London was probably not the best place for him. On 20 March he was still in Kensington but planning to go to London until a chance of 'travelling abroad' should offer. None did, and within a few months he was dead.[41]

A trusted friend in the city, James Keith, dealt with immediate necessities and informed Mackenzie three weeks later:

'This comes to let you know that Dr Martin Martin died here of an Asthma the 9th of October and was decently buried the third day after at St Martin's Church. A few days before his death he desir'd me, when it should happen, to acquaint you or Mr Alexander Macleod with it, that you or he might take the trouble to Signifie it to his Relations in the Isle of Sky who are well knowen to you; that they may empower you or any appointed by you to receive what he has left them.

'By his Will, which is dated the 27th of September last past he leaves the money he had here which is all in one Gentleman's hand to the Children of his deceased Brother Mr Daniel Martin, and likewise disposes of the fifty pound Sterling due to him by his Brother John, but withall desires that if he John cannot recover the money due to him by Sr Donald Mackdonald, He may never be charged with it. But first of all he orders that out of what is owing him here all his Debts and Funeral charges may be taken.

'He nam'd me and one Mr John Gibson an intimate friend of his his Executors. Mr Gibson is since gone beyond Sea, so that I am under a necessity to administer that I may be able to answer the Intention of my deceased Friend.

'The Gentleman in whose hands the money is, is one James Montague Esqr. a Member of Parliament who is not yet come to Town but is expected in a fortnight hence. This I understood but very lately, and it is the reason why I have so long delayed writing to you.'[42]

James Keith, who was evidently a reliable friend, had great difficulty in getting the money out of Montague, but at last he received the sum, also £50, on 9 March 1720. He held a suit of new clothes and some linens left by Martin and valued at £3.6s and £3.10s respectively. These modest amounts would most likely be welcomed by the children of Martin's eldest brother, Donald or Daniel, since, as Keith had heard from John Martin at Flodigarry, they were 'in a very miserable condition'. On 2 January 1721 one of those children, Donald, then staying at 'Mogustot', asked urgently for the money left by his uncle to help out himself and his brothers and sisters.[43]

Martin's late brother Donald, former minister in North Uist, had at least seven children – Donald, Alexander, William, John, Isobell, Florence and Christian. On 21 May 1722, when all but Donald were minors, they received the sum of £87 sterling from John Mackenzie of Delvine, and with the special advice of 'John Martin of Kingsborow More, and Martin Martin indweller in Duntulm our uncles on the father's side, and James McDonald of Cudrich and Normand MackDonald his brother german our uncles on the mother's side' granted their discharge of the amount, the document being written by another Martin Martin, eldest son of John Martin of Kingsborow More, at 'Cudrich'. The existence of an uncle Martin Martin at Duntulm remains a puzzle unless there were two sons of that name in the same family, but John's son Martin is still identifiable twenty years later when two letters were written by him, from Flodigarry on 5 June 1743 and from 'Mougstot' on 6 September in the same year, to a Gilbert Gordon, merchant in Inverness, with directions for the repair and disposal of Martin's old watch and the purchase of a new one.[44]

*

Martin Martin's contribution to the growth of geographical knowledge in the late seventeenth and early eighteenth centuries has been the subject of recent academic study. This has seen considerable importance in his role as 'field worker' for Sir Robert Sibbald and the Royal Society, so much so that he has been called 'perhaps the most famous and the most important of all of Sibbald's collaborators'. Those who wish to pursue this aspect of Martin's career can refer to the short bibliography at the end of this introduction and there is no need to give here more than a brief survey of some of the points of interest arising in his *Description*.

As the principal founder of the Royal College of Physicians in Edinburgh and later Geographer Royal Sir Robert Sibbald was a major influence upon Martin's life and writing. Born in 1641 he developed interests in a wide range of subjects which to him were all part of 'natural history': 'I resolved to make it part of my studies to know what animalls, vegetables, minerals, metalls, and substances cast up by the sea, were found in this country, that might be of use in medicine, or other artes useful to human lyfe, and I began to be curious in searching after them and collecting them.' These words almost set out the pattern of research that Martin was to follow, and so too, but within narrower geographical limits, did Sibbald's ultimate aim which was to 'publish the naturall history of the Country, and the geographical description of the kingdome'.[45]

From the mid 1680s and perhaps earlier Sibbald was in contact with the Royal Society in London and was able to provide information of the kind in which the Society was interested. Both were in search of factual information about the natural world around them, a scientific investigation which needed the material to work on, and each saw in Martin an important source and contributor. As a native of Skye Martin was understood to be a speaker of Gaelic, the 'ancient language' or 'Irish Tongue' to which he several times referred in his book, and this meant, as Sibbald wrote to Sloane, that he had a far closer intimacy with the people of the Hebrides than an investigator from London would have had. In respect of the islands especially, Martin proved an invaluable researcher and informant in one, recognised as such by a group of enquiring learned men including, in addition to Sibbald and Sloane of the Royal Society, Robert Wodrow, Charles Preston, John Adair, and Edward Lhuyd. Martin, whose book seems to suggest by its lay-out that he too worked in accordance with a standard set of 'queries' to be put to the island people, was in contact with Lhuyd, Keeper of the Ashmolean Museum, Oxford. Lhuyd heard that Martin was 'an ingenious Gentleman' who could make a significant contribution to Lhuyd's own collecting project. Martin wrote to Lhuyd between November 1702 and March 1706, sending Gaelic words, comments on Highlanders, and in particular remarking that when, after dedicating his book to a member of the royal family, he went to Windsor he had gained 'nothing by it'. He was depressed thereby, abandoned ideas of further publication, and intended to withdraw 'to some remote corner of Scotland where no books nor Converse are to be looked for'. The last letter added some more natural history comments which elaborated on a few things mentioned in his book. It seems unlikely that, socially, he became very much more than a useful 'servant' to these people.[46]

Not surprisingly therefore Martin has been described as 'a geographical field agent for the Royal Society as well as for Sibbald, directly observing and reporting upon things and transmitting specimens and facts about unknown parts of Britain'. The things he was recommended to look for, and which form the subjects he reported on in his writings, were often called 'curiosities', a word that seemed to cover everything from 'molucca beans' washed up on the shore to superstitious beliefs and antiquities. In a sense Martin, the Gaelic-speaking Hebridean, was himself a curiosity, as were his fellow islanders, to the gentlemen in the south who were to receive his reports and the objects he picked up. On the one hand his education and his duties as 'governor' had brought him into a world which Sibbald and other Royal Society 'virtuosi' inhabited; on the other his island origins and his native language showed that he belonged to a part of Britain and to a people almost unknown to the rest of the country. The region was supposed to be wild and inhospitable, and was virtually unexplored, while the people were understood to be fairly primitive, barbaric and a potential threat to civilisation. Martin had consequently to bridge the gap between the two environments within which he worked and one way of doing so was through what can only have been his genuine interest in both.[47]

Once launched upon his expeditions to the islands he approached them in an honest spirit of enquiry and, quite apart from what he was asked to look out for, he gave in his two books and two articles the impression of having enjoyed describing the distinctive features and odd things he came across, even in his own island of Skye. Of course he did not visit them all, missing out, for example, Lismore and Kerrera as well as smaller but still interesting and inhabited islands like the Garvellach and the Crowlin groups which nevertheless appear on his map. There were no doubt limits to his travels imposed by time, weather and opportunity, and it is perhaps a matter for admiration that he managed to reach as many places as he did. In the case of his journey to St Kilda in 1697 it is clear how he made his voyage; otherwise he said very little about his transport, although when on one occasion describing the custom of going 'deasail' or 'Sun-ways' about a place or object he referred to his departure by boat from Islay:

'I attempted twice to go from *Ila* to *Collonsay*, and at both times they row'd about the Boat Sun-ways, tho' I forbid them to do it, and by a contrary Wind, the Boat and those in it were forc'd back. I took Boat again a third time from *Jura* to *Collonsay*, and at the same time forbid them to row about their Boat, which they obeyed, and when we Landed safely at *Collonsay* without any ill adventure, which some of the Crew did not believe possible, for want of the Round; but this one Instance hath convinced them of the vanity of this Superstitious Ceremony.'

There is something like superstition in reverse in Martin's story, and it may be imagined that the boatmen returned to their ceremony once the visitor was out of the way, but the incident is a good illustration, one of many, of how Martin responded to the island customs he came across and how he probably reported them to the Royal Society. Like many other educated Highlanders and Hebrideans since, Martin almost involuntarily distanced himself, at least in his books, articles and letters, from his own people, in order to make himself acceptable and feel himself acceptable to learned society in the south. He therefore often wrote rather disparagingly and with a tone of superiority about the 'ignorant' natives, and the individuals whom he named as informants were almost all ministers, factors and even landowners, whose social position would give him some air of authority and his reports a greater impression of reliability. Men such as the Morison ministers in Lewis, John Morison tacksman of Bragar in Lewis, Malcolm Campbell steward of Harris, Sir Norman Macleod of Berneray, Lauchlan Mackinnon of Corriechatachan in Skye, and the Skyeman Norman Macleod of Groban in Edinburgh were quoted as valuable sources, and while the 'ordinary' inhabitants were frequently seen as equally valuable in this way Martin did not hesitate to refer to 'The credulous vulgar' of Arran and to inform ' the natives' of South Uist who had just told him one of their 'superstitious' beliefs 'that this was a piece of silly credulity as ever was imposed upon the most ignorant ages'.

He had perhaps an excuse, or more than one. To be treated as a sound and worthy reporter he probably had to be seen as a bit above or separate from the people and places he was writing about. Furthermore, given the religious and political situation in the later 1690s, after the Revolution, as well as the scientific and cultural expectations of his probable readers, the appropriate attitude was that of a disapproving protestant towards island communities which were still in their beliefs and 'superstitions' close to the old Catholic faith at heart. For these reasons Martin had to convey a mood of objectivity and detachment which increased the validity and 'reality' of what he said. The island world was full of 'curiosities', and in writing of them Martin could be believed as an enthusiastic, sincere and reliably honest 'field agent'.

At the same time his frequent remarks on his sources were intended to emphasise his own and the islanders' credibility. He mentioned respectable literary and scientific names such as John Locke, Robert Morison, Dr Pitcairn and James Sutherland, to show that he was acquainted with learned men or with their published works; Locke for instance, in his book on education (1693), had written about how a 'governor' should treat his pupil, guidance which Martin could have found helpful in his duties after 1704. The island people may have been superstitious and 'the ignorant vulgar' in many ways but they were neither unintelligent nor dishonest in what they did or told him. So when Martin uses words like 'The Natives told me' he was intending to indicate both that he had actually been to a particular island and that what he was recording came straight from inhabitants who could be trusted to give factual information. There were few in his day – one of them was probably Edward Lhuyd – who recognised or appreciated that a wealth of history and understanding of nature lay in the oral tradition possessed by remote Highland and island families, and perhaps Martin's books opened up a new field of interest, enquiry and study for early eighteenth century contemporaries as they certainly did for many in later generations, including Dr Johnson and James Boswell, on to the present day.

It would be unfair to view the variety of Martin's interests, in antiquities, diseases, religion, plants, and so on, two or more of them often crammed hurriedly into one paragraph, and his failure to disclose the beliefs and superstitions in which he himself may have shared, as a pretence or piece of cunning concealment. He could follow up his graduation from Edinburgh University with being a 'governor', accompanying John Adair on a voyage round the north of Scotland, serving the interests of the 'virtuosi', turning his collecting of 'curiosities' and specimens into several written accounts of his homeland, and later becoming a doctor, without being criticised for excessive ambition and dishonesty and without being inconsistent with his true self.

*

Editorial Note

The original edition of *A Description of the Western Islands of Scotland*, published in London in 1703, is here reproduced to mark the three hundredth anniversary of the book's first appearance. Since it is not at present known whether Martin's manuscript has survived it may be that the first edition is the nearest that can be reached to it, but the book gives the impression of being published in haste, perhaps to get in ahead of the publication planned by John Adair. Inappropriate punctuation, running two words together, and improbable spellings are three of the features suggesting haste or carelessness. Some of the misprints noticed at the time were corrected in the page of 'Errata'. The spelling of Gaelic words may reflect either Martin's limited ability to read and write Gaelic or the printer's unfamiliarity with them, or both.

In 1716, two years before Martin's death, a second edition was published, 'very much Corrected' and with clearer print. The corrections were chiefly in the punctuation. Though it contained a few changes and errors of its own, this edition has been the one chiefly used for the reprints that have appeared since. In 1884 a reprint was published in Glasgow for the benefit of the members of the Napier Commission. Martin's two books, *A Late Voyage to St Kilda* and *A Description*, were joined by the 1549 account of the Hebrides by Dean Monro in the next publication, from Eneas Mackay, Stirling, in 1934. This had a useful editorial 'Note' which contained various particulars that had 'come to light' since the 1884 reprint; these were mainly the details of the Martin family history given in the third volume of *The Clan Donald*. An introduction, by Donald J Macleod, was largely an essay on the culture and customs of Celtic people.

Two further reprints, from the Mercat Press in 1970 and from Birlinn Ltd in 1999, were again based on the second edition of 1716 though the presentation was modernised for easier reading. The introduction to the latter describes the background and the nature of the content of Martin's work.

The present, new edition, the first to be accompanied with notes, commentary and illustrations, is not intended to be in any way an academic exercise. It is rather an attempt to relate Martin's experience of the western, and northern, islands three centuries ago to the present day, so that the modern reader may find it easier to identify and understand what the author saw and was writing about. In particular it is hoped that the people of the islands today will feel that Martin's book and the circumstances in which he wrote are of even greater interest and relevance than they may previously have realised.

The notes inserted at the end of each 'section' of Martin's book form a somewhat arbitrary and personal commentary, based as they are on a selection from the numerous topics covered in his pages. For instance, there has been no attempt to cover all the diseases and plant cures, dealt with much more expertly than could be done here by Mary Beith in her regular articles in the West Highland Free Press newspaper. It should perhaps be mentioned that a feature of the original 1703 edition of the book is the variability of the printing, including the discontinuation of the bold lettering of names and the apparent additions of information in paragraphs at the ends of some 'sections'.

Notes and References to Introduction

1 MA M Stobie: Plan of the Parish of Kilmuir and Uigg in Trotternish lying in the Isle of Sky etc. 1764

2 Thomson Atlas: 'Skye Island' etc.; Blaeu Atlas. The location of the Campbell of Breadalbane 'seat' at Taymouth near Kenmore, Perthshire, was also once called Beallach.

3 Forfeited Estates Papers NAS E656/2/2; MA GD221 MS4272/1 'At Mogstot'

4 MA GD221 MS4272/4, MS4277/8/3, MS4277/4/4. For further records of the nephew Martin see n.44. Other Martins in the 1718 rental of Trotternish (see n.3) included John Martin in Regndray (Renetra); John Martine in Hoill; Donald Martine in Erisco 'Frail'; John Martine in Flotagarrie Clachglas, Penisheider and Kingsbarrow; Angus Martine in Upper Tout; Alexander Martine in Ellishader; Donald Martine in Graulin; Alexander Martine in Sworbie. In 1738 another of Martin's nephews, Hugh, son of the then deceased John in Flodigarry, received a tack of the pennyland of Grenigile, already possessed by him. The tack was written by Donald Martin, tacksman of Bellach [MA GD221 MS4280/5]. There is a marriage contract between Martin Martin, tacksman of Lachsay next to Bealach, and Margaret Macleod dated 4 September 1776 [NAS GD382/21] and a Martin Martin was tenant of Renetra, formerly possessed by 'Mrs Martin', in January 1827 [MA GD221 MS4289/7].

5 Carmichael Watson Collection EUL nos. 244/123, 200a, 375

6 W. Mackenzie: Skye – Iochdar Trotternish and District Glasgow 1930 pp.121-129; M. Martin: A Description of the Western Islands of Scotland circa 1695 Glasgow 1884

7 Macdonalds Vol. III pp.558-560; J. Macinnes: The Evangelical Movement in the Highlands of Scotland 1688 to 1800 Aberdeen 1951 p.20

8 Information from EUL Special Collections.

9 DJ Macleod (edit.): A Description of the Western Islands of Scotland circa 1695 by Martin Martin, Gent etc. Stirling 1934 pp.10-11, 17, 18; MA GD221 MS5289 Bond by Captain Hugh MacDonald

10 DC Section 3 8/92/1. Some editors (e.g. DJ Macleod 1934) give the date of the receipt as 13 August 1686.

11 DC Section 3 8/92/3,4,6; Section 3/15/2/1,2

12 DC Section 3 13/2/1 Discharge by Rorie McLeoid servitor to John McLeoid of Dunvegan to Normand McLeoid in Groban – 'Written by Mr Martin Martin governour to the Laird of McLeoid younger' 20 October 1686; DC Section 3 8/103,106,112; DC Section 3 9/76, 19/2 8, 19/2/12, 19/2/13. Sibbald's list of people who helped him as sources of information included '[John] Morison indweller in the Lewis' and 'Mr Martin Mac Martin' who 'wrote for me a description of the Hirta or St Kilda with the isles adjacent'. His 'MacMartin' seems to have arisen from a mistaken reading of Martin's signature. Martin commonly signed 'Ma Martin' and the two parts could sometimes appear to be joined by a curl backwards from the second M. [Sibbald MSS NLS Adv. MS 33.3.16 pp.17-30, esp. p.28 (f.15v)]. Martin himself wrote to Edward Lhuyd: 'pray do not add mc to my name since neither myself nor any of my Tribe ever use it' [Emery p.111]. So perhaps Sibbald picked up Mac' some other way.

13 E. Beveridge: North Uist – Its Archaeology and Topography Edinburgh 1911 p.336

14 *DP NLS MS1389 f.75 Letter from London to Mr Alexander McLeod, Advocate, Edinburgh 17 August 1695; NLS MS1389 f.84 Letter from Dunvegan to John Mackenzie of Delvine, Edinburgh. It has been incorrectly stated that this letter was to Mr Alexander McLeod and that 'the president of the Royal Society' had obliged Martin to send all his observations 'to that body'. [Withers (1) p.513]. The letter shows that it was the Viscount Tarbat who directed the sending of the observations.*

15 *DP NLS MS1389 f.85*

16 *DP NLS MS1389 f.86*

17 *RS Copy Letter LBC 11(2) pp.160-161. Withers [(1) p.512, (3) p.88] points out that 'Mr Charleton' was the collector William Courten who went by the name of 'Charleton' for some reason.*

18 *BL Sloane MS4037 f.127 26 September 1696*

19 *BL Sloane MS4036 ff.338-339 Letter from 'Armidill in Skie' 2 August 1697*

20 *BL Sloane MS4036 ff.358-359v. Letter from Edinburgh 30 September 1697*

21 *DP NLS f.90 Letter from London 27 November 1697; RS EL.P1.101, LBC12 pp.344-345*

22 *Sibbald MSS NLS Adv. MS 33.5.19 Essay pp.170, 177; RS LBC12 pp.338-340*

23 *RS EL.P1.102; Withers (1) pp.506, 515*

24 *RS EL.P1.102; RS LBC12 pp.69-72*

25 *RS EL.P1.102; J Moore: 'John Adair's Contribution to the Charting of the Scottish Coasts: a Re-assessment' in Imago Mundi Vol. 52 London 2000 pp.47,57*

26 *BL Sloane MS4060 ff.125-6. The letter is dated in the British Library catalogue 22 November 1698. Contrary to the conclusion drawn from Preston's letter to Sloane of 13 October 1698 that 'Martin Martin undertook at least two of his several Hebridean voyages in the company of John Adair' [Withers (1) p.514] it does not appear from that letter or that of November 1698 that he made more than part of one. A letter from Martin to Mackenzie of Delvine reporting the death of Macleod of Macleod at Fortrose [DP NLS MS1389 f.74] is dated 20 June, with a year that might be read 1695 or 1698. The former seems more likely in view of Martin's voyage with Adair, but the death has also been placed in 1699 [I.F. Grant: The MacLeods – The History of a Clan 1200-1956 London 1959 p.330].*

27 *EUL MS Dc. 8.35 ff.9-10*

28 *BL Sloane MS4039 f.18*

29 *Moore p.57*

30 *BL Sloane MS4060 ff.125-126, RS LBC12 pp.69-72*

31 *RS LBC12 pp.409-412*

32 *DC Section 3 9/87, Section 3 9/97, Section 3 9/101 29 November 1701. Martin had received £5 sterl. (£60 scots) on 8 November 1698 [Discharge of Precept DC Section 3 9/65] For other receipts bearing Martin's name and that of 'Captain Niell MacLeod of the foot Guards' see MA GD221/5346/3 & GD221/5349/4 6 October 1697 and 5 December 1701.*

33 DP NLS MS1389 f.95; BL Sloane MS4040 ff.165-166

34 BL Sloane MS f.384

35 DC Section 3 20/13 22 December 1703; DP NLS MS1389 ff.98-104, also ff.93-94 Letter from London to John Mackenzie 13 April 1703, f.95 Letter from London to John Mackenzie 26 June 1703, ff.96, 100, 105. In his letter of 13 April 1703 Martin expressed his appreciation of further help given by either the Earl of Cromarty or 'My Lord Commissioner': 'My Lord has done me yet a greater honour and kindness in procuring his Royal Highness's the Prince of Denmarks Consent to be patron to my book, of which I am very sensible.' The choice of patron may not therefore have been Martin's, and it came in for criticism from W. Mackenzie (p.124).

36 DP NLS MS1389 f.100

37 DP NLS MS1389 f.100

38 DP NLS MS1389 f.105 Letter from Duntulm: 'I leave this place the end of April. Mr John McLean stays here all summer and will supply the time of my absence till you provide another in my room'; ff.106-112, in which Martin seems to speak of a further 'project', perhaps relating to fisheries as he asks (f.111) John Mackenzie 'what are the two months in spring that the Codd abounds in Garloch [ie. Gairloch, Ross-shire]?'; ff.114-116 Mackenzie's son took his studies almost too seriously: 'I prevailld with him of late to read less for some time, for he is become a skeleton with Studying' (f.114). According to the DNB (1998 reprint pp.1173-1174) 'Martinus Martin, Scoto-Britannus', entered Leyden University 6 March 1710. This is confirmed by records at Leiden which show that he matriculated there on 6 March 1710 when he was aged 41 and that he lodged in the house of one Joannes Ottensteen (or Ottensteyn) on the corner of the street called Diefsteag. Then, according to Innes Smith, Martin was 'M.D.' at Rheims, 12 October 1710.
For instance, Withers [(2) p.5] said he did practice, the Macdonalds [Vol. III p.560] said he didn't.

39 BL Sloane MS4059 f.220

40 DP NLS MS1389 f.126 Letter from London 27 November 1716

41 DP NLS MS1389 ff.145,146

42 DP NLS MS1389 f.159

43 DP NLS MS1389 ff.162,163; ff.162, 184

44 DP NLS MS1389 f.185; Warrand of Bught Papers NAS GD23/6/156. Later Martin Martins continued to appear from time to time (see n.4 above), as for example in the marriage contract between Martin Martin tacksman of Lachsay in Trotternish, and Margaret Macleod 4 September 1776.

45 Withers (1) p.508, (3) pp.70-71

46 Withers (3) p.87. Emery p.111

47 Withers (3) p.88

Introduction: Abbreviations and Bibliography

BL	:	British Library
Blaeu	:	J Blaeu Atlas Novus 1654
DC	:	MacLeod Muniments, Dunvegan Castle
DP	:	Delvine Papers
EUL	:	Edinburgh University Library (Special Collections)
MA	:	Macdonald Archive, Clan Donald Centre, Armadale
NAS	:	National Archives of Scotland
NLS	:	National Library of Scotland

EUL Carmichael Watson Collection
NAS Forfeited Estates Papers
GD382/21
Warrand of Bught Papers
NLS Sibbald MSS

E Beveridge: North Uist – Its Archaeology and Topography Edinburgh 1911
E V Emery: 'Martin Martin (?1660-1719), Naturalist' in Notes and Queries March 1958 pp. 109-111
I F Grant: The MacLeods – The History of a Clan 1200-1956 London 1959
A & A Macdonald: The Clan Donald 3 Vols. Inverness 1896-1904
J Macinnes: The Evangelical Movement in the Highlands of Scotland 1688 to 1800 Aberdeen 1951
W Mackenzie: Skye – Iochdar Trotternish and District Glasgow 1930
D J Macleod (edit.): A Description of the Western Islands of Scotland c.1695 by MartinMartin, Gent etc. Stirling 1934
M Martin: A Description of the Western Islands of Scotland circa 1695 Glasgow 1884
J Moore: 'John Adair's Contribution to the Charting of the Scottish Coasts: a Reassessment' in Imago Mundi Vol.52 London 2000

R W I Smith: English-Speaking Students of Medicine at the University of Leyden Edinburgh 1932
C Withers (1): 'Reporting, Mapping, Trusting' in Isis London 1999
C Withers (2): Introduction to A Description of the Western Islands of Scotland ca. 1695 by Martin Martin Edinburgh 1999
C Withers (3): Geography, Science and National Identity – Scotland since 1520 Cambridge 2001

Note on page numbering

There are two sequences of page numbers:
Martin text pages 1-392
New edition Pages i-xxxii, 1-320
The numbers at the head of the notes pages and the numbers in the index relate to the Martin text.

Note on placenames

The versions of placenames used in the notes are taken from maps previous to the recent Ordnance Survey series which attempts to provide most names in Gaelic.

A
DESCRIPTION
OF THE
Western Islands
OF
SCOTLAND.
CONTAINING

A Full Account of their Situation, Extent, Soils, Product, Harbours, Bays, Tides, Anchoring Places, and Fisheries.

The Ancient and Modern Government, Religion and Customs of the Inhabitants, particularly of their Druids, Heathen Temples, Monasteries, Churches, Chappels, Antiquities, Monuments, Forts, Caves, and other Curiosities of Art and Nature. Of their Admirable and Expeditious way of Curing most Diseases by Simples of their own Product.

A Particular Account of the *Second Sight*, or Faculty of foreseeing things to come, by way of Vision, so common among them.

A Brief Hint of Methods to Improve Trade in that Country, both by Sea and Land.

With a New MAP of the whole, describing the Harbours, Anchoring Places, and dangerous Rocks, for the benefit of Sailers.

To which is added a Brief Description of the Isles of *Orkney*, and *Schetland*.

By *M. MARTIN*, Gent.

LONDON, Printed for *Andrew Bell*, at the *Cross-Keys* and *Bible*, in *Cornhil*, near *Stocks-Market*, 1703.

To His Royal Highness Prince *GEORGE* of *Denmark*, Lord High Admiral of *England*, and *Ireland*, and of all Her Majesties Plantations, and Generalissimo of all Her Majesties Forces, *&c.*

May it please Your Royal Highness,

AMongst the Numerous Croud of Congratulating Addressers, the Islanders described in the following Sheets presume to approach Your Royal Person; they can now without suspicion of Infidelity to the Queen of England, *pay their Duty to a Danish Prince to whose Predecessors all of them*

a 2 *former-*

formerly belonged. They can boast that they are honoured with the Sepulchres of Eight Kings of **Norway**, *who at this day, with forty eight Kings of* Scotland, *and four of* Ireland, *lie Entomb'd in the Island of* Jona; *a Place Fam'd then for some peculiar Sanctity. They presume that it is owing to their great distance from the Imperial Seat, rather than their want of Native Worth, that their Islands have been so little regarded, which by Improvement might render a considerable accession of Strength and Riches to the Crown, as appears by a Scheme annexed to the following Treatise. They have suffer'd hitherto under the want of a powerful and affectionate Patron, Providence*

vidence seems to have given them a Natural Claim to Your Royal Highness; *and tho' it be almost presumption for so Sinful a Nation to hope for so great a Blessing, they do humbly join with their Prayers to God, that the Protection which they hope for from two Princes of so much Native Worth and Goodness, might be continu'd in Your Royal Posterity to all Generations; so Prays*

May it please your Royal Highness,

Your Highnesses most Humble

and most Obedient Servant,

M. Martin.

THE PREFACE.

THE Weſtern Iſlands of *Scotland*, which make the Subject of the following Book, were called by the Ancient Geographers *Æbudæ*, and *Hebrides*, but they knew ſo little of them that they neither agreed in their Name nor Number. Perhaps it is peculiar to thoſe Iſles, that they have never been deſcrib'd till now by any Man that was a Native of the Country, or had travelled them. They were indeed touch'd by *Boethius*, Biſhop *Leſly*, *Buchannan*, and *Johnſton*, in their Hiſtories of *Scotland*, but none of thoſe Authors were ever there in Perſon; ſo that what they wrote concerning 'em was upon truſt from others. *Buchannan* it is true, had his Information from *Donald Monro*, who had been in many of 'em, and therefore his Account is the beſt that has hitherto appear'd, but it muſt be own'd

own'd that it is very imperfect; that Great Man deſign'd the Hiſtory and not the Geography of his Country, and therefore in him it was pardonable. Beſides, ſince his time, there's a great Change in the Humour of the World, and by conſequence in the way of Writing. Natural and Experimental Philoſophy has been much improv'd ſince his days, and therefore Deſcriptions of Countries without the Natural Hiſtory of 'em, are now juſtly reckon'd to be defective.

This I had a particular regard to in the following Deſcription, and have every where taken notice of the Nature of the Climate and Soil, of the Produce of the Places by Sea and Land, and of the Remarkable Cures perform'd by the Natives meerly by the uſe of Simples, and that in ſuch variety as I hope will make amends for what Defects may be found in my Stile and way of Writing; for there's a Wantonneſs in Language as well as in other things, to which my Countrymen of the Iſles are as much ſtrangers, as to other Exceſſes which are

a 4 too

too frequent in many parts of *Europe.* We ſtudy Things there more than Words, tho' thoſe that underſtand our Native Language muſt own that we have enough of the latter to inform the Judgment, and work upon the Affections in as pathetick a manner as any other Languages whatever. But I go on to my Subject;

The Iſles here deſcrib'd are but little known, or conſidered, not only by Strangers, but even by thoſe under the ſame Government and Climate.

The Modern Itch after the Knowledge of Foreign Places is ſo prevalent, that the generality of Mankind beſtow little thought or time upon the Place of their Nativity; it is become Cuſtomary in thoſe of Quality to Travel young into Foreign Countries, whilſt they are abſolute Strangers at home; and many of them when they return, are only loaded with ſuperficial Knowledge, as the bare Names of Famous Libraries, Stately Edifices, Fine Statues, Curious Paintings, late Faſhions, new Diſhes, new

new Tunes, new Dances, Painted Beauties, and the like.

The Places here mentioned afford no ſuch Entertainment, the Inhabitants in general prefer Conveniency to Ornament, both in their Houſes and Apparel, and they rather ſatisfie than oppreſs Nature, in their way of Eating and Drinking; and not a few among them have a Natural Beauty, which excels any that has been drawn by the fineſt *Apelles.*

The Land and the Sea that encompaſſes it, produces many things Uſeful and Curious in their kind, ſeveral of which have not hitherto been mention'd by the Learned; this may afford the Theoriſt ſubject of Contemplation, ſince every Plant of the Field, every Fiber of each Plant, and the leaſt Particle of the ſmalleſt Inſect carries with it the impreſs of its Maker; and if rightly conſider'd, may read us Lectures of Divinity and Morals.

The Inhabitants of theſe Iſlands do for the moſt part labour under the want of of knowledge of Letters, and other uſeful Arts and Sciences ; notwithſtanding which defect, they ſeem to be better vers'd in the Book of Nature, than many that have greater opportunities of improvement ; this will appear plain and evident to the judicious Reader, upon a view of the ſucceſsful Practice of the Iſlanders in the preſervation of their Health, above what the generality of Mankind enjoys, and this is perform'd meerly by Temperance, and the prudent uſe of Simples, which, as we are aſſur'd by repeated Experiments, fail not to remove the moſt ſtubborn Diſtempers, where the beſt prepar'd Medicines have frequently no ſucceſs. This I relate not only from the Authority of many of the Inhabitants, who are Perſons of great integrity, but likewiſe from my own particular Obſervation ; and thus with *Celſus* they firſt make Experiments, and afterwards proceed to reaſon upon the Effects.

Humane Induſtry has of late advanc'd uſeful and experimental Philoſophy very

very much, Women and illiterate Perſons have in ſome meaſure contributed to it by the diſcovery of ſome uſeful Cures ; the Field of Nature is large, and much of it wants ſtill to be cultivated by an ingenious and diſcreet application ; and the Curious by their Obſervations might daily make further advances in the Hiſtory of Nature.

Self preſervation is natural to every living Creature, and thus we ſee the ſeveral Animals of the Sea and the Land ſo careful of themſelves, as to obſerve nicely what is agreeable, and what is hurtful to them, and accordingly they chuſe the one, and reject the other.

The Husbandman and the Fiſher could expect but little ſucceſs without obſervation in their ſeveral Employments, and it is by obſervation that the Phyſician commonly judges of the Condition of his Patient. A Man of Obſervation proves often a Phyſician to himſelf, for it was by this that our Anceſtors preſerv'd their Health till a good old Age, and that Mankind laid up that

that ſtock of Natural Knowlege of which they are now poſſeſs'd.

The Wiſe *Solomon* did not think it beneath him to write of the meaneſt Plant, as well as of the taleſt Cedar. *Hypocrates* was at the Pains and Charge to Travel Foreign Countries with a deſign to learn the Vertues of Plants, Roots, &c. I have in my little Travels endeavour'd among other things in ſome meaſure to imitate ſo great a Pattern, and if I have been ſo happy as to oblige the Republick of Learning with any thing that is uſeful, I have my Deſign. I hold it enough for me to furniſh my Obſervations, without accounting for the Reaſon and Way that thoſe Simples produce them; this I leave to the Learned in that Faculty, and if they would oblige the World with ſuch Theorems from theſe and the like Experiments, as might ſerve for Rules upon Occaſions of this Nature, it would be of great advantage to the Publick.

As for the Improvement of the Iſles in general, it depends upon the Government

ment of *Scotland*, to give Eucouragement for it to ſuch Publick Spirited Perſons or Societies as are willing to lay out their Endeavours that way; and how large a Field they have to work upon, will appear, by taking a Survey of each, and of the Method of Improvement that I have hereunto ſubjoin'd.

There is ſuch an Account given here of the *Second Sight* as the Nature of the thing will bear. This has always been reckon'd ſufficient among the unbiaſs'd part of Mankind; but for thoſe that will not be ſo ſatisfied, they ought to oblige us with a New Scheme, by which we may judge of Matters of Fact.

There are ſeveral Inſtances of Heatheniſm and Pagan Superſtition among the Inhabitants of the Iſlands related here, but I would not have the Reader to think thoſe Practices are chargeable upon the generality of the preſent Inhabitants; ſince only a few of the Oldeſt and moſt Ignorant of the Vulgar are guilty of 'em.

The Preface, &c.

'em. These Practices are only to be found, where the Reform'd Religion has not prevail'd; for 'tis to the Progress of that alone that the Banishment of Evil Spirits, as well as of Evil Customs is owing, when all other Methods prov'd ineffectual. And for the Islanders in general, I may truly say, that in Religion and Vertue they excel many thousands of others, who have greater Advantages of daily Improvement.

THE

THE

CONTENTS.

A Pre-

The CONTENTS.

Hearing

The CONTENTS.

b

Cod

The CONTENTS.

The CONTENTS.

b 2 The

The CONTENTS.

The CONTENTS.

The CONTENTS.

b 4 Cure

The CONTENTS.

The

The CONTENTS.

A

The CONTENTS.

The

The CONTENTS.

The CONTENTS.

The

The CONTENTS.

ERRATA.

PAge 68. *l.* 15. for Vanish, read Vanich, p. 25. *l.* 29. after has been, read quenched. p. 79. *l.* 2. for two, read ten. p. 103. for *Luchkrach*, r. *Luchktaeh*. p. 131. *l.* 19. r. *Innernefs* p. 133. *l.* 25. for *Rofay*, r. *Rafay*. p. 134. *l.* 12. for Bat, r. bot. p. 137. *l.* 25. r. *Dunvegan*. p. 138. *l.* 1. for *Ila* r. *Ifa*. Note, That by mistake the account of *Dulfe* in p, 177. is transposed, to p. 185. p. 2. *ib. l.* 4. r. if before they. p. 263, *For Church-Men*, r. Clergy-Men. p. 357. *l.* 11. for *Serpier*, r. *Cæpier*. p. 361. *l.* 14. for 17. r. 18. The Cutts for the Shells neglected, could not be got ready in time.

A DESCRIPTION OF THE Western Islands OF SCOTLAND, &c.

THE Island of **Lewis** is so call'd from **Leog**, which in the *Irish* Language signifies *Water*, lying on the surface of the Ground; which is very proper to this Island, because of the great number of Fresh-water Lakes that abound in it. The Isle of **Lewis** is by all Strangers and Seafaring-men, accounted the outmost Tract of Islands lying to the Northwest of *Scotland*. It is divided by several narrow Channels, and distinguish'd by several Proprietors as well as by several Names: by the Islanders it is commonly call'd *The Long Island*, being from South to North 100 Miles in length, and from East to West from 3 to 14 in breadth. It lyes in the Shire of *Ross*, and made part of the Diocess of the Isles.

A THE

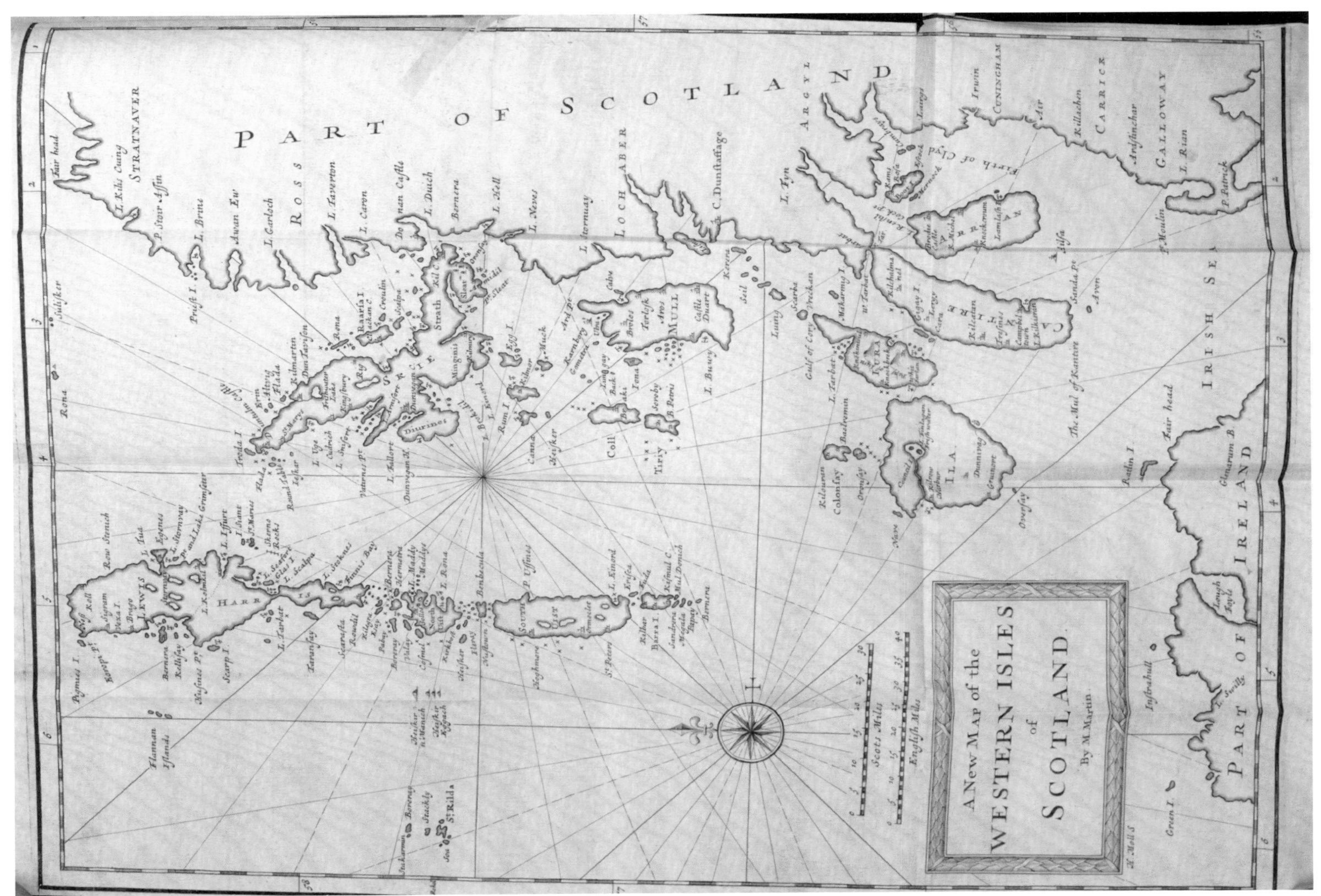
A New Map of the
WESTERN ISLES
of
SCOTLAND.
By M. Martin.
PART OF SCOTLAND
PART OF IRELAND
IRISH SEA
Scots Miles
English Miles

THE Iſle of *Lewis*, properly and ſtrictly ſo call'd, is 36 Miles in length; *viz.* from the North-point of *Bowling-head* to the South-point of *Huſſineſs* in *Harries*: and in ſome places it is 10, and in others 12 Miles in breadth. The Air is temperately cold and moiſt, and for a corrective the Natives uſe a Doſe of *Treſtarig* or *Uſquebaugh*. This Iſland is for the moſt part healthy, eſpecially in the middle from South to North. It is arable on the Weſt ſide, for about ſixteen Miles on the Coaſt, it is likewiſe plain and arable in ſeveral places on the Eaſt: The Soil is generally ſandy, excepting the Heaths, which in ſome places are black, and in others a fine red Clay; as appears by the many Veſſels made of it by their Women; ſome for boiling Meat, and others for preſerving their Ale, for which they are much better than Barrels of Wood.

THIS Iſland was reputed very fruitful in Corn, until the late Years of ſcarcity and bad Seaſons. The Corn ſown here is Barley, Oats and Rye; and they have alſo Flax and Hemp. The beſt increaſe is commonly from the Ground manur'd with Sea ware: They fatten it alſo with Soot; but it is obſerv'd that the Bread made of Corn growing in the Ground ſo fatten'd, occaſions the Jaundice to thoſe that eat it. They obſerve likewiſe that Corn produced in Ground which was never tilled before, occaſions ſeveral Diſorders in thoſe who eat the Bread

Bread, or drink the Ale made of that Corn, ſuch as the Head-ach and Vomiting.

THE Natives are very induſtrious, and undergo a great fatigue by digging the Ground with Spades, and in moſt places they turn the Ground ſo digged upſide down, and cover it with Sea-ware; and in this manner there are about 500 People imploy'd daily for ſome Months. This way of labouring is by them call'd **Timiy**; and certainly produces a greater Increaſe than Digging or Plowing otherwiſe. They have little Harrows with wooden teeth in the firſt and ſecond rows, which breaks the Ground, and in the third row they have rough Heath, which ſmoothes it: This light Harrow is drawn by a Man having a ſtrong rope of Horſe-hair acroſs his breaſt.

THEIR plenty of Corn was ſuch, as diſpos'd the Natives to brew ſeveral ſorts of Liquors, as common *Uſquebaugh*, another call'd *Treſtarig*, *id eſt Aqua vitæ*, three times diſtill'd, which is ſtrong and hot; a third ſort is four times diſtill'd, and this by the Natives is call'd *Uſquebaugh-baul*, *id eſt Uſquebaugh*, which at firſt taſte affects all the Members of the Body: two ſpoonfuls of this laſt Liquor is a ſufficient Doſe; and if any Man exceed this, it would preſently ſtop his Breath, and endanger his Life. The *Treſtarig* and *Uſquebaugh-baul*, are both made of Oats.

A 2 THERE

THERE are ſeveral convenient Bays and Harbours in this Iſland. *Loch Grace* and *Loch-tua*, lying Norweſt, are not to be reckon'd ſuch; tho' Veſſels are forc'd in there ſometimes by ſtorm. *Loch*-**Stornbay** lyes on the Eaſt ſide in the middle of the Iſland, and is 18 Miles directly South from the Norther-moſt Point of the ſame. It is a Harbour well known by Seamen. There are ſeveral places for anchoring about half a League on the South of this Coaſt. About 7 Miles Southward, there is a good Harbour, call'd the *Birkin Iſles*; within the Bay call'd *Loch Colmkill*, 3 Miles further South lies *Loch-Eriſort*, which hath an Anchoring place on the South and North; about 5 Miles South lyes *Loch-ſea-fort*, having two viſible Rocks in the Entry, the beſt Harbour is on the South ſide.

ABOUT 24 Miles South-weſt, lyes *Loch*-**Carlbay**, a very capacious, tho, unknown Harbour, being never frequented by any Veſſels: Tho' the Natives aſſure me that it is in all reſpects a convenient Harbour for Ships of the Firſt rate. The beſt entrance looks North and North-weſt, but there is another from the Weſt. On the South ſide of the Iſland **Bernera**, there are ſmall Iſlands without the entrance, which contribute much to the ſecurity of the Harbour, by breaking the Winds and Seas that come from the great Ocean. Four Miles to the South on this Coaſt, is *Loch-Rogue*, which runs in among the Mountains. All the Coaſts

Coaſts and Bays above mention'd, do in fair weather abound with Cod, Ling, Herring, and all other ſorts of Fiſhes taken in the Weſtern-Iſlands.

COD and Ling are of a very large ſize, and very plentiful near *Loch-Carlvay*; but the Whales very much interrupt the Fiſhing in this place. There is one ſort of Whale remarkable for its Greatneſs, which the Fiſhermen diſtinguiſh from all others by the Name of the *Gallan-Whale*; becauſe they never ſee it but at the Promontory of that Name: I was told by the Natives, that about 15 years ago, this great Whale overturn'd a Fiſhers-boat, and devour'd three of the Crew; the fourth Man was ſav'd by another Boat which happen'd to be near, and ſaw this accident. There are many Whales of different ſizes, that frequent the Herring Bays on the Eaſt ſide; the Natives imploy many Boats together in purſuit of the Whales, chaſing them up into the Bays, till they wound one of them mortally, and then it runs aſhore, and they ſay that all the reſt commonly follow the tract of its Blood, and run themſelves alſo on ſhore in like manner; by which means many of them are kill'd: about five years ago there were fifty young Whales kill'd in this manner, and moſt of them eaten by the common People, who by experience find them to be very nouriſhing Food; this I have been aſſur'd of by ſeveral Perſons, but

A 3 parti-

particularly by ſome poor meagre people, who became plump and luſty by this Food in the ſpace of a Week; they call it *Sea-Pork*, for ſo it ſignifies in their Language: the bigger Whales are more purgative than theſe leſſer ones, but the latter are better for Nouriſhment.

THE Bays afford plenty of Shell-fiſh, as Clams, Oyſters, Cockles, Muſles, Lympits, Wilks, Spout-fiſh; of which laſt there is ſuch a prodigious quantity caſt up out of the Sand of *Loch-tua*, that their noiſome Smell infects the Air, and makes it very unhealthful to the Inhabitants, who are not able to conſume them, by eating or fatning their Ground with them; and this they ſay happens moſt commonly once in ſeven years.

THE Bays and Coaſts of this Iſlands afford great quantity of ſmall Corral, not exceeding 6 Inches in length, and about the bigneſs of a Gooſe's Quill: This abounds moſt in *Loch-Sea-fort*, and there is Corraline likewiſe on this Coaſt.

THERE are a great many Freſh-water Lakes in this Iſland, which abound with Trouts and Eels: The common Bait us'd for catching them is Earthworms, but a handful of parboil'd Muſles thrown into the Water, attracts the Trouts and Eels to the place; the fitteſt time

time for catching them, is, when the Wind blows from the South-weſt: there are ſeveral Rivers on each ſide this Iſland which affords Salmons, as alſo black Muſles, in which many times Pearl is found.

THE Natives in the Village **Barvas** retain an ancient Cuſtom of ſending a Man very early to croſs *Barvas* River, every firſt day of *May*, to prevent any Females croſſing it firſt; for that they ſay would hinder the Salmon from coming into the River all the year round: they pretend to have learn'd this from a foreign Sailer, who was ſhipwreck'd upon that Coaſt, a long time ago. This obſervation they maintain to be true from Experience.

THERE are ſeveral Springs and Fountains of curious Effects; ſuch as that at *Loch-Carlvay*, that never whitens Linnen, which hath often been try'd by the Inhabitants. The Well at St. *Cowſten*'s Church, never boils any kind of Meat, tho' it be kept on fire a whole day. St. *Andrew*'s Well in the Village *Shadar*, is by the vulgar Natives made a Teſt to know if a ſick Perſon will die of the Diſtemper he labours under: they ſend one with a wooden Diſh to bring ſome of the water to the Patient, and if the Diſh which is then laid ſoftly upon the ſurface of the water turn round Sun-ways, they conclude that the Patient will recover of that Diſtemper; but if otherwiſe, that he will die.

A 4 THERE

8 *A Description of the*

THERE are many Caves on the Coast of this Island, in which great numbers of Otters and Seals do lye; there be also many Land and Sea Fowls that build and hatch in them. The Cave in *Loch-Grace* hath several pieces of a hard substance in the bottom, which distil from the top of it. There are several natural and artificial Forts in the Coast of this Island, which are call'd *Dun*, from the *Irish* word *Dain*, which signifies a Fort: The natural Forts here are *Dun-owle*, *Dun-coradil*, *Dun-eisten*.

THE Castle at **Stornway** Village was destroy'd by the *English* Garrison, kept there by *Oliver Cromwell*. Some few Miles to the North of *Brago*, there is a Fort compos'd of large Stones, it is of a round form, made taperwise towards the top, and is three stories high: the Wall is double, and hath several Doors and Stairs, so that one may go round within the Wall. There are some Cairnes or Heaps of Stones gather'd together on Heaths, and some of them at a great distance from any Ground that affords Stones: such as *Cairnwarp* near *Mournagh* Hill, *&c*. These artificial Forts are likewise built upon Heaths at a considerable distance also from stony Ground. The *Thrushel* Stone in the Parish of **Barvas**, is above 20 foot high, and almost as much in breadth. There are three erected Stones upon the North side of **Loch-Carlvay** about 12 foot high each: several other Stones are to be seen here

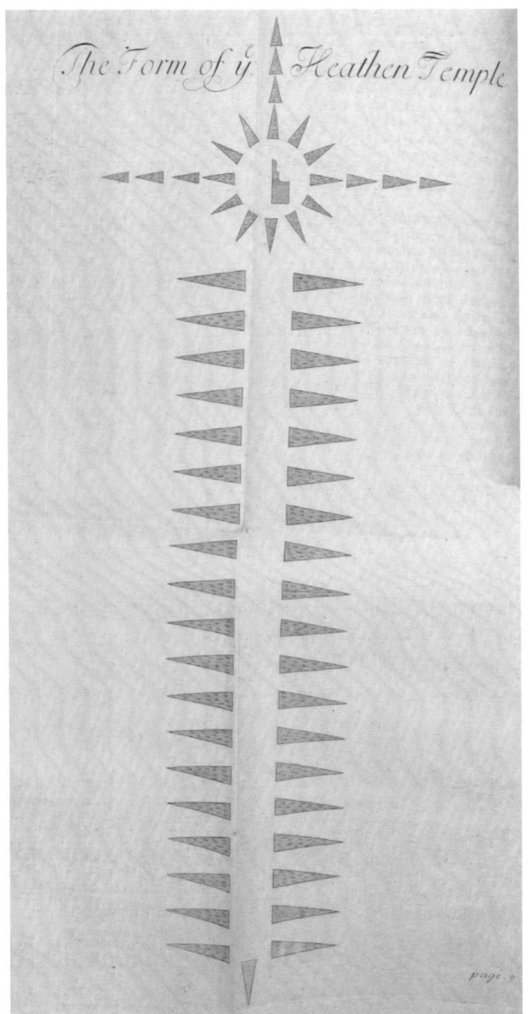

here in remote places, and ſome of them ſtanding on one end; ſome of the ignorant Vulgar ſay, they were Men by Inchantment turn'd into Stones; and others ſay, they are Monuments of Perſons of Note kill'd in Battle.

THE moſt remarkable Stones for Number, Bigneſs, and Order, that fell under my Obſervation, were at the Village of *Claſſerniſs*; where there are 39 Stones ſet up 6 or 7 foot high and two foot in breadth each; they are plac'd in form of an Avenue, the breadth of which is 8 foot, and the diſtance between each Stone ſix: and there is a Stone ſet up in the entrance of this Avenue; at the South end there is join'd to this range of Stone a Circle of 12 Stones of equal diſtance and height with the other 39. There is one ſet up in the center of this Circle, which is 13 foot high, and ſhap'd like the Rudder of a ſhip: without this Circle there are 4 Stones ſtanding to the Weſt, at the ſame diſtance with the Stones in the Circle; and there are 4 Stones ſet up in the ſame manner at the South and Eaſt ſides. I enquir'd of the Inhabitants what Tradition they had from their Anceſtors concerning theſe Stones? and they told me, it was a place appointed for Worſhip in the the time of Heatheniſm, and that the Chief *Druid* or Prieſt ſtood near the big Stone in the center, from whence he addreſs'd himſelf to the People that ſurrounded him.

UPON

UPON the ſame Coaſt alſo there is a Circle of high Stones ſtanding on one end, about a quarter of a Mile's diſtance from thoſe above-mention'd.

THE Shore in *Egginefs* abounds with many little ſmooth Stones prettily variegated with all ſorts of Colours; they are of a round Form, which is probably occaſion'd by the toſſing of the Sea, which in thoſe parts is very violent.

THE Cattle produc'd here are Cows, Horſes, Sheep, Goats, Hogs: theſe Cows are little, but very fruitful, and their Beef very ſweet and tender: the Horſes are conſiderably leſs here, than in the oppoſite continent, yet they plow and harrow as well as bigger Horſes, tho' in the ſpring-time they have nothing to feed upon but Sea ware. There are abundance of Deer in the Chaſe of *Oſervaul*, which is 15 Miles in compaſs, conſiſting in Mountains, and Valleys between them: this affords good paſturage for the Deer, black Cattle, and Sheep. This *Forreſt*, for ſo they call it, is ſurrounded with the Sea, except about one Mile upon the Weſt ſide; the Deer are forc'd to feed on Sea-ware, when the Snow and Froſt continue long, having no Wood to ſhelter in, and ſo are expos'd to the rigor of the Seaſon.

I ſaw big Roots of Trees at the head of *Loch-Eriſport*, and there is about a hundred

young

young Birch and Hazle Trees on the South-west side of *Loch-Stornvay*, but there is no more Wood in the Island. There's great variety of Land and Sea Fowls to be seen in this and the lesser adjacent Islands.

THE *Amphibia* here are Seals, and Otters; the former are eaten by the Vulgar, who find them to be as nourishing as Beef and Mutton.

THE Inhabitants of this Island are well proportion'd, free from any bodily imperfections, and of a good Stature; the colour of their Hair is commonly a light-brown, or red, but few of them are black. They are a healthful and strong bodied People, several arrive to a great Age; Mr. *Daniel Morison*, late Minister of *Barvas*, one of my Acquaintance, died lately in his 86*th*. year.

THEY are generally of a sanguine Constitution; this place hath not been troubl'd with Epidemical Diseases, except the Small Pox, which comes but seldom, and then it sweeps away many young People. The Chin-cough afflicts Children too: the Fever, Diarhea, Dysenteria, and the falling down of the Uvula, Fevers, Jaundies and Stiches, and the ordinary Coughs proceeding from Cold, are the Diseases most prevalent here. The common Cure us'd for removing Fevers and Plurisies, is to let Blood plentifully. For curing the Diarhea

Diarhea and Dysenteria, they take small quantities of the Kernel of the black Molocca Beans, call'd by them *Crospunk*; and this being ground into powder, and drunk in boil'd Milk, is by daily experience found to be very effectual. They likewise use a little Dose of *Trestarig* water with good success. When the Cough affects them, they drink *Brochan* plentifully, which is Oat meal and Water boil'd together; to which they sometimes add Butter: This Drink us'd at going to Bed, disposeth one to sleep and sweat, and is very Diuretick, if it hath no Salt in it. They use also the Roots of Nettles, and the Roots of Reeds boil'd in Water, and add Yeast to it, which provokes it to ferment, and this they find also beneficial for the Cough. When the Uvula falls down, they ordinarily cut it, in this manner: They take a long Quill, and putting a Horse-hair double into it, make a noose at the end of the Quill, and putting it about the lower end of the Uvula, they cut off from the Uvula all that's below the Hair with a pair of Scissers, and then the Patient swallows a little Bread and Cheese, which cures him: This Operation is not attended with the least inconvenience, and cures the Distemper so that it never returns. They cure Green-wounds with Oyntment made of Golden-rod, All-heal, and fresh Butter. The Jaundies they cure two ways; the first is by laying the Patient on his Face, and pretending to look upon his Back-bones, they presently

presently pour a Pail-full of cold Water on his bare Back ; and this proves successful : the second Cure they perform by taking the Tongs, and making them red-hot in the Fire, then pulling off the Clothes from the Patient's Back, he who holds the Tongs, and gently touches the Patient on the *Vertebræ* upwards of the Back, which makes him furiously run out of doors, still supposing the hot Iron is on his Back, till the Pain be abated, which happens very speedily, and the Patient recovers soon after. **Donald-Chuan**, in a Village near *Bragir*, in the Parish of *Barvas*, had by accident cut his Toe at the change of the Moon, and it bleeds a fresh drop at every change of the Moon ever since.

ANNA, Daughter to *George*, in the Village of *Melbost*, in the Parish of *Ey*, having been with Child, and the ordinary time of her Delivery being expir'd, the Child made its passage by the Fundament for some years, coming away Bone after Bone. She liv'd several years after this, but never had any more Children : Some of the Natives both of the Island of *Lewis* and *Harries*, who convers'd with her at the time, when this extraordinary thing happen'd, gave me this Account.

THE Natives are generally ingenious and quick of Apprehension ; they have a Mechanical *Genius*, and several of both Sexes have a Gift

Gift of *Poesy*, and are able to form a *Satyr* or *Panegyrick ex tempore*, without the assistance of any stronger Liquor than Water to raise their Fancy. They are great lovers of *Musick*; and when I was there they gave an account of 18 Men who could play on the Violin pretty well, without being taught : they are still very hospitable, but the late years of Scarcity brought them very low, and many of the poor People have died by Famine. The Inhabitants are very dextrous in the Exercises of Swiming, Archery, Vaulting or Leaping, and are very stout and able Seamen ; they will tug at the Oar all day long upon Bread and Water, and a snush of *Tobacco*.

Of the Inferiour adjacent Islands.

WITHOUT the Mouth of *Loch-Carlvay* lyes the small Island **Garve** ; it is a high Rock about half a Mile in compass and fit only for Pasturage. Not far from this lyes the Island **Berinsay**, which is a quarter of a Mile in compass, naturally a strong Fort, and formerly us'd as such, being almost inaccessible.

THE Island **Fladda**, which is of small compass, lyes betwen *Berinsay* and the main Land. Within

Within these lyes the Island call'd **Bernera** *Minor*, two Miles in length and fruitful in Corn and Grass; within this Island, in the middle of *Loch Carlvay*, lyes the Island **Bernera** *Major*, being 4 Miles in length, and as much in breadth; it is fruitful also in Corn and Grass, and hath 4 Villages. *Alexander Mack-Lenan*, who lives in *Bernera Major*, told me, that some years ago, a very extraordinary Ebb happen'd there, exceeding any that had been seen before or since; it happen'd about the *Vernal Equinox*, the Sea retir'd so far as to discover a Stone-wall, the length of it being about 40 yards, and in some parts about 5, 6 or 7 foot high; they suppose much more of it to be under Water: it lyes opposite to the west side of *Lewis*, to which it adjoins. He says that it is regularly built, and without all doubt the effect of Human Industry; the Natives had no Tradition about this piece of Work, so that I can form no other Conjecture about it, but that it has probably been erected for a defence against the Sea, or for the use of Fishermen, but came in time to be overflow'd. Near to both *Berneras* lyes the small Island of **Kialisay**, **Cavay**, **Carvay**, and **Ozenim**.

NEAR to the North-west Promontory of *Carlvay* Bay, call'd *Galan-head*, are the little Islands of **Pabbay**, **Shirem**, **Varay**, **Kura**, the Great and Lesser. To the North-west of *Gallan-head*, and within 6 Leagues of it,

it, lyes the *Flannan-Islands*, which the Seamen call *North-hunters*; they are but small Islands, and six in number, and maintain about 70 Sheep yearly: The Inhabitants of the adjacent Lands of the *Lewis*, having a right to these Islands, and visit them once every Summer, and there make a great purchase of Fowls, Eggs, Down, Feathers, and Quills: when they go to Sea, they have their Boat well mann'd, and make towards the Islands with an East Wind; but if before, or at the Landing, the Wind turn Westerly, they hoist up Sail, and steer directly home again. If any of their Crew is a Novice, and not vers'd in the Customs of the place, he must be instructed perfectly in all the Punctilio's observ'd here, before Landing; and to prevent Inconveniences that they think may ensue upon the transgression of the least Nicety observ'd here, every Novice is always join'd with another that can instruct him, all the time of their Fowling; so all the Boat's Crew are match'd in this manner: after their Landing they fasten the Boat to the sides of a Rock, and then fix a wooden Ladder, by laying a Stone at the foot of it, to prevent its falling into the Sea; and when they are got up into the Island, all of them uncover their Heads, and make a turn Sun-ways round, thanking God for their Safety. The first Injunction giv'n after Landing, is, not to ease Nature in that place where the Boat lyes, for that they reckon a Crime of the highest nature, and

and of dangerous Conſequence to all their Crew; for they have a great regard to that very piece of the Rock upon which they firſt ſet their Feet, after eſcaping the danger of the Ocean.

The biggeſt of theſe Iſlands is call'd Iſland-More, it has the ruins of a Chappel dedicated to St. *Flannan*, from whom the Iſland derives its Name; when they are come within about 20 paces of the Altar, they all ſtrip themſelves of their upper Garments at once, and their upper Clothes being laid upon a Stone, which ſtands there on purpoſe for that uſe, all the Crew pray three times before they begin Fowling: the firſt day they ſay the firſt Prayer, advancing towards the Chappel upon their Knees; the Second Prayer is ſaid as they go round the Chappel; the Third is ſaid hard-by or at the Chappel, and this is their Morning Service. Their *Veſpers* are perform'd with the like number of Prayers. Another Rule is, That it is abſolutely unlawful to kill a Fowl with a Stone, for that they reckon a great Barbarity, and directly contrary to ancient Cuſtom.

It is alſo unlawful to kill a Fowl before they aſcend by the Ladder. It is abſolutely unlawful to call the Iſland of St. *Kilda* (which lyes thirty Leagues Southward) by its proper *Iriſh* Name Hirt, but only the High Country. They muſt not ſo much as once name the

B Iſlands

Iſlands in which they are Fowling, by the ordinary Name *Flannan*, but only the Country. There are ſeveral other things that muſt not be call'd by their common Names: *E. g.* Viſk, which in the Language of the Natives ſignifies *Water*, they call burn: a *Rock*, which in their Language is Creg, muſt here be call'd Cruey, *i. e. hard*: *Shore* in their Language expreſt by Claddach, muſt here be call'd Vah, *i. e. a Cave*: *Sower*, in their Language is expreſt Gort, but muſt here be call'd Gaire, *i. e. Sharp*: *Slippery*, which is expreſt Bog, muſt be call'd *Soft*: and ſeveral other things to this purpoſe. They account it alſo unlawful to kill a Fowl after Evening Prayers. There is an ancient Cuſtom, by which the Crew is oblig'd not to carry home any Sheep-ſuet, let them kill never ſo many Sheep in theſe Iſlands. One of their principal Cuſtoms is not to ſteal or eat any thing unknown to their Partner, elſe the Tranſgreſſor (they ſay) will certainly vomit it up, which they reckon as a juſt Judgment. When they have loaded their Boat ſufficiently with Sheep, Fowls, Eggs, Down, Fiſh, &c. they make the beſt of their way homeward. It's obſerved of the Sheep of theſe Iſlands that they are exceeding fat, and have long Horns.

I had this ſuperſtitious Account not only from ſeveral of the Natives of the *Lewis*, but likewiſe from two who had been in the *Flannan*

nan Iſlands the preceding Year. I ask'd one of them if he pray'd at home as often, and as fervently as he did when in the *Flannan* Iſlands; and he plainly confeſs'd to me that he did not: adding further, that theſe remote Iſlands were places of inherent Sanctity; and that there was none ever yet landed in them but found himſelf more diſpos'd to Devotion there, than any where elſe. The Iſland of *Pigmies*, or as the Natives call it, *The Iſland of Little Men*, is but of ſmall Extent. There has been many ſmall Bones dug out of the Ground here, reſembling thoſe of Human kind more than any other. This gave ground to a Tradition which the Natives have of a very Low-ſtatur'd People living once here, call'd **Lusbirdan**, *i. e. Pigmies*.

THE Iſland **Rona**, is reckond about 20 Leagues from the North-eaſt Point of *Neſs* in *Lewis*, and counted but a Mile in length and about half a Mile in breadth; it hath a Hill in the Weſt part, and is only viſible from the *Lewis* in a fair Summers-day. I had an Account of this little Iſland, and the Cuſtom of it from ſeveral Natives of *Lewis*, who had been upon the place; but more particularly from Mr. *Daniel Moriſon*, Miniſter of *Barvas*, after his return from *Rona* Iſland, which then belong'd to him, as part of his *Gleib*. Upon my Landing (ſays he) the Natives receiv'd me very affectionately; and ad-

B 2 dreſs'd

dreſs'd me with their uſual Salutation to a Stranger, *God ſave you, Pilgrim, you are heartily welcome here ? for we have had repeated Apparitions of your Perſon among us*, after the manner of the ſecond Sight, *And we heartily congratulate your Arrival in this our remote Country*. One of the Natives would needs expreſs his high eſteem for my Perſon, by making a turn round about me Sun-ways, and at the ſame time Bleſſing me, and wiſhing me all happineſs; but I bid him let alone that piece of Homage, telling him I was ſenſible of his good meaning towards me: but this poor Man was not a little diſappointed, as were alſo his Neighbours; for they doubted not but this ancient Ceremony would have been very acceptable to me; and one of them told me, That this was a thing due to my Character from them, as to their Chief and Patron, and could not, nor wou'd not fail to perform it. They conducted me to the Little Village, where they dwell, and in the way thither there were three Incloſures; and as I entred each of theſe, the Inhabitants ſeverally ſaluted me, taking me by the Hand, and ſaying, *Traveller, you are welcome here*. They went along with me to the Houſe that they had aſſign'd for my Lodging; where there was a bundle of Straw laid on the Floor, for a Seat to me to ſit upon; After a little time was ſpent in general Diſcourſe, the Inhabitants retir'd to their reſpective dwelling Houſes; and in this interval,

they

Western Islands *of* **Scotland**, *&c.* 21

they kill'd each Man a Sheep, being in all Five, answerable to the nnmber of their Families. The Skins of the Sheep were entire, and flea'd off so, from the Neck to the Tail, that they were in form like a Sack: These Skins being flea'd off after this manner, were by the Inhabitants instantly fill'd with Barley-meal; and this they gave me by way of a Present, one of their number acted as Speaker for the rest, saying, *Traveller we are very sensible of the Favour you have done us in coming so far with a Design to instruct us in our way to Happiness, and at the same time to venture your self on the great Ocean: Pray, be pleas'd to accept of this small Present, which we humbly offer as an expression of our sincere Love to you.* This I accepted tho' in a very coarse dress, but it was given with such an Air of Hospitality and Good-will, as deserv'd Thanks: they presented my Man also with some pecks of Meal, as being likewise a Traveller; the Boats-Crew having been in *Rona* before, were not reckon'd Strangers, and therefore there was no Present given them, but their daily Maintenance.

THERE is a Chappel here dedicated to St. **Ronan**, fenc'd with a Stone Wall round it; and they take care to keep it neat and clean, and sweep it every day. There is an Altar in it on which there lies a big Plank of Wood about ten foot in length, every foot has a hole in it, and in every hole a Stone, to which the

B 3 Natives

22 *A* Description *of the*

Natives ascribe several Virtues; one of them is singular, as they say, for promoting speedy delivery to a Woman in Travel.

THEY repeat the Lord's Prayer, Creed and Ten Commandments in the Chappel every Sunday Morning. They have Cows, Sheep, Barley and Oats, and live a harmless Life, being perfectly ignorant of most of those Vices that abound in the World: They know nothing of Money or Gold, having no occasion for either: They neither sell nor buy, but only barter for such little things as they want: they covet no Wealth, being fully content and satisfy'd with Food and Raiment; tho' at the same time they are very precise in the matter of Property among themselves; for none of them will by any means allow his Neighbour to fish within his Property; and every one must exactly observe not to make any incroachment on his Neighbour. They have an agreeable and hospitable Temper for all Strangers: they concern not themselves about the rest of Mankind, except the inhabitants in the North part of *Lewis*. They take their Sirname from the colour of the Sky, Rain-bow, and Clouds. There are only five Families in this small Island, and every Tennant hath his Dwelling-house, a Barn, a House where their best Effects are preserv'd, a House for their Cattle, and a Porch on each side of the Door to keep off the Rain or Snow. Their Houses

are

are built with Stone, and thatched with Straw, which is kept down with Ropes of the ſame, pois'd with Stones. They wear the ſame Habit with thoſe in *Lewis*, and ſpeak only *Iriſh*. When any of them comes to the *Lewis*, which is ſeldom, they are aſtoniſhed to ſee ſo many People. They much admire Grey-hounds, and love to have them in their company. They are mightily pleas'd at the ſight of Horſes, and one of them obſerving a Horſe to neigh, ask'd if that Horſe laugh'd at him: a Boy from *Rona* perceiving a Colt run towards him, was ſo much frighted at it that he jump'd into a buſh of Nettles, where his whole Skin became full of Bliſters.

ANOTHER of the Natives of *Rona*, having had the opportunity of travelling as far as *Coul*, in the Shire of *Roſs*, which is the Seat of Sr. *Alexander Mac-kenzie*, every thing he ſaw there was ſurprizing to him, and when he heard the noiſe of thoſe who walk'd in the Rooms above him, he preſently fell to the Ground, thinking thereby to ſave his Life, for he ſuppos'd that the Houſe was coming down over his head. When Mr. *Moriſon* the Miniſter was in *Rona*, two of the Natives Courted a Maid with intention to marry her, and being married to one of them afterwards, the other was not a little diſappointed becauſe there was no other match for him in this Iſland. The Wind blowing fair, Mr.

B 4 *Moriſon*

Moriſon ſailed directly for *Lewis*, but after 3 hours ſailing was forced back to *Rona* by a contrary Wind, and at his Landing the poor Man that had loſt his Sweet-heart was overjoy'd, and expreſſed himſelf in theſe words; I bleſs God and *Ronan* that you are return'd again, for I hope you will now make me happy, and give me a right to enjoy the Woman every other Year by turns, that ſo we both may have Iſſue by her; Mr. *Moriſon* could not refrain from ſmiling at this unexpected requeſt, chid the poor Man for his unreaſonable demand, and deſir'd him to have patience for a Year longer, and he would ſend him a Wife from *Lewis*; but this did not eaſe the poor Man who was tormented with the thoughts of dying without Iſſue.

ANOTHER who wanted a Wife, and having got a Shilling from a Seaman that happen'd to land there, went and gave this Shilling to Mr. *Moriſon* to purchaſe him a Wife in the *Lewis*, and ſend her to him, for he was told that this piece of Money was a thing of extraordinary Value, and his deſire was gratified the enſuing Year.

ABOUT 14 Years ago a ſwarm of Rats, but none knows how, came into *Rona*, and in a ſhort time eat up all the Corn in the Iſland. In a few Months after ſome Seamen Landed there, who Robbed the poor People of of their Bull. These misfortunes and the want of supply from *Lewis* for the space of a Year, occasion'd the death of all that Ancient Race of People. The Steward of St. *Kilda* being by a Storm driven in there, told me that he found a Woman with her Child on her Breast, both lying dead at the side of a Rock: Some Years after, the Minister (to whom the Island belongeth) sent a new Colony to this Island, with suitable Supplies. The following Year a Boat was sent to them with some more supplies and Orders to receive the Rents, but the Boat being lost as it is supposed, I can give no further account of this late Plantation.

THE Inhabitants of this little Island say that the Cuckow is never seen or heard here; but after the Death of the Earl of *Seaforth*, or the Minister.

The Rock **Soulisker**, lyeth 4 Leagues to the East of *Rona*, it is a quarter of a Mile in Circumference, and abounds with great numbers of Sea-Fowl, such as, *Solan* Geese, Guillamote, Coulter-Neb, Puffin, and several other sorts. The Fowl called the Colk is found here, it is less then a Goose, all covered with Down, and when it hatches it casts its Feathers, which are of divers Colours; It has a Tufft on it's head resembling that of a Peacock, and a Train longer than that of a House-

House-Cock; but the Hen has not so much Ornament and Beauty.

THE Island **Siant**, Or, as the Natives call it *Island-More*, lyes to the East of *Ushiness*, in *Lewis* about a League. There are Three small Islands here, the Two Southern Islands are seperated only by Spring-tides, and are Two Miles in Circumference. *Island-More* hath a Chappel in it Dedicated to the Virgin *Mary*, and is fruitful in Corn and Grass; The Island joyning to it on the West is only for Pasturage, I saw a couple of Eagles here. The Natives told me that these Eagles would never suffer any of their kind to live there but themselves, and that they drove away their Young-ones as soon as they were able to fly, and they told me likewise that those Eagles are so careful of the place of their abode, that they never yet killed any Sheep or Lamb in the Island, tho' the Bones of Lambs, of Fawns, and Wild-Fowls are frequently found in and about their Nests, so that they make their Purchase in the opposite Islands; the nearest of which is a League distant. This Island is very strong and inaccessible, save on one side where the Ascent is narrow, and somewhat resembling a Stair, but a great deal more high and steep, notwithstanding which the Cows pass and repass by it safely, tho' one would think it uneasie for a Man to climb. About a Musket shot further North lies the biggest of the

the Iſlands called *More*, being two Miles in Circumference: It is fruitful in Corn and Paſturage, the Cows here are much fatter than any I ſaw in the Iſland of *Lewis*. There is a blew Stone in the ſurface of the Ground here, moiſt while it lies there, but when dry, it becomes very hard, it is capable of any Impreſſion, and I have ſeen a Sett of Table-Men made of this Stone prettily Carved with different Figures. There is a Promontory in the North-end of the Iſland of *Lewis* called *Eoropy-Point*, which is ſuppoſed to be the furtheſt to North-weſt of any part in *Europe*.

THESE Iſlands are divided into Two Pariſhes, one called *Barvas*, and the other *Ey* or *Y*, both which are Parſonages, and each of them having a Miniſter. The Names of the Churches in *Lewis* Iſles, and the Saints to whom they were Dedicated are *St. Columkil*, in the Iſland of that name; *St. Pharaer* in **Kaerneſs**; *St. Lennan* in **Sternvay**, *St. Collum* in **Ey**, ; *St. Cutchou* in **Garboſt**; *St. Aula* in **Greaſe**; *St. Michael* in **Tolloſta**; *St. Collum* in **Garieu**; *St. Ronan* in **Eorobie**: *St. Thomas* in **Haboſt**: *St. Peter* in **Shanaboſt**; *St. Clement* in **Dell**; *Holy-Croſs* Church in **Galſin**; *St. Brigit* in **Barove**; *St. Peter* in **Shiadir**; *St. Mary* in **Barvas**; *St. John-Baptiſt* in **Bragar**; *St. Kiaran* in **Liant-Shadir**; *St. Michael* in **Kirvig**; *St. Macrel* in **Kirkiboſt**; *St. Dondan* in Little **Berneray**; *St.*

St. Michael in the ſame Iſland; *St. Peter* in **Pabbay** Iſland; *St. Chriſtophers* Chappel in **Uge**; and **Stornbay** Church, all theſe Churches and Chappels were before the Reformation Sanctuaries; and if a Man had committed Murder, he was then ſecure and ſafe when once within their Precincts.

THEY were in greater Veneration in thoſe days than now: it was the conſtant Practice of the Natives to kneel at firſt ſight of the Church, tho' at a great diſtance from 'em. and then they ſaid their *Pater noſter*. *John Moriſon* of **Bragir**, told me that when he was a Boy, and going to the Church of *St. Mulvay*, he obſerv'd the Natives to kneel and repeat the *Pater noſter* at four Miles diſtant from the Church. The Inhabitants of this Iſland had an ancient Cuſtom to ſacrifice to a Sea God call'd *Shony* at Hallow-tide, in the manner following: The Inhabitants round the Iſland came to the Church of *St. Mulvay*, having each Man his Proviſion along with him; every Family furniſh'd a Peck of Malt, and this was brew'd into Ale; one of their number was pickt out to wade into the Sea up to the middle, and carrying a Cup of Ale in his Hand, ſtanding ſtill in that poſture, cry'd out with a loud Voice ſaying. **Shony**, *I give you this Cup of Ale, hoping that you'll be ſo kind as to ſend us plenty of Sea-ware, for inriching our Ground the enſuing Year*; and ſo threw the Cup of Ale into the Sea. This was perform'd form'd in the Night-time; at his return to Land, they all went to Church, where there was a Candle burning upon the Altar; and then ftanding filent for a little time, one of them gave a Signal, at which the Candle was put out, and immediately all of them went to the Fields, where they fell a drinking their Ale, and fpent the remainder of the Night in Dancing, and Singing, &c.

THE next Morning they all return'd home, being well fatisfy'd that they had punctually obferv'd this Solemn Anniverfary, which they believ'd to be a powerful means to procure a plentiful Crop. Mr. *Daniel*, and Mr. *Kenneth Morifon*, Minifters in *Lewis*, told me they fpent feveral Years, before they could perfwade the vulgar Natives to abandon this ridiculous piece of Superftition, which is quite abolifh'd for thefe 32 Years paft.

THE Inhabitants are all Proteftants, except one Family, who are Roman Catholicks. I was told, that about 14 Years ago, three or four Fifhermen, who then forfook the Proteftant Communion, and imbrac'd the Romifh Faith, having the opportunity of a Popifh Prieft on the place, they apply'd themfelves to him for fome of the Holy-water; it being ufual for the Priefts to fprinkle it into the Bays, as an infallible means to procure plenty of Herring, as alfo to bring them into thofe Nets that are befprinkled with

with it: Thefe Fifhers accordingly having got the Water, poured it upon their Nets before they drop'd them into the Sea: They likewife turn'd the infide of their Coats outwards, after which they fet their Nets in the Evening at the ufual hour. The Proteftant Fifhers who us'd no other means than throwing their Nets into the Sea, at the fame time were very unconcern'd; but the Papifts being impatient and full of expectation, got next Morning be times to draw their Nets, and being come to the place, they foon perceiv'd that all their Nets were loft, but the Proteftants found their Nets fafe, and full of Herring; which was no fmall mortification to the Prieft and his Profelytes, and expos'd them to the derifion of their Neighbours.

THE Proteftant Natives obferve the Feftivals of *Chriftmas*, *Good-Friday*, *Eafter*, and *Michaelmas*; upon this laft they have an Anniverfary Cavalcade, and then both Sexes ride on Horfe-back.

THERE is a Village call'd *Storn-Bay*, at the head of the Bay of that Name; it confifts of about fixty Families: there are fome Houfes of entertainment in it; as alfo a Church, and a School, in which *Latin* and *Englifh* are taught. The Steward of the *Lewis* hath his Refidence in this Village. The *Lewis* which was poffefs'd by *Mack-Leod* of *Lewis*, for feveral Centuries, is fince the Reign of King *James* the Sixth, become the Property of the Earl of *Seafort*, who ftill enjoys it. *The*

Dun Othail, Ness

Loch Trealabhal, central Lewis

Garbh Eilean from Eilean Mhuire, Shiant Islands

Brona Cleit through the arches of Roarein, Flannan Isles

Entrance to dwelling, Rona, Lewis

Rona from Sulasgeir

Remains of building on Luchruban, Lewis

Lewis

1. Martin's early remarks on Lewis raise questions as to what area he was describing. He refers to it as 'the outmost Tract of Islands ... divided by several narrow Channels, and distinguish'd by several Proprietors as well as by several Names'. There is therefore at first some doubt as to whether he writes of Lewis 'properly and strictly so call'd' or of the whole length of the Outer Hebrides.

Several dividing channels, proprietors and names would suggest in turn more than one or two islands. In Martin's time Lewis proper had only one proprietor, the Earl of Seaforth, and while there were sea lochs which to some extent separated districts there were no dividing channels. If by 'Lewis' Martin understood a combination of at least Lewis itself and much of Harris, this would bear comparison with the opening paragraph of a description of the isles of Scotland dated around 1595: 'The haill Iles of Scotland were devidit in four pairts of auld, viz. Lewis, Sky, Mule, and Yla...First to the Ile of Lewis wes annext the Iles of Wist, Barra, Harragis, Ronalewis, Pabla in Harreik, Helsker, Collismown, and Iit.'

This 16th century account indicates that the boundary between Lewis and that part called Harris was at the Tarbert isthmus, which may explain Martin's comment that Lewis reached as far as 'the South-point of *Hussiness.*' Husinish is now accepted as being clearly in Harris. Martin's 'several Names' were presumably those of various islands.

[Skene Vol. III (Appendix III) p.428. Iit is Irt or Hirt (St Kilda)]

2. Lewis and Harris, or the entire Outer Hebrides, went under the name of 'the Long Island', which description is still used from time to time without consistency.

3. The 'north-point' of Lewis, now known as the Butt of Lewis, appears to have been called 'Bowling-Head' well before Martin's day. On a sketch map of Lewis and Harris dated c.1630 and held in the National Library of Ireland the name occurs as 'Bollin head'; and '*A Descriptione of the Lewes*' has 'Bowlin-head'. Again 'Bowling Head' appears on Mark Tiddeman's map of 1730, but by this time Martin's book was well-known. Being in English form, the name may have been given by an English ship.

[Copy of MS Map in NLS; NLS Adv.MS 13.3.8 p.114]

4. It is possible that 'healthy', perhaps a mis-print, should really be 'heathy'.

5. The word '*Trestarig*', evidently a powerful form of '*Usquebaugh*', whisky, was noted by Sibbald: 'of Corne of Oats they make severall Drinks such as Trestarig which is Aqua vita, three times distilled, which is strong and hot'.

[NLS Adv. MS 33.5.19 p.8 'Of the Diet of the Highlanders']

6. The vessels made by women with 'fine red Clay' come within the probably ancient tradition of such pottery, of which the well-known Barvas craggan ware is an example.

7. The process of cultivation as described by Martin is a brief indication of how the feannagan or lazybeds were made; the instrument used being perhaps the 'cas chrom'. 'Timiy', turning and manuring the ground, could be a version of 'Tionndadh', turning.

8. Sibbald also noted the powerful '*Usquebaugh-baul*' again in Martin's own words. Nothing was added nor any other explanation or derivation of the term given.

[See n.5 above].

9. The series of 'convenient Bays and Harbours' is on the east coast of Lewis. '*Loch- Grace*' – the bay or Loch of Gress, '*Loch-tua*' – the earlier name of Broad Bay, are both north of '*Loch-Stornvay*', while southwards are the Birkin or Barkin Isles at the entrance of Loch Leurbost where that loch joins Loch Erisort, and '*Loch Colmkill*' clearly comprises the entrance to Loch Erisort. Today's maps have no Loch Colmkill, but evidently the bay so called took its name from Eilean Chaluim Chille. The tidal rocks at the mouth of Loch Seaforth were probably Sgeir Hal and Bogha Bridog, the latter being close to the Lewis shore.

10. Loch Carloway ('*Loch-Carlvay*') was soon to become an important anchorage for fishing boats, as were the inner bays of Loch Roag; and in the late 18th century a pier and associated buildings were established at the head of Loch Carloway.

[cf NLS Adv. MS 13.2.8 '*A Descriptione of the Lewes*' p.116]

11. Martin's outsize whale reappears in Sibbald's notes for his essay relating to the natural history of Scotland: 'In the Sea Loughs of the Liewes there is a sorte of Whale remarkable for its Bigness which the Fishermen call the Gallan whale for that they sie it only at the Gallan promontorie. This not long since overturn'd a fisher boate and devoured three of the men.' The practice of running whales of another kind ashore or into a bay is well known in the Faroe Islands and took place about 1818 at Isle Ornsay in the south of Skye, where William Daniell captured the scene in an engraving. These were probably pilot whales but there were several other kinds around.

[NLS Adv MS 33.5.19 p.284]

12. The revival of 'poor meagre people' was also recorded by Martin at St Kilda.

13. The 'spout-fish', in Gaelic muirsgian (sea knife), is known commonly as the razor-fish and in many parts of Scotland as 'spouts'. Martin described spout-fish at greater length in a letter to Edward Lhuyd: 'Spout fish is of 2 shells about 7 or 8 inches long, 1 in breadth, all the fish comes out of the shell, and pierces 5 or 6 foot perpendicularly in the sands, the shell sticking to the fish yet hath a void passage from one end neer the other, out of which it spouts a water; for this reason it is called spout fish, it is called murskin in Irish, and that from Muir the sea and skien a knife for the shell is sharp on each side; it is eaten boyld, or fried and is had in every sandy coast of this nature' [Emery p.111].

14. Martin's observations on coral in Lewis, Skye and elsewhere were noted by Sibbald after seeing some samples:

'Mr Martin showed me some pieces of white Corall taken up about the West Isles of Scotland, some at 20, some at 30, some at one Fathom deep, he sayeth some of it growth to the Rocks, some of it he brought up redish, some of it of a pale colour, there is some of it still of a Flesh colour, but most of it is Greyish, some of it has the Fibers of a plant sticking to it and twisted about it.'

More particularly, Martin's own words regarding the Lewis location are repeated with only the slightest of changes: 'In Lough Seafort in the Lewis and in severall other Bayes ther is Corrall found, of the bigness of a Goose Quill, and in Length some 6 Inches.'

[NLS Adv. MS 33.5.19 p.177. See Skye n.19]

15. It is considered that Martin's comments on the 'black Musles' in rivers constitute a first record of the Freshwater Pearl Mussel, which occurs in some rivers not only in Lewis but also in Mull and Skye.

[Currie; See Skye nn.13, 15]

16. Every now and again Martin relates ancient custom, often of a deeply-ingrained superstitious kind. Examples include 1 May at Barvas, and the beliefs related to wells.

'St Cowsten' was another form of St Constantine. The chapel dedicated to this saint was at Garrabost, in the old pre-Reformation parish of Eye. But 'levelled' before 1833, nothing of it remains: 'The building has disappeared, and its site is under tillage.' Nearby was the well, 'in a steep bank beside the shore.' Rev. John Cameron, minister of Stornoway in the 1830s, was not a believer in the failure of the well water to boil meat: 'this holds true, I presume, of every water, when the fuel is wet and the fire of insufficient strength'.

The well of St Andrew, Tobar Andrais, is still present on the sea-ward side of Shader, Barvas.

[MacKinlay 1914 p.203; NSA pp.120, 126]

17.The cave in the shore at Gress [by '*Loch-Grace*'], known even today as Geodha nan Ron, the seals' cave, was reputed a remarkable feature, one of the places considered worth a visit by early tourists to Lewis. Two accounts of 1796, not much different, describe the main features:

'In this parish there is a remarkable cave, into which the sea goes at high water. When it was first noticed, vast numbers of seals were killed in it; and the practice is still continued once a-year, about Michaelmas. It is only accessible from sea; the people land from their boat opposite to the cave in time of low water, at spring-tide; they walk forward, and being furnished with fire, they light torches at the entry to the cave, which is dark far in, and they knock to death all the seals found there with heavy bludgeons armed with iron. At first it was not uncommon to see 50 killed at a time; but now the number does not exceed from 7 to 12. At the farthest end, there is a small apartment, the top of which is lined with stalactitae, or icicles, of a very firm consistence; it is about an eighth part of an English mile in length, and its height is variable.'

The other account adds a few details. The cave is only accessible by sea. The killing of 'vast numbers' of seals took place annually about 50 years earlier. The people assembled at low water and carried a boat into the cave as far as possible, then took from it a pot filled with live coals from which they lit torches. By this light the seals were killed. 'The entry of the cave is very steep and narrow on its sides, and does not admit more than the breadth of a six-oared boat.' When a long way in the day light was dim and there was a large pillar dividing the cave into two openings or arches, through one of which the people passed and, walking a long way further, met 'with large tumbling round stones, surrounded in part with water'. Going on they came to 'a fine pleasant beach' where the seals were, and beyond that point was the 'small chamber' of stalactites hanging from the roof. The total distance in was said to be an eighth of an English mile.

[OSA pp.31, 34]

18. Martin's distinction between natural and artificial forts on the coast is of interest. The former were all in the Ness district – Dun Othail ('*Dun-owle*', cf 'Dun-Owle' in Bute), Dun Eorodale ('*Dun-coradil*'), and Dun Eistean ('*Dun-eisten*'), two of them islands at high tide and all naturally defended by steep, cliff-bound sides. Only one or two artificial forts were named, perhaps because they were too numerous to mention in detail. One of them was the castle at Stornoway, the other a broch which if 'Brago' were Bragar was probably that at Dun Carloway, even though this was to the south rather than the north.

19. '*Mournagh* Hill', Muirneag today, though not very high is nevertheless a distinctive hill rising from the great stretches of moor around it. The name '*Cairnwarp*', associated as it seems to be by Martin with 'Cairnes or Heaps of Stones,' suggests a similarity with the great cairns further south such as Barpa Langass in North Uist. It is probably now Carn a' Mharc, the chambered cairn up the slope on the east side of the Gress river on Cnoc a' Chairn, with Loch a' Chairn, Druim a' Chairn and Sidhean Blar a Chairn nearby.

'The *Thrushel* Stone', Clach an Truiseil, is still a conspicuous feature of Balantrushel near Barvas, but the three standing stones north of Loch Carloway have been reduced to one, known as Clach an Tursa, standing in the croft lands on the slope running down to the inner end of the loch. In 1914 the broken remains of two other pillar stones lay nearby.

[Inventory p.16 no 55; p.7 no.16, p.24 no.87]

20. Much has been written already about the 'remarkable stones' at Callanish, but it is worth pointing out that many such groups, large or small, seem to be accompanied by the name of 'na fir bhreige', the falsemen, or of men transformed, perhaps partly because, assembled on a piece of higher ground, the stones, when silhouetted against the sky, can give the impression of a human gathering.

21. '*Egginess*' is shown as 'Egenes' on Martin's own map and is the later Aignish.

22. Martin's 'Chase of *Oservaul*', otherwise a forest, 'for so they call it', was a 'forest' in the sense of a wild area where deer were hunted rather than an extensive cover of trees. Three hunting forests existed in the island in the 17th century, the mountainous district of north Harris, stretching from east to west coast and along the undefined border with Lewis, the Lewis side of this border, and the Park district on the north side of Loch Seaforth. The Blaeu map of Lewis and Harris is so confused to be of little use in defining the bounds of the forest but it does have 'Bin Ostrafeald' across a wide stretch of hills. The map of Lewis and Harris of c.1630 names both forest areas: 'the hille forrist' (Harris/Lewis) and 'The Great Forrist' (Park). William Bald's Map of Harris (1804-5) has 'Forrest' right across North Harris. Versions of John Morrison's *Descriptione of the Lewes* refer to the Park forest:

'It is also served with a most plentiful Forrest of Deer naturally environed with the sea, and as it were inclosed betwixt the Lochs Seafort and Herrigh [Harris], having 2 miles of ground only twixt both Loch ends full of goodly Hills and vast bounds.'

By the 'Chase of *Oservaul*' Martin probably meant no more than the general forest area of Lewis and Harris, as in the case of the description of the isles c.1595: 'Thair is na woods in the Lewis, but ane great wildernes or forrest callit Osirsdaill quhairin is sustenit mony deir'. Here there was 'pleasant hunting'. In 1630 Captain Dymes refers to 'the two Forrests' in his description of Lewis.

[NLS Adv. MS 13.2.8 '*Descriptione of the Lewes*' pp.121-122; cf MacIver p.28; Skene Vol. III p.429; Mackenzie (1903) p.593]

23. Indicating that there were or had been some woods on Lewis Martin noted 'big Roots of Trees' at the head of Loch Erisort ('*Loch-Erisport*'), and birch and hazel beside '*Loch-Stornvay*', probably within and near the area of the castle grounds now covered with well-grown plantation. Tree roots and fragments are still found under peat in parts of the Lewis moors.

24. For the eating of seals see n.17

25. Rev. Daniel or Donald Morison was at various times minister in Ness, in Stornoway, and of Barvas, and at one stage possibly the only minister in Lewis. He and his descendants have been described in some detail.

[Matheson (1970) Appendix G pp.245-254]

26. Sibbald's account of the diet of the Highlanders contains extracts from Martin's remarks on various ailments and refers to the virtues of 'Molucca Beans', a subject which is more extensively dealt with elsewhere in his manuscript. The 'beans' have been identified as including a variety of nuts brought to the shores of the Hebrides via the Gulf Stream from a Caribbean origin. Martin also refers to them as 'black and white *Indian Nuts*' (Mull) and '*Molluka*' beans or 'the White Nut, called the *Virgin Marie's* Nut' (Harris).

[NLS Adv MS 33.5.19 pp. 234, 236-238; see Mull n.6 and Harris nn.10, 11]

27. There was apparently a tradition which claimed that 'Domhnall a' Chuain was an old bachelor who had nothing to do but to go rock and loch fishing, and when lucky to get some fish and gorge himself, he would go and lie on the hillside'.John Morison addressed him in verses:

'Is buidhe dhuit fhein, Dhomh'ill a' Chuain,
's tu 'nad laigh' air do chluain thaobh:
cha tog pracadair do ghealL,
ni mo tha thu'n taing nam maor.'

Various references to a tenant of the same name in South Bragar in the later 18th century have been found: 'Donald Choin' (1766), 'Dond. Ochoin' (1780), 'Donald O chuinn' (1787). Martin's Donald of the Ocean was 'apparently a poor landless man'.

[Matheson (1970) Appendix E pp.215-216, 232]

28. It would obviously be difficult to identify '*George*, in the village of *Melbost*', but it may be worth noting that 'George' was quite a distinctive first name in Lewis and that in a 1718 rental of the island there was a George Mackenzie, tacksman of 'Shadder' in the parish of Ey, who could perhaps have moved from Melbost where in 1718 the tacksman was Alexander Campbell.

[FEP NAS E655/1/2 p.16]

29. The 'late years of scarcity' were the well-known period in the 1690s which proved disastrous for many rural districts of Scotland.

30. The 'small Island' called Garve is now known as 'The Old Hill' or 'Seanabheinn', at the mouth of Loch Roag (Thomson: 'Shenevin'). Its steep cliffs and its position on the edge of the open ocean make it very difficult both to land and to ascend. It appears in some accounts as 'Garvellan', in English the appropriate 'rough island.'

[Monro p.87 no.212; NLS Adv. MS 33.3.20 f.23]

31. Martin's 'Berinsay' was already known by the name which survives in use today, Bearasay, the 'roke within the sea' to which Neil Macleod withdrew around 1610. It seems to have been the island which Monro knew as Lambay.

NLS Adv MS 22.7.11 ff. 24-25; Monro p.82 no. 213]

32. The islands of Flodda ('*Fladda*'), '*Bernera Minor*' and '*Bernera Major*', are all easily recognisable, but the partly submerged wall seen by Alexander MacLennan remains a mystery unless it was the enclosure of a lobster pond. Kealasay ('*Kialisay*') and Greinam ('*Grenim*'), there being two of the latter,

are also to be found still in Loch Roag, while Keava and Eilean Kearstay may today represent *Cavay* and *Carvay* respectively. In that case Martin does not refer to Campay and Craigeam, while Monro mentions only 'Keallasay' and 'Kirtay'(Kearstay).

[Monro pp.81-82]

33. The islands of Pabbay, Vacsay ('*Vaxay*'), Vuia Mor and Vuia Beag all lie between Bernera and the districts of Valtos, Reef and Carishader. So too does the smaller island of Shiaram Mor ('*Shirim*'), which is close in to Kneep and Traigh na Berie.

34. Martin's description of the Flannan Isles is the principal source of information about those islands in earlier days. The rituals and 'Customs of the place' are some of the most interesting of those he recorded in the Hebrides, and, in the case of substitute terms and names and the matter of 'easing nature' at sea, are paralleled by observations made in one or two other islands. Some of the preferred terms at the Flannan Isles are usual in Lewis Gaelic.

[see Skye n.43, Bute n.5, Eigg n.6]

35. Since the 1630 description of Lewis by Captain John Dymes the 'Island of *Pigmies*, or, as the Natives call it, *The Island of Little Men*', has been a subject for conjecture and exploration. What appeared on the Blaeu map as 'Ylen Dunibeg', situated close to the Butt of Lewis, is now known locally as 'Luchruban', to which Martin's '*Lusbirdan*' may be related. Access to the island is difficult, and the structural remains have been subject at various times to random digging. Monro refers to 'ane little kirk in it'.

[Mackenzie (1903) p.592; Inventory pp.9-10 no.22; Monro pp.82-83 no.225; see also Colonsay n.5]

36. Martin's account of Rona, largely based on what he heard from Rev. Donald Morison (see n.25), is, like those of St Kilda and the Flannan Isles, an exceptionally detailed description and is clear evidence of his interest in such very remote and somewhat mysterious places, two of them with populations whose origins were obscure.

[see Robson (1991)]

37. The 'Colk' is generally understood to be the eider.

38. '*Island-More*', if not the name of the whole Shiants group, should be Eilean Mhuire, Mary's Island, which is separate from the other two, linked islands. Martin, however, refers to an island 'joyning to it on the West' where there was a pair of eagles; since this would be Garbh Eilean, joined to Eilean Tighe by a shingle bar, it could be that Martin's '*Island-More*' is now Eilean Tighe. But his later reference to 'the biggest of the Islands called *More*' lying further north suggests that some confusion existed between 'More' indicating 'big' and 'Island-More', Mary's Island. Even so, Martin seems to have visited the Shiant islands in person since he was given information by 'the natives', and saw the sea eagles, which continued to have their home on Garbh Eilean for nearly two centuries after 1700.

The Blaeu map of Lewis and Harris, though having 'Garvellan' and 'Yl-Kil' close to each other, places a group of islands which includes Scalpay to the east of Lewis but is not helpful so far as exact location is concerned. Martin's own map, while naming one island 'St Maries', adds nothing. Fifty years later Murdo Mackenzie's map of 'The Lewis' shows the Shiant islands in accurate relationship, naming the southern one as 'Ilanakily' (Island of the cell or chapel) and that to the east 'Ilan Wirray' (Eilean Mhuire). Uisinis ('Ushineis') is a point on the coast of the Park deer forest north of Loch Bhrollum.

39.Monro said that Lewis had 'four paroche kirks'. These would have been in the parishes of Ey, Uig, Ness and Barvas. In view of Martin's statement that there were only two parishes, it is said that either a reduction in number took place after the Reformation or that two ministers served the four parishes.

[Monro p.87' Macdonald p.108; Mackenzie (1903) p.524. see also n.25 above]

40. Martin's list of churches in 'Lewis Isles' includes many pre-Reformation chapels. Most can be identified:

'*St. Columkil* in the Island of that name' - on Eilean Chaluim Chille, off Cromore, Lochs

'*St Pharaer* in Kaerness'- has been located at Swordale on Loch Leurbost, Lochs [Macdonald p.108]

'*St. Lennan* in Sternvay' - ?

'*St. Collum* in Ey' – the old church at Aignish

'*St. Cutchou* in Garbost' – St Cowsten's chapel at Garrabost (see n.16) [Muir (1885) p.40]

'*St. Aula* in Grease' – St Olaf's chapel at Gress [Inventory p.14 no.95]

'*St. Michael* in Tollosta' – St Michael's chapel and burial ground at Tolsta [Inventory p.17 no.60]

'*St. Collum* in Garieu' – a chapel (site now unknown) dedicated to St. Columba at Garinen, near Fivepenny, Ness [Blaeu: Ghearen]

'*St Ronan* in Eorobie' – site on top of rising ground between Eoropie and Sto, Ness

'*St Thomas* in Habost' – site on small area of rising ground on the coast near Habost cemetery, Ness

'*St Peter* in Shanabost' – church or chapel in the burial ground at Swainbost, Ness

'*St Clement* in Dell' – site roughly located near a Clement's Well in North Dell, Ness

'*Holy-Cross* Church in Galsin' – church or chapel on coast at South Galson. 'Galsin' was incorrectly changed to 'Galan' in the 1716 Martin edition.

'*St. Brigit* in Barove' – site of chapel at the southern end of Melbost Borve

'*St. Peter* in Shiadir' – site of chapel on coast at Shader, Barvas

'*St. Mary* in Barvas' – site of church in the sandy, eroded area near the coast at Barvas

'*St. John-Baptist* in Bragar' – chapel found to be 'pretty entire' in the 1850s [Muir (1861) p.186]

'*St. Kiaran* in Liani-Shadir' – unlocated site of chapel at Laimishader, Carloway

'*St. Michael* in Kirvig' – slight traces of this chapel at 'Cirabhig', Carloway, were seen in the mid 19th century [Muir (1885) p.41]. Baile an Teampuill is nearby

'*St. Macrel* in Kirkibost' – reckoned to be the only chapel in Scotland with a dedication possibly to St. Macra, a female French martyr. 'Macrel' was altered, for no stated reason, to 'Marcel' in the 1999 Martin reprint [Mackinlay p.328; OPS Vol.II p.386; Inventory p.18 no.65; Muir (1861) p.177]

'*St. Dondan* in Little Berneray' – site of chapel dedicated to St. Donnan [Muir (1861) p.177]

'*St. Michael* in the same island' – 'groundwork' of the chapel on top of a rock [Muir (1861) p.177]

'*St. Peter* in Pabbay Island' – remains of chapel in turf-covered sand on the east side of Pabbay, Loch Roag [Inventory p.18 no.64]

'*St. Christophers* Chappel in Uge' – church supposed to have stood at Bailenacille, Uig

[Inventory p.18 no.67]

The list is not comprehensive as there were further chapels and sacred sites elsewhere. Omitted here but mentioned a little later was the church in Eoropie dedicated to St. Maolrubha (or St. Moluag), which Martin calls 'the Church of *St Mulvay*'.

[Robson (1997) pp.50-67]

41. An account of John Morison of Bragar is given by Matheson. A letter written by Morison in 1700 is clearly connected with what Martin says about the 'Church of *St Mulvay*' and it is evident that Morison was not only a correspondent of Sibbald and author of *A Descriptione of the Lewes*, but an important source for Martin. The two certainly met.

[Matheson (1970) Appendices E & F pp.206-244; EUL Colin Campbell Collection MS3097.12; NLS Adv. MS 34.2.8 ff.193-194; Maciver pp.23-31]

42. Mr Kenneth Morison was minister of Stornoway where he was predecessor, and father-in-law, of Rev. Donald Morison. Kenneth graduated at Aberdeen in 1667 and died at Stornoway in 1720.

[Matheson (1970) Appendix C 189-192]

43. The priest who converted the fishermen may have been Cornelius Con, attached to the family of George Mackenzie of Kildun, possibly at Aignish.

[Robson (2002)]

44. The steward of Lewis to whom Martin refers was Zachary Macaulay.

[Morrison MS pp.205-214]

The Isle of HARRIES.

THE *Harries* being seperated from *Lewis* is 18 Miles, from the *Hushiness* on the West Ocean, to *Loch-Seafort* in the East, from this bounding to the Point of *Strond* in the South of *Harries*, it is 24 Miles, and in some places, 4, 5, and 6 Miles in breadth: The Soil is almost the same with that of *Lewis*, and it produces the same sorts of Corn, but a greater increase.

THE Air is temperately Cold, and the Natives endeavour to qualify it by taking a Dose of *Aquavitæ*, or *Brandy*, for they brew no such Liquours as *Trestarig*, or *Usquebaugh-baul*. The Eastern Coast of *Harries* is generally Rocky, and Mountainous, covered with Grass, and Heath. The West-side is for the most part Arable on the Sea-Coast; some parts of the Hills on the East side, are naked without Earth, The Soil being dry and Sandy, is Fruitful when Manur'd with Sea-ware. The Grass on the West side is most Clover and Dasie, which in the Summer yields a most fragrant smell. Next to *Loch-Seafort*, which for some Miles divides the *Lewis* from *Harries*, is the notable Harbour within the Island, by Sea-

Sea-faring Men call'd *Glass*, and by the Natives **Scalpa**; it is a Mile and an half long from South to North, and a Mile in breadth. There is an Entrance on the South and North ends of the Isle, and several good Harbours in each, well known to the generality of Seamen. Within the Isle is *Loch-Tarbat*, running 4 Miles West; it hath several small Isles, and is sometimes frequented by Herring. Without the *Loch* there is plenty of Cod, Ling, and large Eels.

ABOUT half a League further on the same Coast, lies *Loch-Stokness*, which is about a Mile in length; there is a fresh-water Lake at the entrance of the Island, which affords Oysters, and several sorts of Fish, the Sea having access to it at Spring-tides.

ABOUT a League and a half farther South, is *Loch-Finisbay*, an excellent tho' unknown Harbour; the Land lies low, and hides it from the sight of the Sea-faring Men, till they come very near the Coast. There are besides this Harbour, many Creeks on this side, for Barks and lesser Boats.

FRESH-Water Lakes abound in this Island, and are well stor'd with Trout, Eels, and Salmon; each Lake has a River running from it to the Sea, from whence the Salmon comes, about the beginning of *May*, and sooner if the Season be be warm. The beſt time for Angling for Salmon and Trout is when a warm South-weſt Wind blows. They uſe Earth-Worms commonly for Bait, but Cockles attract the Salmon better than any other.

THERE is variety of excellent Springs iſſuing from all the Mountains of this Iſland, but the Wells on the Plains near the Sea are not good. There is one remarkable Fountain lately diſcovered near *Marvag* houſes, on the Eaſtern Coaſt, and has a large Stone by it, which is ſufficient to direct a Stranger to it. The Natives find by experience that it is very effectual for reſtoring loſt Appetite, all that drink of it become very ſoon hungry, though they have eat plentifully but an Hour before; the truth of this was confirmed to me by thoſe that were perfectly well, and alſo by thoſe that were Infirm, for it had the ſame effect on both.

THERE is a Well in the Heath, a Mile to the Eaſt from the Village Borve, the Natives ſay that they find it Efficacious againſt Collicks, Stiches, and Gravel.

THERE are ſeveral Caves in the Mountains, and on each ſide the Coaſt; the largeſt and beſt fortify'd by Nature, is that in the Hill *Ulweal*, in the middle of a high Rock, the Paſſage leading to it is ſo narrow, that one

C only

only can enter at a time: This advantage renders it ſecure from any attempt, for one ſingle Man is able to keep off a Thouſand, if he have but a Staff in his Hand, ſince with the leaſt touch of it he may throw the ſtrongeſt Man down the Rock. The Cave is capacious enough for 50 Men to lodge in; it hath two Wells in it, one of which is excluded from Dogs; for they ſay that if a Dog do but taſt of the Water, the Well preſently dryeth up; and for this reaſon, all ſuch as have occaſion to Lodge there, take care to tye their Dogs that they may not have acceſs to the Water; the other Well is called the Dogs Well, and is only drunk by them.

THERE are ſeveral ancient Forts erected here, which the Natives ſay, were built by the *Danes*; they are of a round form, and have very thick Walls, and a paſſage in 'em by which one can go round the Fort. Some of the Stones that compoſe 'em are very large, theſe Forts are named after the Villages in which they are built, as that in *Borve* is call'd *Down-Borve*, &c. They are built at convenient diſtances on each ſide the Coaſt, and there is a Fort built in every one of the leſſer Iſles.

THERE are ſeveral Stones here erected on one end, one of which is in the Village of *Borve*, about 7 Foot high. There is another Stone of the ſame hight to be ſeen in the op-

poſite

poſite Iſle of Faranſay. There are ſeveral Heaps of Stones, commonly called *Karnes*, on the tops of Hills, and riſing Grounds on the the Coaſt upon which they us'd to burn Heath, as a Signal of an approaching Enemy. There was always a Sentinel at each *Karne* to obſerve the Sea-coaſt; the Steward of the Iſle made frequent Rounds to take notice of the Sentinels, and if he found any of them a ſleep, he ſtrip'd them of their Cloths, and deferred their Perſonal Puniſhments to the Proprietor of the Place. This Iſle produceth the ſame kind of Cattle, Sheep, and Goats that are in the *Lewis*; the Natives gave me an account that a couple of Goats did grow wild on the Hills, and after they had increaſed, they were obſerv'd to bring forth their Young twice a Year.

THERE are abundance of Deer in the Hills and Mountains here, commonly called the Forreſt; which is 18 Miles in length from Eaſt to Weſt; the number of Deer computed to be in this place, is at leaſt 2000; and there is none permitted to Hunt there without a Licence from the Steward to the Forreſter. There is a particular Mountain, and above a Mile of Ground ſurrounding it, to which no Man hath acceſs to Hunt, this place being reſerved for *Mack-leod* himſelf, who when he is diſpos'd to Hunt, is ſure to find Game enough there.

C 2 BOTH

BOTH Hills and Valleys in the Forreſt are well provided with plenty of good Graſs mix'd with Heath, which is all the ſhelter theſe Deer have during the Winter and Spring; there is not a ſhrub of Wood to be ſeen in all the Forreſt, and when a Storm comes, the Deer betake themſelves to the Sea-Coaſt, where they feed upon the *Alga Marina*, or *Sea-ware*.

THE *Mertrick*, a four-footed Creature, about the ſize of a big Cat, is pretty numerous in this Iſle; they have a fine Skin, which is ſmooth as any Fur, and of a brown Colour; they ſay that the Dung of this Animal yields a ſcent like Musk.

THE *Amphibia*, here are *Otters* and *Seals*, the latter are eat by the meaner ſort of People, who ſay they are very nouriſhing. The Natives take them with Nets, whoſe ends are tyed by a Rope to the ſtrong *Alga*, or *Sea-ware*, growing on the Rocks.

THIS Iſland abounds with variety of Land and Sea Fowl, and particularly with very good Hawks.

THERE are Eagles here of two ſorts, the one is of a large ſize, and gray colour, and theſe are very deſtructive to the Fawns, Sheep, and Lambs.

THE

THE other is confiderably lefs, and black, and fhap'd like a Hawk, and more diftructive to the Deer, &c. than the bigger fort.

THERE is no Venemous Creatures of any kind here, except a little *Viper*, which was not thought Venemous till of late, that a Woman dyed of a Wound fhe received from one of them.

I have feen a great many *Rats* in the Village *Rowdil*, which became very troublefome to the Natives, and deftroy'd all their Corn, Milk, Butter, Cheefe, &c. They could not extirpate thefe Vermin for fome time by all their endeavours. A confiderable number of *Cats* was employed for this end, but were ftill worfted, and became perfectly faint, becaufe overpower'd by the *Rats*, who were twenty to one; at length one of the Natives of more fagacity than his Neighbours, found an expedient to renew his *Cats* Strength and Courage, which was by giving it warm Milk after every Encounter with the *Rats*, and the like being given to all the other *Cats* after every Battle, fucceeded fo well, that they left not one *Rat* alive, notwithftanding it great number of them in the Place.

ON the Eaft-fide the Village *Rowdil*, there is a Circle of Stone, within 8 Yards of the

C 3 Shore,

Shore, it's about 3 Fathom under Water, and about two ftories high; it is in form, broader above than below, like to the lower ftory of a Kiln: I faw it perfectly on one fide, but the feafon being then Windy, hinder'd me from a full view of it. The Natives fay that there is fuch another Circle of lefs compafs, in the Pool *Borodil*, on the other fide the Bay.

THE Shore on the Weft Coaft of this Ifland, affords variety of curious Shells, and Walks; as *Tellinæ*, and *Turbines*, of various kinds; thin *Patellæ*, *Streaked-blue*, various colour'd; *Pectenes*, fome blue, and fome of Orange colours.

THE *Os Sepie* is found on the Sand in great quantities. The Natives pulverize it, and take a Dofe of it in boiled Milk, which is found by experience to be an effectual Remedy againft the *Diarhea*, and *Dyfenteria*. They rub this Powder likewife, to take off the Film on the Eyes of Sheep.

THERE is variety of Nuts, called *Molluka*, Beans, fome of which are ufed as Amulets againft Witch-craft, or an Evil Eye, particularly the white one, and upon this account they are wore about Childrens Necks, and if any Evil is intended to them, they fay, the Nut changes into a black colour: That they did change colour, I found true by my own ob-

fervation

servation, but cannot be positive as to the Cause of it.

MALCOM CAMPBELL, Steward of *Harries*, told me that some Weeks before my arrival there, all his Cows gave Blood instead of Milk, for several days together, one of the Neighbours told his Wife that this must be Witchcraft, and it would be easie to remove it, if she would but take the White Nut, called the *Virgin Maries* Nut, and lay it in the Pale into which she was to milk the Cows; this advice she presently follow'd, and having milked one Cow into the Pale with the Nut in it, the Milk was all Blood, and the Nut changed its colour into dark brown, she used the Nut again, and all the Cows gave pure good Milk, which they ascribe to the virtue of the Nut. This very Nut Mr. *Campbel* presented me with, and I keep it still by me.

SOME small quantity of *Ambergreese* hath been found on the Coast of the Island *Barnera*. I was told that a Weaver in this Island had burnt a lump of it, to show him a Light for the most part of the Night, but the strong scent of it made his Head ake exceedingly, by which it was discover'd.

AN Ancient Woman, about 60 Years of age, here lost her Hearing, and having no Physitian to give her advice, she would needs

C 4 try

try an experiment her self, which was thus; she took a Quill with which she ordinarily snushed her Tobacco, and filling it with the Powder of Tobacco, pour'd it into her Ear, which had the desired effect, for she could hear perfectly well next day. Another Neighbour about the same Age, having lost her Hearing sometime after, recover'd it by the same Experiment, as I was told by the Natives.

THE Sheep which feed here on Sandy Ground, become blind sometimes, and are cur'd by rubbing Chalk in their Eyes.

A Servant of Sr. *Normond Mackcleods*, living in the Island of **Bernera**, had a Mare that brought forth a Fole with both the hinder Feet Cloven, which dyed about a Year after; the Natives concluded that it was a bad Omen to the Owner, and his death which follow'd in a few Years after, confirmed them in their Opinion.

THE Natives make use of the Seeds of a White wild Carrot, instead of Hops for brewing their Beer, and they say that it answers the end sufficiently well, and gives the Drink a good relish besides.

JOHN CAMPBELL Forrester of **Harries**, makes use of this singular Remedy for the

the Cold, he walks into the Sea up to the middle with his Cloths on, and immediatly after goes to bed in his wet Cloths, and then laying the Bed-cloths over him, procures a Sweat, which removes the Diſtemper, and this he told me is his only Remedy for all manner of Colds. One of the ſaid *John Campbel's* Servants having his Cheek ſwell'd, and there being no Phyſitian near, he asked his Maſters advice; he knew nothing proper for him but however, bid him apply a Plaiſter of warm Barley Dough to the place affected, this aſſwaged the ſwelling, and drew out of the Fleſh a little Worm, about half an Inch in length, and about the bigneſs of a Gooſe-quill, having a pointed Head, and many little Feet on each ſide, this Worm they call *Fillan*, and it hath been found in the Head and Neck of ſeveral Perſons that I have ſeen in the Iſle of Skie.

ALLIUM Latifolium, a kind of Wild *Garlick*, is much uſed by ſome of the Natives, as a Remedy againſt the Stone; they boil it in Water, and Drink the infuſion, and it expels Sand powerfully with great eaſe.

THE Natives told me that the Rock on the Eaſt-ſide of Harries, in the ſound of Iſland Glaſs, hath a Vacuity near the front, on the North-weſt ſide of the ſound, in which they ſay there is a Stone that they call the *Lunar-Stone*, which advances and retires according to the increaſe and decreaſe of the Moon. A

A poor Man Born in the Village Rowdil, commonly called *St. Clements-blind*, loſt his ſight at every Change of the Moon, which obliged him to keep his Bed for a Day or two, and then he recover'd his ſight.

THE inferiour Iſlands belonging to Harries are as follow. The Iſland Bernera, is Five Miles in Circumference, and lies about Two Leagues to the South of Harries. The Soil is Sandy for the moſt part, and yields a great Product of Barly and Rye in a plentiful Year, eſpecially if the Ground be enriched by *Sea-ware*, and that there be Rain enough to ſatisfie the dry Soil. I had the opportunity to travel this Iſland ſeveral times, and upon a ſtrict enquiry, I found the Product of Barley to be ſometimes 20 fold and upwards, and at that time all the Eaſt-ſide of the Iſland produced 30 fold; this hath been confirmed to me by the Natives, particularly, by Sr. *Normond-Mackleod*, who poſſeſſes the Iſland, he likewiſe confirmed to me the account given by all the Natives of Harries and South-Uiſt, *viz.* that one Barley Grain produceth in ſome places 7, 10, 12, and 14 Ears of Barley, of which he himſelf being diffident for ſometime, he was at the pains to ſearch nicely the Root of one Grain after ſome Weeks growth, and found that from this One Grain many Ears had been grown up. But this happens not except

cept when the Seaſon is very favourable, or in Grounds that have not been cultivated ſome Years before, which if Manur'd with *Sea-ware*, ſeldom fails to produce an extraordinary Crop. It is obſerved in this Iſland, as elſewhere, that when the Ground is dug up with Spades, and the Turfs turn'd upſide down, and cover'd with *Sea-ware*, it yields a better product than when it is plow'd.

THERE is a Freſh-water Lake in this Iſland called *Loch-Bruiſt*, in which there are ſmall Iſlands abounding with Land and Sea Fowl, which build there in the Summer. There is likewiſe plenty of Eels in this Lake, which are eaſieſt caught in *September*, and then the Natives carry Lights with them in the Night time to the Rivulet running from the Lake, in which the Eels fall down to the Sea in heaps together.

This Iſland in the Summer is covered all over with Clover, and Daſie, except in the Corn-fields: There is to be ſeen about the Houſes of **Bernera**, for the ſpace of a Mile a ſoft Subſtance in ſhew and colour, exactly reſembling the *Sea-plant*, called *Slake*, and grows very thick among the Graſs. The Natives ſay that it is the Product of a dry hot Soil, it grows likewiſe in the tops of ſeveral Hills in the Iſland of **Harries**.

IT'S

IT'S proper to add here an account of ſeveral ſtrange irregularities in the Tides, on **Bernera** Coaſt, by Sr. *Robert Murray*, mention'd in the *Phil. Tranſactions*.

THE Tides increaſe and decreaſe gradually according to the Moons Age ſo as about the third day after the New and full Moon, in the Weſtern Iſles and Continent they are commonly at the higheſt, and about the quarter Moons, at the loweſt. (The former called Spring-Tide, the other Neap Tides) the Tides from the quarter to the higheſt Spring Tide increaſe in a certain proportion, and from the Spring Tide to the Quarter Tide in like proportion; and the Ebbs riſe and fall always after the ſame manner.

IT's ſuppos'd that the increaſe of Tides is made in the proportion of ſines; the firſt increaſe exceeds the loweſt in a ſmall proportion, the next in a greater, the third greater than that, and ſo on to the middle-moſt, whereof the exceſs is the greateſt, diminiſhing again from that to the higheſt Spring-Tide, ſo as the proportions before and after the middle, do anſwer one another. And likewiſe from the higheſt Spring-Tide, to the loweſt Neap-Tide, the decreaſes ſeem to keep the like proportions. And this commonly falls out when no Wind, or other Accident cauſes an alteration. At the begining beginning of each Flood on the Coast, the Tide moves faster, but in a small degree, increasing its swiftness till towards the middle of the Flood, and then decreasing in swiftness again from the middle to the top of the High-water, it's supposed that the inequal spaces of time, the increase and decrease of swiftness, and consequently the degrees of the Risings and Fallings of the same inequal spaces of time, are performed according to the proportion of Sines. The proportion cannot hold precisely and exactly in regard of the inequalities that fall out in the Periods, of the Tides, which are believed to follow certain positions of the Moon in regard of the Equinox, which are known not to keep a precise constant Course, so that there not being equal Portions of Time between one New Moon and another, the Moons return to the same Meridian cannot be always performed in the same time. And the Tides from New-Moon, being not always the same in Number, or sometimes but 57, sometimes 58, sometimes 59, (without any certain order or succession) is another evidence of the difficulty of reduceing this to any great exactness.

AT the East end of this Isle, there is a strange reciprocation of the flux and reflux of the Sea. There is another no less remarkable upon the West side of the Long Island, the Tides which come from the South-west, run along

along the Coast Northward; so that during the ordinary course of the Tides, the Flood runs East in the *Frith*, where **Berneray** lies, and the Ebb West, and thus the Sea Ebbs and Flows orderly, some Four days before the Full and Change; and as long after, (the ordinary Spring-Tides rising some 14 or 15 foot upright, and all the rest proportionably, as in other places) but afterwards, for Four Days before the Quarter Moons, and as long after, there is constantly a great and singular Variation. For then (a Southerly Moon making there the full Sea) the Course of the Tide being Eastward: When it begins to flow, which is about 9½ of the Clock, it not only continues so about 3½ in the Afternoon, that it be high-water, but after it begins to Ebb, the Current runs on still Eastward, during the Whole Ebb, so that it runs Eastward 12 hours together, that is, all day long, from about 9½ in the Morning, till about 9½ at Night. But then when the Night-Tide begins to Flow, the Current turns, and runs Westward all Night, during both Flood and Ebb for some 12 hours more, as it did Eastward the day before, and thus the Reciprocations continue, one Flood and Ebb and running 12 hours Eastward, and another 12 hours Westward, till 4 days before the Full and New Moon; and then they resume their ordinary regular Course as before, running East during the Six hours of Flood, and West during the Six of Ebb.

THERE

THERE is another extraordinary Irregularity in the Tides, which never fail: That whereas between the *Vernal* and *Autumnal* Equinox, that is for ſix Months together, the Courſe of irregular Tides about the Quarter Moons, is to run all day, 12 hours, as from about 9½ to 9½ to 10 exact Eaſtward all night, that is, 12 hours more Weſtward, during the other ſix Months, from the *Autumnal* to the *Vernal* Equinox, the Current runs all Day Weſtward, and all Night Eaſtward. I have obſerved the Tides as above, for the ſpace of ſome Days both in *April*, *May*, *July*, and *Auguſt*. The Natives have frequent opportunities to ſee this both Day and Night, and they all agree that the Tides run as mention'd above.

THERE's a Couple of Ravens in this Iſland, which beat away all Ravenous Fowls, and when their Young are able to fly abroad, they beat them alſo out of the Iſland, but not without many blows, and a great Noiſe.

THERE are two Chappels in this Iſle, to wit, *St. Aſaphs*, and *St. Columbus*'s Chappel There is a Stone erected near the former, which is 8 Foot high, and 2 Foot thick.

ABOUT half a League from Bernera, to the Weſtward, lies the Iſland Pabbay, 3 Miles in Circumference, and having a Mountain in the middle; the Soil is Sandy, and fruitful

fruitful in Corn and Graſs, and the Natives have lately diſcovered here a white Marle. The Weſt end of this Iſland which looks to St *Kilda*, is called the Wooden Harbour, becauſe the Sands at Low-water, diſcover ſeveral Trees that have formerly grown there. Sir *Normand Mackleod* told me that he had ſeen a Tree cut there, which was afterwards made into a Harrow.

THERE are two Chappels in this Iſland, one of which is Dedicated to the Virgin *Mary*, the other to St. *Muluag*.

THE Steward of Kilda, who lives in Pabbay, is accuſtomed in time of a Storm, to tie a bundle of Puddings made of the Fat of Sea-Fowl to the end of his Cable, and lets it fall into the Sea, behind the Rudder, this he ſays hinders the Waves from breaking, and calms the Sea; but the ſcent of the Greaſe attracts the Whales, which put the Veſſel in danger.

ABOUT half a League to the North of Pabbay, lies the Iſle Sellay, a Mile in Circumference, that yields extraordinary Paſturage for Sheep, ſo that they become fat very ſoon; they have the biggeſt Horns that ever I ſaw on Sheep.

About a League farther to the North, lies the Iſle Taranſay, very fruitful in Corn and Graſs,

Graſs, and yeilds much yellow Talk. It is 3 Miles in Circumference, and has two Chappels, one dedicated to *St. Tarran*, the other to *St. Keith*.

THERE is an ancient Tradition among the Natives here, that a Man muſt not be Buried in *St. Tarrans*, nor a Woman in *St. Kieth's*, becauſe otherwiſe the Corps would be found above Ground the day after it is Interred. I told them this was a moſt ridiculous fancy, which they might ſoon perceive by experience, if they would but put it to a tryal. *Roderick Campbel*, who reſides there, being of my opinion, reſolved to embrace the firſt opportunity that offer'd, in order to undeceive the Credulous Vulgar, and accordingly a poor Man in this Iſland who dyed a Year after, was buried in *St. Tarrans* Chappel, contrary to the ancient Cuſtom and Tradition of this place, but his Corps are ſtill in the Grave, from whence it is not like to riſe until the general Reſurrection. This inſtance has delivered the credulous Natives from this unreaſonable fancy. This Iſland is a Mile diſtant from the main Land of **Harries**, and when the Inhabitants go from this Iſland to **Harries** with a deſign to ſtay for any time, they agree with thoſe that carry them over, on a particular motion of walking upon a certain peice of Ground, unknown to every body but themſelves as a ſignal to bring 'em back.

D THREE

THREE Leagues to the Weſtward of this Iſland, lies **Gasker**, about half a Mile in circumference, it excels any other plot of its extent, for fruitfulneſs in Graſs and Product of Milk, it maintains 8 or 10 Cows; the Natives kill Seals here which are very big.

ABOUT two Leagues farther North lies the Iſland **Scarp**, 2 Miles in Circumference, and is a high Land covered with Heath and Graſs.

BETWEEN **Bernera** and the Main Land of **Harries** lies the Iſland **Ensay**, which is above 2 Miles in Circumference, and for the moſt part Arable Ground, which is fruitful in Corn and Graſs; there is an old Chappel here for the uſe of the Natives, and there was lately diſcovered a Grave in the Weſt end of the Iſland, in which was found a pair of Scales made of Braſs, and a little Hammer, both which were finely poliſhed.

BETWEEN **Ensay** and the main Land of **Harries**, lies ſeveral ſmall Iſlands, fitter for Paſturage then Cultivation.

THE little Iſland **Quedam**, hath a Vein of Adamant Stone, in the front of the Rock; the Natives ſay that Mice don't live in this Iſland, and when they chance to be carried thither

among

aoming Corn, they die quickly after, without these small Islands, there is a Tract of small Isles in the same Line with the Eastside of the Harries, and North-vist, They are in all respects of the same Nature with those two Islands, so that the sight of them is apt to dispose one to think that they have been once united together.

THE most Southerly of these Islands, and the nearest to North-vist is Hermetra, two miles in Circumference, it is a Moorish Soil, covered all over almost with Heath, except here and there a few Piles of Grass, and the Plant *Milk-wort*, yet notwithstanding this disadvantage, it is certainly the best spot of its extent for Pasturage, among these Isles, and affords great plenty of Milk in *January* and *February* beyond what can be seen in the other Islands.

I saw here the foundation of a House built by the *English*, in K. *Charles* the First's time, for one of their Magazines to lay up the Cask, Salt, &c. for carrying on the Fishery, which was then begun in the Western Islands, but this design miscarried because of the Civil Wars, which then broke out.

THE Channel between Harries and North-vist, is above three Leagues in breadth, and abounds with Rocks, as well under as above Water, Tho' at the same time, Vessels of

D 2 300

300 Tuns have gone through it, from East to West, having the advantage of one of the Natives for a Pilot, some 16 years ago, one Captain *Frost* was safely conducted in this manner. The Harries belongs in property to the Laird of *Mack Leod*, he and all the Inhabitants are Protestants, and observe the Festivals of *Christmass*, *Goodfriday*, and St. *Michaels* day, upon the latter, they Rendezvous on Horse-back, and make their Cavalcade on the Sands at low water.

THE Island of North vist lyes about three Leagues to the South of the Island of Harries, being in form of a Semi-circle, the Diameter of which looks to the East and is Mountainous and full of Heath, and fitter for Pasturage then Cultivation. The West side is of a quite different Soil, Arable and Plain, the whole is in length from South to North Nine Miles, and about Thirty in Circumference.

THERE are Four Mountains in the middle, Two lie within less then a Mile of each other, and are called South and North-Lee; all the Hills and Heath afford good Pasturage, tho' it consists as much of Heath as Grass. The Arable Ground hath a mixture of Clay in some places, and it is covered all over in Summer-time, and Harvest with Clover, Dasie, and Variety of other Plants, pleasant to the sight, and of a fragrant smell, and abounds with

in

with black Cattle, and Sheep. The Soil is very grateful to the Husband-man, yielding a Produce of Barley, from Ten to Thirty fold in a plentiful Year; provided the Ground be manur'd with *Sea-ware*, and that it have Rain proportionable to the Soil. I have upon several occasions enquired concerning the produce of Barley, in this and the Neighbouring Islands; the same being much doubted in the South of *Scotland*, as well as in *England*; and upon the whole, I have been assured by the most Antient and Industrious of the Natives, that the increase is the same as mentioned before in Harries.

THEY told me likewise, that a Plot of Ground which hath lain unmanur'd for some Years, would in a Plentiful season produce Fourteen Ears of Barley from One Grain; and several Ridges were then shewed me of this extraordinary Growth in different places. The Grain sow'n here is Barley, Oats, Rye; and it's not to be doubted, but the Soil would also produce Wheat. The way of Tillage here is commonly by Ploughing, and some by Digging; the ordinary Plough is drawn by four Horses, and they have a little Plough also call'd Ristle, *i.e.* a thing that cleaves, the Culter of, which is in Form of a Sickle, and it is drawn sometimes by One, and sometimes by Two Horses, according as the Ground is; the design of this little Plow is to draw a deep

D 3 Line

Line in the Ground, to make it the more easie for the big Plow to follow, which otherwise would be much retarded by the strong Roots of Bent lying deep in the Ground, that are cut by the little Plow. When they dig with Spades, it produceth more increase; the little Plow is likewise used to facilitate Digging as well as Plowing; they continue to Manure the Ground until the 10*th*. of *June*, if they have plenty of *Braggir*, *i.e.* the broad Leaves growing on the top of the *Alga-Marina*.

ABOUT a League and a half to the South of the Island Hermetra in Harries, lies Loch-Maddy, so called from the three Rocks without the Entry on the South side: They are called *Maddies*, from the great quantity of big Muscles call'd *Maddies* that grows upon them. This Harbour is Capacious enough for some hundreds of Vessels of any Burthen; it hath several Isles within it, and they contribute to the security of the Harbour, for a Vessel may safely come close to the Key; the Seamen divide the Harbour in two parts, calling the South-side Loch-Maddy, and the North-side Loch-Partan. There is one Island in the South Loch which for its Commodiousness is by the *English* call'd Nonsuch; this Loch hath been famous for the great quantity of Herrings yearly taken in it within these 50 Years last past: The Natives told me that in the Memory of some yet alive, there had

been

been 400 Sail Loaded in it with Herrings at one Seaſon; but it is not now frequented for Fiſhing, tho' the Herrings do ſtill abound in it, and on this Coaſt every Summer and Harveſt, the Natives ſit Angling on the Rocks, and as they pull up their Hooks, do many times bring up Herrings; That they are always on the Coaſt, appears from the Birds, Whales, and other Fiſhes, that are their forerunners every where, and yet it is ſtrange that in all this Iſland there is not one Herring Net to be had; but if the Natives ſaw any Encouragement, they could ſoon provide 'em. Cod, Ling, and all ſorts of Fiſh taken in theſe Iſlands abound in and about this Lake.

IN this Harbour there is a ſmall Iſland called **Wackſay**, in which there is ſtill to be ſeen the Foundation of a Houſe, built by the *Engliſh*, for a Magazine to keep their Cask, Salt, *&c.* for carrying on a great Fiſhery which was then begun there. The Natives told me that King *Charles* the *1ſt.* had a ſhare in it: This Lake with the convenience of its Fiſhings and Iſlands is certainly capable of great improvement; much of the Ground about the Bay is capable of Cultivation, and affords a great deal of Fuel, as Turff, Peats, and plenty of Freſh-Water. It alſo affords a good quantity of Oyſters, and Clam-ſhell-fiſh, the former grows on Rocks, and are ſo big that they are cut in four peices before they are eat.

D 4 ABOUT

ABOUT half a Mile further South is **Loch-Eport**, having a Rock without the Mouth of the Entry, which is narrow; the Lake penetrates ſome Miles towards the Weſt, and is a good Harbour, having ſeveral ſmall Iſles within it. The Seals are very numerous here. In the Month of *July* the Spring-Tides carry in a great quantity of Macrel, and at the return of the Water, they are found many times lying on the Rocks. The Vulgar Natives make uſe of the Aſhes of burnt *Sea-ware*, which preſerves them for ſome time inſtead of Salt.

ABOUT two Miles to the South of **Loch-Eport** lies the Bay, called the **Kyle** of **Rona**; having the Iſland of that Name (which is a little Hill) within the Bay; there is a Harbour on each ſide of it, this Place hath been found of great convenience for the Fiſhing of Cod, and Ling, which abounds on this Coaſt; there is a little Chappel in the Iſland **Rona**, called the *Low-landers* Chappel, becauſe Seamen who dye in time of Fiſhing, are buried in that place.

THERE is a Harbour on the South ſide the Iſland **Borera**, the Entry ſeems to be narrower then really it is; the Iſland and the oppoſite Point of Land appear like two little Promontories off at Sea. Some Veſſels have been forced in there by Storm, as was Captain *Peter's* *ters* a Dutch Man, and after him an *Engliſh* Ship, who both approved of this Harbour; the former built a Cock-boat there on a Sunday, at which the Natives were much offended. The latter having Landed in the Iſland, happened to come into a Houſe where he found only Ten Women, and they were imploy'd (as he ſuppos'd) in a ſtrange manner, *viz.* their Arms and Legs were bare, being Five on a ſide, and between them lay a Board, upon which they had laid a piece of Cloth, and were thickning of it with their Hands and Feet, and Singing all the while, the *Engliſh* Man, preſently concluded it to be a little Bedlam, which he did not expect in ſo remote a Corner, and this he told to Mr. *John Macklean*, who poſſeſſes the Iſland; Mr. *Macklean* anſwer'd he never ſaw any Mad People in thoſe Iſlands, but this would not ſatisfie him, till they both went to the place where the Women were at work, and then Mr. *Macklean* having told him, that it was their common way of thickning Cloth, he was convinced, tho' ſurpriz'd at the manner of it.

THERE is ſuch a number of Freſh-water Lakes here, as can hardly be believed, I my ſelf and ſeveral others indeavour'd to number them, but in vain, for they are ſo diſpos'd into turnings, that it is impracticable. They are generally well ſtock'd with Trouts and Eels, and ſome of 'em with Salmon, and which is yet

yet more ſtrange, Cod, Ling, Macrel *&c.* are taken in theſe Lakes into which they are brought by the Spring Tides.

THESE Lakes have many ſmall Iſlands which in Summer abound with variety of Land and Sea Fowls, that build and hatch there. There be alſo ſeveral Rivers here, which afford Salmon, one ſort of them is very ſingular, that is called Marled Salmon, or as the Natives call it *ieskdrumin*, being leſſer then the ordinary Salmon, and full of ſtrong Large Scales, no bait can allure it, and a ſhadow frights it away, being the wildeſt of fiſhes, it leaps high above water, and delights to be in the ſurface of it.

THERE's great plenty of Shell-fiſh round this Iſland, more particularly Cockles, the Iſlands do alſo afford many ſmall Fiſh called Eels of a whitiſh colour, they are picked out of the Sand with a ſmall crooked Iron made on purpoſe. There is plenty of Lobſters on the weſt ſide of this Iſland, and one ſort bigger then the reſt, having the Toe ſhorter and broader.

THERE are ſeveral antient Forts in this Iſland, built upon Eminences, or in the middle of freſh water Lakes.

HERE are likewiſe ſeveral Kairns or Heaps of Stones, the biggeſt I obſerved was on a hill near to Loch-Eport. There are three Stones erected

erected about five foot high, at the diftance of a quarter of a mile from one another, on E-minences about a mile from Loch-Maddy, to a-mufe Invaders, for which reafon they are ftill called falfe fentinels.

THERE is a Stone of 24 foot long and 4 in breadth in the hill *Criniveal*, the Natives fay a Giant of a month old was buried under it. There is a very confpicuous Stone in the face of the Hill above *St. Peters*, village, aboue 8 foot high.

THERE is another about 8 foot high at Down-roffel which the natives call a Crofs, There are two broad Sones about 8 foot high on the hill two miles to the South of **Valay**.

THERE is another at the Key oppofite to **Kirkibaft** 12 foot high, the Natives fay that delinquenrs were tyed to this Stone in time of Divine Service.

THERE is a Stone in form of a Crofs in the Row, oppofite to *St. Maries* Church about 5 foot high, the Natives call it the water Crofs, for the antient Inhabitants had a Cuftom of erecting this fort of Crofs to procure rain, and when they had got enough they laid it flat on the ground, but this cuftom is now disufed. The inferior Ifland is the Ifland of **Heiskir** which lyes near three

three Leagues weftward of **North-Vift** is three miles in Circumference of a fandy foil, and very fruitful in Corn and Grafs, Black Cattle and the Inhabitants labour under want of Fuel of all forts, which obliges them to burn Cows Dung, Barley ftraw, and dry'd Sea-ware; the Natives told me that bread baked by the Fuel of Sea-ware, relifhes better than that done otherwife. They are accuftomed to Salt their Cheefe with the Afhes of Barley Straw, which they fuffer not to ly on it above 12 hours time, becaufe otherwife it would fpoil it. There was a Stone Cheft lately difcovered here, having an earthen Pitcher in it which was full of Bones, and affoon as touched they to Duft.

THERE are two fmall Iflands feparated by narrow Channels from the Northweft of this Ifland, and are of the fame Mold with the big Ifland. The Natives fay that there is a Couple of Ravens there, which fuffer no other of their kind to approach this Ifland, and if any fuch Chance to come, this Couple immediately drive them away, with fuch a noife as is heard by all the Inhabitants: They are obferved like-wife to beat away their young as foon as they be able topurchafe for themfelves; the Natives told me that when one of this Couple happened to be Wounded by Gun-fhot, it lay ftill in the Corner of a Rock for a week or two, du-ing which time its Mate brought Provifion to it it daily, until it recovered perfectly: the Natives add further that one of theſe two Ravens having dyed ſome time after; the ſurviving one abandoned the Iſland for a few days, and then was ſeen to return with about ten or 12 more of its kind and having choſen a Mate out of this number all the reſt went quite off, leaving theſe two in Poſſeſſion of their little Kingdom, they do by a certain ſagacity diſcover to the Inhabitants any Carcaſe, on the Shoar or in the fields (whereof I have ſeen ſeveral inſtances;) The inhabitants pretend to know by their noiſe, whether it be Fleſh or Fiſh, I told them,this was ſuch a Nicety that I could ſcarcely give it credit,but they anſwered me that they came to the knowledge of it by obſervation, and that they make their loudeſt noiſe for Fleſh. There is a narrow Channel between the Iſland of Heiskir and one of the leſſer Iſlands in which the Natives formerly killed many Seals, in this manner, they twiſted together ſeveral ſmall Ropes of Horſe Hair in form of a Net contracted at one end like a Purſe, and ſo by opening and ſhutting this Hair Net, theſe Seals were catched in the narrow Channel. On the South Side of *Northviſt* are the Iſlands of *Illeray* which are acceſſible at low Water, each of them being 3 miles in compaſs and are very fertile in Corn and Cattle.

ON the weſtern Coaſt, of this Iſland lyes the Rock Coufinil, about a quarter of a mile in

in circumference, and it is ſtill famous for the yearly fiſhing of Seals there, in the end of *October*, this Rock belongs to the Farmers of the next adjacent Lands, there is one who furniſheth a Boat, to whom there is a particular ſhare due on that account, beſides his proportion as Tenant, the Pariſh Miniſter hath his choice of all the Young Seals, and that which he takes is called by the Natives, Cullen Mory, that is, the Virgin Marys Seal. The Steward of the Iſland hath one paid to him, his Officer hath another, and this by vertue of their Offices. Theſe Farmers man their Boat with a competent number fit for the buſineſs, and they always imbarque with a contrary wind, for their ſecurity againſt being driven away by the Ocean, and likewiſe to prevent them from being diſcovered, by the Seals, who are apt to ſmell the ſcent of them, and preſenely run to ſea.

WHEN this Crew is quietly landed, they ſurround the Paſſes, and then the ſignal for the general attacque is given from the Boat, and ſo they beat them down with bigſtaves. The Seals at this On-ſet make towards the Sea with all ſpeed, and often force their paſſage over the necks of the ſtouteſt aſſailants, who aim always at the Forehead of the Seals, giving many blows before they be killed, and if they be not hit exactly on the front they contract a Lump on their Forehead which makes them look very fierce, and if they get hold of the Staff with their

their Teeth, they carry it along to Sea with them. Thoſe that are in the Boat ſhoot at them as they run to Sea, but few are catch'd that way. The Natives told me that ſeveral of the biggeſt Seals loſe their Lives by endeavouring to Save their Young ones, whom they tumble before them, towards the Sea. I was told alſo that 320 Seals Young and Old have been killed at one time in this Place. The reaſon of attacking 'em in *October*, is, becauſe in the beginning of this month the Seals bring forth their Young on the Ocean Side, but theſe on the Eaſt Side who are of the leſſer ſtature bring forth their Young in the middle of *June*.

THE Seals eat no Fiſh till they firſt take off the Skin, they hold the Head of the Fiſh between their Teeth, and pluck the Skin off each Side with their ſharp pointed Nails, this I obſerved ſeveral times. The Natives told me, that the Seals are regularly coupled, and reſent an Encroachment on their Mates at an extraordinary rate, the Natives have obſerved that when a Male had invaded a Female, already coupled to another the injured Male upon its return to its Mate would by a ſtrange Sagacity find it out and reſent it againſt the aggreſſor by a bloody conflict, which gives a red Tincture to the Sea in that part where they Fight; this piece of revenge has been often obſerved by Seal Hunters, and many others of unqueſtionable

ble Integrity, whoſe occaſions obliged them to be much on this Caaſt, I was aſſured by good Hands that the Seals make their addreſſes to each other by kiſſes, this hath been obſerved often by Men and Women as Fiſhing on the Coaſt in a clear Day: the Female puts away its Young from ſucking, as ſoon as it is able to provide for it ſelf, and this is not done without many ſevere blows.

THERE is a Hole in the Skin of the Female, within which the Teats are ſecured from being hurt, as it creeps along the Rocks and Stones, for which cauſe nature hath formed the point of the Tongue of the Young one cloven without which it could not ſuck.

THE Natives Salt the Seals with the aſhes of burnt Sea-ware, and ſay they are good Food, the vulgar eat them commonly in the Spring time with a long pointed Stick inſtead of a Fork, to prevent the ſtrong ſmell which their hands would otherwiſe have for ſeveral Hours after. The Fleſh and Broth of freſh Young *Seals*, is by experience known to be Pectoral; the Meat is Aſtringent, and uſed as an effectual remedy againſt the *Diarrhea* and *Dyſenteria*; the Liver of a *Seal* being dry'd and pulveriz'd, and afterwards a little of it drunk with Milk, *Aquavitæ* or Red-Wine, is alſo good againſt *Fluxes*.

SOME

SOME of the Natives wear a Girdle of the *Seals-skin* about their middle for removing the *Sciatica,* as thoſe of the Shire of Aberdeen wear it to remove the *Chin-cough.* This four-footed Creature is reckon'd one of the ſwifteſt in the Sea; they ſay likewiſe that it leaps in Cold Weather the height of a Pike above Water, and that the Skin of it is white in Summer and darker in Winter, and that their Hair ſtands on end with the Flood, and falls again at the Ebb: The Skin is by the Natives cut in long pieces, and then made uſe of inſtead of Ropes to fix the Plow to their Horſes when they Till the Ground.

THE *Seal,* tho' eſteemed fit only for the Vulgar, is alſo eaten by Perſons of Diſtinction, tho' under a different Name, to wit, *Hamm*; this I have been aſſur'd of by good hands, and thus we ſee that the generality of Men are as much led by fancy as judgment in their Palates as well as in other things. The Popiſh Vulgar in the Iſlands Southward from this, eat theſe *Seals* in Lent inſtead of Fiſh, this occaſion'd a debate between a *Proteſtant* Gentleman and a *Papiſt* of my Acquaintance, the former alledged that the other had tranſgreſſed the Rules of his Church, by eating Fleſh in Lent, the latter anſwer'd, that he did not, for ſays he I have eat a Sea Creature, which only lives and feeds upon Fiſh, the *Proteſtant* reply'd, that this

E Creature

Creature is Amphibious, lies, creeps, eats, ſleeps, and ſo ſpends much of its time on Land, which no Fiſh can do and live. It hath alſo another faculty that no Fiſh has, that is, it breaks Wind backward ſo loudly, that one may hear it at a great diſtance; but the Papiſt ſtill maintain'd that he muſt believe it to be Fiſh till ſuch time as the Pope and his Prieſts decide the queſtion.

ABOUT Three Leagues and an half to the Weſt, lies the ſmall Iſlands called Hawsker, Rocks, and Hawsker Eggath, and Hawsker-Nimannich, id, eſt, *Monks-Rock,* which hath an Altar in it, the firſt called ſo from the Ocean as being near to it, for *Haw* or *Thau* in the Ancient Language ſignifies the Ocean, the more Southerly Rocks are 6 or 7 big ones nicked or indented, for *Eggath* ſignifies ſo much the largeſt Iſland which is Northward, is near half a Mile in Circumference, and it is covered with long Graſs, only ſmall Veſſels can paſs between this and the Southern Rocks, being neareſt to *St. Kilda* of all the Weſt Iſlands; both of 'em abound with Fowls as much as any Iſles of their extent in *St. Kilda.* The Coulterneb Guillemot, and Scarts are moſt numerous here, the *Seals* likewiſe abound very much in and about theſe Rocks.

THE Iſland of Valay lies on the Weſt near the main Land of North-viſt, it is about 4

Miles

Miles in Circumference, arable and a dry Sandy Soil, very fruitful in Corn and Grafs, Clover and Dasie. It hath Three Chappels, One Dedicated to *St. Ulton*, and another to the *Virgin Mary.* There are Two Crosses of Stone, each of them about 7 Foot high, and a Foot and a half broad.

THERE is a little Font on an Altar, being a big Stone, round in like of a Cannon Ball, and having in the upper end a little Vacuity capable of two Spoonfuls of water; below the Chappels there is a flat thin Stone, called *Brownies* Stone, upon which the ancient Inhabitants offered a Cows Milk every Sunday, but this Custom is now quite abolish'd. Some Thirty Paces on this side is to be seen a little Stone House under Ground, it is very low and long, having an entry on the Sea side; I saw an entry in the middle of it, which was discover'd by the falling of the Stones and Earth.

ABOUT a League to the North-east of **Valay** is the Island of **Borera**, about 4 Miles in Circumference, the Mold in some places is Sandy, and in others black Earth, it is very fruitful in Cattle and Grafs; I saw a Mare here, which I was told brought forth a Fole in her Second Year.

THERE is a Cow here that brought forth two Female Calves at once, in all things so very

E 2 like

like one another that they could not be distinguished by any outward mark, and had such a simpathy, that they were never separate, except in time of sucking, and then they kep'd still their own side of their Dam, which was not observed until a distinguishing Mark was put about one of their Necks by the Milk-maid. in the middle of this Island, there's a Fresh-water Lake, well stock'd with very big Eels, some of them as long as Cod, or Ling-Fish; there is a passage under the Stony Ground, which is between the Sea and the Lake, through which it's the suppos'd Eels come in with the Spring Tides; one of the Inhabitants called *Muck-van-sh*, i. e. *Monks-Son*, had the curiosity to creep naked through this Passage.

THIS Island affords the largest and best Dulse for eating, it requires less Butter than any other of this sort, and has a mellowish Taste.

THE Burial place near the Houses, is called the Monks-Field, for all the Monks that dyed in the islands that lye Northward from **Egg**, were buried in this little Plot, each Grave hath a Stone at both ends, some of which are 3 and others 4 Foot high. There are big Stones without the Burial place even with the Ground, several of them have little Vacuities in them as if made by Art; the Tradition is that these Vacuities were dug for receiving the Monks Knees when they prayed upon 'em. THE

THE Island Lingay, lyes half a League South on the side of Boreray, it is singular in respect of all the Lands of Uist and the other Islands that surround it, for they a e all composed of Sand, and this on the contrary, is altogether Moss covered with Heath, affording five Peats in depth, and is very serviceable and useful, furnishing the Island Boreray, &c. with Plenty of good Fuel: This Island was held as Consecrated for several Ages, in so much that the Natives would not then presume to cut any Fuel in it.

THE Cattle produced here, are Horses, Cows, Sheep and Hogs, generally of a low stature: the Horses are very strong and fit for Pads, tho' exposed to the rigour of the weather all the Winter and Spring in the open Fields. Their Cows are also in the Fields all the Spring, and their Beef is sweet and tender as any can be; they live upon *Sea-ware* in the Winter and Spring, and are fatned by it, nor are they slaughtered before they eat plentifully of it in *December*. The Natives are accustomed to salt their Beef in a Cows Hide, which keeps it close from Air, and preserves it as well, if not better, then Barrels, and tasts they say best when this way used: This Beef is transported to Glasgow, a City in the West of *Scotland*, and from thence (being put into Barrels there) exported to the *Indies* in good Condition. The Hills

afford some hundreds of Deer, who eat *Sea-ware* also in Winter and Spring-time.

THE *Amphibia* produced here are Seals, and Otters. There is no Fox or venemous Creature in this Island. The great Eagles here fasten their Tallons in the back of Fish, and commonly of Salmon, which is often above Water and in the surface. The Natives who in the Summer time live on the Coast, do sometimes rob the Eagle of its Prey after its Landing.

HERE are Hawks, Eagles, Pheasants, Moor-Fowls, Tarmogan, Plover, Pigeons, Crows, Swans, and all the ordinary Sea-Fowls in the West Islands. The Eagles are very destructive to the Fawns and Lambs, especially the black Eagle, which is of a lesser size then the other. The Natives observe that it fixes its Tallons between the Deers Horns, and beats its Wings constantly about its Eyes, which puts the Deer to run continually till it fall into a Ditch, or over a Precipice, where it dies, and so becomes a Prey to this cunning Hunter. There are at the same time several other Eagles of this kind which flye on both sides of the Deer, which frights it extreamly, and contributes much to its more sudden destruction.

THE Forester and several of the Natives assured me, that they had seen both sorts of Eagles

Eagles kill Deer in this manner. The Swans come hither in great Numbers in the Month of *October*, with North East Winds, and live in the fresh Lakes, where they feed upon Trout and Water Plants till *March*, at which time they fly away again with a South-east Wind. When the Natives kill a Swan it is common for the Eaters of it to make a *Negative-vow* (i. e. they swear never to do something that is in it self impracticable.) before they taste of the Fowl.

THE Bird *Corn-Craker*, is about the bigness of a *Pigeon*, having a longer Neck, and being of a brown Colour, but blacker in harvest then in Summer; the Natives say it lives by the Water, and under the Ice in Winter and Spring.

THE *Colk* is a Fowl somewhat less than a *Goose*, hath Feathers of divers colours, as White, Gray, Green and Black, and is beautiful to the Eye; it hath a Tuft on the Crown of its Head like that of a *Peacock*, and a Train longer then that of *House-Cock*. This Fowl looseth its Feathers in time of Hatching, and lives mostly in the remotest Islands, as **Heisker** and **Rona**.

THE *Gawlin*, is a Fowl less than a *Duck*, it is reckon'd a true Prognosticator of fair weather, for when it sings fair and good weather always follows, as the Natives commonly

E 4 observe;

observe; the Piper of St. *Kilda* plays the Notes which it sings, and hath composed a Tune of 'em, which the Natives judge to be very fine Musick.

THE *Rain-goose* bigger then a *Duck*, makes a doleful Noise before a great Rain, it builds its Nest always upon the brink of fresh water Lakes, so as it may reach the water.

THE *Bonnivochil*, so called by the Natives, and by the Seamen, *Bishop*, and *Carara*, as big as a *Goose*, having a white spot on the Breast, and the rest party coloured, it seldom flies, but is exceeding quick in diving; the Minister of **Northvist** told me that he kill'd one of them which weighed Sixteen Pound and an Ounce; there is about an Inch deep of Fat upon the Skin of it, which the Natives apply to the Hip Bone, and by experience find it a succesful Remedy for removing the *Sciatica*.

THE Bird *Goylir*, about the bigness of a *Swallow*, is observed never to Land but in the Month of *January*, at which time it is supposed to hatch, it dives with a violent swiftness; when any number of these Fowls are seen together, its concluded to be an undoubted sign of an approaching storm, and when the storm ceases they disappear under the Water, the Seamen call them *Malifigies*, from *Maliceffigies*, which they often find to be true.

THE

THE Bird *Sereachan-aittin*, is about the bigneſs of a large *Mall* but having a longer Body, and a blewiſh Colour, The Bill is of a Carnation Colour, This Bird ſhreiks moſt hideouſly, and is obſerved to have a greater affection for its Mate, than any Fowl whatſoever, for when the Cock or Hen is killed, the ſurviving one doth for 8 or 10 Days afterward make a Lamentable Noiſe about the place.

THE Bird *Faskidar*, about the bigneſs of a *Sea-maw* of the middle ſize is obſerved to fly with greater ſwiftneſs than any other fowl in thoſe parts, and purſues leſſer fowls, and forces them in their flight to let fall the Food which they have got, and by its nimbleneſs catches it, before it touch the Ground.

THE Natives obſerve that an extraordinary heat without Rain at the uſual time the Sea-fouls lay their Eggs, hinders them from laying any Eggs, for about 8 or ten Days, whereas warm Weather accompanied with Rain diſpoſes them to lay much ſooner.

THE *Wild Geeſe* are plentiul here and very deſtructive to the Barley, notwithſtanding the many methods uſed for driving them away both by Traps and Gun-ſhot. There are ſome flocks of barren Fowls of all kinds, which are diſtinguiſhed by their not joyning with the

the reſt of their kind, and they are ſeen commonly upon the bare Rocks, without any Neſts.

THE Air here is moiſt and moderately Cold, the Natives qualify it ſometimes by drinking a Glaſs of *Uſquebaugh*, the moiſture of this Place is ſuch that a Loaf of Sugar is in Danger to be diſſolved, if it be not preſerved by being near the Fire, or laying it among Oat Meal, in ſome cloſe place; Iron here becomes quickly ruſty, and Iron which is on the Sea ſide of a Houſe grows ſooner ruſty than that which is on the Land ſide.

THE greateſt Snow falls here with the *South-weſt* Winds, and ſeldom continues above three or four Days. The ordinary Snow falls with the *North* and *Northweſt* Winds, and dos not lye ſo deep on the Ground near the Sea, as on the tops of Mountains.

THE Froſt continues till the Spring is pretty far advanced,the ſeverity of which occaſions Great numbers of Trouts and Eles to Dye, but the Winter Froſts have not this effect, for which the Inhabitants give this reaſon *viz.* That the rains being more frequent in *October*, do in their opinion carry the Juice and Quinteſſence of the Plants into the Lakes, whereby they think theFiſh are nouriſhed during the winter and there being no ſuch nouriſhment in the Spring,

Spring, in regard of the uninterrupted running of the Water which carries the Juice with it to the Sea, it deprives the Fiſh of this nouriſhment, and conſequently of Life, and they add further, that the Fiſh have no acceſs to the Superficies of the Water, or to the brink of it, where the Juice might be had. The Natives are the more confirmed in their opinion, that the Fiſhes in Lakes and Mariſhes are obſerved to out-Live both Winter and Spring Froſts. The Eaſt North Eaſt Winds always procure fair weather here as they do in all the North Weſt Iſlands, and the rains are more frequent in this place in *October* and *February*, than at any other time of the Year.

FOUNTAIN Water drunk in Winter, is reckoned by the Natives to be much more wholeſome than in the Spring, for in the latter it cauſeth the Diarrhea and Diſenteria.

THE diſeaſes that prevail here are, Fevers, Diarhea and Diſenteria, ſtitch Coughs, Sciatica, Megrim, the ſmall Pox which commonly come once in 17 Years time, the ordinary cure for feavers is letting Blood plentifully. The Diarhea is cured by drinking Aqua vitæ and the Stronger the better: the Fleſh and Liver of Seals are uſed as above mentioned both for the Diarhea and Diſenteria, milk wherein hectick Stone has been quehed, being frequently drunk is likewiſe a good remedie for the two Diſeaſes laſt mentioned.

THE

THE Kernel of the black Nut found on the Shore, being beat to powder and drunk in milk or *Aqua Vitæ*, is reckoned a good remedy for the ſaid two diſeaſes, Stitches are cured ſometimes by Letting blood.

THEIR common cure for Coughs is *Brochan* formerly mentioned: The caſe of the *Carrara* foul with the fat being powdered a little, and applyed to the Hip-bone is an approved remedy for the *Sciatica.* Since the great Change of the Seaſons, which of late Years is become more piercing and cold, by which the growth of the Corn, both in the Spring and Summer Seaſons are retarded; there are ſome diſeaſes diſcovered, which were not known here before, *viz.* a ſpoted Fever, which is commonly cured by drinking a glaſs of Brandy or *Aqua Vitæ* liberally when the diſeaſe ſeizes them, and uſing it till the Spots appear outwardly. This Fever was brought hither by a Stranger from the Iſland of Mull, who infected theſe other Iſlands; when the Fever is violent the Spots appear the 2*d* Day, but commonly on the 4*th* Day, and then the Diſeaſe comes to a Criſis the 7*th* Day, but if the Spots don't appear the 4*th*. Day, the Diſeaſe is reckoned mortal, yet it hath not prov'd ſo here, tho' it has carried off ſeveral in the other adjacent Southern Iſlands. The vulgar accuſtomed to apply *flamula Jovis*, for evacuating Noxious Humours ſuch as Cauſe the Headach,

Western Islands of Scotland, &c. 77

ach, and pains in the Arms or Leggs, and they find great Advantage by it, the way of using it is thus, they take a quantity of it, bruised small and put into a *Patella* and apply it so to the Skin a little below the place affected, in a small time it raises a Blister about the bigness of an Egg, which when broke, voids all the matter that is in it, then the Skin fills and swells twice again and as often voids this matter ; they use the Sea-plant *Linarich* to cure the Wound, and it proves effectual for this purpose, and also for the Megrim and Burning.

THE Broth of a *Lamb* in which the Plants *Shunnish* and *Alexander* have been boiled is found by Experience to be good against *Consumptions*. The green Sea-plant *Linarich* is by them applyed to the Temples and Forehead to dry up Defluctions, and also for drawing up the Tonsels. *Neil Mackdonald* in the Island **Heiskir** is subject to the falling of the Tonsels at every change of the *Moon*, and they continue only for the first Quarter, this infirmity hath continued with him all his days, yet he is now 72 Years of Age.

JOHN FAKE who lives in **Pabble** in the Parish of *Kilmoor*, alias St. *Maries* is constantly troubled with a great Sneezing a day or two before Rain, and if the Sneezing be more than usual, the Rain is said to be the greater ; Therefore he is called the Rain *Almanack*. He has had this faculty, these 9 Years past.

THERE

78 A Description of the.

THERE is a House in the Village called **Ard-Nim-boothin** in the Parish of St. *Maries*, and the house Cock there never crows from the tenth of *September* till the middle of *March*. This was told me two Years ago, and since confirmed to me by the Natives, and the present Minister of the Parish.

THE Inhabitants of this Island are generally well Proportioned, of an ordinary Stature and a good Complection, healthful, and some of 'em come to a great Age, several of my Acquaintance arrived at the Age of 90, and upwards, *John Mackdonald* of **Griminis** was of this Number, ad died lately in the 93*d* Year of his Age. *Donald Roy* who lived in the Isle of **Sand**, and died lately in the hundreth Year of his Age, was able to travel and manage his Affairs till about two Years before his Death. They are a very Charitable and Hospitable People as is any where to be found. There was never an Inn here till of late, and now there is but one, which is not at all frequented for eating, but only for drinking, for the Natives by their hospitality render this new invented House in a manner useless, the great Produce of Barley draws many Strangers to this Island, with a design to procure as much of this Grain as they can, which they get of the Inhabitants *gratis* only for asking, as they do Horses, Cows, Sheep, Wool, &c. I was told some

Months

Months before my Laſt arrival there, that there had been two Men in that Place at one time to ask Corn *gratis*, and every one of theſe had ſome one, ſome two, and others three Attendants, and during their abode there, were all entertained *gratis*, no one returning empty.

THIS a great, yet voluntary Tax, which has continued for many Ages, but the late general ſcarcity, has given them an occaſion to alter this Cuſtom, by making Acts againſt liberality, except to Poor Natives, and Objects of Charity.

THE Natives are much addicted to riding, the plainneſs of the Country diſpoſing both Men and Horſes to it. They obſerve an Anniverſary Cavalcade on *Michaelmas* Day, and then all ranks of both Sexes appear on Horſeback. The place for this Randezvous is a large Piece of firm ſandy Ground on the Sea-ſhore, and there they have Horſe racing for ſmall prizes, for which they contend eagerly. There is an Antient Cuſtom, by which it is lawful for any of the Inhabitants to ſteal his Neighbours Horſe the Night before the race, and ride him, all next Day, provided he deliver him ſafe and ſound to the Owner after the race; the manner of running is, by a few Young Men, who uſe neither Sadles, nor Bridles, except two ſmall Ropes made of

of Bent inſtead of a Bridle nor any ſort of Spurs, but their bare heels, and when they begin the race they throw theſe Ropes on their Horſes Necks, and drive them on vigorouſly with a piece of long Sea-ware in each hand, inſtead of a Whip, and this is dry'd, in the Sun ſeveral Months before for that purpoſe. This is a happy opportunity for the Vulgar, who have few occaſions for meeting, except on Sundays, the Men have their Sweet-hearts behind them on Horſe-back, and give and receiving mutual Preſents, the Men preſent the Women with Knives and Purſes, the Women preſent the Men with a pair of fine Garters of divers Colours, they give them likewiſe a quantity of Wild Carrots. This Iſle belongs in Property to Sir. *Donald-Mack-Donald* of Sleat; he and all the Inhabitants are Proteſtants, one only excepted, they obſerve *Chriſtmaſs*, *Goodfriday*, and St. *Michaels* Day.

The

Nutrients from the shore

In the Forest of Harris

Tacksman's house in Taransay

Sunset over Coppay, Sound of Harris

South over North Uist from South Clettraval

Teampall na Trionaid

Cave on Ullaval, Harris

Harris and (North) Uist

Harris

1.The 'Point of *Strond*' is probably Renish Point, a short way south of Rodel.

2.Martin's sentence 'The Grass on the West side…fragrant smell' is a good brief description of the machair land at Husinish and from Luskentyre round to Northton. For some time 'Eilean Glas' was used as a name for the whole of Scalpay but eventually was applied mainly to the lighthouse built 1787-89. '*Loch-Stokness*', now Loch Stockinish on the coast of south Harris, has Stockinish Island at its mouth with a distinctive 'fresh-water Lake' in the middle. This loch had a dam put across the narrow channel leading to the sea, but as Martin noticed the sea had 'access to it at spring-tides', so that the loch would count as the brackish water habitat which is 'actively being researched at present' and which could be used for the storage of lobsters.

[Currie; Lawson (2002) p.116]

3.'*Marvag* houses' signifies the settlement of Maaruig on an inlet of Loch Seaforth. The well used to supply water for the houses of Maaruig but is now mostly out of use. About 1954 the road down to Maaruig was improved and the large rock blasted away. A concrete box was put over the well.

4.The location of the well east of Borve, a settlement on the west coast of south Harris, is not now generally known.

5.The cave in the cliffs near Sron Ulladale, the northern end of Ullaval ('*Ulweal*') is much as Martin describes it, though the 'wells' within are not immediately apparent, perhaps because of the accumulated earth and debris. There are several stories relating to the cave and its occupants over the centuries.

6.The remains of Dun Borve ('*Down-Borve*') are on a hill near the south end of Loch an Duin at Borve on the west coast of south Harris. At the south-west end of Borve there was a stone circle, close to the coast, but it would appear that the standing stone 'about 7 feet high' was Clach MhicLeoid, on the headland of Aird Nisabost, still a prominent landmark opposite the point of Taransay at Paible on that island. The stone on Taransay is that known as Clach an Teampuill, standing above the beach near the old settlement at Uidh. It has a Christian cross cut into its face.

[Inventory p.40 no.125, p.43 nos.136, 135, p.38 no.116]

7.It is not known which hill on the Harris forest was Macleod's special reserve. The '*Mertrick*' seems to be the pine martin, once in Harris and Lewis but extinct in south Harris by 1886. The two sorts of eagle were the sea eagle, the larger, greyer one, and the golden eagle, quite often known as the black eagle. The 'little viper' could have been the slow worm, which is not venomous.

[Currie; Harvie-Brown & Buckley (1888) pp.16-18, pp.80-87 where the name of 'Iolair Dhubh', black eagle, is noted from Alexander Carmichael.]

8.The Rodel rats were the brown species, to be found on many islands, where they are thought to have arrived from wrecked ships, and even on inland moors. The best known island rats are those of the Shiant Islands, but these are the much rarer black rats.

[Harvie-Brown & Buckley (1888) pp.36-37; Nicolson pp.353-356]

9.The underwater circles of stones remain mysterious. The 'Pool *Borodil*' must be the narrow Borosdale Bay west of the inner part of Loch Rodel.

10. Martin's records of nature, including shells, reveal his own interests and education in such matters, not shared by the average island inhabitants who would not use such words as 'turbines', the gastropod category of molluscs which include whelks and limpets. The 'patellae' would also include limpets, while '*Pectenes*', toothed structures, might include cowrie shells. For the '*Molluka*' beans see also Lewis n.26 and n.11 below.

11. The chamberlain (steward) of Harris in the 1660s was Finlay MacKenzie, in the later 1680s and earlier 1690s he was Roderick ('Rorie') Campbell, merchant at Rodel and tacksman of Uidh in Taransay, and Malcolm Campbell held the office in 1699 and 1700. It seems probable that Malcolm like Rorie before him lived at Rodel much of the time. Information on 'the *Virgin Maries* Nut', otherwise the '*Molluka*' bean, can be found on a website: www.waynesword.palomar.cdv/plmay96.htm.

12. Ambergris is a grey substance, with a strong scent, originating in the intestines of the spermaceti whale, and cast up on the shore. In the context '*Barnera*' was probably Berneray, Sound of Harris.

13. John Campbell, forester of Harris, was the leading local figure in north Harris around 1700. He was tacksman of Scalpay and Maaruig, and had charge of the forest, giving or refusing permission to hunt.

[Lawson (2002) pp.163-165]

14. The north-west side of the 'sound of Island *Glass*' should be the Harris shore of the Sound of Scalpay, but there seems to be no placename there with 'lunar' implications.

15. The name of the man in Rodel who lost his sight at the change of the moon derives in part from the dedication of the church there to St Clement, the building being generally known as Tur Chliamain. This dedication is an unusual one, the saint's name occurring at Northton, Harris, and at North Dell, Ness, Lewis, as well as in the Strath parish of Skye and at Tigharry in North Uist.

16. For digging the ground with spades in preference to ploughing see Lewis n.7, Uist n.2.

17. The 'Fresh-water Lake' called Loch Bhruist ('*Loch-Bruist*') in Berneray was dammed in order to enable the loch to serve as a reservoir, but it seems the 'small islands' in it disappeared as a result of sand blown into the loch in the earlier part of the 18th century. The stream that drains the loch flows into the fine cockle beach of Loch Borve. Martin again mentions the machair qualities of Berneray; the 'soft Substance' growing about the houses in summer might be silverweed.

[Mackay p.54. For the 'Ceannaichean Loch Bhruist', the eels in Loch Bhruist, see Ferguson p.130]

18. Sir Robert Murray's article on tides was published in the Royal Society's Philosophical Transactions Vol.I Pt.4 pp.53-55 – 'A Relation of Some Extraordinary Tydes in the West-Isles of Scotland, as it was communicated by Sir Robert Moray'.

Martin's account of them is a lengthy example of his reporting island curiosities and perhaps intended as a kind of pilot guide for mariners, as Captain Otter and others composed sailing directions for the same useful purpose in the 1860s.

19.The chapel which Martin oddly mentions as dedicated to St Asaph, a saint not otherwise known in the Hebrides, is supposed to have stood in a level area among rocks north-east of the road out to Bruist where the placename Cill Eiseam occurs. It may be that both names, Asaph and Eiseam, should be interpreted in some other way. The tall stone which Martin located nearby seems to have vanished, though a carved stone with a panel of interlacing was sent from this site to Edinburgh by Alexander Carmichael.

The site of a chapel dedicated to St Columba has not been identified.

[Inventory p.38 no.115; Ferguson pp.150-151; EUL Carmichael Watson Coll. no.457]

20. Stumps of trees embedded in peat can still be seen on the south-west coast of Pabbay. The two chapels, one called Teampall Mhoire and the other Teampall Beag or, more properly, Teampall Mholuaig, also remain amid the sandy ground of Baile na Cille, though not much is left of either of them. The stewards or tacksmen of St Kilda, successively members of a Macleod family in Martin's time, lived in Pabbay and made a long visit to St Kilda each summer.

21. Roderick ('Rorie') Campbell was living or staying temporarily on his tack at the Eye (Uidh) of Taransay in 1698 and 1699, when Martin could have met him. The distinction between a burial place for men and another for women may be compared to Martin's mention of the two churches built by St Columba on Iona.

[DC Section 3 8/54/4, 5 & 8/113/7; see Iona n.6]

22. The small island of Gasker used to have cattle put on it from Taransay and with pools of brackish water in the middle area still attracts numerous seals, especially in the autumnal breeding season. Around 1840 the natives of Harris were said to 'slaughter with clubs a considerable number of seals in the island of Gaasker'.

[OSA p.56; NSA p.156]

23. The old chapel on Ensay has been much altered by restoration work. Near it is a standing stone, and across at Traigh Mhanais, Manish Strand, are the remains of a burial area where the discovery of a grave reported by Martin was probably made.

[Inventory p.37 no.113, p.44 no.137]

24. The 'little Island *Quedam*' could be either Coitem at the entrance to the bay at Leverburgh or Coddem off the southern tip of Ensay, but more probably the former.

25. Hermetray was linked to Berneray in earlier days, when it was a source of peats and used for grazing. In 1827 it was taken from Berneray, but it remained on the Harris side of the boundary with North Uist. It is a little surprising that Martin went close enough to Hermetray to see the remains of the unsuccessful fishing station.

[see Uist n.6]

Uist

1. The higher hills of North Uist are around the western, northern and eastern edges of the island, from the Lees and Eaval in the east across to South and North Clettraval, Maari and Crogary Mor in the north and Beinn Mhor and Beinn Bhreac east of the road to Newton. Marrival and Marrugh are two of the few more central hills.

2. Writing in 1793 the North Uist parish minister, Rev. Allan Macqueen, gave a description of 'implements of husbandry', particularly the plough, which was little different from Martin's account:

'The implements of husbandry, with very few exceptions, are the same kind that were used a century back. The plough generally used is little known any where else beyond the Long Island. It is drawn by 4 horses, has only one handle, which the person who directs it holds in his right hand, as he walks beside it, having in his left a lash to drive the horses. Before this plough is a machine drawn by one horse, to which is fixed a crooked iron, of the form of a reaping-hook, to cut the ground, so that the plough may turn it up with greater facility. The number of men and horses requisite to keep this plough a-going, makes it very expensive. It requires one man to direct the plough, and another to lead the horse that draws it… The thin ground, which does not admit of the plough is turned up with an instrument called the crooked spade…'

[OSA pp.107-108. See also Beveridge pp.314-315, with n. and illustration]

3. MacLennan's Gaelic Dictionary gives: bragaire – tangle tops (cf. Armstrong: Bragair: 'the broad leaves that grow on the top of the alga marina' – presumably derived from Martin).

4. There are three 'Madadh' islands ('*Maddies*'), two of them, Madadh Beag and Madadh Mor, north and south of the main channel into Loch Maddy; and the third, Madadh Gruamach, south again and close to the shore at Aird nam Madadh. At the point near Madadh Mor is Leac nam Madadh. The word 'madadh', normally associated with the Gaelic for wolf, fox or otter, is also given the meaning 'a kind of shell-fish (of the mussel type)' in MacLennan's Dictionary but this may be based only on Martin's comments. In 1837 Rev. Finlay Macrae said the loch derived its name from 'three bold rocks called Madies or dogs'.

[NSA pp.162-163]

5. Loch Portain ('*Loch Partan*') is an inlet of the broad island-filled bay north of Loch Maddy reaching in to the foot of the hill called Crogary Beag. There are several islands in the more southerly part of Loch na Madadh, so that '*Nonsuch*' could be a matter of choice, but it has been identified with the island called 'Faihore' in the midst of Loch nam Madadh and also with a fishing store house.

[see n.6 below. Beveridge p.107]

6. Martin's 'small Island called *Vacksay*' [Blaeu: 'Vexa'] is thought to be Vaccasay in the Sound of Harris next to Hermetray. In that case the 'Magazine' house would be that built on Hermetray in the mid 17th century (prior to 1640), although there was also one in Loch nam Madadh.

[Beveridge p.107. See no.5 above]

7. Loch Eport could be properly 'Loch Eford', the second part of the name deriving from Norse and signifying 'island fjord'. The loch is about 2 miles south of Loch nam Madadh.

[Beveridge p.106]

8. The island of Rona is between 3 and 4 miles south of Loch Eport and is much larger than 'a little Hill'. There seems to be at present no known site of a chapel on Rona, but the existence of Cnoc nan Gall towards the west side of the island suggests a link with lowlanders, and there are also two relevant placenames, Rudh' an t-Sagairt and Beinn an t-Sagairt.

[Beveridge pp.278-279]

9. The 'Harbour' to the south of Boreray results from shelter provided by the island of Boreray itself and the prominent headland of Aird a' Mhorain with its remarkable settlement site at Udal. The building of the boat on a Sunday may have taken place at Traigh na Luibe, the 'Natives' being inhabitants of Boreray. It was evidently on Boreray that the crew of the English ship found women waulking cloth.

[Beveridge pp.321-322]

10. John MacLean was, according to Beveridge (p.322), tacksman of the island of Boreray, chamberlain or factor of North Uist for the Macdonald proprietor, and sheriff depute of the Western Isles. He married Marion, daughter of Kenneth Campbell, third son of Malcolm Campbell in Harris. There was thus a link between the two factors, Maclean for North Uist and Campbell for Harris.

[Mackenzie (1946) pp.85-86]

11. The '*iesk-druimin*' or 'Marled Salmon' has been explained as the grey mullet. Cockles occur in several places (e.g. Vallay strand), as also sandeels which in many parts of the islands are drawn out of the shore sand with the *corran siol*, Martin's 'small crooked Iron'.

[Beveridge p.330]

12. There are many 'ancient forts' in North Uist, especially in coastal areas and on small islands in fresh-water lochs. Loch an Duin alone, in the north-east of the island, has the remains of at least three. The cairn near Loch Eport is that known as Barpa Langass. West from Lochmaddy on a slope of the hill Blashaval is a row of three standing stones which are supposed not to be those three mentioned by Martin as being erected 'to amuse Invaders', but they are known as Na Fir Bhreige, the false men.

[Beveridge pp.261-262]

13. The hill named '*Criniveal*' may be either Cringraval or Craonaval. The latter is the more likely as on its summit are two slabs, one of which may be broken off from the other and which together would measure about 20 feet in length. These slabs go under the name of Leac a' Mhiosachan, the slab of 'the month-old little one', which would associate them with the giant's stone. On the other hand there is another slab over 23 feet long on the slope of Craonaval known as Ultach Fhinn, Fingal's Lift, which also may be the stone Martin mentioned.

[Beveridge p.256]

14. The 'very conspicuous Stone' above what Martin calls '*St Peters*, village' is reckoned to be a broken monolith on the hill at Balelone. Between Balelone and the coast is Kilphedder, not a village now at any rate but the site of a chapel dedicated to St Peter with a burial ground. In 1837 the parish minister wrote of a large 'obelisk' at 'Balmartin, near the centre of the parish named Caracrom, regarding the erection of which tradition is totally silent'. Caracrom is the name of the hill at the back of Balelone.

[Beveridge pp.263, 295-296; NSA p.169]

15. The fort at 'Down-rossel' has almost entirely disappeared, but the 8 feet high stone to which Martin refers is still to be seen. With a cross cut into its south face the stone is known as Clach an t-Sagairt and by other names. The two stones south of Vallay may be the two on the southern slope of the hill called Toroghas or possibly the fallen two further east at the

back of Grenitote. The former are at least three miles from Vallay. The stone at Kirkibost is Clach Mhor a' Che.

[Beveridge pp.226, 277-278, 262-263]

16. The 'Stone in form of a Cross' was situated on Aird an Runair ('the Row'), perhaps at the site of Cladh Chothain which was 'opposite' to the cemetery of Kilmuir, St Mary's Chapel or Church.

[Beveridge p.292 and map]

17. Heisgeir ('*Heiskir*', The Monach Islands) is today at least three islands, none now inhabited. Martin seems to treat those known as Ceann Iar and Ceann Ear, along with the intermediate Shivinish, as one, which at low tide they are. The narrow channel was probably that between Ceann Iar and Shillay. The islands of Illeray must be Kirkibost island and Baleshare, and perhaps including Vorogay, Eilean Mor and Stromay.

18. '*Eousmil*', probably a misprinting of 'Cousmil', is Causamul, the small island, little more than a rock, a mile and a half west of Aird an Runair. It was long 'famous for the yearly fishing of seals' in the autumn. A 'cuilean' is a pup or whelp and in 'Cullen-Mory' would signify a young seal. Alexander Carmichael referred to seal-hunting at Heisgeir and Causamul, describing how it was done, and writing of other 'seal' customs.

[Carmichael (1884) pp.464-466; EUL Carmichael Watson Coll. No.112 pp.183, 187, 211, 213; no.380; see Lewis n.17]

19. The small islands called '*Hawsker-Rocks*' and '*Hawsker Eggath*' are now known as Haisgeir (the ocean rock) and Haisgeir Eagach (the notched ocean rock), both distinct from the islands called Heisgeir. On the other hand, '*Hawsker-Nimannich*', the Monk's ocean rock, gives the alternative English name 'The Monach Isles' for Heisgeir and is thought to be only Shillay, the western island of the group. Haisgeir has sometimes been called Haisgeir na Meul [Blaeu: 'Havelskyr na meul'].

[Beveridge pp.67-76]

20. Of the three chapels on Vallay that dedicated to St Mary is the best preserved. Beside it is a burying-ground. Neither the building nor the site of the chapel of St Ulton is known. The third chapel was apparently dedicated to St Orain and situated on Oransay, attached to Vallay's north coast.

[Beveridge pp.297-299]

21. The '*Brownies* Stone', a translation of Clach na Gruagach, is one among several examples to be found in various Hebridean islands e.g. on Rona (Lewis), on Habost machair in Ness, on Trodda(y) in northern Skye.

[See Skye n.34; Ancient Customs n.13; Pennant (1776) p.437; Beveridge p.117. The Habost stone is also near an 'earth-house'.]

22. The 'little Stone House under Ground' is said by Beveridge to be an earth-house but his explorations in search of it led to no satisfactory conclusion.

[Beveridge pp.117-121]

23. Loch Mor in the midst of Boreray was reduced in area by a culvert through the shingle on the west coast of the island. The original structure must have been old by Martin's time.

[Mackenzie (1946) p.15]

24. The old burying-ground on Boreray and its stones are described by Beveridge.

[Beveridge pp.301-302; Mackenzie (1946) pp.15-16]

25. The heathery island of Lingay was part of the Boreray grazing and supplied the Boreray people with peats until they had to move to the much less accessible Stromay for this purpose.

[Beveridge p.83]

26. Martin's account of cattle and other domestic animals applies to North Uist as a whole, as in the case of deer.

27. The '*Colk*' is generally believed to have been the eider duck. The '*Rain-goose*' is either the red-throated or black-throated diver, or perhaps both, and the '*Bonnivochill*' (bunabhuachaille) is the great northern diver. The '*Sereachan-aittin*' may be the arctic tern; the '*Faskidar*' is the arctic skua. To identify the '*Gawlin*' as the 'gobhlan', a swallow, seems inappropriate in view of size. The '*Goylir*' might be either the stormy or Leach's petrel.

[See Lewis n.37]

28. The black nut found on the shore is elsewhere called the Molucca bean. 'Brochan' is porridge or a gruel, and '*Linarich*' is a type of sea plant, identified by Dwelly as sea-fennel or samphire but possibly a seaweed. '*Shunnish*' (sunais) is explained by Dwelly as loveage, '*Alexander*' as lus nan gran dubh – called in English 'Alexanders'. In a letter to Lhuyd Martin wrote: 'The skunnis or carmel herbs cannot be had before the end of april' [Emery p.110].

[see Jura n.3, Skye n.19]

29. It seems likely that Neil Macdonald in Heisgeir was one of the two of that name in the pedigree of Rachael Macdonald in Grenetote and later in Liniclate, Benbecula.

John Fake may have been a MacPhaic, a surname which in Berneray developed into MacKillop and is related to 'Paul'. The settlement of '*Ard-Nim-boothin*' has not been located.

[Matheson (1982) p.320; MacKillop (1989) pp.480-482]

30. John Macdonald was tacksman of Griminish. He was one of the descendants of 'Domhnall Hearach', son of Hugh Macdonald of Sleat. A century after Martin payments were made 'to Donald Roy the herd's son' and 'to Donald Roy mac Innish, servant', but there is no need to suppose that either of the transactions involved a descendant of the otherwise unidentified Donald Roy in Sand. Sand is a district, north of Trumisgarry, and not an island.

[Matheson (1982) pp.326, 327]

31. The inn, it has been suggested, might have been at Carinish, the other possible location being at Lochmaddy.

[Beveridge pp.327-328]

32. Martin mentions the annual cavalcade at Michaelmas several times, but the description of the event in North Uist is the fullest. It is more usually associated with Catholic islands such as South Uist and Barra, but Martin records it as taking place in Protestant areas, for instance in Lewis: 'The Protestant Natives observe the Festivals of *Christmas*, *Good Friday*, *Easter*, and *Michaelmas*; upon this last they have an Anniversary Cavalcade, and then both Sexes ride on Horseback.'

Where in Lewis the calvalcade took place was not recorded by Martin. Perhaps the long beach at Tolsta called Traigh Mhor would have been a suitable location. In Harris the sands at Northton, Traigh Chliamain, were the setting, whereas in South Uist almost the whole west coast would have served the purpose. It was here that Martin provided one of his most vivid scenes:

'As I came from *Southuist*, I perceived about sixty Horsemen riding along the Sands, directing their Course for the East-sea, and being between me and the Sun, they made a great figure on the plain Sands; we discover'd them to be Natives of *Southuist*, for they alighted from their Horses, and went to gather Cockles in the sands…'

In South Uist the people 'have a general Cavalcade…and then they bake *St Michael's* Cake at Night, and the Family and Strangers eat it at Supper'.

The cavalcade in Barra took place 'in *Kilbar* Village', perhaps on unenclosed machair land. The much larger island of Skye saw a cavalcade in each parish, and here too, as elsewhere, 'the Cake called *St Michael's Bannock*' (struthan) was baked and eaten. Other islands which enjoyed the festival according to Martin, were Tiree, Coll and even St Kilda where cavalcade ground might have been thought to be lacking:

'The Inhabitants ride their Horses (which were but eighteen in all) at the Anniversary Cavalcade of *All Saints;* this they never fail to observe. They begin at the shoar, and ride as far as the Houses; they use no Saddles of any kind, nor Bridle, except a Rope of Straw which manages the Horses head; and when they have all taken the Horses by turns, the Show is over for that time.'

The celebrations at all the festival seasons in Lewis indicate the persistence of ancient custom among protestants more than a century after the Reformation. Carmichael described the Michaelmas festival twice at length.

[Martin pp.79-80, 30, 52, 88-89, 100, 213, 270-271, 295; Carmichael Vol. I pp.198-211, Vol III pp.138-143]

Western Islands of Scotland, &c. 81

The Isle Benbecula, *it's Distance, Length, Bay, Mold, Grain, Fish, Cattle, Fresh Lakes, Forts, a Stone Vault, Nunnery, Proprietor.*

THE Island of Benbecula lyes directly to the *South* of Northvist from which, it is two Miles distant, the Ground being all plain and sandy between them, having two little Rivers or Channels no higher than ones Knee at a Tide of *Ebb*; this Passage is overflow'd by the Sea every Tide of Flood, nor is it Navigable except by Boats. There are several small Islands on the *East-side* of this Channel. This Island is three Miles in length from *South* to *North*, and three from *East* to *West*, and ten Miles in Compass. The *East-side* is covered with Heath, it hath a *Bay* called Uiskway, in which small Vessels do sometimes harbour, and now and then Herrings are taken in it.

THE Mountain Benbecula, from which the Isle hath its Name, lies in the middle of it; the *Eastern* part of this Island is all arable, but the Soil sandy, the Mold is the same with that of Northvist, and affords the same Corn, Fish, Cattle, Amphibia, &c. There is no Venemous Creature here. It hath several Fresh-water Lakes well stock'd with Fish, and Fowl. There are some ruines of old Forts to be seen in the small Islands, in the Lakes and on the Plain.

F

82 *A Description of the*

THERE are also some small Chapels here, one of them at Bael-nin-Killach, *id est*, Nuns Town, for there were *Nunnerys* here in time of Popery; the Natives have lately discovered a Stone Vault on the *East-side* the Town, in which there are abundance of small Bones which have occasioned many uncertain Conjectures, some said they were the Bones of Birds, others judged them rather to be the Bones of Pigmies, the Proprietor of the Town enquiring Sir. *Normand Mackleods* Opinion concerning them, he told him that the matter was plain as he supposed, and that they must be the Bones of Infants born by the Nuns there. This was very disagreeable to the Roman Catholick Inhabitants who laugh'd it over. But in the mean time the Natives out of Zeal took care to shut up the Vault, that no access can be had to it since, so that it would seem they believe what Sir *Normand* said or else fear'd that it might gain Credit by such as afterward had Occasion to see them. This Island belongs properly to Ranal Mackdonald of Benbecula, who, with all the Inhabitants are Roman Catholicks, and I remember I have seen an old *Lay Capuchin* here, called in the Language *Brahir bocht*,

bocht, that is, *Poor Brother*, which is litterally true, for he anſwers this Character, having nothing but what is given him, he holds himſelf fully ſatisfied with Food and Rayment, and lives in as great ſimplicity as any of his Order, his Diet is very mean, and he drinks only Fair Water; his habit is no leſs Mortifying than that of his Brethren elſewhere, he wears a ſhort Coat which comes no further than his Middle, with narrow Sleeves like a Waſtcoat, he wears a Plad above it girt about the Middle which reaches to his Knee, the Plade is faſtened on his Breaſt with a Wooden Pin, his Neck bare, and his feet often ſo to, he wears a Hat for Ornament, and the ſtring about it is a bit of a Fiſhers Line made of Horſes Hair, this Plad he wears inſtead of a Gown worn by thoſe of his Order in other Countrys, I told him he wanted the Flaxen Girdle that Men of his Order uſually wear, he anſwered me that he wore a Leather one, which was the ſame thing upon the matter, if he is ſpoke to when at Meat, he anſwers again, which is contrary to the Cuſtom of his Order; this Poor Man frequently diverts himſelf with Angling of Trouts, he lyes upon Straw, and had no Bell (as others have) to call him to his Devotion, but only his Conſcience, as he told me.

THE ſpeckled Salmons, deſcribed in N'uiſt are very plentifull on the Weſt ſide of this Iſland.

F 2 THE

THE Iſland of South-uiſt lyes directly two Miles to the *South* of Benbecula, being in length one and twenty Miles, and three in breadth, and in ſome places four, the *Eaſt-ſide* is Mountainous on the Coaſt, and heathy for the moſt part, the *Weſt-ſide* is plain arable Ground, the Soil is generally ſandy, yielding a good produce of Barley, Oats, and Rye, in proportion to that of N. Uiſt: And has the ſame ſort of Cattle; both *Eaſt* and *Weſt-ſides* of this Iſland abound in Freſh-water Lakes, which afford Trouts and Eels, beſides variety of Land and Sea-fowls, the arable Land is much damnified by the overflowing of theſe Lakes in divers Places which they have not hitherto been able to drain, tho the thing be practicable. Several Lakes have old Forts built upon the ſmall Iſlands in the middle of them. About four Miles on the *South-eaſt* end of this Iſland, is Loch-eynord, it reaches ſeveral Miles *Weſtward*, having a narrow Entry which makes a violent Current, and within this entry there's a Rock, upon which there was ſtaved to pieces a Frigat of *Cromwels*, which he ſent there to ſubdue the Natives. Ambergreaſe hath been found by ſeveral of the Inhabitants on the *Weſt* Coaſt of this Iſland, and they ſold it at Glaſgow at a very low rate, not knowing the value of it at firſt, but when they knew it, they raiſed the price to the other extream. Upon a Thaw after a long Froſt,

Froſt, the South-eaſt Winds caſt many dead Fiſhes on the ſhoar. The Inhabitants are generally of the ſame Nature and Complection with thoſe of the next adjacent Northern Iſlands, they wear the ſame Habit, and uſe the ſame Diet; one of the Natives is very Famous for his great Age, being as it's ſaid, an hundred and thirty years old, and retains his Appetite and Underſtanding; he can walk abroad, and did Labour with his hands as uſually, 'till within theſe three years, and for any thing I know, is yet living.

THERE are ſeveral big *Kairnes* of Stone on the Eaſt ſide this Iſland, and the Vulgar retain the ancient Cuſtom of making a Religious Tour round them on Sundays, and Holidays.

THERE is a Valley between two Mountains on the eaſt ſide, called *Glenſlyte*, which affords good Paſturage. The Natives who Farm it, come thither with their Cattle in the Summer time, and are poſſeſſed with a firm belief that this Valley is haunted by Spirits, who by the Inhabitants are called the great Men; and that whatſoever Man or Woman enters the Valley without making firſt an entire reſignation of themſelves to the Conduct of the great Men, will infallibly grow Mad. The words by which he or ſhe gives up himſelf to theſe Mens Conduct, are comprehen-

F 3 ded

ded in three Sentences, wherein the *Glen* is twice named; to which they add, that it is Inhabited by theſe great Men, and that ſuch as enter depend on their protection. I told the Natives that this was a piece of ſilly Credulity as ever was impoſed upon the moſt ignorant Ages, and that their imaginary Protectors deſerved no ſuch Invocation. They anſwer'd, That there had hapened a late inſtance of a Woman who went into that *Glen* without reſigning her ſelf to the Conduct of theſe Men and immediately after ſhe became Mad, which confirmed them in their unreaſonable fancy.

THE People reſiding here in Summer ſay, they ſometimes hear a loud noiſe in the Air, like Men ſpeaking: I enquired if their Prieſt had Preach'd or Argu'd againſt this ſuperſtitious Cuſtom? They told me he knew better things, and would not be guilty of diſſwading Men from doing their Duty, which they doubted not he judged this to be, and that they reſolv'd to perſiſt in the belief of it, until they found better Motives to the contrary, than hath been ſhewed them hitherto. The Proteſtant Miniſter hath often endeavour'd to undeceive them, but in vain, becauſe of an Implicit Faith they have in their Prieſt; and when the Topicks of Perſwaſion, tho' never ſo urgent, comes from one they believe to be an Heretick, there is little hope of ſucceſs.

THE

THE Island **Erisca**, about a Mile in length, and three in Circumference, is partly heathy, and partly arable, and yields a good produce. The innerside hath a wide Anchorage, there is excellent Cod and Ling in it, the Natives begin to manage it better, but not to that advantage it is capable of. The small Island near it was overgrown with Heath, and about three years ago the ground threw up all that Heath from the very root, so that there is not now one shrub of it in all this Island. Such as have occasion to Travel by Land between *Southuist*, and *Benbecula*, or *Benbecula* and *Northuist*, had need of a Guide to direct them, and to observe the Tide when low, and also for crossing the Channel at the right Fords, else they cannot pass without danger.

THERE are some houses under ground in this Island, and they are in all points like those described in *Northuist*; one of them is in the South Ferry-Town, opposite to *Barray*. The Cattle produced here, be like those of *Northuist*, and there are above three hundred Deer in this Island; it was believ'd generally, that no Venomous Creature was here, yet of late some little Vipers have been seen in the South end of the Island.

THE Natives speak the Irish Tongue more perfectly here, than in most of the other Islands;

F 4

Islands; partly because of the remoteness, and the small number of those that speak *English*, and partly because some of 'em are Scholars, and versed in the *Irish* Language. They wear the same habit with the Neighbouring Islanders.

THE more Ancient People continue to wear the old Dress, especially Women; they are a hospitable well-meaning People, but the misfortune of their education disposes them to Uncharitableness, and rigid thoughts of their Protestant Neighbours; tho' at the same time they find it convenient to make Alliances with them. The Churches here are *St. Columba*, and *St. Maries* in *Hogh-more*, the most Centrical place in the Island. *St. Jeremy's Chappels*, *St. Peter's*, *St. Bannan*, *St. Michael*, *St. Donnan*.

THERE is a Stone set up near a Mile to the *S.* of *Columbus*'s Church, about eight foot high, and two foot broad, it is called by the Natives the *Bowing-Stone*; for when the Inhabitants had the first sight of the Church, they set up this Stone, and there bowed and said the Lord's Prayer. There was a Buckle of Gold found in *Einort* ground some twenty years ago, which was about the value of seven Guineas.

AS I came from *Southuist*, I perceived about sixty Horsemen riding along the Sands, directing

ing their Course for the East-sea, and being between me and the Sun, they made a great figure on the plain Sands; we discover'd them to be Natives of *Southuist*, for they alighted from their Horses, and went to gather Cockles in the sands, which are exceeding plentiful there. This Island is the Property of *Allan Macdonald* of *Moydart*, head of the Tribe of *Mackdonald* called *Clanronalds*, one of the Chief Families descended of *Mackdonald*, who was Lord and King of the Islands. He, and all the Inhabitants are Papists, except sixty, who are Protestants; the Papists observe all the Festivals of their Church, they have a general Cavalcade on *All Saints Day*, and then they bake *St. Michael's* Cake at Night, and the Family and Strangers eat it at Supper.

FERGUS BEATON hath the following Ancient *Irish* Manuscripts in the *Irish* Character; to wit, *A.Vicenna*, *A.Verroes*, *Joannes de Vigo*, *Bernardus Gordonus*, and several Volumes of *Hypocrates*.

THE Island of **Barray** lies about two Leagues and a half to the South West of the Island *Southuist*, it is five Miles in length, and three in breadth, being in all respects like the Islands lying directly North from it. The East side is Rocky, and the West Arable Ground, and yields a good produce of the same Graine that both *Uists* do: They use likewise the same

same way for enriching their Land with *Sea-Ware*. There is plenty of Cod and Ling got on the East and South sides of this Island; several small Ships from *Orkney* come hither in Summer, and afterwarward return Loaden with Cod, and Ling.

THERE is a safe Harbour on the North East side of **Barray**, where there is great plenty of Fish.

THE Rivers on the East side afford Salmons some of which are speckled like these mentioned in *Northuist*, but they are more successful here in Catching them. The Natives go with with three several Herring-Nets, and lay them cross-ways in the River where the Salmon are most numerous, and betwixt them and the Sea. These Salmon at the sight or shadow of the People make towards the Sea, and feeling the Net from the surfaee to the ground, jump over the first, then the second, but being weakned, cannot get over the third Net, and so are catched. They delight to leap above Water, and swim on the surface; one of the Natives told me that he killed a Salmon with a Gun, as jumping above Water.

THEY inform'd me also that many Barrels of them might be taken in the River above-mention'd, if there was any encouragement for cureing

Weſtern Iſlands *of* **Scotland,** *&c.* 91

cureing and tranſporting them. There are ſeveral old Forts to be ſeen here, in form like thoſe in the other Iſlands. In the South end of this Iſland there is an Orchard which produces Trees, but few of them bear Fruit, in regard of their nearneſs to the Sea; all ſorts of Roots and Plants grow plentifully in it; ſome years ago Tobacco did grow here, being of all Plants the moſt grateful to the Natives, for the Iſlanders love it mightily.

THE little Iſland **Kiſmul,** lies about a quarter of a Mile from the ſouth of this Iſle, it is the Seat of *Mackneil* of *Barra*, there is a ſtone Wall round it two ſtories high, reaching the Sea, and within the Wall there is an old Tower and an Hall, with other Houſes about it. There is a little Magazine in the Tower, to which no Stranger has acceſs. I ſaw the Officer call'd the *Cockman*, and an old Cock he is, when I bid him Ferry me over the Water to the Iſland, he told me that he was but an inferior Officer, his buſineſs being to attend in the Tower; but if (ſays he) the Conſtable, who then ſtood on the Wall will give you acceſs, I'll Ferry you over. *I* deſir'd him to procure me the Conſtables permiſſion, and *I* would reward him; but having waited ſome hours for the Conſtable's Anſwer, and not receiving any, I was oblig'd to return without ſeeing this famous Fort. *Mackneill* and his Lady being abſent was the cauſe of this difficulty, and of my

92 *A* Deſcription *of the*

my not ſeeing the Place: I was told ſome weeks after that the Conſtable was very apprehenſive of ſome Deſign I might have in viewing the Fort, and thereby to expoſe it to the Conqueſt of a Foreign Power, of which I ſuppos'd there was no great cauſe of fear. The Natives told me there is a Well in the Village *Tangſtill*, the Water of which being boiled, grows thick like puddle. There is another Well not far from *Tangſtill*, which the Inhabitants ſay in a fertile year throws up many grains of Barley in *July*, and *Auguſt*. And they ſay that the Well of *Kilbar* throws up embrioes of Cockles, but I could not diſcern any in the Rivulet, the Air being at that time foggy. The Church in this Iſland is called *Kilbarr*, i.e. *St. Barr*'s *Church*. There is a little Chappel by it, in which *Mackneil*, and thoſe deſcended of his Family are uſually interred. The Natives have *St. Barr's* Wooden Image ſtanding on the Altar covered with Linen in form of a ſhirt, all their greateſt Aſſeverations are by this Saint. I came very early in the Morning with an intention to ſee this Image, but was diſappointed, for the Natives prevented me, by carrying it away, leſt I might take occaſion to ridicule their ſuperſtition, as ſome Proteſtants have done formerly, and when I was gone, it was again expoſed on the Altar. They have ſeveral Traditions concerning this great Saint. There is a Chappel (about half a mile on the ſouth ſide of the Hill

Hill near *St. Barr's* Church) where I had occaſion to get an account of a Tradition concerning this Saint, which was thus. *The Inhabitants having begun to build the Church, which they dedicated to him, they laid this Wooden Image within it, but it was inviſibly tranſported* (as they ſay) *to the Place where the Church now ſtands, and found there every morning.* This Miraculous Conveyance is the Reaſon they give for deſiſting to Work where they firſt began. I told my Informer that this extraordinary Motive was ſufficient to determine the Caſe, if true, but ask'd his Pardon to diſſent from him, for I had not Faith enough to believe this Miracle; at which he was ſurpriz'd, telling me in the mean time, That this Tradition hath been faithfully conveyed by the Prieſts and Natives ſucceſſively to this day. The ſouthern Iſlands are, (1) Muldonich, about a Mile in Circumference, it is high in the middle, cover'd over with Heath and Graſs, and is the only Forreſt here for maintaining the Deer, being commonly about ſeventy or eighty in number. (2) The Iſland Sandreray, lies ſoutherly of *Barra*, from which it is ſeparated by a narrow Channel, and is three Miles in Circumference, having a Mountain in the middle, it is deſign'd for Paſturage and Cultivation. On the ſouth ſide there is an Harbour convenient for ſmall Veſſels, that come yearly here to Fiſh for Cod, and Ling, which abound

abound on the Coaſt of this Iſland. (3) The Iſland Sandreray, two Miles in Circumference, is Fruitful in Corn and Graſs, and ſeparated by a narrow Channel from *Vatterſay.*

(4) TO the ſouth of theſe lies the Iſland Bernera, about two Miles in Circumference; it excels other Iſlands of the ſame extent for Cultivation, and Fiſhing. The Natives never go a Fiſhing while *Mackneil* or his Steward is in the Iſland, leſt ſeeing their plenty of Fiſh, perhaps they might take occaſion to raiſe their Rents. There is an old Fort in this Iſland, having a vacuity round the Walls, divided in little Apartments; the Natives endure a great fatigue in Manuring their Ground with Sea-ware, which they carry in Ropes upon their backs over high Rocks; they likewiſe faſten a Cow to a Stake, and ſpread a quantity of Sand on the ground, upon which the Cows dung falls, and this they mingle together, and lay it on the arable Land. They take great numbers of Sea-Fowls from the adjacent Rocks, and ſalt them with the aſhes of burnt ſea-ware in Cows hides, which preſerves them from putrefaction.

THERE is a ſort of Stone in this Iſland, with which the Natives frequently rub their Breaſts by way of prevention, and ſay it is a good

good prefervative for Health, this is all the Medicine they ufe, Providence is very favourable to them, in granting them a good State of Health, fince they have no Phyfician among them.

THE Inhabitants are very Hofpitable, and have a Cuftom, that when any Strangers from the *Northern* Iflands refort thither, the Natives immediately after their landing oblige them to eat, even tho' they fhould have liberally eat and drunk but an Hour before their landing there. And this Meal they call *Bieyta'v*, id eft Ocean Meat, for they prefume that the fharp Air of the Ocean, which indeed furrounds them muft needs give them a good Appetite: And whatever number of Strangers come there, or of whatfoever Quality or Sex, they are regularly lodged according to Antient Cuftom, that is, one only in a Family, by which Cuftom a Man cannot lodge with his own Wife, while in this Ifland, Mr. *John Campbell* the prefent Minifter of **Harries**, told me that his Father being then Parfon of **Harries** and Minifter of **Barray** (for the Natives at that time were Proteftants) carried his Wife along with him, and refided in this Ifland for fome time,and they difpofed of him,is Wife and Servants in manner above mentioned, and fuppofe *Mackneil* of **Barra** and his Lady fhould go thither, he would be obliged to comply with this Ancient Cuftom.

THERE

THERE is a Large Root grows among the Rocks of this Ifland lately difcovered, the Natives call it *Curran-Petris*, of a whitifh colour, and upwards of two foot in Length where the Ground is deep, and in fhape and fize like a large Carret, where the Ground is not fo deep, it grows much thicker, but fhorter, the top of it is like that of a Carret.

THE Rock *Linmull* about half a Mile in Circumference, is indifferently high, and almoft Inacceffible, except in on Place, and that is by climbing which is very Difficult, this Rock abounds with Sea-fowls that build and hatch here in Summer, fuch as the *Gillemot*, *Coulter-neb*, *Puffin*, &c. The chief Climber is commonly called *Gingich*, and this Name imports, a Big Man having Strength and Courage proportionable, when they approach the Rock with the Boat Mr. *Gingich* jumps out firft upon a Stone on the Rock-fide, and then by the affiftance of a Rope of Horfe-hair, he draws his Fellows out of the Boat upon this high Rock, and draws the reft up after him with the Rope, till they all arive at the Top, where they purchafe a Confiderable Quantity of Fowls and Eggs; upon their return to the Boat, this *Gringich* runs a great hazzard by jumping firft into the Boat again, where the violent Sea continually rages, having but a few Fowls more than his Fellows, befides a a greater eſteem to compenſate his Courage. When a Tenants Wife in this or the adjacent Iſlands Dies, he then addreſſes himſelf to *Mackneill* of Barra, repreſenting his Loſs, and at the ſame time deſires that he would be pleaſed to recommend a Wife to him, without, which he cannot manage his Affairs, nor beget followers to *Mackneill* which would prove a publick Loſs to him; upon this Repreſentation *Mackneill* finds out a ſuitable Match for him, and the Womans Name being told him, immediately he goes to her carrying with him a Bottle of Strong-waters for their Entertainment at Marriage which is then Conſummated.

WHEN a Tennant Dyes, the Widdow addreſſeth her ſelf to *Mackneill* in the ſame manner, who likewiſe provides her with a Husband, and they are married without any further Courtſhip. There is in this Iſland an Altar dedicated to *St. Chriſtopher* at which the Natives perform their Devotion. There is a Stone ſet up here, about ſeven foot high, and when the Inhabitants come near it, they take a Religious turn round it.

IF a Tenant chance to loſe his Milk Cows by the Severity of the Seaſon, or any other Misfortune. In this Caſe *Mackneill* of Barra, ſupplies him with the like Number that he loſt.

G WHEN

WHEN any of theſe Tenants are ſo far advanced in Years as they are uncapable to till the Ground, *Mackneill* takes ſuch Old Men into his own Family and Maintains them all their Life after. The Natives obſerve that if ſixSheep are put a graſing in the little Iſland Pabbay, five of them ſtill appear Fat, but the ſixth a Poor Skeleton, but any Number in this Iſland not exceeding five are always very Fat. There is a little Iſland not far from this called Micklay of the ſame extent as Pabbay, and hath the ſame way of feeding of Sheep. Theſe little Iſlands afford excellent Hawks.

THE Iſles above mentioned lying near to the *South* of Barray are commonly called the Biſhops Iſles becauſe they held of the Biſhop, ſome Iſles, ly on the *Eaſt* and *North* of Barray, as, Fiaray, Mellisay, Buya, *Major* and *Minor*, Lingay, Fuda, they afford Paſturage and are Commodious for Fiſhing, and the latter being above two Miles in Circumference, is fertile in Corn and Graſs. There is a good anchoring Place next to the Iſle on the *North-Eaſt* ſide.

THE Steward of the Leſſer and *Southern* Iſlands is reckoned a Great Man here, in regard of the Perquiſits due to him ſuch as a particular Share of all the Lands, Corn, Butter, Cheeſe, Fiſh &c. which theſe Iſlands pro-

duce

duce, the Meaſure of Barley paid him by each Family yearly is an Omer as they call it containing about two Pecks.

THERE is an inferiour Officer who alſo hath a right to a ſhare of all the ſame Products: Next to theſe comes in courſe thoſe of the loweſt Poſts, ſuch as the Cockman and Porter, each of whom hath his reſpective due which is punctually paid.

Mackneil of Barra and all his Followers are Roman Catholick, one only excepted, *viz.* *Murdock Mackneil*, and it may perhaps be thought no ſmall Vertue in him to adhere to the Proteſtant Communion conſidering the diſadvantages he labours under by the want of his Chief's Favour, which is much leſſened, for being a Heretick, as they call him. All the Inhabitants obſerve the Anniverſary of St. *Barr* being the 27*th* of *September*, it is performed riding on Horſe-back, and the ſolemnity is concluded by three turns round St. Barrs Church: This brings into my Mind a Story which was told me concerning a Foreign Prieſt and the entertainment he met with after his arrival there ſome Years ago, as follows. This Prieſt hapned to land here upon the very Day and at the particular Hour of this ſolemnity, which was the more acceptable to the Inhabitants, who then deſired him to preach a Commemoration Sermon to the

G 2 Honour

Honour of their Patron St. *Barr*, according to the Antient Cuſtom of the Place; at this the Prieſt was ſurpriſed, he never having heard of St. *Barr* before that Day, and therefore knowing nothing of his Vertues could ſay nothing concerning him, but told them that if a Sermon to the honour of St. *Paul* or St. *Peter* could pleaſe them, they might have it inſtantly, this Anſwer of his was ſo diſagreeable to them, that they plainly told him he could be no true Prieſt, if he had no heard of St. *Barr*; for the Pope himſelf had heard of him, but this would not perſuade the Prieſt ſo that they parted much diſſatisfied with one another. They have likewiſe a general Cavalcade on St. *Michaels* Day in Kilbar Village, and do then alſo take a turn round their Church: Every Family as ſoon as the ſolemnity is ended, is accuſtomed to bake St. *Michaels* Cake as above deſcrib'd, and all Strangers together with thoſe of the Family muſt eat the Bread that Night.

THIS Iſland and the adjacent leſſer Iſlands belong in property to *Mackneil* being the 34 of that Name by Lineal deſcent, that has poſſeſſed this Iſland if the preſent *Genealogers* may be credited: He holds his Lands in vaſſallage of Sr. *Donald* Mc. *Donald* of *Slate* to whom he pays 40 *l.* *per Annum* and a Hawk if required, and is oblig'd to furniſh him a certain Number of Men upon extraordinary Occaſions.

The

Churches and Chapels at Howmore, South Uist

The South Uist mountains

Corodale, South Uist

Loch Cracavaig, Eriskay

On Barra's east coast

West side of Vatersay

Field pattern on Berneray, Barra

Landing at Mingulay

Benbecula - Barra

Benbecula, South Uist and Eriskay

1. The bay called 'Uiskway' is Loch Uiskevagh on recent OS maps.

2. There does not appear to be a mountain known as Benbecula either in the middle or anywhere else in the island. The most conspicuous hill, and fairly central, is Rueval. Derived from Norse this seems to be a more likely name in an area where 'Ben' or 'Beinn' is almost entirely absent as a placename element.

Martin first of all describes the east side of the island as 'covered with Heath', but within a few lines appears to contradict himself by saying that 'the *Eastern* part of this Island is all arable'. This should perhaps have been 'the western part', where settlements and arable ground are mainly located.

[Carmichael Vol. II p.80; Caird p.68]

3. Several freshwater lochs have 'old Forts' on small islands, e.g. Loch Iain, Loch Dun Mhurchaidh (Dun Buidhe), Loch Toraisay; and there are the remains of Borve Castle and Dun Shunish on what might be called 'the plain' of the south-west part of the island.

4. Baile nan Cailleach ('*Bael-nin-Killach*'), generally known by the English name of Nunton ('Nun's-town'), is reputed to have received its name from a nunnery nearby, one of the only accounts of which is that of Rev. Roderick MacLean in 1837:

'In the island of Benbecula, there was a nunnery on the farm now called Nuntown. The building was taken down, and the stones used in the building of Clanranald's mansion and office-houses.'

[NSA p.188; Inventory pp.99-100 no.340; Carmichael Vol.II p.202]

5. The brathair bochd ('*Brahir bocht*') or 'poor brother' can be identified as a wandering friar, comparable with the friar recorded as frequenting the parish of Ewes in eastern Dumfriesshire at much the same time. He may have found some sustenance at 'Clanranald's mansion', supposed to have been at Aird, next to Nunton. An earlier association with Clanranald was attached to Borve Castle:

'There are also at Benbecula, on the west side, the remains of an old castle named Caistal Bhuirbh, or the Castle of Borve, a very ancient building, the residence of the lairds of Benbecula in ancient times.'

[NSA p.188]

6. The 'old Forts' on 'small Islands' in South Uist can be seen at Eochar and West Gerinish to the north and south respectively of Loch Bee, and at various points further south from Loch Druidibeg to North and South Boisdale and on almost to Pollachar. There are few, if any, on or near the east coast of the island.

7. The rock on which Cromwell's frigate was wrecked was probably that in the outer part of Sruthan Beag, the narrow channel leading in to the shelter of Loch Eynort. Although it has the appearance of remoteness and of being rather difficult of access from the central and western part of the island the loch was a trading point in the earlier 19th century when large quantities of eggs were marketed:

'These are shipped off for Glasgow and Greenock from Loch Boisdale, Loch Eynort, and the Sound of Eriscay, in open boats, of from 17 to 20 feet keel; in return for which, the dealers bring home goods, such as dye-stuffs, tobacco, cotton goods, crockery,and some other articles of convenience.'

Loch Eynort was also considered one of the 'three principal harbours' of South Uist, in spite of its being 'very narrow at the entrance, where there is a low flat rock in the middle covered at high water'.

[NSA pp.193, 195]

8. Ambegris – see Harris n.12.

9. A 'native' of great age was of interest to Martin on more than one occasion – probably as a curiosity.

10. Big cairns of stone may be the same as burial cairns, but there are few obvious examples near the east coast; the heap of stones at Gro Ghot may be one.

[Inventory p.121 no.418. Perhaps some of the chambered cairns may also count.]

11.The valley on the east side of South Uist, lying 'between two Mountains', has been identified with Glen Liadale (Gleann Liadail or Liathadail) on the basis of a traditional song taken down from John Maclellan, a crofter at 'Hacleit an Iochdair, Benbecula'. 'No one dared to go into Gleann Liadail without singing the song to propitiate....the little folk of the glen. The only persons who could go were Clann 'ic Iosaig, the MacIsaacs...' It was noted that from Martin's account and from the song or poem about Liadail the little people should be 'the great men of the glen'.

[Carmichael Vol. 5 pp.386-387; MacLean p.503]

12.The houses underground are probably the structures later called earth-houses or souterrains, as at Usinish. Perhaps the one in 'the South Ferry-Town' is the mound called 'Sithean' in Smerclate ('Smerclett').

[Inventory p.119 no.463]

13. The churches dedicated to St Columba and St Mary at Howmore are well known, the chapels less so. Three chapels in the vicinity of the churches are mentioned, along with others further off. The larger church appears to have been known as 'Teampull Mor', the smaller as 'Caibeal Dhiarmaid', neither name bearing any evident relationship to the recorded dedications. Of the three chapels one was known as 'Caibeal nan Sagairt', while another was totally removed around 1860. T.S. Muir's list of 'the old ecclesiastical sites' contains, in addition to Howmore, the names of Kilaulay, Kilivanan, Ardmichael, Kildonnan and Kilpeader, all except the first representing Martin's chapels of St. Bannan , St. Michael, St. Donnan and St. Peter, with locations at Kilaulay near Ardivachar, near Loch Cille Bhanain at West Gerinish, Rubh' Aird-mhicheil west of Stoneybridge, at Kildonan between Loch Kildonan and the sea, and at Kilpheder near the north end of Loch Duin na Cille.

Several other chapels are known to have existed, some of which are said to have been eroded away by the sea on the west coast.

[Inventory pp.106 no.367, 120 nos.411-416; Muir (1885) p.50]

14. The stone south of St Columba's church might be that of An Carra on the western slope of Beinn a' Charra, though its height and the distance from Howmore do not match those given by Martin.

[Inventory p.119 no.407]

15. Martin's vivid picture of the horsemen suggests that he was moving northwards to Benbecula, since they were riding towards 'the East-sea' which could mean along the sands of the South Ford, where cockles could be found in plenty.

'The most important and useful shell-fish on the shores of this parish, is the cockle. It is found in great abundance in the sands between Benbecula and North Uist, and between South Uist and Benbecula. Great crowds of people, with horses and baskets or creels, are seen every summer, but especially in years of scarcity, picking up this shell-fish, as a most useful article of food...'

The cockle shells also 'make excellent lime for building, and particularly for plastering', and were sold by the barrel.

[NSA p.187]

16. For Allan Macdonald of Moydart see Eigg n.5.

17. The Beatons in South Uist included Fergus, 'chirurgione in Uist' in 1683 and 'doctor of phisick in South Wist' in 1700. He must have been the possessor of the 'ancient Irish manuscripts' recorded by Martin and probably physician to Clanranald.

[Bannerman pp.41-43, 89-91, 112, 114, 121, 126, 128]

Barra

18.The ruins of 'old Forts' in this island can be seen at Dun Scurrival at Eoligarry, Dun Cuier above Allasdale, Loch an Duin near Northbay, and elsewhere. Confusion between fort and chambered cairn appears in the name 'Dun Bharpa' north-east of Borve.

19. For the Cockman or Gockman see Ancient Customs n.3.

20. The village called '*Tangstill*' is Tangasdale, but no well seems now to have the powers mentioned to Martin. As for 'the Well of *Kilbar*', the cockle story seems to be first told by Monro in 1549:

'In the north end of this countrey of Barray thair is ane round heich know mayne girs and grene about all to the heid thairof. Upon the heid of this know thair is ane spring and fresh water well. This well treulie springis up certane little round quhyte things les nor the quantitie of ane quhyte virne, likest to the shape, figure and form of ane little Cockle as it appeirit to me'.

The cockles in the Traigh Mhor were 'alledgit be the ancient cuntrymen' to come down in small form to the sands and there grow into 'great Cockles'. 'But alwayis thair is not ane fairer and mair profitable sandis for Cockles in ony pairt of the warld.' Here again came horsemen to gather them.

[Munro pp.73-74; Campbell (1936) pp.33-34, 44]

21.The subsequent disappearance of the old 'Wooden Image', or statue as Compton MacKenzie called it, remains an unsolved mystery, although MacKenzie had heard it 'darkly said' that it would be found 'in the keeping of a certain family'.

[Campbell (1936) p.26; cf. the instruction from the Synod of Argyll to MacNeil of Barra in 1643 to deliver for destruction 'two idols' kept by him in his private chapel (MacTavish Vol.I p.68)]

22. '*Muldonish*' appears on the OS map as 'Muldoanich', a curious name for an island, although the syllable 'mul' is common as a suffix in the area. When given to a person the name is said to denote an unbaptised child or adult, but it also had religious connotations.

[Carmichael Vol.II pp.74-75]

23. The first '*Sandreray*' should really be Vatersay. It has been stated that by Bernera Martin really meant Mingulay, but for the most part the description would be appropriate to either island, with the 'old Fort' being the dun at Barra Head lighthouse on Berneray.

[Campbell (1936) p.53]

24. The compulsory meal called '*Biey-ta'v*' (Biadh an t-haf), ocean food, was explained as 'Biadh an t-saimh', the latter word being a Gaelic form of the Norse 'haf'.

25. It was not necessary for Martin to conclude that the 'Natives' of Barra were protestants, as a protestant minister could be held responsible for serving an island even though the inhabitants were catholics. The inconvenient link between Harris and Barra indicates that Campbell's visits to Barra were probably very rare.

26. The '*Curran-Petris*' or 'curran peatrais' has been explained as the wild parsnip or rock carrot, which was found growing in the walls of an old house at Griminish, North Uist. Father Allan MacDonald recorded it as 'curran phetruis' and was told 'that it grew on the Borrilean in Barra Head'.

[Carmichael Vol. VI p.57; Macdonald (1958) p.94]

27. '*Linmull*', usually Lianamul, is on the west side of Mingulay. The 'coulterneb' here seems to be the razorbill.

28. Martin himself seems to give the only explanation for the word '*Gingich*'/'*Gringich*'.

29. J L Campbell stated that 'Martin mixes the southern islands up' and consequently he was not always sure which 'this island' was; nor is it clear, therefore, whether the altar dedicated to St Christopher was on Barra or one of the lesser isles to the south. The same uncertainty surrounds the 7 feet high standing stone, though it seems likely that both altar and stone were on Barra itself.

30. '*Micklay*' is evidently Mingulay but might have been dealt with more fully. Fiaray, Fuday, Hellisay (not '*Mellisay*'), Lingay and Fuiay ('*Buya*'), are all to the north or north-east of Barra itself. Gighay was omitted from Martin's list, and Flodday may once have been 'Buya Minor' (Beag).

31. 'The Steward of the Lesser and *Southern* Islands' was presumably one of MacNeil of Barra's chief officers.

The Ancient and Modern Cuſtoms of the Inhabitants of the Weſtern Iſlands of Scotland.

EVERY Heir, or young Chieſtain of a Tribe, was oblig'd in Honour to give a Publick Specimen of his Valour, before he was owned and declared Governour or Leader of his People, who obey'd and follow'd him upon all Occaſions.

THIS Chieſtain was uſually attended with a Retinue of Young Men of Quality, who had not before hand given any proof of their Valour, and were ambitious of ſuch an opportunity to ſignalize themſelves.

IT was uſual for the Captain to lead them, to make a deſperate Incurſion upon ſome Neighbour or other that they were in ſewd with, and they were obliged to bring by open force the Cattle they found in the Lands they attacked, or to die in the attempt.

AFTER the performance of this Atchievement, the young Chieſtain was ever after reputed Valiant, and worthy of Government, and ſuch as were of his Retinue acquired the like reputation. This Cuſtom being reciprocally uſed among them, was not reputed

G 3 Robbery;

Robbery; for the Damage which one Tribe ſuſtained by this Eſſay of the Chieſtain of another, was repaired when their Chieſtain came in his turn to make his Specimen; but I have not heard an inſtance of this practiſe for theſe ſixty years paſt.

THE Formalities obſerved at the entrance of theſe Chieſtains upon the Government of their Clans, were as follow;

A heap of ſtones was erected in form of a Pyramid, on the top of which the young Chieſtain was placed, his Friends and Followers ſtanding in a Circle round about him, his elevation ſignifying his Authority over them, and their ſtanding below, their ſubjection to him. One of his principal Friends deliver'd into his hands the Sword wore by his Father, and there was a white Rod delivered to him likewiſe at the ſame time.

IMMEDIATELY after the Chief Druid (or Orator) ſtood cloſe to the Pyramid, and pronounc'd a Rhetorical Panegyrick, ſetting forth the ancient Pedigree, Valour, and Liberality of the Family, as Incentives to the young Chieſtain, and fit for his imitation.

IT was their Cuſtom, when any Chieſtain marched upon a Military Expedition, to draw ſome fome blood from the firft Animal that chanced to meet them upon the Enemies ground, and thereafter to fprinkle fome of it upon their Colours ; this they reckon'd as a good Omen of future Succefs.

THEY had their fixed Officers who were ready to attend them upon all occafions, whither Military or Civil; fome Families continue them from Father to Son, particularly Sir *Donald Macdonald* has his principal Standard Bearer, and Quartermafter. The latter has a right to all the hides of Cows killed upon any of the occafions mention'd above, and this I have feen exacted punctually, tho' the Officer had no Charter for the fame, but only Cuftom.

THEY had a conftant Sentinel on the top of their Houfes called *Gockmin*, or in the *Englifh* Tongue *Cockman*, who was obliged to Watch Day and Night, and at the approach of any body, to ask *Who comes there ?* This Officer is continu'd in *Barra* ftill, and has the Perquifites due to his Place paid him duly at two Terms in the year.

THERE was a competent number of young Gentlemen called *Luchktach*, or *Guard de Corps*, who always attended the Chieftain at home, and abroad; they were well Train'd in managing the Sword, and Target, in Wreft-

G 4 ling,

ling, Swimming, Jumping, Dancing, Shooting with Bows and Arrows, and were ftout Seamen.

EVERY Chieftain had a bold Armour-Bearer, whofe Bufinefs was always to attend the Perfon of his Mafter Night and Day to prevent any furprize, and this Man was called *Galloglach* ; he had likewife a double portion of Meat affigned him at every Meal. The meafure of Meat ufually given him, is called to this day *Bieyfir*, that is, a Man's portion, meaning thereby an extraordinary Man, whofe Strength and Courage diftinguifhed him from the common fort.

BEFORE they engaged the Enemy in Battle, the Chief *Druid* harangu'd the Army to excite their Courage ; he was placed on an Eminence, from whence he Addreffed himfelf to all of 'em ftanding about him, putting them in mind of what great things were perform'd by the Valour of their Anceftors, rais'd their hopes with the Noble Rewards of Honour and Victory, and difpell'd their fears by all the Topicks that Natural Courage could fuggeft. After this Harangue, the Army gave a general fhout, and then charged the Enemy ftoutly. This in the ancient Language was called *Brofnichiy Kab*, *i. e.* an Incentive to War. This Cuftom of fhouting aloud, is believed to have taken its rife from

an

an instinct of Nature, it being attributed to most Nations that have been of a Martial Genius. As by *Homer* to the *Trojans*, by *Tacitus* to the *Germans*, by *Livy* to the *Gauls*. Every great Family in the Isles had a Chief *Druid* who foretold future Events, and decided all Causes Civil and Ecclesiastical. It is reported of them that they wrought in the Night time, and rested all Day. *Cæsar* says they Worshipped a Deity under the Name of *Taramis*, or *Taran*, which in *Welsh* signifies Thunder, and in the ancient Language of the Highlanders, *Torin* signifies Thunder also.

ANOTHER God of the *Britains* was *Belus*, or *Belinus*, which seems to have been the *Assyrian* God *Bel*, or *Belus*; and probably from this Pagan Deity comes the *Scots* term of *Beltin*, the Day of *May*, having its first rise from the Custom practised by the *Druids* in the Isles, of extinguishing all the Fires in the Parish until the Tithes were paid; and upon payment of them, the Fires were kindled in each Family, and never till then. In those Days Malefactors were burnt between two Fires; hence when they would express a Man to be in a great strait, they say, *he is between two Fires of Bel*, which in their Language they express thus. *Edir da hin Veaul or Bel.* Some object that the *Druids* could not be in the Isles, because no Oaks grow there. To which I answer, That in those Days

Days Oaks did grow there, and to this day there be Oaks growing in some of them, particularly in *Sleat*, the most Southern part of the Isle of *Skie*. The Houses Named after those *Druids*, shall be described elsewhere.

The manner of Drinking used by the Chief Men of the Isles, is called in their Language *Streah*, i. e. a *round*, for the Company sate in a Circle, the Cup-bearer filled the Drink round to them, and all was drank out, whatever the Liquor was, whether strong, or weak; they continued drinking sometimes twenty four, sometimes forty eight hours: It was reckon'd a piece of Manhood to drink until they became drunk, and there were two Men with a Barrow attending punctually on such Occasions. They stood at the door until some became drunk, and they carried them upon the Barrow to Bed, and returned again to their Post as long as any continued fresh, and so carried off the whole Company one by one as they became drunk. Several of my Acquaintance have been Witnesses to this Custom of drinking, but it is now abolish'd.

AMONG Persons of distinction it was reckon'd an affront put upon any Company, to broach a piece of Wine, Ale, or *Aqua Vitæ*, and not to see it all drank out at one Meeting. If any Man chance to go out from the Company, tho' but for a few Minutes, he is obliged

ged upon his return, and before he take his Seat, to make an Apology for his abfence in Rhyme, which if he cannot perform, he is liable to fuch a fhare of the Reckoning as the Company thinks fit to impofe ; which Cuftom obtains in many Places ftill, and is called *Beanchiy Bard,* which in their Language fignifies the Poets congratulating the Company.

IT hath been an ancient Cuftom in thefe Ifles, and ftill continues, when any number of Men retire into an Houfe, either to Difcourfe of ferious Bufinefs, or to pafs fome time in drinking; upon thefe occafions the door of the Houfe ftands open, and a Rod is put crofs the fame, which is underftood to be a fign to all Perfons without diftinction not to approach ; and if any fhould be fo rude as to take up this Rod, and come in uncalled, he is fure to be no welcome Gueft ; for this is accounted fuch an affront to the Company, that they are bound in honour to refent it ; and the Perfon offending, may come to have his Head broken, if he do not meet with a harfher reception.

THE Chieftain is ufually attended with a numerous Retinue when he goes a Hunting the Deer, this being his firft Specimen of Manly Exercife: all his Cloaths, Arms, and Hunting equipage is upon his return from the Hills,

Hills, given to the Forrefter, according to Cuftom.

EVERY Family had commonly two Stewards, which in their Language were called *Marifchall Taeh* ; the firft of thefe ferv'd always at home, and was oblig'd to be well verfed in the Pedigree of all the Tribes in the Ifles, and in the Highlands of *Scotland* ; for it was his Province to affign every Man at Table his Seat according to his Quality, and this was done without one word fpeaking, only by drawing a Score with a white Rod which this *Marifchall* had in his hand, before the Perfon he was bid to fit down, and this was neceffary to prevent diforder and contention ; and tho' the *Marifchall* might fometimes be miftaken, the Mafter of the Family incurr'd no cenfure by fuch an efcape ; but this Cuftom has been laid afide of late. They had alfo Cup-bearers, who always filled and carried the Cup round the Company, and he himfelf drank off the firft draught. They had likewife Purfe-mafters, who kept their Money ; both thefe Officers had an hereditary right to their Office in Writing, and each of them had a Town and Land for his Service; fome of thofe Rights I have feen fairly written on good Parchment.

BESIDES the ordinary Rent paid by the Tenant to his Mafter, if a Cow brought forth

forth two Calves at a time, which indeed is extraordinary, or an Ewe two Lambs, which is frequent, the Tenant paid to the Master one of the Calves, or Lambs; and the Master on his part was obliged, if any of his Tenants Wives bore Twins, to take one of them, and breed him in his own Family. I have known a Gentleman who had sixteen of these Twins in his Family at a time.

THEIR ancient Leagues of Friendship were ratified, by drinking a drop of each others Blood, which was commonly drawn out of the little Finger. This was Religiously observ'd as a sacred Bond; and if any Person after such an Alliance happened to violate the same, he was from that time reputed unworthy of all honest Mens Conversation. Before Money became current, the Chieftains in the Isles bestowed the Cows head, feet, and all the intrails upon their Dependants; such as the Physician, Orator, Poet, Bard, Musicians, *&c.* and the same was divided thus: The Smith had the head, the Piper had the, *&c.*

IT was an ancient Custom among the Islanders to hang a He Goat to the Boats Mast, hoping thereby to procure a favourable Wind, but this is not practised at present; tho' I am told it hath been done once by some of the Vulgar within these 13 years last past.

THEY

THEY had an Universal Custom, of powring a Cows Milk upon a little Hill, or big Stone where the Spirit call'd *Browny* was believed to lodge, this Spirit always appeared in the shape of a Tall Man having very long brown Hair: There was scarce any the least Village in which this Superstitious Custom did not prevail, I enquired the reason of it from several well meaning Women, who, until of late had practised it, and they told me that it had been transmitted to them by their Ancestors successfully, who believed it was attended with good Fortune, but the most Credulous of the Vulgar had now laid it aside. It was an ordinary thing among the over-curious to consult an invisible Oracle, concerning the fate of Families, and Battles &c, This was performed three different Ways, the first was by a Company of Men, one of whom being detached by Lot, was afterwards carried to a River, which was the Boundary between two Villages, four of the Company laid hold on him, and having shut his Eyes, they took him by the Legs and Arms, and then tossing him to and again, struck his Hipps with force against the Bank, one of them cry'd out what is it you have got here, another answers a Log of *Birch-wood*, the other crys again, let his invisible Friends appear from all quarters and let them relieve him by giving an Answer to our present demands; and in a few

Minutes

Minutes after, a Number of little Creatures came from the Sea who anſwered the Queſtion, and diſappeared ſuddenly, the Man was then ſet at liberty, and they all returned home, to take their Meaſures according to the prediction of their falſe Prophets, but the poor deluded Fools were abuſed for the Anſwer was ſtill Ambiguous. This was always practiſed in the Night, and may litterally be called the Works of Darkneſs.

I had an account from the moſt Intelligent and Judicious Men in the I e of Skie, that about 62 Years ago, the Oracle was thus conſulted only once, and that was in the Pariſh of *Kilmartin*, on the *Eaſt* ſide, by a Wicked and Miſchievous race of People, who are now extinguiſh'd, both Root and Branch.

THE ſecond way of conſulting the Oracle was, by a Party of Men, who firſt retired to Solitary Places, remote from any Houſe, and there they ſingled out one of their Number, and wrap'd him in a big Cows Hide which they folded about him, his whole Body was covered with it except his Head, and ſo left in this Poſture all night until his inviſible Friends reliev'd him, by giving a proper Anſwer to the Queſtion in hand, which he received, as he fancied, from ſeveral Perſons that he found about him all that time, his conſorts return'd to him

him at break of Day, and then he communicated his News to them, which often proved fatal to thoſe concerned in ſuch unwarrantable enquiries.

THERE was a third way of conſulting, which was a Confirmation of the ſecond abovementioned. The ſame Company who put the Man into the Hide, took a live Cat and put him on a Spit, one of the Number was imployed to turn the Spit, and one of his Conſorts enquired at him, what are you doing? He anſwered, I roaſt this Cat, until his Friends anſwer the Queſtion, which muſt be the ſame that was propoſed by the Man ſhut up in the Hide, and afterwards a very big Cat comes attended by a Number of leſſer Cats, deſiring to relieve the Cat turned upon the Spit, and then anſwers the Queſtion: If this Anſwer prove the ſame that was given to the Man in the Hide, then it was taken as a Confirmation of the other which in this caſe was believed Infallible.

Mr. *Alexander Cooper* preſent Miniſter of *North-viſt* told me that one *John Erach* in the Iſle of Lewis aſſured him it was his fate to have been led by his Curioſity with ſome who conſulted this Oracle, and that he was a Night within the Hide as above mentioned, during which time he felt and heard ſuch terrible things that he could not expreſs them, the

the Impression it made on him was such as could never go off, and he said that for a thousand Worlds he would never again be concern'd in the like performance, for this had disordered him to a high degree; he confessed it ingenuously and with an Air of great Remorse, and seem'd to be very Penitent under a just sense of so great a Crime, he declared this about five Years since, and is still living in the *Lewis* for any thing I know. The Inhabitants here did also make use of a Fire called *Tin-Egin*, (i. e.) a forced Fire, or Fire of necessity, which they used as an Antidote against the *Plague* or *Murrain* in Cattle; and it was performed thus, all the Fires in the Parish were extinguished, and then eighty one married Men being thought the necessary number for effecting this design, took two great Planks of Wood, and nine of 'em were imploy'd by turns vvho by their repeated Efforts rubb'd one of the Planks against the other until the heat thereof produced Fire, and from this forced Fire, each Family is supplyed with new Fire, which is no sooner kindled, than a Potfull of Water is quickly set on it, and afterwards sprinkled upon the People infected with the Plague, or upon the Cattle that have the Murrain, and this they all say they find succesful by Experience, it was practis'd in the main Land opposite to the South of Skie, within these thirty Years.

H THEY

THEY preserve their Boundaries from being lyable to any debates by their Successors, thus, they lay a quantity of the Ashes of burnt wood in the Ground, and put big Stones above the same: And for conveying the knowledge of this to Posterity, they carry some Boys from both Villages next the *Boundary*, and there whip 'em soundly, which they will be sure to remember and tell it to their Children. A debate having risen betwixt the Village of Ose and Groban in Skie, they found Ashes as above mentioned under a Stone which decided the Controversy. It was an Ancient Custom in the Islands, that a Man should take a Maid to his Wife and keep her the space of a Year without marrying her, and if she pleased him all the while, he married her at the end of the Year, and legitimated these Children, but if he did not love Her, he return'd her to her Parents and her Portion also, and if there happened to be any Children, they were kept by the Father, but this unreasonable Custom was long ago brought in disuse.

IT is common in these Islands, when a Tenant Dies, for the Master to have his choice of all the Horses which belonged to the Deceas'd, and this was called the *Eachfuin Horizeilda*, (i. e.) a Lord's Gift, for the first use of it was from a Gift of a Horse granted by all the Subjects in *Scotland* for relieving King

from

from his Impriſonment in *England*. There was another Duty payable by all the Tenants, to their Chief, tho' they did not live upon his Lands and this is called *Calpich*, there was a ſtanding Law for it alſo, called *Calpich* Law, and I am informed that this is exacted by ſome in the main Land to this Day.

WOMEN were anciently denyed the uſe of Writing in the Iſlands to prevent Love intrigues, their Parents believ'd, that Nature was too skilful in that matter, and needed not the help of Education, and by Conſequence that Writing would be of Dangerous Conſequence to the weaker Sex.

THE Orators, in their Language call'd *Iſ-Dane*, were in high eſteem both in theſe Iſlands, and the Continent, until within theſe forty Years, they ſate always among the Nobles and Chiefs of Families in the *Streah* or Circle: Their Houſes and little Villages were Sanctuaries, as well as Churches, and they took place before Doctors of Phyſick. The Orators after the *Druids* were extinct, were brought in to preſerve the Geneaogly of Families, and to repeat the ſame at every ſucceſſion of a Chief, and upon the occaſion of Marriages and Births they made *Epithalamiums* and *Penegyricks*, which the Poet or Bard pronounc'd. The Orators by the force of their Eloquence, had a powerful Aſcendant over the greateſt Men in their

H 2 time,

time, for if any Orator did but ask the Habit, Arms, Horſe, or any other being belonging to the greateſt Man in theſe Iſlands, it was readily granted them, ſometimes out of reſpect, and ſometimes for fear of being exclaimed againſt by a Satyr, which in thoſe days was reckoned a great diſhonour, but theſe Gentlemen becoming inſolent, loſt ever ſince both the Profit, and Eſteem which was formerly due to their Character; for neither their *Panegyricks* nor *Satyrs* are regarded to what they have been, and they are now allowed but a ſmall Sallary. I muſt not omit to relate their way of Study, which is very ſingular, they ſhut their Doors and Windows for a days time, and lie on their Backs, with a Stone upon their Belly, and Plaids about their Heads, and their Eyes being covered, they pump their Brains Rhetorical Encomium or *Panegerick*, and indeed they furniſh ſuch a Stile from this dark Cell, as is underſtood by very few, and if they purchaſe a couple of Horſes as the Reward of their Meditation, they think they have done a great matter. The Poet, or Bard, had a Title to the Bridegrooms upper Garb, that is, the Plade and Bonnet, but now he is ſatisfied with what the Bridegroom pleaſes to give him on ſuch occaſions.

THERE was an ancient Cuſtom in the Iſland of **Lewis**, to make a fiery Circle about the Houſes, Corn, Cattle, &c. belonging

ing to each particular Family; a Man carried fire in his right hand and went round, and it was called *Deſſil*, from the right hand, which in the ancient Language is called *Deſs*; an inſtance of this Round was performed in the Village *Shadir* in *Lewis*, about ſixteen years ago (as I was told) but it proved fatal to the Practiſer, called *Mac-Callum*; for after he had carefully performed this Round, that very Night following he and his Family were ſadly ſurpriz'd, and all his Houſes,Corn,Cattle, &c. were conſumed with fire. This ſuperſtitious Cuſtom is quite aboliſhed now, for there has not been above this one inſtance of it in forty years paſt.

THERE is another way of the *Deſſil*, or carrying Fire round about Women before they are Churched, after Child-bearing, and it is us'd likewiſe about Children until they be Chriſtened; both which are performed in the Morning, and at Night. This is only practiſed now by ſome of the ancient Midwives; I enquired their Reaſons for this Cuſtom, which I told them was altogether unlawful; this diſobliged them mightily, inſomuch that they would give me no ſatisfaction. But others that were of a more agreeable temper, told me the fire-round was an effectual means to preſerve both the Mother and the Infant from the power of evil Spirits, who are ready at ſuch times to do miſchief, and ſometimes

H 3 carry

carry away the Infant; and when they get them once in their poſſeſſion, return them poor meager Skeletons; and theſe Infants are ſaid to have voracious Appetites, conſtantly craving for meat. In this caſe it was uſual with thoſe who believed that their Children were thus taken away, to dig a Grave in the Fields upon Quarter Day, and there to lay the Fairy Skeleton till next Morning; at which time the Parents went to the Place, where they doubted not to find their own Child inſtead of this Skeleton. Some of the poorer ſort of People in theſe Iſlands retain the Cuſtom of performing theſe Rounds Sun-ways, about the Perſons of their Benefactors three times, when they bleſs them, and wiſh good ſucceſs to all their Enterprizes. Some are very careful when they ſet out to Sea, that the Boat be firſt rowed about Sun-ways, and if this be neglected, they are afraid their Voyage may prove unfortunate. I had this Ceremony paid me (when in the Iſland of *Ila*) by a poor Woman after I had given her an Alms: I deſired her to let alone that Complement, for I did not care for it, but ſhe inſiſted to make theſe three ordinary turns, and then Pray'd that God and *Mac Charmig*, the Patron Saint of that Iſland, might bleſs and proſper me in all my deſigns and affairs.

I at-

I attempted twice to go from *Ila* to *Collonsay*, and at both times they row'd about the Boat Sun-ways, tho' I forbid them to do it, and by a contrary Wind, the Boat and those in it were forc'd back. I took Boat again a third time from *Jura* to *Collonsay*, and at the same time forbid them to row about their Boat, which they obeyed, and then we Landed safely at *Collonsay* without any ill adventure, which some of the Crew did not believe possible, for want of the Round; but this one Instance hath convinced them of the vanity of this Superstitious Ceremony. Another ancient Custom observ'd on the second of *February*, which the Papists there yet retain, is this. The Mistriss and Servants of each Family take a Sheaf of Oats, and dress it up in Womens Apparel, put it in a large Basket, and lay a Wooden Club by it, and this they call *Briids-bed*, and then the Mistriss and Servants cry three times *Briid* is come, *Briid* is welcome. This they do just before going to Bed, and when they rise in the Morning, they look among the ashes, expecting to see the impression of *Briids* Club there, which if they do, they reckon it a true presage of a good Crop, and prosperous Year, and the contrary they take as an ill Omen.

IT has been an ancient Custom amongst the Natives, and now only used by some old

H 4 People,

People, to Swear by their Chief, or Laird's Hand.

WHEN a Debate arises between two Persons, if one of them assert the Matter by your Fathers hand, they reckon it a great indignity; but if they go a degree higher, and out of spite say, by your Father and Grandfather's hand, the next word is commonly accompanied with a blow.

IT is a receiv'd Opinion in these Islands, as well as in the neighbouring part of the main Land, That Women by a Charm, or some other secret way, are able to convey the increase of their Neighbours Cows Milk to their own use, and that the Milk so charmed, doth not produce the ordinary quantity of Butter; and the Curds made of that Milk are so tough, that it cannot be made so firm as other Cheese, and is also much lighter in weighr. The Butter so taken away, and joyned to the Charmer's Butter, is evidently discernable by a Mark of separation, *viz.* The diversity of colours, that which is charmed being still paler than that part of the Butter which hath not been charmed; and if Butter having these Marks be found with a suspected Woman, she is presently said to be guilty. Their usual way of recovering this Loss, is to take a little of the Rennet from all the suspected Persons, and to put it in an egg-shell full of Milk, and when

when that from the Charmer is mingled with it, it presently curdles, and not before.

THIS was asserted to me by the generality of the most Judicious People in these Islands; some of them having, as they told me, come to the knowledge of it to their cost. Some Women make use of the root of Groundsel as an Amulet against such Charms, by putting it among their Cream.

BOTH Men and Women in those Islands, and in the Neibouring Main Land, affirm that the increase of Milk is likewise taken away by Trouts, if it happen that the Dishes or Pales wherein the Milk is kept, be washed in the Rivulets where Trouts are. And the way to recover this damage, is by taking a live Trout, and pouring Milk into its mouth, which they say doth presently curdle, if it was taken away by Trouts, but otherwise they say it is not.

THEY affirm likewise, that some Women have an Art to take away the Milk of Nurses.

I saw four Women whose Milk were tried, that one might be chosen for a Nurse; and the Woman pitch'd upon, was after three days Suckling, depriv'd of her Milk, whereupon she was sent away, and another put in her Place;

Place; and on the third day after, she that was first chosen recover'd her Milk again. This was concluded to be the effects of Witchcraft by some of her Neighbours.

THEY also say that some have an Art of taking away the increase of Malt, and that the Drink made of this Malt, hath neither life nor good taste in it; and on the contrary, the Charmer hath very good Ale all this time. A Gentleman of my acquaintance, for the space of a year, could not have a drop of good Ale in his House; and having complained of it to all that conversed with him, he was at last advised to get some Yest from every Alehouse in the Parish; and having got a little from one particular Man, he put it among his Wort, which became as good Ale as could be drank, and so defeated the Charm. After which the Gentleman in whose Land this Man lived, Banished him thirty six Miles from thence.

THEY say there be Women who have an Art of taking a Moat out of ones Eye, tho' at some Miles distance from the Party griev'd, and this is the only Charm these Women will avouch themselves to understand, as some of them told me, and several of these Men out of whose Eyes Moats were then taken confirm'd the truth of it to me.

ALL

ALL these Islanders, and several thousands on the neighbouring Continent are of Opinion that some particular Persons have an evil Eye, which affects Children and Cattle, this they say occasions frequent Mischances, and sometimes Death, I could name some who are believed to have this unhappy faculty, tho' at the same time void of any ill design: This hath been an ancient opinion as appears from that of the Poet.

Nescio quis teneros Oculus mihi fascinat Agnos.

COURTS

COURTS of Judicatory.

AT the first Plantatation of these Isles, all Matters were Managed by the sole Authority of the Heads of Tribes, called in the Irish *Thiarna*, which was the same with *Tyrannus*, and now it signifies Lord or Chief; there being no Standard of Equity or Justice but what flowed from them. And when their Numbers increased, they erected Courts called *Mode*, and in the *English* Baron-Courts.

THE Proprietor has the Nomination of the Members of this Court, he himself is President of it, and in his absence, his Bayliff; the Minister of the Parish is always a Member of it. There are no Attorneys to plead the Cause of either Party, for both Men and Women represent their respective Causes, and there is always a speedy decision, if the Parties have their Witnesses present, &c.

THERE is a peremptory Sentence passes in Court for ready Payment, and if the Party against whom Judgment is given prove refractory, the other may send the common Officer, who has power to Distrain, and at the same time to exact a Fine of 20 *l.* Scots, for the use of the Proprietor, and about two Marks for himself.

THE

THE Heads of Tribes had their Offensive and Defensive Leagues, called Bonds of *Mandrate*, and *Manrent* in the Lowlands, by which each Party was oblig'd to assist one another upon all extraordinary emergencies. And tho' the differences between those Chieftains involved several Confederates in a Civil War, yet they oblig'd themselves by the Bond mention'd above, to continue stedfast in their Duty to their Sovereign.

WHEN the Proprietor gives a Farm to his Tenant, whether for one or more Years, it is customary to give the Tenant a Stick of Wood, and some Straw in his hand; this is immediately return'd by the Tenant again to his Master, and then both Parties are as much oblig'd to perform their respective Conditions, as if they had Sign'd a Lease, or any other Deed.

CHURCH

CHURCH *Discipline.*

EVERY Parish in the Western Isles has a Church Judicature, called the *Consistory*, or *Kirk-Session*, where the Minister presides, and a competent number of Laymen call'd Elders meet with him they take cognisance of Scandals, censure faulty Persons, and with that strictness, as to give an Oath to those who are suspected of Adultery, or Fornication, for which they are to be proceeded against according to the Custom of the Country. They meet after Divine Service, the Chief Heretor of the Parish is present, to concurr with them, and enforce their Acts by his Authority, which is irresistable within the bounds of his Jurisdiction.

A

A Form of Prayer us'd by many of the Iſlanders at Sea, after the Sails are hoiſted.

☞ This Form is contain'd in the *Iriſh* Liturgy Compos'd by Mr. *John Kerſwell*, afterwards Biſhop of *Argile*, Printed in the Year 1566, and Dedicated to the Earl of *Argile*; I have ſet down the Original for the ſatisfaction of ſuch Readers as underſtand it.

MOdh Bendaighto luingo ag dul dionſa idhe na fairrge.

Abrah aon dá chaeh Marſo.

Da.

An Stioradoir.

Beanighidh ar Long.

Fregra Cháich.

Go mbeandaighe Dia Athair i.

An Stioradoir.

Beanoaidhidh ar Long.

Fregra.

Go mbeandaighe Joſa Crioſd i.

An Stíoradoir.

Beanoaidhidh ar Long.

Fregra.

Go mbeandaighe an Shiorad Naomh i.

An Stioradoir.

Cred

Cred is egail Libh is Dhia Athair libh.

Fregra.

Ni heagal en ni.

An Stioradoir.

Cred is egil libh is Dia an Mac Libh.

Fregra.

Ni heagal en ni.

An Stioradoir.

Cred is eagail Libh is Dia an ſbiorad Naomh libh.

Fregra.

Ni beagail en ni.

An Stioradoir.

Dia Athair Vile Chumhaehtach ar Grádh a Mhic Joſa Crioſd, le Comh ſhurtach an Spioraid Naomh, An taon Dhia tug Cland Iſrael trid an Muir ruaigh go mirbhuileach, agas tug Jonas ad tir ambroind an Mbil mhoie, & tug Pol Eaſpol, agas a long gon, foirind o an ſadh iomarcach, agas o dheartan dominde dar ſa oradhne, agas dar ſenadh, agas dar mbeandrghadh, agas dar m breith le ſen, agas le ſoinind, agas le ſolas do chum chnain, agas chalaidh do reir a theile diadha fein.

Ar ni iarrmoid air ag radha.

Ar Nathairne ata ar Neamh, &c.

Abradh Cach Vile.

Bionh Amhlvidh.

The

The manner of Blessing the Ship when they put to Sea.

THE Steers-Man *says,*
Let us Bless our Ship :
The Answer by all the Crew,
God the Father Bless her.

Steers Man.

Let us Bless our Ship.

Answer,

Jesus Christ Bless Her.

Steers-Man.

Let us Bless our Ship.

Answer.

The Holy Ghost Bless her.

Steers-Man.

What do you fear since God the Father is with you ?

Answer.

We do not fear any thing.

Steers-Man.

What do you fear since God the Son is with you ?

Answer.

We do not fear any thing.

Steers-Man.

What are you afraid of since God the Holy Ghost is with you ?

Answer.

We do not fear any thing.

I Steers-

Steers-Man.

God the Father Almighty, for the love of Jesus Christ his Son, by the comfort of the Holy Ghost, the One God, who miraculously brought the Children of Israel *through the Red-Sea, and brought* Jonas *to Land out of the Belly of the Whale, and the Apostle St.* Paul, *and his Ship to safety, from the troubled raging Sea, and from the violence of a tempestuous Storm, deliver, sanctifie, bless and conduct us peaceably, calmly, and comfortably through the Sea to our Harbour, according to his Divine Will ; which we beg, saying,* Our Father, *&c.*

A Descrip-

Sound of Hellisay, Barra

Cattle sale in Skye

Ancient Customs

1.The various Gaelic words for 'tribe' include 'treubh', 'fine', 'cinne', 'clann', 'sliochd' and 'siol'. These all have different shades of context, 'treubh' for instance being somewhat biblical, and perhaps either 'fine' or 'sliochd' is the appropriate word for tribe as Martin uses it here.

[Dwelly p.435; A.I. Macinnes: Clanship, Commerce and the House of Stuart, 1603-1788 East Linton 1996 pp.2-8, index p.271; R.A. Dodgshon: From Chiefs to Landlords – Social and Economic Change in the Western Highlands and Islands, c.1493-1820 Edinburgh 1998 pp.8,10-11; J Bannerman: 'MacDuff of Fife' in A Grant and K J Stringer: Medieval Scotland – Crown, Lordship and Community Edinburgh 1993 pp.20-38]

2. Martin's 'Chief Druid' would be either the bard or the historian (seanchaidh) serving a chief and his family, two of the 'fixed Officers' to whom Martin refers. These 'officers' amounted to professionals, hereditary bards, physicians and the like. Both the Macdonalds of Sleat and the MacLeods of Dunvegan kept up at least some of the offices in the 1680s and 1690s when Martin was 'governor' in each family.

[W J Watson: 'Classic Gaelic Poetry of Panegyric in Scotland' in TGSI Vol. XXIX (1914-19) pp.194-235; J MacInnes; 'The Panegyric Code in Gaelic Poetry and its Historical Background' in TGSI Vol. L (1976-78) pp.435-498; MacPhail Vol.I pp.45-46]

3. At the 'little Island *Kismul*' in Barra Martin 'saw the Officer call'd the *Cockman*' who told him he was 'but an inferior Officer' who had 'to attend in the Tower'. In North Uist near Loch Eport was Airigh Ghocmain.

4. For the 'Galloglach' see J Marsden: Galloglas – Hebridean and West Highland Mercenary Warrior Kindreds in Medieval Ireland East Linton 2003. Martin's '*Bieyfir*' is the Gaelic 'biadh fir' (cf. Barra n.24)

5.The words '*Brosnichiy Kah*' are Martin's version of 'brosnachadh catha', explained by Dwelly (p.129) as 'a battlesong'.

6. Dwelly (pp.965, 935) has 'torrunn' for thunder, 'tarnach' a thunder-clap.

7. Tithes or teinds of stock produce were normally paid in May. The proverb heard by Carmichael in Lewis in 1873 includes a phrase closely similar to Martin's '*Edir da hin Veaul*': 'A Mhoire! Mhicean, bu dora dhomhsa sin a dheanamh dhuit na dhol eadar dha theine mhoir Bheaill'. The custom of the two fires at Beltane, 1 May, is also described, with mention of an oak log.

[Carmichael Vol. I pp.182-183, Vol. II pp.369-371]

8. Dwelly (pp.892-893) has 'sreath' for Martin's '*Streah*' and gives a variety of English meanings including an account of the drinking circle which may be derived from Martin's version.

9. The '*Beanchiy Bard*', i.e. 'beannachadh' or blessing of the bard, is to be included along with the other customs and expectations associated with the bard's role as described by Martin.

10. Forests, otherwise hunting areas for the chiefs and their 'retinues', existed and are still known in several islands, for instance, the Cuillin range and the 'Red Hills' in Skye, the mountains of Rum, the hills in the south-east of Lewis and in

north Harris, the hills of Jura, each area at one time being under the control of a forester.

11. The '*Marischall Taeh*', the house marshal or steward, evidently supervised domestic arrangements. Gaelic: 'marasgal'; 'marasglachd' – office of marshal. Most of the chief's officers had not only 'an hereditary right' but also hereditary possession of a farm or other distinct holding of land.

[Dwelly p.632]

12. For blood-drinking and 'blood-brothering' see Carmichael Vol.II pp.296-297, Vol.VI p.34; EUL Carmichael Watson Collection nos.63, 239, 244.

13. The 'Browny' seems to have been the same as the 'Gruagach' (see Skye n.34).

14. Mr Alexander Cooper, 'late Episcopal incumbent' in North Uist, had 'intruded himself' into the charge at Clachan Sand, North Uist, in place of Mr Allan Moryson by July 1696 and had possibly done so in 1692. He 'submitted to Presbyterianism' in June 1699 and was drowned in August 1706.

[Minutes of the Synod of Argyll NAS CH2/557/14 6 June 1695, 1696; Fasti Vol. VII p.191]

15. Judging from his name, John Erach may have been a Harrisman.

16. For the 'Tin-Egin' see n.7 above.

17. The use of ashes and the whipping of boys as a means of ensuring that boundary lines were not forgotten were once widely practised and appear in the case of the disputed boundary between Lewis and Harris (c.1800-1850).

18. Both Ose and Groban are not far from the shore of Loch Bracadale in Skye – There was another Groban in Waternish. The custom involving a trial wife was generally known in many parts of Scotland, being called hand-fasting or just an 'irregular' form of marriage.

19. Dwelly (p.377) has 'each-fuinn', signifying 'herezeld'; see also Macdonalds Vol.III p.118, where 'calp' is mentioned as if the same as 'herezeld' and presumably related to Martin's '*Calpich*'. Dwelly (p.235) quotes Martin's explanation as the meaning of 'colpach'.

20. For the orators or 'Aos-dana' (Martin's '*Is-Dane*') see the brief comment in I.F. Grant and H. Cheape: Periods in Highland History London 1987 pp.96-97.

21. The custom of going 'sunwise' or 'deasail' around something is frequently mentioned by Martin and must have been one of the most common 'superstitious' practices.

[Carmichael Vol.VI p.60 and index of subjects p.162 'Sunwise Turn']

22. The custom of making St Bride's bed appears to be associated by Martin with Colonsay. The second day of February was Candlemas, the first day of Spring – however, John Morison in his letter relating to superstitions in Lewis wrote:

'Another custome was upon Candlesmes Even or in Irish Feil bride after supper, St Brigida's bed was made in a Seive with a litle straw and clean cloaths, a handfull of barly and oats unthressed was taken and wrapped about with Linnens well pinned, and maid into the fashion of a womans body. Then every persone in the family man woman and child put in something which he daily wore into the bed, and after all was compleet for the service, all the familie fell on ther faces and with high voices cryed ndanig briid, gun di riist.'

Thus there is some doubt about where 'the Papists' were, and Martin may have just fitted in information received from Morison at random.

[EUL Colin Campbell Collection MS 3097.12]

23. Carmichael collected numerous charms associated with milk and milking and the evil eye.

[Carmichael Vol.I pp.258-271, Vol.II pp.143, 319, Vol.VI Index p.150]

24. Presumably Martin's '*Thiarna*' is Gaelic 'Tighearna', lord or chief ruler, people of this rank in society having the right to hold courts within their territories such as baron courts until the mid eighteenth century. Bonds of manrent were widely used to build up often military support.

25. It seems to have been an overstatement on Martin's part to say that every parish in 'the Western Isles' had a kirk session by 1700, since the Protestant church situation was not clear cut nor so organised, but in theory the system is correctly described.

26. Bishop John Carswell's translation into Gaelic of The Book of Common Order was printed in 1567 and indeed contains the prayer quoted by Martin.

A Deſcription of the Iſle of SKIE.

SKIE (in the ancient Language *Skianach* i. e. wing'd ;) is ſo called becauſe the two oppoſite *Northern* Promontories *Vaternis* lying *Northweſt* and *Troternis* *North-eaſt*, reſemble two Wings. This Iſle lies for the moſt part half way in *Weſtern-Sea* between the main Land on the *Eaſt*, the Shire of *Roſſe*, and the *Weſtern* Iſle of *Lewis* &c.

THE Iſle is very high Land, as well on the Coaſt, as higher up in the Country, and there are ſeven high Mountains near one another, almoſt in the center of the Iſle.

THIS Iſland is forty Miles in length from *South* to *North*, and in ſome Places twenty and in others thirty in breadth, the whole may amount to a hundred Miles in Circumference.

THE Channel between the *South* of Skie and oppoſite main Land (which is part of the Shire of *Inderneſs*) is not above three Leagues in breadth, and were the Ferry-boat croſſeth to *Glenelg*, it's ſo narrow, that one may call for the Ferry-boat and be eaſily heard on the other ſide, this Iſle is a part of the Sheriffdom *Inverneſs*, and formerly of the Dioceſs of the Iſles, which was united to that of *Argyle* ; a. *S. E.* Moon cauſeth a Spring Tide here.

I 2 THE

THE Mold is generally Black, eſpecially in the Mountains, but there is ſome of a red Colour, in which Iron is found.

THE arable Land is for the moſt part Black, yet affords Clay, of different Colours, as White, Red, and Blue ; the Rivulet at *Dunvegan* Church, and that of *Nisboſt* hath Fullers-earth.

THE Village *Borve*, and *Glenmore* afford two very fine ſorts of Earth, the one Red, the other White, and they both feel, and cut like melted Tallow. There are other Places that afford plenty of very fine white Marle which cuts like Butter, it abounds moſt in *Corchattachan*, where an Experiment has been made of its Vertue ; a quantity of it being ſpread on a ſloping Hill, covered with Heath, ſoon after all the Heath fell to the Ground, as if it had been cut with a Knife, they afterwards ſowed Barley on the Ground, which tho' it grew but unequally, ſome places producing no Grain, becauſe perhaps it was unequally laid on, yet the produce was thirty five fold, and many ſtalks carried five Ears of Barley. · This account was given me by the preſent poſſeſſor of the Ground *Lachlin-Mac-Kinon.*

THERE

THERE are *Marcaſites* black and White reſembling Silver-Ore near the Village *Sartle*; there likewiſe in the ſame place ſeveral Stones which in bigneſs, ſhape, *&c.* reſemble Nutmegs, and many Rivulets here afford variegated Stones of all Colours. The *Apples-glen* near *Loch-fallart* has *Aggat* growing in it of different Sizes and Colours, ſome are Green on the out-ſide, ſome are of a pale Skie colour, and they all ſtrike fire as well as Flint, I have one of them by me which for ſhape and bigneſs is proper for a Sword Handle. Stones of a Purple Colour flow down the Rivulets here after great Rains.

THERE is Chryſtal in ſeveral Places of this Iſland as at *Portry*, *Quillin*, and *Mingnis*, its of different Sizes and Colours, ſome is ſexangular, as that of *Quilling*, and *Mingnis*, and there is ſome in *Minrineſs*, of a Purple Colour, the Village *Torrin* in *Strath*, affords a great deal of good White and Black Marble, I have ſeen Cups made of the White which is very fine. There are large Quarries of Freeſtone in ſeveral parts of this Iſle, as at *Sniſneſs* in *Strath*, in the *South* of *Borrie*, and Iſle of *Roſay*. There is abundance of Lime-ſtone in *Strath* and *Trotterneſs*, ſome Banks of Clay on the *Eaſt* Coaſt are overflow'd by the Tide, and in theſe grow the *Lapis Ceranius, or Cerna Amonis* of different Shapes. Some of the breadth of a Crown-piece bearing an Impreſſi-

I 3 on

on reſembling the Sun. Some are as big as a Man's Finger in form of a *Semicircle*, and furrowed on the Inner ſide, others are leſs and have furrows of a Yellow Colour on both ſides. Theſe Stones are by the Natives called Cramp ſtones, becauſe as they ſay they cure the Cramp in Cows, by waſhing the part affected with Water in which this Stone has been ſteep'd for ſome Hours. The *Velumnites*, grows likewiſe in theſe Banks of Clay, ſome of 'em are twelve Inches long, and tapering towards one end, the Natives call them *Bat Stones*, becauſe they believe them to cure the Horſes of the Worms which occaſion that Diſtemper, by giving them Water to drink in which this Stone has been Steept for ſome Hours.

THIS Stone grows likewiſe in the middle of a very hard grey Stone on the ſhore. There is a Black Stone in the ſurface of the Rock on *Rig* ſhore, which reſembles Goats Horns.

THE *Lapis Hecticus*, or white *Hectic* Stone abounds here both in the Land and Water, the Natives uſe this Stone as a remedy againſt the *Diſenteria* and *Diarrhea*; they make them red-hot in the Fire, and then quenche them in Milk, and ſome in Water, which they drink with good ſucceſs. They uſe this Stone after the ſame manner for *Conſumptions*, and they likewiſe quench theſe Stones in Water, with which they bathe their feet and hands.

THE

Weſtern Iſlands *of* Scotland, *&c.* 135

THE Stones on which the Scurf called *Corkir* grows, are to be had in many Places on the Coaſt and in the Hills, this Scurf dyes a pretty Crimſon Colour; firſt well dryed and then ground to Powder, after which it's ſteep'd in Urine, the Veſſel being well ſecured from Air, and in three Weeks its ready to boyl with the Yarn that is to be Dyed. The Natives obſerve the decreaſe of the Moon for ſcraping this Scurf from the Stone, and ſay its ripeſt in *Auguſt*.

THERE are many White Scurfs on Stone, ſomewhat like theſe on which the *Corkir* grovvs, but the *Corkir* is White and thinner than any other that reſembles it.

THERE is another coarſer Scurf called *Croſtil*, its of a dark colour, and only dyes a Philamot.

THE Rocks in the Village *Ord*, have much *Talk* grovving on them like the *Venice-talk*.

THIS Iſle is naturally vvell provided vvith variety of excellent Bays and Harbours. In the *South* of it lies the *Peninſula* called *Oronſa*, *alias* Iſland *Dierman*, it has an excellent Place for Anchorage on the *Eaſt* ſide, and is generally known by moſt *Scots-Sea-men*. About a

I 4 League

136 *A* Deſcription *of the*

League more *Eaſterly* on the ſame Coaſt there is a ſmall Rock viſible only at half Low water, but may be avoided by ſteering through the middle of the Channel. About a League more *Eaſterly* on the ſame Coaſt, there is an Anchorage pretty near the Shore, within leſs than a Mile further is the narrow Sound called the *Kyle*, in order to paſs which its abſolutely neceſſary to have the Tide of Flood, for ſuch as are *Northward* bound, elſe they will be obliged to retire in diſorder, becauſe of the violence of the Current; for no Wind is able to carry a Veſſel againſt it. The quite contrary Courſe is to be obſerved by Veſſels coming from the *North*. A Mile due *Eaſt* from the *Kyle* there is a big Rock on the *South* ſide, the point of Land on *Skie* ſide called *Kaillach* which is overflow'd by the Tide of Flood, a Veſſel may go near its outſide; above a Mile further due *North*, there are two Rocks in the paſſage through the *Kyle* they are on the Caſtle ſide, and may be avoided by keeping the middle of the Channel, about eight Miles more to the *Northward* or the *Eaſt* of *Skie*, there is ſecure anchorage between the Iſle *Scalpa* and *Skie* in the middle of the Cannel, but one muſt not come to it by the *South* Entry of *Scalpa*, and in coming between *Raſay* and this Iſle, there are Rocks without the Entry, which may be avoided beſt, by having a Pilot of the Country, more to the North is *Lockſligichan*, on the Coaſt of *Skie*, where is good anchorage the

the Entry is not deep enough for Vessels of any burden except at high Water, but three Miles further *North* lyes *Loch-port-ry* a capacious and convenient Harbour of above a Mile in length.

THE Island *Tulm* which is within half a Mile of the *Northermost* point of *Skie*, has an Harbour on the inside. The entrance between the Isle, and *Duntulm* Castle is the best.

ON the *West* of the same Wing of *Skie*, and about five Miles more *Southerly*, lies *Loch-uge*, about a Mile in Length, and a very good Harbour for Vessels of the greatest burden, about two Miles on this Coast further *South* is *Loch-snijsort*, it's three Miles in length, and half a Mile in breadth, it is free from Rocks, and has convenient Anchorage.

ON the *West-side* the Promontory at the Mouth of *Loch snijsort*, lies *Loch-arnisort*, being about two Miles in length, and half a Mile in breadth; there are two small Isles in the mouth of the Entry, and a Rock near the *West-side*, a little within the Entry.

SOME five Miles to the *West* of *Arnisort* lies *Loch-fallart*, the Entry is between *Vaternis-head* on the *East-side*, and *Duntegon-head* on the *West-side*, the *Loch* is six Miles in length, and about a League in breadth for some Miles. It hath

hath the Island **Isa** about the middle, on the *East-side*. There is a Rock between the *North-end* and the Land and there Vessels may anchor between the *N. E.* side of the Isle and the Land, there is also good anchorage near *Duntegon* Castle, two Miles further to the *Southward*.

LOCH-BRAKADIL, lies two Miles *South* of *Loch-fallart*, it is seven Miles in length, and has several good anchoring Places, on the *North-side* the Entry lies two Rocks called *Mack-lleods Maidens*. About three Miles *South-west* is *Loch-einard* a Mile in length, it has a Rock in the Entry, and is not visible but at an Ebb.

ABOUT two Miles to the *Eastward*, there is an anchoring place for Barks between *Skie* and the Isle **Soa**.

ABOUT a League further *East* lies *Loch-slapan*, and *Loch-essort*, the first reaches about four Miles to the *North*, and the second about six Miles to the *East*.

THERE are several Mountains in the Isle of considerable height and extent, as *Quillin*, *Scornifiey*, *Bein-store*, *Bein-vore-scowe*, *Bein-chro*, *Bein-nin*, *Kaillach*, some of them are covered with Snow on the top in Summer, others are almost quite covered with Sand in the top, which is much wash'd down with the great Rains: All these Mountains abound with Heath, and Grass, which serve as good Pastorage for black Cattle and Sheep. THE

THE *Quillin* which exceeds any of thoſe Hills in height, is ſaid to be the cauſe of much Rain, by breaking the Clouds that hover about it,which quickly after pour down inRain upon the quarter on which theWind then blows.There is a high ridge of one continued Mountain of conſiderable height, and fifteen Miles in length, running along the middle of the *Eaſt-wing* of *Skie* called *Troterneſs*, and that part above the Sea is faced with a ſteep Rock.

THE arable Ground is generally along the Coaſt, and in the Valleys between the Mountains having always a River running in the middle; the ſoil is very grateful to the Husband-man: I have been ſhew'd ſeveral Places that had not been till'd for ſeven Years before, which yielded a good product of Oats by Diging,tho theGround was not dung'd,particularly near the Village *Kilmartin*, which the Natives told me had not been dung'd theſe forty Years laſt. Several pieces of Ground yield twenty,and ſome thirty fold when dung'd with Sea-ware. I had an account that a ſmall tract of Ground in the Village *Skerybreck*, yielded an hundred fold of Barley.

THE Iſle of *Altig*, which is generally covered with Heath, being manur'd with Sea-ware, the Owner ſow'd Barley in the Ground, and it yielded a very good Product, many Stalks

Stalks had five Ears growing upon them. In plentiful Years *Skie* furniſhes the oppoſite continent with Oats and Barley. The way of tillage here is after the ſame manner that is already deſcrib'd in the Iſles of *Lewis*, &c: And diging doth always produce a better Increaſe here than plowing.

ALL the Mountains in this Iſle are plentifully furniſhed with Varietie of excellent Springs and Fountains, ſome of them have Rivulets with Water-mills upon them. The moſt celebrated Well in *Skie*, is *Loch ſiant* Well, it is much frequented by Strangers, as well as by the Inhabitants of the Iſle, who generally believe it to be a Specifick for ſeveral Diſeaſes, ſuch as *Stitches, Head-aches, Stone, Conſumptions, Megrim.* Several of the common People oblige themſelves by a Vow to come to this Well, and make the ordinary Touer about it, call'd *Deſſil*, which is performed thus; they move thrice round the Well proceeding Sunways from *Eaſt* to *Weſt* and ſo on, this is done after drinking of the Water, and when one goes away from the Well, it's a never failing cuſtom, to leave ſome ſmall offering on the Stone which covers the Well, there are nine Springs iſſuing out of the Hill above the Well, and all of them pay the tribute of their Water to a Rivulet that falls from the Well. There is a little Freſh water Lake within ten Yards of the ſaid Well, it abounds with Trouts, but neither

neither the Natives nor Strangers will ever prefume to deftroy any of them, fuch is the efteem they have for the Water.

THERE is a fmall Coppice near to the Well, and there is none of the Natives dare venture to cut the leaft Branch of it, for fear of fome fignal Judgment to follow upon it.

THERE are many Wells here efteemed effectual to remove feveral Diftempers, the Lighteft and wholefomeft Water in all the Ifle is that of *Tonbir Tellibreck* in *Uge*, the Natives fay that the Water of this Well, and the Sea-plant call'd *Dulfe* would ferve inftead of Food for a confiderable time, and own that they have experienc'd it in time of War. I faw a little Well in *Kilbride* in the *South* of *Sky*, with one Trout only in it, the Natives are very tender it,and tho' they often chance to catch it in their wooden Pales, they are very careful to preferve it from being deftroy'd, it has been feen there for many Years, there is a Rivulet, not far diftant from the Well, to which it hath probably had accefs through fome narrow Paffage.

THERE are many Rivers on all quarters of the Ifle, about thirty of them afford Salmon, and fome of 'em black Mufles,in which Pearl do breed particularly the River of *Kilmartin*, and the River *Ord*.The Proprietor told me that fome Years ago a Pearl had been taken out of the former

former valued at 20 *l. Sterling.* There are feveral Cataracts as that in *Sker-horen*, *Holm*, *Rig* and *Tont*. When a River makes a great noife in time of fair Weather, it's a fure Prognoftick here of Rain to enfue.

THERE are many Frefh-water Lakes in *Skie*, and generally well ftockt with Trout and Eels, the Common Flie, and the Earth-worms are ordinarily us'd for angling Trout, the beft Seafon for it is a Calm, or a *South-weft* Wind.

THE largeft of the Frefh-water Lakes is that nam'd after St. *Columbus*, on the account of the Chappel dedicated to that Saint, it ftands in the Ifle, about the middle of the Lake.

THERE is a little Frefh-water Lake near the *South-fide* of *Loch-einordftard*, in which Mufces grow that breed Pearl.

THIS Ifle hath anciently been covered all over with Woods, as appears from the great Trunks of Fir-trees, *&c.* dug out of the Bogs, frequently, *&c.* there are feveral Coppices of Wood, fcattered up and down the Ifle, the largeft called *Lettir-hurr*, exceeds not three Miles in length.

HERRINGS are often taken in moft or all the Bays mention'd above, *Loch-effort*, *Slapan*, *Loch-fallort*,

Loch-fallort, *Loch-ſcowſar*, and the *Kyle* of *Scalpa*, are generally known to Strangers, for the great quantities of Herring taken in them. This ſort of Fiſh is commonly ſeen without the Bays, and on the Coaſt all the Summer. All other Fiſh follow the Herring and their Fry, from the Whale to the leaſt Fiſh that ſwims, the biggeſt ſtill deſtroying the leſſer.

THE Fiſhers and others told me that there is big Herring almoſt double the ſize of any of its kind, which leads all that are in a Bay, and the Shoal follows it wherever it goes. This Leader is by the Fiſhers called the King of Herring, and when they chance to catch it alive, they drop it carefully into the Sea, for they judge it Petty Treaſon to deſtroy a Fiſh of that Name.

THE Fiſhers ſay, that all ſorts of Fiſh from the greateſt to the leaſt, have a Leader, who is follow'd by all of its kind.

IT is a General Obſervation all *Scotland* over, that if a Quarrel happen on the Coaſt where Herring is caught, and that Blood be drawn violently, then the Herring go away from the Coaſt without returning, during that Seaſon. This they ſay has been obſerv'd in all paſt Ages, as well as at preſent; but this I relate only as a common Tradition, and ſubmit it to the Judgment of the Learned.

THE

THE Natives preſerve and dry their Herring without Salt, for the ſpace of eight Months, provided they be taken after the tenth of *September*; they uſe no other Art in it, but take out their Guts, and then tying a ruſh about their Necks, hang them by Pairs upon a Rope made of Heath, croſs a Houſe, and they eat well, and free from Putrefaction, after eight Months, keeping in this manner. Cod, Ling, Herring, Mackrel, Haddock, Whiting, Turbat, together with all other Fiſh that are in the *Scots* Seas, abound on the Coaſts of this Iſland.

THE beſt time of taking Fiſh with an Angle is in warm weather, which diſpoſes them to come near the ſurface of the Water, whenas in cold weather, or rain, they go to the bottom. The beſt Bait for Cod and Ling is a piece of Herring, Whiting, Thornback, Haddock, or Eel. The Grey-Lord, *alias* Black-mouth, a Fiſh of the ſize and ſhape of a Salmon, takes the Limpet for Bait. There is another way of Angling for this Fiſh, by faſtning a ſhort white Down of a Gooſe behind the Hook, and the Boat being continually row'd, the Fiſh run greedily after the Down, and are eaſily caught. The Gray-Lord ſwims in the ſurface of the Water, and then is caught with a Spear, a Rope being tied to the further end of it, and ſecur'd in the Fiſhermans hand.

ALL

ALL the Bays and Places of Anchorage here, abound with most kinds of shell-fish; The Kyle of *Scalpa* affords Oysters in such Plenty, that commonly a Spring-Tide of Ebb leaves fifteen, sometimes twenty Horse Load of them on the sands.

THE Sands on the Coast of *Bernstill* Village at the Spring Tides afford daily such plenty of Muscles, as is sufficient to maintain sixty Persons *per* day; and this was a great support to many poor Families of the Neighbourhood in the late years of scarcity. The Natives observe that all shell-fish are plumper at the increase than decrease of the Moon; they observe likewise that all shell-fish are plumper during a south west wind, than when it blows from the north, or north east quarters.

THE Limpet being parboil'd with a very little quantity of water, the Broth is drank to increase Milk in Nurses, and likewise when the Milk proves astringent to the Infants. The Broth of the black Periwinkle is us'd in the same Cases. It's observ'd that Limpets being frequently eat in *June*, are apt to occasion the Jaundice; the outside of the Fish is colour'd like the skin of a Person that has the Jaundice; the tender yellow part of the Limpet which is next to the shell, is reckon'd good nourishment, and very easie of digestion.

K I had

I had an Account of a poor Woman who was a Native of the Isle of *Jura*, and by the Troubles in King *Charles* the First's Reign was almost reduc'd to a starving Condition, so that she lost her Milk quite, by which her Infant had nothing proper for its sustenance; upon this she boyl'd some of the tender Fat of the Limpets, and gave it to her Infant, to whom it became so agreeable, that it had no other Food for several Months together; and yet there was not a Child in *Jura*, or any of the adjacent Isles wholsomer than this poor Infant, which was expos'd to so great a strait.

THE Limpet creeps on the Stone and Rock in the night time, and in a warm day, but if any thing touch the shell, it instantly clings to the stone, and then no hand is able to pluck it off without some Instrument; and therefore such as take 'em, have little Hammers, call'd Limpet-hammers, with which they beat it from the Rock; but if they watch its motion, and surprize it, the least touch of the hand pulls it away; and this that is taken creeping, they say is larger and better than that which is pull'd off by force. The motion, fixation, taste and feeding, &c. of this little Animal being very curious, I have here exhibited its Figure, for the satisfaction of the inquisitive Reader.

I have

I have likewise here exhibited the Figure of the *Balanos*, growing on Stone, and Shells, in which, very small *Wilks* are found to lodge, and grow.

THE pale *Wilk*, which in length and smalness exceeds the black *Periwinkle*, and by the Natives call'd *Gil-fiunt*, is by them beat in pieces, and both Shell and Fish boyl'd; the Broth being strain'd and drunk for some days together, is accounted a good Remedy against the Stone; it is call'd a *Dead Mans Eye* at *Dover*. It is observ'd of *Cockles*, and *Spout-Fish*, that they go deeper in the Sands with North Winds, than any other; and on the contrary, they are easier reach'd with South Winds, which are still warmest.

IT is a General Observation of all such as live on the Sea Coast, that they are more prolifick than any other People whatsoever.

The Sea-Plants here, are as follows.

LINARICH, a very thin small green Plant, about eight, ten, or twelve inches in length, it grows on Stone, on Shells, and on the bare Sand; this Plant is applied Plaisterwise to the Forehead and Temples to procure Sleep, for such as have a Fever, and they say it is effectual for this purpose.

The *Linarich* is likewise applied to the Crown of the Head, and Temples, for removing the Megrim, and also to heal the Skin after a Blister Plaister, of *Flammula Jovis*.

Slake, a very thin Plant, almost round, about ten or twelve inches in circumference, grows on the Rocks, and Sands; the Natives eat it boil'd, and it dissolves into Oil; they say that if a little Butter be added to it, one might live many years on this alone, without Bread, or any other Food, and at the same time, undergo any laborious exercise: This Plant boil'd with some Butter, is given to Cows in the Spring, to remove Costiveness.

Dulſe is of a reddiſh brown Colour, about ten or twelve inches long, and above half an inch in breadth, it is eat raw, and then reckon'd to be looſning, and very good for the ſight; But if boil'd it proves more looſning, if the juice be drank with it. This Plant applied Plaiſter wiſe to the Temples, is reckon'd effectual againſt the Megrim; the Plant boil'd, and eat with its infuſion, is us'd againſt the Cholick, and Stone, and dried without waſhing it in water, pulveriz'd and given in any convenient Vehicle Faſting, it kills Worms: the Natives eat it boil'd with Butter, and reckon it very wholſom. The *Dulſe* recommended here, is that which grows on Stone, and not that which grows on the *Alga Marina*, or *Sea Tangle*; for tho' that be likewiſe eaten, it will not ſerve in any of the Caſes above mention'd.

THE *Alga Marina*, or *Sea-Tangle*, or as ſome call it *Sea-ware*, is a Rod about four, ſix, eight or ten Foot long, having at the end a Blade commonly ſlit into ſeven or eight pieces, and about a foot and half in length; it grows on Stone, the Blade is eat by the Vulgar Natives. I had an Account of a young Man who had loſt his Appetite, and taken Pills to no purpoſe, and being adviſed to boil the Blade of the *Alga*, and drink the infuſion boil'd with a little Butter, was reſtor'd to his former ſtate of health.

K 3 THERE

THERE is abundance of White and Red Coral growing on the S. and W. Coaſt of this Iſle, it grows on the Rocks, and is frequently interwoven with the roots of the *Alga*; the Red ſeems to be a good freſh Colour when firſt taken out of the Sea, but in a few hours after it becomes pale. Some of the Natives take a quantity of the red Coral, adding the yolk of an Egg roaſted to it, for the *Diarrhea*: Both the Red and White Corral here is not above five inches long, and about the bigneſs of a Gooſes Quill.

THERE are many Caves to be ſeen on each quarter of this Iſle, ſome of them are believ'd to be ſeveral Miles in length; there is a big Cave in the Village *Bornskittag*, which is ſuppos'd to exceed a Mile in length. The Natives told me that a Piper who was over curious, went into the Cave with a deſign to find out the length of it, and after he entred, began to play on his Pipe, but never return'd to give an account of his Progreſs.

THERE is a Cave in the Village *Kigg*, wherein drops of water that iſſue from the roof, petrifie into a white Limy ſubſtance, and hang down from the roof and ſides of the Cave.

THERE

THERE is a Cave in the Village *Holm*, having many petrified Twigs hanging from the top, they are hollow from one end to the other, and from five to ten inches in length.

THERE is a big Cave in the Rock on the east side *Portrie*, large enough for eighty Persons; there is a Well within it, which together with its Scituation and narrow Entry, renders it an inaccessible Fort, one Man only can enter it at a time, by the side of a Rock, so that with a Staff in in his hand, he is able by the least touch to cast over the Rock as many as shall attempt to come into the Cave.

ON the South side *Loch Portry*, there is a large Cave in which many Sea Cormorants do Build; the Natives carry a bundle of straw to the door of the Cave in the Night time, and there setting it on fire, the Fowls fly with all speed to the Light, and so are caught in Baskets laid for that purpose. The Golden Cave in *Sleat* is said to be seven Miles in length, from the West to East.

THERE are many *Cairns*, or heaps of Stones in this Island. Some of the Natives say they were erected in the times of *Heathenism*, and that the ancient Inhabitants Worshipped about them. In Popish Countries the People still

K 4 retain

retain the ancient Custom of making a Tour round them.

OTHERS say, these *Cairns* were erected where Persons of Distinction, killed in Battle, had been Buried, and that their Urns were laid in the ground under the *Cairns*. I had an account of a *Cairn* in *Knapdale* in the Shire of *Argyle*, underneath which an Urn was found. There are little *Cairns* to be seen in some places on the common Road, which were made only where Corpses happen'd to rest for some minutes; but they have laid aside the making such *Cairns* now.

THERE is an erected Stone in *Kilbride* in *Strath*, which is ten Foot high, and one and a half broad.

THERE is another of five Foot high plac'd in the middle of the *Cairn*, on the South side *Loch Uge*, and is call'd the high Stone of *Uge*.

THERE are three such Stones on the Sea Coast, opposite to *Skerinefs*, each of them three Foot high; the Natives have a Tradition, that upon these Stones a big Caldron was set for Boyling *Fin Mack Coul*'s Meat. This Gigantick Man is reported to have been General of a Militia that came from *Spain*, to *Ireland*, and from thence to those Isles; all his

Western Islands of Scotland, &c. 153

his Soldiers are called *Fienty* from *Fiun*, he is believed to have arrived in the Isles, in the reign of King *Evan*, the Natives have many Stories of this General and his Army with which I will not trouble the Reader. He is mentioned in Bishop *Lesly*'s History.

THERE are many Forts erected on the Coast of this Isle, and suppos'd to have been built by the *Danes*; they are called by the Name of *Dun* from *Dain*, which in the ancient Language signify'd a Fort; they are round in form, and they have a Passage all round within the Wall, the Door of 'em is low, and many of the Stones are of such bulk that no number of the present Inhabitants could raise them without an Engine.

ALL these Forts stand upon eminences, and are so disposed, that there is not one of them, which is not in view of some other; and by this means when a Fire is made upon a Beacon, in any one Fort, it's in a few Moments after communicated to all the rest, and this hath been always observed upon sight of any number of foreign Vessels, or Boats approaching the Coast.

THE Forts are commonly named after the Place where they are, or the Person that built them, as *Dun-Skudborg*, *Dun-Derig*, *Dun-Skerinefs*, *Dun-David*, &c.

THERE

154 A Description of the

THERE are several little Stone-houses, built under Ground, called Earth-houses, which served to hide a few People and their Goods in time of War, the Entry to them was on the Sea, or River side; there is one of them in the Village *Lachsay*, and another in *Camstinvag*.

THERE are several little Stone-houses built above ground, capable only of one Person, and round in form, one of 'em is to be seen in *Portry*, another at *Lincro*, and at *Culuknock*; they are called *Tey-nin-druinich* (i. e.) *Druids-house*, *Druinich* signifies a retired Person, much devoted to Contemplation.

THE Fewel us'd here is Peats dug out of the Heaths, there are Cakes of Iron found in the Ashes of some of 'em, and at *Flodgery* Village, there are Peats from which *Salt-peter* sparkles. There is a Coal lately discovered at *Holm* in *Portry*, some of which I have seen, there are pieces of Coal dug out likewise of the Sea-sand in *Heldersta* of *Vaternis*, and some found in the Village *Mogstat*.

THE Cattle produced here are Horses, Cows, Sheep, Goats and Hogs: The common work-horses are expos'd to the rigour of the Season during the Winter and Spring, and tho they have neither Corn, Hay, or but seldom Straw, yet they undergo all the Labour that other Horses better treated are liable to. THE

THE Cows are likewise expos'd to the rigour of the coldest Seasons, and become meer Skeletons in the Spring, many of them not being able to rise from the Ground without help, but they recover as the Season becomes more favourable, and the Grass grows up, then they acquire New-beef, which is both sweet and tender; the Fat and Lean is not so much separated in them as in other Cows, but as it were larded, which renders it very agreeable to the Taste, a Cow in this Isle, may be twelve Years old, when at the same time, its Beef, is not above four, five, or six Months Old. When a Calf is slain its an usual Custom to cover another Calf with its Skin to suck the Cow whose Calf hath been slain, or else she gives no Milk, nor suffers her self to be approach'd by any body, and if she discover the Cheat, then she grows enraged for some days, and the last remedy us'd to pacifie her is to use the sweetest Voice, and sing all the time of milking her. When any Man is troubled with his Neighbours Cows, by breaking into his Inclosures, he brings all to the utmost boundary of his Ground, and there, drawing a quantity of Blood from each Cow, he leaves them upon the spot, from whence they go away, without ever returning again to trouble him, during all that Season. The Cows often feed upon the *Alga Marina* or Sea-ware; and they can exactly distinguish the Tide of Ebb from the Tide

Tide of Flood, tho' at the same time they are not within view of the Sea, and if one meet them running to the shore at the Tide of Ebb, and offer to turn them again to the Hills to graze they will not return, when the Tide has Ebb'd about two hours, so as to uncover the Sea-ware, then they steer their course directly to the nearest Coast, in their usual order, one after another, whatever their number be, there are as many Instances of this, as there are Tides of Ebb on the shore. I had occasion to make this Observation thirteen times in one Week, for tho' the Natives gave me repeated assurances of the truth of it, I did not fully believe it, till I saw many Instances of it in my Travels along the Coast. The Natives have a remark that when the Cows belonging to one Person do of a sudden become very irregular and run up and down the Fields, and make a lowd noise, without any visible cause, that it is a presage of the Master or Mistress's Death, of which there were several late Instances given me, *James Mack-Donald* of *Capstil*, having been killed at the Battle of *Kelicrankie*, it was Observed that night, that his Cows gave Blood instead of Milk, his Family and other Neighbours concluded this a bad Omen, The Minister of the Place, and the Mistriss of the Cows, together with several Neighbours assured me of the truth of this.

THERE

THERE was a Calf brought forth in *Vaternis* without Legs, it leaped very far, bellowed louder than any other Calf, and drank much more Milk, at laſt the Owner killed it. *Kenneth* the *Carpenter*, who lives there told me that he had ſeen the Calf. I was alſo informed that a Cow in *Vaternis*, brought forth five Calves at a time, of which, three died.

THERE was a Calf at *Skerineſs*, having all its Legs double, but the Bones had but one Skin to cover both, the Owner fancying it to be Ominous killed it, after having lived nine Months. Several of the Natives there abouts told me that they had ſeen it.

THERE are ſeveral Calves that have a ſlit in the top of their Ears, and theſe the Natives fancy to be the Iſſue of a Wild-bull, that comes from the Sea or freſh Lakes, and this Calf is by them call'd *Corky-ſyre*.

THERE's Plenty of Land and Water Fowl in this Iſle as Hawks, Eagles of two kinds, the one Gray and of a larger ſize, the other much leſs and Black, but more deſtructive to young Cattle. *Black-cock*, *Heath-hen*, *Plovers*, *Pigeons*, *Wild-Geeſe*, *Tarmagan*, and *Cranes*, of this latter ſort, I have ſeen ſixty on the ſhore in a flock together. The Sea Fowls are *Malls* of all kinds, *Coalterneb*, *Guillamet*, *Sea-Cormorant*,

Cormorant, &c. The Natives obſerve that the latter if perfectly Black, make no good Broth, nor is its Fleſh worth eating, but that a *Cormorant*, which has any white Feathers or Down, makes good Broth, and the Fleſh of it is good Food, and the Broth is uſually drunk by Nurſes to encreaſe their Milk.

THE Natives obſerve that this Fowl flutters with its Wings towards the quarter from which the Wind is ſoon after to blow.

THE Sea-fowl *Bunivochil*, or as ſome Seamen call it *Carara*, and others *Biſhop*, is as big as a Gooſe, of a brown Colour, and the inſide of the Wings white, the Bill is long and broad,& it is footed like a Gooſe,it dives quicker than any other Fowl whatever, its very Fat. The Caſe of this Fowl being flea'd off with the Fat, and a little Salt laid on to preſerve it, and then applied to the Thigh-bone, where it muſt lie for ſome Weeks together, is an effectual remedy againſt the *Sciatica*, of which I ſaw two Inſtances. It is obſerved of Fire-arms that are rubb'd over (as the cuſtom is here) with the Oyl or Fat of Sea-Fowls, that they contract ruſt much ſooner, than when done with the Fat of Land-Fowl; the *Fulmar* Oyl from St. *Kilda* only exceptd, for it preſerves Iron from contracting ruſt much longer than any other Oyl or Greaſe whatſoever, the Natives obſerve, that when the Sea-Pye, warbles it Notes inceſſantly,

inceſſantly, it is a ſure preſage of Fair Weather to follow in a few hours after.

THE *Amphibia* to be ſeen in this Iſle, are Seals, Otters, Vipers, Frogs, Toads and Asks, the Otter ſhuts its Eyes when it eats, and this is a conſiderable diſadvantage to it, for then ſeveral ravenous Fowls lay hold on this opportunity, and rob it of its Fiſh.

THE Hunters ſay there is a big Otter above the ordinary ſize with a White Spot on its Breaſt, and this they call the King of Otters, it is rarely ſeen and very hard to be killed, Seamen aſcribe great Vertues to the skin; for they ſay that it is fortunate in Battle, and that Victory is always on its ſide. Serpents abound in ſeveral parts of this Iſle, there are three kinds of them, the firſt Black and White ſpotted, which is the moſt Poyſonous, and if a ſpeedy remedy be not made uſe of after the Wound given, the Party is in danger. I had an Account that a Man at *Glenmore*, a Boy at *Portry*, and a Woman at *Loch-ſcah-vag*, did all die of Wounds given by this ſort of Serpents; ſome believe that the Serpents wound with the Sting only, and not with their Teeth, but this Opinion is founded upon a bare Conjecture becauſe the Sting is expoſed to view, but the Teeth very rarely ſeen, they are ſecured within a Hoſe of Fleſh, which prevents their being broke, the end of them being hook'd and exceeding

ſmall, would ſoon be deſtroy'd, if it had not been for this Fence, that Nature has given them. The longeſt of the black Serpents mention'd above, is from two to three, or at moſt four foot long.

THE yellow Serpent with brown ſpots, is not ſo poyſonous, nor ſo long as the black and white one.

THE brown Serpent is of all three the leaſt poyſonous, and ſmalleſt and ſhorteſt in ſize.

THE Remedies uſed here to extract the poy- of Serpents are various. The Rump of a Houſe Cock ſtrip'd of its Feathers, and applied to the Wound, doth powerfully extract the poyſon, if timely applied. The Cock is obſerv'd after this to ſwell to a great bulk, far above its former ſize, and being thrown out into the Fields, no Ravenous Bird, or Beaſt, will ever offer to taſte of it.

THE Fork'd Sting taken out of an Adder's Tongue, is by the Natives ſteep'd in water, with which they waſh and cure the wound.

THE Serpent's Head that gives the wound, being applied, is found to be a good Remedy.

NEW Cheeſe applied timely, extracts the Poyſon well.

THERE

THERE are two forts of *Weafles* in the Ifle, one of which exceeds that of the common fize in bignefs; the Natives fay that the breath of it kills Calves, and Lambs, and that the leffer fort is apt to occafion a decay in fuch as frequently have them tame about them; efpecially fuch as fuffer them to fuck and lick about their mouths.

The Inferiour Ifles about SKIE.

SOA-BRETTIL lies within a quarter of a Mile to the South of the Mountain *Quillin*, it's five Miles in Circumference, and full of Bogs, and fitter for Pafturage than Cultivation. About a Mile on the Weft fide it is cover'd with Wood, and the reft confifts of Heath, and Grafs, having a mixture of the *Mertillo* all over. The Red Garden Currants grow in this Ifle, and are fuppos'd to have been carried thither by Birds. There has been no Venomous Creature ever feen in this little Ifle, until within thefe two years laft, that a black and white big Serpent was feen by one of the Inhabitants who kill'd it; they believe it came from the oppofite Coaft of *Skie*, where there are many big Serpents. There is abundance of *Cod* and *Ling* round this Ifle.

ON the South of *Sleat* lies Iland *Oronfa*, which is a *Peninfula* at low water; it's a Mile in

L

in Circumference, and very Fruitful in Corn, and Grafs. As for the latter, it's faid to excell any piece of ground of its extent in thofe parts

IN the North entry to *Kyle-Akin*, lie feveral fmall Ifles; the biggeft and next to *Skie* is *Ilan Nin Gillin*, about half a Mile in Circumference, cover'd all over with long Heath, and the *Erica Baccifera*, there is abundance of *Seals*, and *Sea Fowls* about it.

A League further North lies the Ifle *Pabbay*, about two Miles in Circumference, it excells in Pafturage, the Cows in it afford near double the Milk that they yield in *Skie*. In the Dog Days there is a big Flye in this Ifle, which infefts the Cows, makes them run up and down, difcompofes them exceedingly, and hinders their Feeding, infomuch that they muft be brought out of the Ifle, to the Ifle of *Skie*; this Ifle affords abundance of *Lobfters*, *Limpets*, *Wilks*, *Crabs*, and ordinary Sea Plants.

ABOUT half a League further North lies the fmall Ifle *Gilliman*, being a quarter of a Mile in Circumference; the whole is cover'd with long Heath, and the *Erica Baccifera*. Within a call further North lies the Ifle *Scalpa*, very near to *Skie*, five Miles in Circumference, it is Mountanous from the South end, almoft to the North end, it has Wood in feveral

ral parts of it; the South end is moft arable, and is Fruitful in Corn andGrafs.

ABOUT a Mile further North is the Ifle *Rafay*, being feven Miles in length, and three in breadth, floaping on the Weft and Eaft fides; it has fome Wood on all the Quarters of it, the whole is fitter for Pafturage than Cultivation, the Ground being generally very unequal, but very well watered with Rivulets and Springs. There's a Spring running down the face of a high Rock on the Eaft fide of the Ifle, it petrifies into a white fubftance, of which very fine Lime is made, and there's a great quantity of it. There's a Quarry of good Stone one the fame fide of the Ifle; there is abundance of Caves on the Weft fide, which ferve to lodge feveral Families; who for their convenience in Grazing, Fifhing, &c. refort thither in the Summmer. On the Weft fide, particulary near to the Village *Clachan*, the Shoar abounds with fmooth Stones of different fizes, variegated all over. The fame Cattle, Fowl and Fifh are produc'd here, that are found in the Ifle of *Skie*. There is a Law obferv'd by the Natives, that all their Fifhing-Lines muft be of equal length, for the longeft is always fuppos'd to have beft accefs to the Fifh, which would prove a difadvantage to fuch as might have fhorter ones.

THERE are fome Forts in this Ifle, the higheft is in the South end, it is a Natural ftrength, and in form like the Crown of a Hat; it's called *Dun-Cann*, which the Natives will needs have to be from one Canne Coufen to the King of *Denmark*. The other lies on fide, is an Artificial Fort, three Stories high, and is called *Caftle Vreokle*.

THE Proprietor of the Ifle is Mr. *Mack Leod*, a Cadet of the Family of that Name; his Seat is in the Village *Clachan*, the Inhabitants have as great a veneration for him, as any Subjects can have for their King. They preferve the Memory of the deceafed Ladies of the Place, by erecting a little Pyramid of Stone for each of them, with the Ladies Name. Thefe Pyramids are by them called Croffes; feveral of them are built of Stone and Lime, and have three fteps of gradual afcent to 'em. There are eight fuchCroffes about the Village, which is adorn'd with a little Tower, and leffer Houfes, and an Orchard with feveral forts of Berries, Pot-herbs, &c. The Inhabitants are all *Proteftants*, and ufe the fame Language, Habit, and Diet, with the Natives of *Skie*.

ABOUT a quarter of a Mile further North lies the Ifle *Rona*, which is three Miles in length, Veffels pafs through the narrow Channel

Channel between *Rofay*, and *Rona*, this little Ifle is the moft unequal rocky piece of Ground to be feen any where ; there's but very few Acres fit for digging, the whole is covered with long Heath, *Erica-baccifera*, *Mertillus*, and fome mixture of Grafs, it is reckoned very fruitful in Pafturage, moft of the Rocks confift of the *Hectic* Stone, and a confiderable part of 'em is of a Red Colour.

THERE is a Bay on the *South-weft* end of the Ifle, with two Entries, the one is on the *Weft-fide*, the other on the *South*, but the latter is only acceffible, it has a Rock within the Entry, and a good Fifhing.

ABOUT three Leagues to the *North-weft* of *Rona*, is the Ifle *Fladda* being almoft joyn'd to *Skie*, it is all plain arable Ground, and about a Mile in Circumference.

ABOUT a Mile to the *North*, lies the Ifle *Altvig*, it has a high Rock facing the *Eaft*, is near two Miles in Circumference, and is reputed fruitful in Corn and Grafs, there is a little old Chappel in it, dedicated to St. *Turos*. There is a Rock of about forty Yards in length at the *North-end* of the Ifle diftinguifhed for its commodioufnefs in Fifhing. Herrings are feen about this Rock in great Numbers all Summer, infomuch that the Fifher-boats are fometimes as it were entangled among the fhoals of them.

L 3 THE

THE Ifle *Troda*, lies within half a League to the Northermoft point of *Skie*, called *Hunifh*, it is two Miles in Circumference, fruitful in Corn, and Grafs, and had a Chappel dedicated to St. *Columbus*. The Natives told me that, there is a couple of Ravens in the Ifle, which fuffer none other of their kind to come thither, and when their own Young are able to flie, they beat them alfo away from the Ifle.

FLADDA-Chuan(i.e.)*Fladda* of the *Ocean*,lies about two Leagues diftant from the *Weft-fide* of *Hunifh-point*, it is two Miles in Compafs, the Ground is boggy, and but indifferent for Corn or Grafs ; the Ifle is much frequented for the plenty of Fifh of all kinds, on each quarter of it. There are very big Whales which purfue the Fifh on the Coaft,theNatives diftinguifh one Whale for its bignefs above all others, and told me that it had many big Limpets growing upon its Back, and that the Eyes of it were of fuch a prodigious bignefs, as ftruck no fmallTerror into the Beholders. There is a Chappel in the Ifle dedicated to St. *Columbus*, it has an Altar in the *Eaft-end*, and there is a blue Stone of a round Form on it, which is always moift ; It is an ordinary Cuftom, when any of the Fifhermen are detain'd in the Ifle, by contrary Winds, to wafh the blue Stone with Water all round, expecting thereby to procure a favourable Wind, which the Credulous Tenant living

living in the Iſle ſays never fails, eſpecially if a Stranger waſh the Stone; The Stone is likewiſe applied to the ſides of People troubled with Stitches, and they ſay it is effectual for that purpoſe. And ſo great is the regard they have for this Stone, that they ſwear deciſive Oaths on it.

THE Monk *O Gorgon* is buried near to this Chappel, and there is a Stone five foot high at each end of his Grave. There's abundance of Sea-fowl that come to hatch their Young in the Iſle; the *Coulter-nebs* are very numerous here, it comes in the middle of *March*, and goes away in the middle of *Auguſt*, it makes a Tour round the Iſle Sunways, before it ſettles on the Ground, and another at going away in *Auguſt*; which Ceremony is much approved by the Tenant of the Iſle, and is one of the chief Arguments, he made uſe for making the like round, as he ſets out to Sea with his Boat.

THERE is a great Flock of Plovers, that come to this Iſle frome *Skie*, in the beginning of *September*, they return again in *April*, and are ſaid to be neer two thouſand in all; I told the Tenant he might have a Couple of theſe at every meal during the Winter and Spring, but my motion ſeem'd very diſagreeable to him: For he declared that he had never once attempted to take any of them, tho he might if he would,

L 4 and

and at the ſame time told me, he wondred how I could imagine, that he would be ſo Barbarous as to take the lives of ſuch innocent Creatures as came to him only for Self-preſervation.

THERE are ſix or ſeven Rocks within diſtance of a Musket-ſhot, on the *South-eaſt* ſide the Iſle, the Sea running between each of them; that lying more *Eaſterly* is the Fort called *bord Cruin*, (i. e.) a round Table, from its round Form, it is about three hundred Paces in Circumference, flat in the toep, has a deep Well within it, the whole is ſurrounded with a ſteep Rock, and has only one Place that is acceſſible by climbing, and that only by one Man at a time, there is a violent current of a Tide on each ſide of it, which contributes to render it an Impregnable Fort, it belongs to Sr. *Donald Mac Donald*, one ſingle Man above the Entry, without being expos'd to ſhot, is able with a Staff in his hand, to keep off five hundred Attaquers, for one only can climb the Rock at a time, and that not without difficulty.

THERE is a high Rock on the *Weſt ſide* the Fort, which may be ſecured alſo by a few hands.

ABOUT half a League on the *South-ſide* the round Table, lies the Rock called *Jeskar* (i. e.) *Fiſher*, becauſe many Fiſhing-boats reſort to it, it it is not higher than a ſmall Veſſel under Sail. This Rock affords a great quantity of Scurvy-graſs, of an extraordinary ſize, and very thick, the Natives eat it frequently, as well Boyl'd as Raw, two of them told me that they happen'd to be confin'd there, for the ſpace of thirty hours by a contrary Wind; and being without Victuals, fell to eating this Scurvy-graſs, and finding it of a ſweet Taſte, far different from the Land Scurvy-graſs, they eat a large Basket full of it, which did abundantly ſatisfie their Appetites untill their return home; they told me alſo that it was not in the leaſt windy, or any other way troubleſome to them.

ISLAND *Tulm* on the *Weſt* of the wing of *Skie*, called *Troterneſs*, lies within Muſquet-ſhot of the Caſtle of the Name, it is a hard Rock, and cloathed with Graſs, there are two Caves on the *Weſt-ſide*, in which abundance of Sea *Cormorants* build and hatch.

ABOUT 5 Leagues to the *South-weſt* from *Tulm*, lies the Iſland *Aſcrib*, which is divided into ſeveral parts by the Sea, it is about two Miles in Compaſs, and affords very good Paſturage, all kind of Fiſh abound in the neighbouring Sea, on the *South-weſt* ſide of the Iſle *Aſcrib*, at the diſtance of two Leagues, lies the two ſmall Iſles of *Timan*, directly in the mouth of *Loch-arniſort*, they are only fit for Paſturage.

ON

ON the *Weſt-ſide* of *Vaterniſ* Promontory, within the mouth of *Loch-fallart*, lies *Iſa*, two Miles in Compaſs, being fruitful in Corn and Graſs, and is Commodious for fiſhing of Cod and Ling.

THERE are two ſmall Iſles, called *Mingoy*, on the *North-eaſt* ſide this Iſle which afford good Paſturage.

THERE is a red ſhort kind of *Dulſe*, growing in the *South-end* of the Iſle, which occaſions a pain in the Head when eaten, a property not known in any other *Dulſe* whatever.

THE two Iſles *Bnia* and *Harlas*, lies in the mouth of *Loch-Brakadil*, they are both pretty high Rocks, each of them about a Mile in Circumference, they afford good Paſturage & there are red Currants in theſe ſmall Iſles, ſuppoſed to have been carried thither at firſt by Birds.

THE *Southern* parts of *Skie*, as *Sleat*, and *Strath*, are a Month earlier with their Graſs than the *Northern* parts, and this is the reaſon that the Cattle and Sheep, &c. bring forth their Young ſooner than in the *North-ſide*.

THE days in Summer are much longer here than in the *South* of *England*, or *Scotland*, and the Nights ſhorter, which about the Summer *Sol-*
ſtice

ſtice is not above an hour and an half in length, and the further we come *South*, the contrary is is to be obſerved in Proportion.

THE Air here is commonly moiſt and Cold, this diſpoſes the Inhabitants to take a larger Doſe of Brandy, or other ſtrong Liquors, than in the *South* of *Scotland*, by which they fancy that they qualify the Moiſture of the Air; this is the Opinion of all Strangers, as well as of the Natives, ſince the one as well as the other, drinks at leaſt treble the quantity of Brandy in *Skie* and the adjacent Iſles, that they do in the more *Southern* Climate.

THE height of the Mountains contributes much to the moiſture of the Place, but more eſpecially the Mountain *Quillin*, which is the Husbandmans Almanack, for it is commonly obſerved that if the Heavens above that Mountain be clear and without Clouds in the Morning, then it is not doubted but the Weather will prove fair; & *è contra*. Tthe height of that Hill reaching to the Clouds breaks them, and and then they preſently after fall down in great Rains according as the Wind blows; thus when the Wind blows from the *South*, then all the Ground lying to the *North* of *Quillin* Hills is wet with Rains, whereas all the other three Quarters are dry.

THE

THE *South-weſt* Winds, are obſerved to carry more Rain with them than any other, and blow much higher in the moſt *Northern* point of *Skie*, than they do two Miles further *South*, for which I could perceive no viſible cauſe, unleſs it be the height of the Hill; about two Miles *South* from that point, for after we come to the *South-ſide* of it, the Wind is not perceived to be ſo high as on the *North-ſide* by half.

IT'S obſerved of the *Eaſt-wind*, that tho it blow but very gently in the Iſle of *Skie*, and on the *Weſt-ſide* of it, for the ſpace of about three or four Leagues towards the *Weſt*, yet as we advance more *Weſterly*, it is ſenſibly higher, and when we come near to the Coaſt of the more *Weſtern* Iſles of *Uiſt*, *Harries*, &c. It is obſerved to blow very freſh, tho at the ſame time it is almoſt Calm on the *Weſt-ſide* the Iſle of *Skie*, the Wind is attended with fair Weather, both in this and other *Weſtern* Iſles.

THE Sea in time of a Calm, is obſerved to have a riſing motion, before the *North-wind* blows, which it has not before the approaching of any other Wind.

THE *North-wind* is ſtill colder, and more deſtructive to Corn, Cattle, &c. than any other.

WOMEN

WOMEN obſerve that their Breaſts contract to a leſſer bulk when the Wind blows from the *North*, and that then they yield leſs Milk, than when it blows from any other Quarter; and they make the like obſervation in other Creatures that give Milk.

THEY obſerve that when the Sea yields a kind of Pleaſant and ſweet ſcent, it is a ſure preſage of fair Weather to enſue.

THE Wind in Summer blows ſtronger by Land, than by Sea, and the contrary in Winter.

IN the Summer, the Wind is ſometimes obſerved to blow from different Quarters at the ſame time, I have ſeen two Boats ſail quite contrary ways, until they came within leſs than a League of each other, and then one of them was becalm'd, and the other continu'd to ſail forward.

THE Tide of Ebb, here runs *Southerly*, and the Tide of Flood *Northerly*, where no Head Lands or Promontories are in the way to interpoſe, for in ſuch caſes the Tides are obſerved to hold a courſe quite contrary to the ordinary motion in theſe Iſles, and the oppoſite main Land: This is obſerved between the *Eaſt-ſide* of *Skie* and the oppoſite continent, where the Tide

Tide of Ebb runs *Northerly*, and the Tide of Flood *Southerly*, as far as *Killach-ſtone*, on the *South-eaſt* of *Skie*, both Tides running directly contrary to what is to be ſeen in all the *Weſtern* Iſles, and oppoſite Continent; The Natives at *Kylakin*, told me that they had ſeen three different ebbings ſucceſſively on that part of *Skie*.

THE Tide of Ebb is always greater with *North-winds*, than when it blows from any other Quarter, and the Tide of Flood is always higher with *South-winds*, than any other.

THE two chief Spring-tides are on the tenth of *September*, and on the tenth or twentieth of *March*,

THE Natives are very much diſpos'd to obſerve the influence of the Moon on humane Bodies, and for that cauſe they never dig their Peats but in the decreaſe, for they obſerve that if they are cut in the increaſe, they continue ſtill moiſt, and never burn clear, nor are they without Smoak, but the contrary is dayly obſerved of Peats cut in the increaſe.

THEY make up their earthen Dykes, in the decreaſe only, for ſuch as are made at the Increaſe are ſtill obſerved to fall.

THEY

THEY fell their Timber, and cut their Ruſhes in time of the decreaſe.

The Diſeaſes, known and not known in SKIE, *and the adjacent Iſles.*

THE *Gout*, *Corns* in the Feet, *Convulſions*, *Madneſs*, *Fits* of the Mother, *Vapours*, *Palſy*, *Lethargy*, *Rheumatiſms*, *Wens*, *Ganglions*, *Kings-evil*, *Ague Surfeits* and *Conſumptions* are not frequent, and *Barenneſs*, and *Abortion* very rare.

THE Diſeaſes that prevail here are *Feavers*, *Stitches*, *Collick*, *Head-ach*, *Megrim*, *Jaundiſe*, *Sciatica*, *Stone*, *Small-pox*, *Meaſles*, *Rickets*, *Scurvy*, *Worms*, *Fluxes*, *Tooth-ach*, *Cough* and *Squinance*.

THE ordinary Remedies us'd by the Natives, are taken from Plants, Roots, Stones, Animals, &c.

TO cure a *Pleuriſie*, the letting of Blood plentifully, is an ordinary Remedy.

WHEY in which Violets have been boyl'd, is us'd as a cooling and refreſhing Drink for ſuch as are ill of *Fevers*. When the Patient has not a ſweat duly, their Shirt is boyl'd in Water,

Water, and afterwards put on them, which cauſes a ſpeedy ſweat. When the Patient is very Coſtive, and without paſſage by Stool or Urine, or paſſes the ordinary time of ſweating in *Fevers*, two or three handfulls of the Sea plant call'd *Dulſe*, boyl'd in a little Water, and ſome freſh Butter with it, and the Infuſion drunk, procures Paſſage both ways, and ſweat ſhortly after: The *Dulſe*, growing on Stone, not that on the Sea-ware is only proper in this caſe.

TO procure Sleep after a *Feaver*, the Feet, Knees, and Ancles of the Patient are waſhed in warm Water, into which a good quantity of Chick-weed is put, and afterwards ſome of the Plant is applied warm to the Neck, and between the Shoulders, as the Patient goes to Bed.

THE tops of *Nettles*, chop'd ſmall, and mix'd with a few whites of raw Eggs, applied to the Fore-head, and Temples, by way of a Frontell, is us'd to procure Sleep.

FOXGLOVE, applied warm plaſterwiſe to the part affected; removes pains that follow after *Fevers*.

THE Sea-plant *Linarich*, is us'd to procure Sleep as is mentioned among its Vertues.

ERICA-BACCIFERA,

ERICA-BACCIFERA boyl'd a little in Water, and applied warm to the Crown of the Head and Temples, is us'd likewise as a Remedy to procure Sleep.

TO remove *Stitches*, when letting Blood does not prevail, the part affected is rubb'd with an Oyntment made of Camomile and fresh Butter: Or of Brandy with fresh Butter, and others apply a quantity of raw Scurvy-grass chop'd small.

THE *Scarlet-fever*, which appeared in this Isle, only within these two Years last, is ordinarily Cur'd by drinking now and then a glass of Brandy. If an Infant happen to be taken with it, the Nurse drinks some Brandy, which qualifies the Milk, and proves a successful Remedy.

THE Sea-plant *Dulse*, is us'd as is said above, to remove *Collicks*, and to remove that distemper and *Costiveness*, a little quantity of Fresh-butter, and some Scurvy-grass boyl'd, and eaten with its Infusion, is an usual and and effectual Remedy.

A large handful of the Sea-plant *Dulse*, growing upon Stone, being applied outwardly, as is mentioned above, against the *Iliaca Passio*, takes away the *After-birth*, with great ease and

M safety;

safety; this Remedy is to be repeated until it produce the desired effect, tho some hours may be intermitted; the fresher the *Dulse* is, the operation is the stronger, for if it is above two or three days old, little is to be expected from it in this case. This Plant seldom or never fails of success, tho the Patient had been delivered several days before; and of this I have lately seen an extraordinary instance at *Edinburgh* in *Scotland*, when the Patient was given over as dead.

DULSE, being eaten raw or boyl'd, is by dayly experience found to be an excellent *Antiscorbutick*, it is better raw in this case, and must be first wash'd in cold Water.

THE Common *Alga*, or *Sea-Ware*, is yearly us'd with success, to Manure the Fruit Trees in Sr. *Donald Mock Donalds* Orchard at *Armidill*; several affirm that if a quantity of Sea-ware be us'd about the roots of Fruit-trees, whose growth is hindred by the Sea-air, this will make them grow and produce Fruit.

HEAD-ACH, is removed by taking raw *Dulse*, and *Linarich* applied cold by way of a Plaister to the Temples. This likewise is us'd as a Remedy to remove the *Megrim*.

THE

THE *Jaundiſe* is cured by the Vulgar, as follows; the Patient being ſtript naked behind to the middle of the Back, he who acts the Surgeons part, marks the 11th Bone from the Rump on the Back, with a black ſtroak, in order to touch it, with his Tongs as mention'd already.

SCIATICA is cured by applying the Caſe with the fat of the *Carara-fowl*, to the Thigh-bone, and it muſt not be removed from thence, till the Cure is perform'd.

FLAMULA JOVIS or *Spire-wort*, being cut ſmall, and a Limpet-ſhell filled with it, and applied to the Thigh-bone, cauſes a Bliſter to riſe about the bigneſs of an Egg, which being cut, a quantity of watry matter iſſues from it, the Bliſter riſes three times, and being emptied as often, the Cure is performed; the Sea-plant *Linarich*, is applied to the Place to Cure and dry the Wound.

CROW-FOOT of the *Moor*, is more effectual for raiſing a Bliſter, and Curing the *Sciatica*, than *Flammula Jovis*, for that ſometimes fails of breaking, or raiſing the skin, but the *Crowfoot* ſeldom fails.

M 2 SEVERAL

SEVERAL of the common People have the boldneſs to venture upon the *Flammula Jovis*, inſtead of a Purge, they take a little of the infuſion and drink it in melted freſh Butter,as the propereſt Vehicle, and this preſerves the Throat from being excoriated.

FOR the Stone they drink Water-gruel without Salt: They likewiſe eat *Allium*,or wild *Garlick*, and drink the Infuſion of it boyl'd in Water, which they find effectual both ways. The Infuſion of the Sea plant *Dulſe* boyl'd, is alſo good againſt the Stone, as is likewiſe the Broth of *Wilks* and *Limpets*, and againſt the *Collick*, *Coſtiveneſs*, and *Stitches*, a quantity of Scurvy-graſs boyl'd in Water with ſome freſh Butter added and eaten for ſome days, is an effectual Remedy.

TO kill Worms, the Infuſion of Tanſy in Whey, or *Aqua vitæ*, taken faſting, is an ordinary Medicine with the *Iſlanders*.

CARYOPHYLATA Alpina Chamedreos fol. It grows on Marble in divers Parts, about *Chriſt-Church* in *Strath*: Never obſerved before in *Britain*, and but once in *Ireland*, by Mr. *Hiaton*. *Moriſons* Hiſt. Ray *Synopſis* 137.

Carmel,alias *Knaphard*,by Mr. *James Sutherland*, call'd *Argatilis Sylvaticus*, it has a blew Flower

Flower in *July*, the Plant it self is not us'd, but the Root is eaten to expel Wind, and they say it prevents Drunkenness, by frequent chewing of it, and being so us'd gives a good relish to all Liquors, Milk only excepted; it is *Aromatick*, and the Natives prefer it to Spice, for brewing *aqua vitæ*, the Root will keep for many Years; some say that it is Cordial, and allays Hunger.

SHUNNIS is a Plant highly valued by the Natives who eat it raw, and also boyl'd with Fish, Flesh, and Milk, it is us'd as a Sovereign Remedy to cure the Sheep of the Cough, the Root eaten fasting expels Wind, it was not known in *Britain*, except in the *North-west* Isles, and some parts of the opposite Continent, Mr. *James Sutherland* sent it to *France* some Years ago.

A quantity of wild Sage chewed between ones Teeth, and put into the Ears of Cows or Sheep that become Blind, they are thereby Cured, and their Sight perfectly restored; of which there are many fresh Instances both in *Skie* and *Harries*, by Persons of great Integrity.

A quantity of wild Sage chop'd small and eaten by Horses mixed with their Corn kills Worms, the Horse must not drink for 10 hours after eating it.

M 3 THE

THE Infusion of wild Sage after the same manner produces the like effect.

WILD Sage cut small, and mix'd among Oats given to a Horse fasting, and kept without Drink for seven or eight hours after, kills Worms.

FLUXES are Cur'd by taking now and then a spoonful of the Syrup of blew Berries that grow on the *Mertillus*.

PLANTAIN boyl'd in Water, and the *Hectic stone* heated Red-hot quenched in the same, is succesfsfully us'd for *Fluxes*.

Some cure the *Tooth-ach*, by applying a little of the *Flammula Jovis* in a *Limpet* shell, to the Temples.

A Green Turf heated among Embers, as hot as can be endured and by the Patient applied to the side of the Head affected, is likewise us'd for the Tooth-ach.

FOR *Coughs* and *Colds*, Water-gruel with a little Butter is the ordinary Cure.

FOR *Coughs* and *Hoarsness*, they use to bath the Feet in warm Water, for the space of a quarter of an hour at least; and then rub a little quantity

quantity of Deers greaſe (the older the better) to the ſoles of their Feet by the Fire, the Deers greaſe alone is ſufficient in the Morning, and this method muſt be continued until the Cure is perform'd, and it may be us'd by Young or Old, except Women with Child, for the firſt four Months, and ſuch as are troubled with Vapours.

HARTS-TONGUE and *Maiden-hair*, boyl'd in Wort, and the Ale drunk, is us'd for *Coughs* and *Conſumptions*.

MILK or Water wherein the *Hectic-ſtone* hath been boyl'd or quench'd Red-hot, and being taken for ordinary Drink, is alſo efficacious againſt a *Conſumption*.

THE Hands and Feet often waſhed in Water, in which the *Hectic-ſtone* has been boyl'd is eſteemed Reſtorative.

YARROW with the *Hectic-ſtone* boyl'd in Milk, and frequently drunk, is us'd for *Conſumptions*.

WATER-GRUEL is alſo found by experience to be good for *Conſumptions*, it purifies the Blood and procures Appetite, when Drunk without Salt.

M 4 THERE

THERE is a Smith in the Pariſh of *Kilmartin*, who is reckoned a Doctor for Curing faintneſs of the Spirits. This he performs in the following manner.

THE Patient being laid on the Anvil with his Face uppermoſt, the Smith takes a big Hammer in both his hands, and making his Face all Grimace, he approaches his Patient, and then drawing his Hammer from the Ground, as if he deſign'd to hit him with his full Strength on the Forehead, he ends in a Faint, elſe he would be ſure to Cure the Patient of all Diſeaſes; but the Smith being accuſtomed with the performance has a dexterity of Managing his Hammer with Deſcretion; tho at the ſame time he muſt do it ſo as to ſtrike Terror in the Patient, and this they ſay has always the deſign'd effect.

THE Smith is Famous for his Pedegree, for it has been obſerved of a long time, that there has been but one only Child born in the Family, and that always a Son, and when he arrived to Man's eſtate, the Father died preſently after; the preſent Smith makes up the thirteenth Generation of that Race of People who are bred to be Smiths, and all of them pretend to this Cure.

ILICA

ILICA PASSIO, or *Twiſting of the Guts*, has been ſeveral times Cured by drinking a draught of cold Water, with a little Oatmeal in it, and then hanging the Patient by the heels for ſome time. The laſt Inſtance in *Skie* was by *John Moriſon*, in the Village of *Taliſker*, who by this Remedy alone Cur'd a Boy of fourteen years of age. Dr. *Pitcairn* told me that the like Cure had been perform'd in the Shire of *Fife* for the ſame Diſeaſe. A *Cataplaſm* of hot *Dulſe*, with its juice, applied ſeveral times to the lower part of the Belly, Cured the *Illiac Paſſion*.

FOR a *Fracture*, the firſt thing they apply to a broken Bone, is the white of an Egg, and ſome Barley Meal; and then they tie Splinters round it, and keep it ſo tied for ſome days. When the Splinters are untied, they make uſe of the following Ointment, *viz.* a like quantity of *Betonica Pauli*, *St. John's Wort*, *Golden-Rod*, all cut and bruis'd in Sheeps-greaſe, or Freſh Butter, to a conſiſtence, ſome of this they ſpread on a Cloath, and lay on the Wound, which continues untied for a few days.

GIBEN of *St. Kilda*, i. e. the Fat of Sea Fowls made into a Pudding in the Stomach of the Fowl, is alſo an approved Vulnerary for Man or Beaſt.

THE

THE Vulgar make Purges of the Infuſion of *Scurvygraſs*, and ſome Freſh Butter; and this they continue to take for the ſpace of a Week or two, becauſe it is mild in its operation.

THEY uſe the Infuſion of the Sea-plant *Dulſe* after the ſame manner, inſtead of a Purge.

EYES that are Blood-ſhot, or become blind for ſome days, are Cur'd here by applying ſome blades of the Plant *Fern*, and the yellow is by them reckon'd beſt; this they mix with the white of an Egg, and lay it on ſome coarſe Flax——and the Egg next to the Face and Brows, and the Patient is order'd to lie on his back.

TO Ripen a *Tumor*, or *Boil*, they cut Female *Jacobea* ſmall, mix it with ſome freſh Butter on a hot ſtone, and apply it warm, and this ripens and draws the *Tumor* quickly, and without pain; the ſame Remedy is us'd for Womens Breaſts that are hard, or ſwell'd.

FOR taking the *Syroms* out of the hands, they uſe aſhes of burnt *Sea-ware*, mix'd with Salt water, and waſhing their hands in it, without drying them, it kills the Worms.

BURNT Aſhes of *Sea-ware* preſerves Cheeſe inſtead of Salt, which is frequently practis'd in in this Isle. Ashes of burnt *Sea-ware* scowers Flaxen Thread better, and makes it whiter than any thing else.

WHEN their Feet are swell'd and benum'd with Cold, they scarifie their Heels with a Lancet.

THEY make Glisters of the Plant *Mercury*, and some of the Vulgar use it as a Purge, for which it serves both ways.

THEY make Glisters also of the Roots of Flags, Water, and salt Butter.

THEY have found out a strange Remedy for such as could never ease Nature at Sea by Stool, or Urine; there were three such Men in the Parish of St. *Maries* in *Trotternefs*, two of them I knew, to wit, *John Mack Phade*, and *Finlay Mack Phade*, they liv'd on the Coast, and went often a Fishing, and after they had spent some nine or ten hours at Sea, their Bellies would swell; for after all their endeavours to get passage either ways, it was impracticable untill they came to Land, and then they found no difficulty in the thing. This was a great inconvenience to any Boats-Crew in which either of these three Men had been Fishing, for it oblig'd them often to forbear when the Fishing was most plentiful, and to Row to the shoar with any of these Men that happened to become

become Sick, for Landing was the only Remedy. At length one of their Companions thought of an Experiment to remove this inconvenience; he consider'd that when any of these Men had got their feet on dry ground, they could then ease Nature with as much freedom as any other Person; and therefore he carried a large green Turff of Earth to the Boat, and placed the green side uppermost, without telling the reason. One of these Men who was subject to the Infirmity above-mention'd, perceiving an Earthen Turff in the Boat, was surpriz'd at the sight of it, and enquir'd for what purpose it was brought thither? He that laid it there answer'd, that he had done it to serve him, and that when he was dispos'd to ease Nature, he might find himself on Land, tho' he was at Sea. The other took this as an Affront, so that from words, they came to blows; their fellows with much ado did separate them, and blam'd him that brought the Turff into the Boat, since such a Fancy could produce no other effect than a Quarrel. All of them employ'd their time eagerly in Fishing, untill some hours after, that the angry Man who before was so much affronted at the Turff, was so ill of the Swelling of his Belly as usual, that he begg'd of the Crew to row to the Shoar, but this was very disobliging to them all; he that intended to try the Experiment with the Turff, bid the Sick Man stand on it, and he might expect to have success by it; but

but he refus'd, and ſtill reſented the affront which he thought was intended upon him; but at laſt all the Boats Crew urg'd him to try what the Turff might produce, ſince it could not make him worſe than he was. The Man being in great pain, was by their repeated Importunities prevail'd upon to ſtand with his Feet on the Turff, and it had the wiſhed effect, for Nature became obedient both ways, and then the angry Man changed his note, for he thanked his Doctor, whom he had ſome hours before beat; and from that time none of theſe three Men ever went to Sea without a green Turff in their Boat, which prov'd effectual. This is matter of Fact ſufficiently known and atteſted by the better part of the Pariſhioners ſtill living upon the Place.

THE ancient way the Iſlanders us'd to procure Sweat was thus; a part of an Earthen Floor was cover'd withFire,and when it was ſufficiently heated, the Fire was taken away, and the ground cover'd with a heap of Straw, upon this Straw a quantity of Water was poured, and thePatient lying on the Straw,the heat of it put his whole Body into a ſweat.

TO cauſe any particular part of the Body to Sweat, they dig an hole in an Earthen Floor, and fill it with Hazel Sticks, and dry Ruſhes; above theſe they put a Hectick Stone red hot, and pouring ſome water into the hole, the Patient

tient holds the part affected over it, and this procures a ſpeedy Sweat.

THEIR common way of procuring Sweat, is by drinking a large draught of Water-gruel, with ſome Butter, as they go to Bed.

Of the various effects of Fiſhes on ſeveral Conſtitutions in theſe Iſlands.

DONGAL-MACK-EWAN became Feveriſh always after eating Fiſh of any kind, except *Thornback*, and *Dog-Fiſh.*

A *Ling-Fiſh* having brown ſpots on the Skin, cauſes ſuch as eat of its Liver, to caſt their Skin from head to foot. This happened to three Children in the Hamlet *Taliskir*, after eating the Liver of a brown ſpotted *Ling*.

FINLAY ROSS, and his Family, in the Pariſh of *Uge*, having eat a freſh *Ling-Fiſh*, with brown ſpots on its Skin, he and they became indiſpoſed and Feveriſh for ſome few days, and in a little time after they were bliſter'd all over. They ſay that when the freſh *Ling* is ſalted a few days, it has no ſuch effect.
THERE

THERE was a Horfe in the Village *Bretill*, which had the Erection backward, contrary to all other of its kind.

A Weaver in *Portrie* has a Faculty of erecting and letting fall his Ears at pleafure, and opens and fhuts his mouth on fuch occafions.

A Boy in the Caftle of *Duntulm*, called *Mifter* to a By-Name, hath a Pain and Swelling in his great Toe at every Change of the Moon, and it continues only for the fpace of one day, or two at moft.

ALLEN-MAC-LEOD being about ten years of age, was taken ill of a Pain which moved from one part of his Body to another, and where it was felt the Skin appeared blue; it came to his Toe, Thigh, Tefticles, Arms and Head, when the Boy was bath'd in warm water he found moft eafe; the hinder part of his Head which was laft affected, had a little fwelling, and a Woman endeavouring to fqueeze the Humour out of it, by bruifing it on each fide with her Nails, fhe forc'd out at the fame time a little Animal near an inch in length, having a white Head fharp pointed, the reft of its Body of a red colour, and full of fmall feet on each fide; Animals of this fort have been feen in the Head and Legs of feveral

feveral Perfons in the Ifles, and is diftinguifh'd by the name of *Fillan*.

Yeft how preferv'd by the Natives.

A ROD of Oak of four, five, fix or eight inches about, twifted round like a Wyth, boil'd in Wort, well dried and kept in a little bundle of Barley Straw, and being fteep'd again in Wort, caufeth it to ferment, and procures *Yeft*; the Rod is cut before the middle of *May*, and is frequently us'd to furnifh *Yeft*, and being preferved and us'd in this manner, it ferves for many years together. I have feen the Experiment tried, and was fhew'd a piece of a thick Wyth which hath been preferved for making Ale with, for above twenty or thirty years.

The

The Effects of eating Hemlock-Root.

FERGUS KAIRD an Emperick, living in the Village *Talisker*, having by a miſtake eaten a *Hemlock-Root*, inſtead of the White Wild Carrot; his Eyes did preſently roll about, his Countenance became very pale, his Sight had almoſt fail'd him, the Frame of his Body was all in a ſtrange Convulſion, and his *Pudenda* retir'd ſo inwardly, that there was no diſcerning whether he had then been Male, or Female. All the Remedy given him in this State was a draught of hot Milk, and a little *Aqua-Vitæ* added to it, which he no ſooner drank, but he Vomited preſently after, yet the Root ſtill remain'd in his Stomach. They continu'd to adminiſter the ſame Remedy for the ſpace of four or five hours together, but in vain, and about an hour after they ceas'd to give him any thing, he voided the Root by Stool, and then was reſtor'd to his former ſtate of health; he is ſtill living, for any thing I know, and is of a ſtrong healthful Conſtitution.

SOME few years ago, all the Flax in the Barrony of *Troterneſs* was over-run with a great quantity of Green Worms, which in a few days would have deſtroy'd it, had not a Flock of Ravens made a Tour round the

N ground

ground where the Flax grew, for the ſpace of fourteen Miles, and eat up the Worms in a very ſhort time.

THE Inhabitants of this Iſle are generally well proportion'd, and their Complection is for the moſt part black. They are not oblig'd to Art in forming their Bodies, for Nature never fails to act her part bountifully to them; and perhaps there is no part of the habitable Globe where ſo few Bodily Imperfections are to be ſeen, nor any Children that go more early. I have obſerv'd ſeveral of them walk alone before they were ten Months old; they are bath'd all over every Morning and Evening, ſome in cold, ſome in warm water; but the latter is moſt commonly us'd, and they wear nothing ſtrait about them. The Mother generally ſuckles the Child, failing of which, a Nurſe is provided, for they ſeldom bring up any by hand; they give New-born Infants freſh Butter to take away the *Miconium*, and this they do for ſeveral days; they taſte neither Sugar, nor Cinamon, nor have they any daily allowance of Sack beſtowed on them, as the Cuſtom is elſewhere, nor is the Nurſe allowed to taſte Ale.

THE Generality wear neither Shooes or Stockings before they are ſeven, eight or ten years old, and many among them wear no Night-Caps before they are ſixteen years old, and

and upwards; fome ufe none all their life time, and thefe are not fo liable to Headaches, as others who keep their Heads warm.

THEY ufe nothing by way of prevention of Sicknefs, obferving it as a Rule to do little or nothing of that nature. The abftreniouf-nefs of the Mothers is no fmall advantage to the Children; they are a very prolifick People, fo that many of their numerous Iffue muft feek their Fortune on the Continent, and not a few in Foreign Countries, for want of Imployment at home. When they are any way Fatigu'd by Travel, or otherways, they fail not to bath their Feet in warm water, wherein red Mofs has been boil'd, and rub them with it going to bed.

THE ancient Cuftom of rubbing the Body by a warm hand oppofite to the fire, is now laid afide, except from the lower part of the Thigh, downwards to the Ankle; this they rub before and behind, in cold weather, and at going to bed. Their fimple Diet contributes much to their Sate of Health, and long Life; feveral among them of my Acquaintance arriv'd at the Age of Eighty, Ninety, and upwards; but the Lady *Mack Leod* liv'd to the Age of one hundred and three years; fhe had then a comely head of hair, and a cafe of good teeth, and always enjoy'd the free ufe of her underftanding, untill the Week in which fhe died.

N 2 THE

THE Inhabitants of this and all the Weftern Ifles, do wear their Shooes after Mr. *Lock's* mode, in his Book of Education; and among other great advantages by it, they reckon thefe two: That they are never troubled with the Gout, or Corns in their Feet.

THEY lie for the moft part on Beds of Straw, and fome on Beds of Heath; which latter being made after their way, with the tops uppermoft, are almoft as foft as a Feather-bed, it yields a pleafant fcent after lying on it once. The Natives by experience have found it to be effectual for drying fuperfluous Humours, and ftrengthning the Nerves. It is very refrefhing after a Fatigue of any kind. The *Picts* are faid to have had an Art of Brewing curious Ale with the tops of Heath, but they refus'd to communicate it to the *Scots*, and fo 'tis quite loft.

A Native of this Ifle requires treble the Dofe of Phyfick that will ferve one living in the South of *Scotland* for a Purge; yet an Iflander is eafier Purged in the South, than at home. Thofe of the beft Rank are eafier wrought on by Purging Medicines, than the Vulgar.

THE Inhabitants are of all People eafieft Cured of green Wounds; they are not fo liable to

Weſtern Iſlands *of* Scotland, *&c.* 197

to Fevers as others on ſuch Occaſions; and therefore they never cut off Arm, or Leg, tho never ſo ill broke, and take the freedom to venture on all kind of Meat and Drink, contrary to all Rule in ſuch caſes, and yet commonly recover of their Wounds.

MANY of the Natives upon occaſion of ſickneſs, are diſpoſed to try Experiments, in which they ſucceed ſo well, that I could not hear of the leaſt inconvenience attending their Practice. I ſhall only bring one Inſtance more of this, and that is of the illiterate Emperick *Neil Beaton* in *Skie*; who of late is ſo well known in the Iſles and Continent, for his great ſucceſs in curing ſeveral dangerous Diſtempers, tho he never appeared in the quality of a *Phyſician* until he arrived at the age of Forty Years, and then alſo without the advantage of Education: He pretends to judge of the various qualities of Plants, and Roots, by their different Taſtes, he has likewiſe a Nice Obſervation of the Colours of their Flowers, from which he learns their Aſtingent and Looſening qualities; he extracts the Juice of Plants and Roots, after a Chymical way, peculiar to himſelf, and with little or no charge.

HE conſiders his Patients conſtitution before any Medicine is adminiſtred to them; and he has form'd ſuch a Syſtem for curing Diſeaſes, as ſerves for a Rule to him upon all Occaſions of this Nature.

N 3 HE

198 *A* Deſcription *of the*

HE treats *Riverius's*, *Lilium Medicinæ*, and ſome other Practical Pieces that he has heard of with Contempt, ſince in ſeveral Inſtances it appears that their Method of Curing has fail'd, where his had good Succeſs.

SOME of the Diſeaſes Cured by him are as follows. Running Sores in Legs and Arms, grievous Head-aches; he had the boldneſs to cut a piece out of a Womans Skull broader than half a Crown, and by this reſtored her to perfect Health. A Gentlewoman of my Acquaintance having contracted a dangerous Pain in her Belly, ſome days after her being delivered of a Child, and ſeveral Medicines were us'd ſhe was thought paſt recovery, if ſhe continued in that Condition a few hours longer; at laſt this Doctor happen'd to come there, and being imploy'd, apply'd a Simple Plant to the part affected, and reſtored the Patient in a quarter of an hour after the Application.

One of his Patients told me that he ſent him a Cap interlined with ſome Seeds, *&c.* to wear for the Cough, which it remov'd in a little time, and it had the like effect upon his Brother.

THE Succeſs attending this Mans Cures were ſo extraordinary, that ſeveral People thought his Performances to have proceeded rather

rather from a Compact with the Devil, than from the Vertue of Simples. To obviate this Mr. *Beaton* pretends to have had ſome Education from his Father, tho he died when he himſelf was but a Boy. I have diſcours'd him ſeriouſly at different times, and am fully ſatisfied, that he uſes no unlawful means for obtaining his end.

HIS diſcourſe of the ſeveral Conſtitutions, the qualities of Plants, *&c.* were more ſolid than could be expected from one of his Education. Several Sick People from remote Iſles came to him, and ſome from the Shire of *Roſs*, at 70 Miles diſtance, ſent for his Advice, I left him very ſucceſsful, but can give no further Account of him ſince that time.

THEY are generally a very Sagacious People, quick of Apprehenſion, and even the Vulgar exceed all thoſe of their Rank, and Education, I ever yet ſaw in any other Country. They have a great Genius for Muſick and Mechanicks. I have obſerved ſeveral of their Children, that before they could ſpeak, were capable to diſtinguiſh and make choice of one Tune before another upon the Violin, for they appear'd always uneaſie until the Tune which they fancied beſt was play'd, and then they expreſs'd their ſatisfaction by the motions of their Head and Hands.

N 4 THERE

THERE are ſeveral of 'em, who Invent Tunes very taking in the *South* of *Scotland*, and elſewhere; ſome Muſitians have endeavoured to paſs for firſt Inventers of them by changing their Name, but this has been Impracticable, for whatever Language gives the Modern Name, the Tune ſtill continues to ſpeak its true Original, and of this I have been ſhew'd ſeveral Inſtances.

SOME of the Natives are very dextrous in engraving Trees, Birds, Deer, Dogs, *&c.* upon Bone, and Horn, or Wood, without any other Tool than a ſharp pointed Knife.

SEVERAL of both Sexes have a quick Vein of Poeſie, and in their Language (which is very Emphatick) they compoſe Rhyme and Verſe, both which powerfuly affect the Fancy. And in my Judgment (which is not ſingular in this matter) with as great force as that of any Ancient or Modern Poet I ever yet read. They have generally very retentive Memories, they ſee things at a great diſtance. The unhappineſs of their Education, and their want of Converſe with Foreign Nations, deprives them of the opportunity to Cultivate and Beautify their Genius, which ſeems to have been form'd by Nature for great Attainments. And on the other hand, their Retireneſs may be rather thought an advantage, at leaſt to their better part; according to that of the Hiſtorian.

Plus

Plus valuit apud hos Ignorantia Vitiorum, quam apud Grecos omnia precepta in Philosophorum. The Ignorance of Vices is more powerful among those, than all the Precepts of Philosophy are among the *Greeks*.

FOR they are to this day happily Ignorant of many Vices, that are practised in the Learn'd and Polite World: I could mention several, for which they have not as yet got a Name, or so much, as a Notion of them.

THE Diet generally us'd by the Natives, consists of fresh Food, for they seldom tast any that is salted, except Butter; the generality eat but little Flesh, and only Persons of distinction eat it every day, and make three Meals, for all the rest eat only two, and they eat more Boyl'd than Roasted. Their ordinary Diet is Butter, Cheese, Milk, Potatoes, Colworts, *Brochan* i. e. Oatmeal and Water boyl'd; the latter taken with some Bread is the constant Food of several Thousands of both Sexes in this and other Isles, during the Winter, and Spring; yet they undergo many Fatigues both by Sea and Land, and are very healthful. This verifies what the Poet saith. *Populis sat est Lymphaque Cerésque.* Nature is satisfied with Bread and Water.

THERE

THERE is no Place so well stored with such great quantity of good Beef and Mutton, where so little of both is consum'd by eating. They generally use no fine Sawces to entice a false Appetite, nor Brandy, or Tea for Digestion, the purest Water serves them in such Cases; this together with their ordinary Exercise, and the free Air, preserves their Bodies and Minds in a regular Frame, free from the various Convulsions that ordinarily attend Luxury. There is not one of them too Corpulent, nor too Meagre.

THE Men-servants have always double the quantity of Bread, &c. that is given to Women-Servants, at which the latter are no ways offended, in regard of the many Fatigues by Sea and Land, which the former undergo.

OON, which in English signify's Froath, is a Dish us'd by several of the *Islanders*, and some on the opposite Main-land, in time of scarcity, when they want Bread, it is made in the following manner. A quantity of Milk, or Whey is boyl'd in a Pot, and then it is wrought up to the mouth of the Pot with a long Stick of Wood, having a Cross at the lower-end; it is turn'd about like the Stick for making Chocolat, and being thus made it is supp'd with Spoons; it is made up five or six times, in the same manner, and the last is always reckon'd best, and

and the first two or three froathings the worst; the Milk or Whey that is in the bottom of the Pot is reckon'd much better in all respects than simple Milk. It may be thought that such as feed after this rate, are not fit for action of any kind, but I have seen several that liv'd upon this sort of Food, made of Whey only, for some Months together, and yet they were able to undergo the ordinary Fatigue of their Imployments, whether by Sea or Land, and I have seen them travel to the tops of high Mountains, as briskly as any I ever saw.

SOME who live plentifully, make this Dish as above said of Goats Milk, which is said to be nourishing; the Milk is thickned and taste much better after so much working; some add a little Butter and Nutmeg to it. I was treated with this Dish in several Places, and being ask'd whether this said Dish or Chocolat was best, I told them that if we judged by the Effects, this Dish was preferable to Chocolat, for such as drink often of the former, enjoy a better state of Health, than those who use the latter.

Graddan

Graddan.

THE ancient way of dressing Corn, which is yet us'd in several Isles, is call'd *Graddan*, from the Irish word *Grad*; which signifies quick. A Woman sitting down, takes a handful of Corn, holding it by the Stalks in her left hand, and then sets fire to the Ears, which are presently in a flame; she has a Stick in her right hand, which she manages very dextrously, beating off the Grain at the very Instant, when the Husk is quite burnt, for if she miss of that, she must use the Kiln, but Experience has taught them this Art to perfection. The Corn may be so dressed, winowed ground, and backed, within an Hour after reaping from the Ground. The Oat-bread dressed as above is loosening, and that dress'd in the Kiln, Astringent, and of greater strength for Labourers: But they love the *Graddan*, as being more agreeable to their taste. This barbarous Custom is much laid aside, since the Number of their Mills encreas'd; Captain *Fairweather*, Master of an English Vessel, having dropt Anchor at *Bernera* of *Glenelg* over against *Skie*, saw two Women at this Imployment, and wondring to see so much Flame and Smoak, he came near, and finding that it was Corn they burnt, he run away in great hast, telling the Natives that he he had ſeen two Mad-women very buſie burning Corn; the People came to ſee what the matter was, and laugh'd at the Captain's Miſtake, tho' he was not a little ſurpriz'd at the ſtrangeneſs of a Cuſtom that he had never ſeen or heard of before.

THERE are two Fairs of late held yearly at *Portry* on the Eaſt ſide of *Skie*: the Convenience of the Harbour which is in the middle of the Iſle, made 'em chuſe this for the fitteſt Place. The firſt holds about the middle of *June*, the ſecond about the beginning of *September*. The various Products of this and the adjacent Iſles and Continent, are Sold here: *viz.* Horſes, Cows, Sheep, Goats, Hides, Skins, Butter, Cheeſe, Fiſh, Wooll, &c.

ALL the Horſes and Cows Sold at the Fair, ſwim to the Main Land over one of the Ferries or Sounds called *Kyles*, one of which is on the Eaſt, the other on the South ſide of *Skie*. That on the Eaſt is about a Mile broad, and the other on the South is half a Mile: They begin when it is near Low Water, and faſten a twiſted *Wyth* about the lower Jaw of each Cow, the other end of the *Wyth* is faſtned to another Cows Tail, and the number ſo tied together is commonly five. A Boat with four Oars rows off, and a Man ſitting in the Stern, holds the *Wyth* in his hand to keep up the foremoſt Cows head, and thus all the five

five Cows ſwim as faſt as the Boat rows; and in this manner above an hundred may be Ferried over in one day. Theſe Cows are ſometimes drove above 400 Miles further South; they ſoon grow Fat, and prove ſweet and tender Beef.

Their Habit.

THE firſt Habit wore by Perſons of Diſtinction in the Iſlands, was the *Leni-Croich*, from the *Iriſh* word *Leni*, which ſignifies a Shirt, and *Croch* Saffron, becauſe their Shirt was died with that Herb: the ordinary number of Ells us'd to make this Robe was twenty four; it was the upper Garb, reaching below the knees, and was tied with a Belt round the middle; but the Iſlanders have laid it aſide about a hundred years ago.

THEY now generally uſe Coat, Waſtcoat, and Breeches, as elſewhere, and on their Heads wear Bonnets made of thick Cloth, ſome blew, ſome black, and ſome gray.

MANY of the People wear *Trowis*, ſome have them very fine Woven like Stockings of thoſe made of Cloath; ſome are colour'd, and

and others ſtriped; the latter are as well ſhap'd as the former, lying cloſe to the Body from the middle downwards, and tied round with a Belt above the Haunches. There is a ſquare piece of Cloth which hangs down before. The meaſure for ſhaping the *Trowis* is a Stick of Wood whoſe length is a Cubit, and that divided into the length of a finger, and half a finger; ſo that it requires more skill to make it, than the ordinary Habit.

THE Shooes anciently wore, was a piece of the Hide of a Deer, Cow, or Horſe, with the Hair on, being tied behind and before with a Point of Leather. The Generality now wear Shooes having one thin Sole only, and ſhaped after the right and left Foot; ſo that what is for one Foot, will not ſerve the other.

BUT Perſons of Diſtinction wear the Garb in Faſhion in the South of *Scotland*.

THE *Plad* wore only by the Men, is made of fine Wool, the Thread as fine as can be made of that kind; it conſiſts of divers Colours, and there is a great deal of ingenuity requir'd in ſorting the Colours, ſo as to be agreeable to the niceſt Fancy. For this reaſon the Women are at great pains, firſt to give an exact Pattern of the *Plade* upon a piece of Wood, having the number of every thread of the

the ſtripe on it. The length of it is commonly ſeven double Ells; the one end hangs by the middle over the left Arm, the other going round the Body, hangs by the end over the left Arm alſo. The right hand above it is to be at liberty to do any thing upon occaſion. Every I[illegible]e differs from each other in their Fancy of making *Plaids*, as to the Stripes in Breadth, and Colours. This Humour is as different thro' the main Land of the *Highlands*, inſofar that they who have ſeen thoſe Places, is able at the firſt view of a Man's *Plaid*, to gueſs the place of his Reſidence.

WHEN they Travel on Foot, the *Plaid* is tied on the breaſt with a Bodkin of Bone or Wood, (juſt as the *Spina* wore by the *Germans*, according to the deſcription of *C. Tacitus*;) the *Plaid* is tied round the middle with a Leather Belt; it is pleated from the Belt to the Knee very nicely; this Dreſs for Footmen is found much eaſier and lighter than *Breeches*, or *Trowis*.

THE ancient Dreſs wore by the Women, and which is yet wore by ſome of the Vulgar, called *Ariſad*, is a white *Plade*, having a few ſmall Stripes of black, blew, and red; it reached from the Neck to the Heels, and was tied before on the Breaſt with a Buckle of Silver, or Braſs, according to the Quality of the Perſon. I have ſeen ſome of the former of of an hundred Marks value; it was broad as any ordinary Pewter Plate, the whole curiouſly engraven with various Animals, &c. There was a leſſer Buckle which was wore in the middle of the larger, and above two Ounces weight; it had in the Center a large piece of Chryſtal, or ſome finer Stone, and this was ſet all round with ſeveral finer Stones of a leſſer ſize.

THE *Plad* being pleated all round, was tied with a Belt below the Breaſt; the Belt was of Leather, and ſeveral pieces of Silver intermix'd with the Leather like a Chain. The lower end of the Belt has a piece of Plate about eight inches long, and three in breadth, curiouſly engraven; the end of which was adorned with fine Stones, or pieces of Red Corral. They wore Sleeves of Scarlet Cloth, clos'd at the end as Mens Veſts, with gold Lace round 'em, having Plate Buttons ſet with fine Stones. The Head dreſs was a fine *Kerchief* of Linen ſtrait about the Head, hanging down the back taper-wiſe; a large Lock of Hair hangs down their Cheeks above their Breaſt, the lower end tied with a knot of Ribbands.

THE Iſlanders have a great reſpect for their Chief and Head of Tribes, and they conclude Grace after every Meal, with a Petition to God for their Welfare and Proſperity. Neither

O

will they, as far as in them lies, ſuffer them to ſink under any Misfortune: But in caſe of a decay of Eſtate, make a voluntary Contribution on their behalf, as a common Duty, to ſupport the Credit of their Families.

Way of Fighting.

THE Ancient way of Fighting was by ſet Battles, and for Arms ſome had broad two handed Swords, and Head-pieces, and others Bows and Arrows. When all their Arrows were ſpent, they attack'd one another with Sword in hand. Since the Invention of Guns, they aere very early accuſtomed to uſe them, and carry their Pieces with them wherever they go: They likewiſe learn to handle the broad Sword, and Target. The *Chief* of each Tribe advances with his Followers within ſhot of the Enemy, having firſt laid aſide their upper Garments; and after one General diſcharge, they attack them with Sword in hand, having their Target on their left hand, (as they did at *Kelicranky*) which ſoon brings the Matter to an Iſſue, and verifies the Obſervation made of 'em by our Hiſtorians,

Aut mors cito, aut victoria læta.

THIS

THIS Isle is divided into three Parts, which are possess'd by different Proprietors. The Southern part call'd *Slait*, is the Property and Title of Sir *Donald Mack Donald*, Knight and Baronet; his Family is always distinguish'd from all the Tribes of his Name, by the *Irish* as well as *English*, and call'd *Mack Donald* absolutely, and by way of Excellence; he being reckoned by *Genealogists*, and all others, the first for Antiquity among all the Ancient Tribes, both in the Isles and Continent. He is Lineally descended from *Sommerled*, who according to *Buchannan*, was *Thane* of *Argyle*; he got the Isles into his Possession by Vertue of his Wifes Right; his Son was called *Donald*, and from him all the Families of the Name *Mack Donald* are descended. He was the first of that Name, who had the Title of King of the Isles. One of that Name Subscribing a Charter granted by the King of *Scots* to the Family of *Roxburgh*, writes as follows: *Donald King of the Isles Witness*. He would not pay Homage to the King for the Isles, but only for the Lands which he held of him on the Continent.

ONE of *Donald*'s Successors Married a Daughter of King *Robert* the 2d, the first of the Name of *Stuart*, by whom he acquired several Lands in the Highlands. The Earldom of *Ross* came to this Family, by Marrying the

O 2

the Heiress of the House of *Lesly*. One of the Earls of *Ross* called *John*, being of an easie Temper, and too liberal to the Church, and to his Vassals and Friends, his Son *Æneas*, (by *Buchannan* called *Donald*) was so opposite to his Father's Conduct, that he gather'd together an Army to oblige him from giving away any more of his Estate. The Father rais'd an Army against his Son, and Fought him at Sea, on the Coast of *Mull*, the Place is since call'd the *Bloody-Bay*; the Son however had the Victory. This dispos'd the Father to go straight to the King, and make over the Right of all his Estate to him. The Son kept Possession some time after; however this occasion'd the fall of that great Family, tho' there are yet extant several ancient Tribes of the Name, both in the Isles and Continent. Thus far the Genealogist *Mack Vurich*, and *Hugh Mack Donald* in their *Manuscripts*.

THE next adjacent Part to *Slait*, and joyning it on the North side, is *Strath*; it is the Property of the Laird of *Mack Kinnon*, Head of an ancient Tribe.

ON the North West side of *Strath* lies that part of *Skie* called *Mackleod*'s Countrey, Possess'd by *Mackleod*. Genealogists say he is Lineally descended from *Leod*, Son to the

the Black *Prince of Man*; he is Head of an ancient Tribe.

THE Baronny of *Troternefs* on the North fide *Skie*, belongs to Sir *Donald Mack Donald*; the Proprietors and all the Inhabitants are Proteftants, except twelve, who are Roman-Catholicks. The former obferve the Feftivals of *Chriftmafs*, *Eafter*, *Good-Friday*, and that of St. *Michael's*. Upon the latter they have a Cavalcade in each Parifh, and feveral Families bake the Cake called St. *Michael's Bannock*.

O 3 BOOT

Tombstone effigy at Skeabost

Underground chamber near Lachsay, Trotternish

Preshal Mor above Talisker

Dun Grungaig, Strathaird

Raasay from Beinn Tianavaig

Dun Caan (Cana), Raasay

Brochil Castle, Raasay

On Fladday Chuain, Trotternish

Skye

1.The idea, or tradition, presented by Martin that 'Skie' and '*Skianach*' shared the meaning of 'winged' has long been popularly accepted though the latter is more commonly used to mean 'belonging to Skye' or 'a Skye person'. There is reference in accounts of 1706-1707 to an allowance to 'Neill Skiannich'. However it is possible that this traditional belief may only be an attempt to find an explanation for a placename so old that its original significance was lost long before the 17th century. The placenames mentioned in the Norse Magnus Barefoot's Saga include 'Skith' (Skye), but it has been pointed out that 'most of the Hebridean names in the sagas appear to be adaptations of earlier (Celtic) names, even though they give the impression of being Norse'. Martin's 'ancient Language' was Gaelic ('Irish').

The circumference of the whole island is a great deal more than 100 miles; some earlier estimates went up to 900.

[DC Section 3 29/25; Watson (1926) pp.38-40; Palsson p.22]

2.Martin's description of the 'geological' aspects of Skye involves a variety of locations and placenames.

The ferry-boat crossing to Glenelg around 1700 was in the narrows at Kylerhea, where it still is [see n.50 below]. The stream at '*Nisbost*' is that just south of Claigan (Claggan) between four and five miles north of Dunvegan Castle; it entered the sea at 'Port Nisabost'. *Borve* is four miles from Portree beside the road to Uig, and the settlements of '*Glenmore*' and Mugeary are near the head of the Glenmore river, a tributary of the Snizort river, and about three miles west of the Varragill bridge. Coirechatachan, near Broadford, was for many generations in the possession of the Mackinnons, most of them called Lachlan [see n.53 below]. It has been stated that 'Lachlan Mackinnon was possessor of Corriechatachin in 1700' and that he was married to Margaret, daughter of John Macrae, Episcopalian minister in Dingwall. From what he says about the experiment with marle Martin must have met Lachlan more than once. A report of 1799 by David Wilson on minerals discovered on the MacDonald estate in Skye refers to the Strath district: 'The fine Marle and Marble in this parish I reckon out of my department as Mr Blackadder paid particular attention to them and I am sensible he is much better qualified than I am to give you a proper account of their Quality.'

[Thomson; Cameron p.80; MA GD221/4441/1(3)]

3. Marcasites, defined as white iron pyrites, could be found according to Martin at 'Sartle', still the pronunciation of Sarthill near Balmeanach at Staffin in Trotternish. '*Loch-fallart*,' later 'Loch Follart', was the name of the sea loch now called Loch Dunvegan, shown on the Blaeu map of Skye as 'Loch Faillord'; but the identification or location of the '*Apples-glen*' has so far not been discovered. '*Quillin*' is an older version of 'Cuillin', relating to the mountain range once known as MacLeod's 'Forest' [Blaeu: 'Culluelun or Gulluin hils'; Thomson: 'Cuillen Hills']. '*Mingis*' [Blaeu: 'Mingenes'] is the Minginish region of the MacLeod estate in Skye, extending from the southern margin of Loch Bracadale to Loch Scavaig. '*Minriness*' might be the same.

[H.H. Read (edit.): Rutley's Elements of Minerology 24th Edition 1949 p.493; NSA p.323]

4.The marble, limestone and freestone of areas such as Torrin and Suisnish ('*Snisness*')[Thomson: 'Torrins', 'Suishnish'] are well known. '*Borrie*' may be Boreraig near Suishnish; and the 'Isle of Rosay' is probably Raasay (see p. 16 Errata). '*Rig*' is probably Rigg, on the east coast of Trotternish just north of the Storr. '*Lapis Ceranius*' denotes ammonite fossils, usually found in clay soils in limestone areas.

[Lamont pp.160-161, with illustration; OSA p.223; NSA pp.310-311]

5. Martin frequently mentions '(white) hectic stone', by which it is understood that he refers to quartz.

[Pennant p.304]

6. Martin also mentions 'the Scurf called *Corkir*' in his account of Gigha [Martin p.229], and a note to that island explains it as a mossy white lichen giving a crimson or scarlet dye. The lichen 'crostil' is no doubt 'crotal'('*Crottil*' in Gigha), while 'Talk' may be another, yellow kind of lichen.

[Dwelly p.253]

7. Ord is on the north side of the Sleat district. Across the hill to the coast of the Sound of Sleat is what Martin rightly calls the '*Peninsula*' of '*Oronsa*', extending out to the tidal island of Oronsay (Ornsay), this name appearing for many such islands throughout the Hebrides. Martin says it is '*alias* Island *Dierman*', the 'Eilean Iarmain' of today. Isleornsay is the name of the nearby settlement on the 'mainland' of Skye. Martin praises the anchorage beside the island, what Rev. Macpherson called in 1794 'an excellent and well-known harbour'.

[OSA p.193]

8. The description of 'the *Kyle*' relates to Kyle Rhea, known for its powerful currents. As the Kyle widens into Loch Alsh the 'big Rock' called '*Kaillach*', otherwise Sgeir na Caillich, lies just beyond Rudha na Caillich. Most of the harbours located by Martin are easily recognisable today from his account. Loch Snizort is evidently the name of what has more recently been known as Loch Snizort Beag, since on the west side of the Lynedale promontory was Loch Arnisort, now Loch Greshornish, with the 'two small isles in the mouth of the Entry' called Eilean Beag and Eilean Mor though later referred to by Martin as 'Timan'. The settlements of Arnisort and Flashader, under 2 miles north of Edinbane, confirm the locations of the lochs. Next to the west was 'Loch Fallart' [see n.3 above], and south of Loch Bracadale and Loch Harport is Loch Eynort ('*Loch-einard*'), the rock at the entrance being An Dubh-Sgeir. Loch Eishort ('*Loch- essort*') succeeds Loch Slapin in the southward direction.

9. Most of the mountains listed can be identified – *Quillin* (Cuillin), *Bein-store* (The Storr), *Bein-vore-scowe* (Marsco), *Bein-chro* (Beinn na Cro – between Loch Ainort and Loch Slapin), *Bein-nin,Kaillach* (Beinn na Caillich – there are two, that near Broadford being the more probable). 'Scornifiey' remains uncertain.

10. The village of Kilmartin was situated near the burial ground beside the Kilmartin river a mile south of the shore of Staffin Bay. In the 17th and 18th centuries it was known as 'Clachan of Kilmartin' and survives now as the Clachan part of Staffin. The settlement at '*Skerybreck*' [Thomson: 'Scoribreac'] was at the eastern edge of Portree. The 'Isle of *Altig*' [Blaeu: 'Altavick'; Thomson: 'Aultbheig'; OSA p.168 and NSA p.240: 'Aultbheig'] is now called Flodigarry Island or Eilean Flodigarry. As the 'Isle of Altivick' it was included in a tack of the 7 penny lands of Flodigarry in 1732.

[WDH Sellar & A Maclean: The Highland Clan MacNeacail (MacNicol) – A History of the Nicolsons of Scorrybreac Waternish 1999; MA GD221/4272/4]

11. There have been various descriptions of the well at '*Loch siant*', one of the more curious being that by Rev. Donald Martin of Kilmuir parish in 1790:

'In a low valley, there is a small hill, shaped like a house, and covered with small trees, or rather shrubs, of natural growth. At one side of it, there is a lake of soft water, from which there is no visible discharge. Its water finds many passages through the hill, and makes its appearance, on the other side, in a great number of springs, of the very purest kind: They all run into an oval bason below, which has a bottom of white sand, and is the habitation of many small fish. From that pond, the water runs, in a copious stream, to the sea. At the side of this rivulet, there is a bath, made of stone, and concealed from public view, by small trees surrounding it. Its name is Loch Shiant, or the sacred lake. There was once a great resort of people, afflicted with ailments, to this place. They bathed themselves, and drank of the water, though it has no mineral quality; and, on a shelf, made for the purpose, in the wall of a contiguous inclosure, they left offerings of small rags, pins, and coloured threads, to the divinity of the place.'

A rather 'superior' account was provided by Rev. Robert MacGregor, of the same parish, in 1840, which concluded with a characteristic sentence. 'These superstitions have, however, long ago ceased, and Loch Sianta, though beautiful as ever, has lost its ancient charms in this more enlightened age.'

[OSA p.175; NSA p.245]

12. The well at Uig, '*Tonbir Tellibreck*', has not been located. That which Martin saw in Kilbride, near Torrin, is Tobar na h-Annait. In his history of the parish of Srath Rev. Lamont wrote of this well: 'Tobar na h-annait was no doubt considered a holy well. It was emphatically asserted that a little fish lived in it – immortal from age to age.' Unless he had heard some local tradition he seems to have added to Martin's description, which seeks some rational explanation for the presence of the trout, a measure of exaggeration.

[Lamont p.162]

13. The rivers of Kilmartin and Ord still contain salmon. The 'black mussel' is the Freshwater Pearl Mussel and occurs in rivers in Lewis as well as in Skye and Mull (see Lewis n.15). The waterfalls of '*Holm*', '*Rig*' (Rigg) and '*Tont*' (Tote), all on the east coast of Trotternish, are given by Martin in a northward sequence. It may be therefore that the unidentified '*Sker – horen*', first in the list, was further to the south.

14. The story of the former Loch Chaluim Chille at Balgown in Kilmuir, which contained the chapel dedicated to St Columba to which Martin refers as well as the remains of a monastic settlement, was outlined in 1840:

'It was proposed to drain this sheet of water as early as the year 1715, and the work was commenced under the superintendence of Sir Donald Macdonald, who, from his great achievements, was commonly called Donull a' chogaidh, that is warlike Donald. The work was, however, relinquished in an unfinished state, owing to the disturbances occasioned in this and other parts of the kingdom by the battle of Sheriffmuir. It is said that although the draining was not then thoroughly accomplished, yet it was so to such an extent, that a considerable quantity of water escaped. The proprietor set about redraining this loch about the year 1763, and succeeded; but, from neglect in keeping the trenches in proper repair, it was allowed again to fill. The work was commenced anew in 1824, by the late Right Honourable Lord Macdonald, and after a period of five years, during which time a great number of labourers were employed, the lake was converted into arable land.'

The work was calculated to have cost around £1000 and led to the reclamation of about 230 acres 'of the finest alluvial soil imaginable', which was either cultivated or produced 'an abundant crop of natural grasses'. The main trench was, at one place, 35 feet deep, 114 feet wide at the top, and nine feet wide at the bottom.

[NSA pp.246-247, 279]

15. If '*Loch-einordstard*' is identified as the present Loch Ainort then the 'little Fresh-water Lake' would be Loch nam Madadh Uisge at the back of Luib. The 'madadh-uisge' can be a freshwater pearl mussel as well as an otter (Dwelly p.621). At the head of Loch Ainort the Blaeu map has 'Bun Skard'.

16. The largest piece of woodland, which Martin places at '*Lettir-hurr*', was probably that along the hillside to the east of Kinloch Lodge in Sleat, where later the name 'Letterfurre' occurs, and where there is now a mixture of 'natural' wood and a large modern plantation of conifers.

[Thomson]

17. In the list of lochs where herring were often taken '*Loch scowsar*' (Loch Sconsor) [Blaeu: 'Scosa'] is the Loch Sligachan of more recent times. The nearby '*Kyle* of *Scalpa*', the channel between the island of Scalpay and the opposite Skye shore at Dunan and Strollamus, is precisely the place where, in a shorter and less exact description of Skye possibly by Martin, it was possible to find 'an infinit number of Oysters'. The numerous mussels said to have been collected at '*Bernstill Village*' (Bernisdale) were presumably to be collected towards the head of Loch Snizort Beag.

[MGC Vol. II pp.220-221]

18. His writing on limpets is evidence of Martin's 'scientific' approach on behalf of the Royal Society, as are his comments on the 'pale *Wilk*' which he calls '*Gil-fiunt*'. The name is his version of 'Gille-Fionn', a large periwinkle, or 'Gille-Fiunnd', 'that species of shell-fish called *wilk*'.

[Dictionarium Scoto-Celticum Vol. II p.482; Armstrong]

19. Martin's 'Linarich' appears as 'Linnearaich' in Armstrong's Dictionary (p.355) where it is defined in terms which are clearly derived from Martin: 'A sea-green plant, often applied by the Hebrideans to the temple and forehead, to dry up the defluxions; and also to draw up the tonsils, which, among that people, are apt to swell at certain seasons.' The Enteromorpha and Ulva (sea lettuce) have both been suggested. Suggestions for 'slake' include seaweed in general, Porphyra spp., and 'laver', called in Irish 'sloke'. One reddish weed that was cooked until dissolved, eaten with bread and butter, and given to cows, was called 'slabhacan', the same as 'sloke'. Carmichael explains 'slabhacan' and gives a recipe. Dulse and tangle are both much better known.

The red coral, found for instance on beaches at Ashaig, Ord and Claigan, is probably maerl (Lithothamnion) and is live, whereas the white is the dead calcareous skeleton. Another suggestion for the coral is that it might be phymatolithon or Lithothamnion glaciale.

[Currie; the Dwelly and MacLennan dictionaries include 'slabhacan'. EUL Carmichael Watson Collection no.58A p.27]

20. The 'big Cave in the Village *Bornskittag*' is that later called 'Uamh an oir' or 'Uamh Oir', 'respecting which several traditions are afloat among the natives', in the headland of Bornaskitaig in Kilmuir. The story of the piper entering it has been told more than once. The caves at Rigg and Holm were presumably among the numerous 'caves and underground openings' which 'fantastically penetrated' the coast of that area, although it is possible that what was eventually called Prince Charlie's Cave might have been that in 'the Village *Holm*', since Martin's use of 'village' seems generally to denote the associated land as well as the houses of a settlement. The big cave in the rock east of Portree could have been that known as 'Mac Choiteir's Cave', in the face of a cliff below Torvaig. Its internal space has been altered by roof collapses. Across the mouth of Portree bay on the south side are what appear on the OS map as 'Scarf caves,' caves of cormorants, where, according to Martin, 'many Sea Cormorants do Build'. 'The Golden Cave' in Sleat could be the 'Uamh Tarskavaig' near Ord.

[NSA p.240; Mackenzie (1930) pp.73-74; Gordon (1950) p.102; Mackenzie p.10]

21. Many of the burial cairns mentioned by Martin have either disappeared or been much reduced because stones have been taken to build walls. The Inventory describes a few. Small cairns where coffins were placed when a funeral procession rested were to be found in many places and some can still be seen. The standing stone at Kilbride, Clach na h-Annait, was described in 1914 as being 7 feet 9 inches in height; that of Uig, above South Cuil, called the Clach Ard and measuring 5 feet 2 inches in length, was found lying on top of 'a stony mound resembling a denuded cairn' in the same year.

'*Skeriness*', otherwise Skerinish near Kensaleyre on the road north to Uig, is on the opposite side of the tidal Loch Eyre from the two standing stones which the Inventory names as 'Sornaichean Coir' Fhinn', in approximate English the stones of Finn's cauldron. The Inventory also noted: 'It is said that there was once a third stone here.'

[Inventory: pp.147-148 nos.491-493, p.164 nos.523-524, p.175 nos.550-552, pp.203-204 nos.631-635, p.214 no.666, pp.204-205 no.637, p.205 no.638]

22. Martin's description of the 'round forts' in Skye gives the impression that they were far from being still complete. His use of 'Dun' covers brochs, as it does in placenames.

The remains of Dun Skudiburgh, just north of Idrigil at Uig, and of duns at Skerinish near the mouth of the Haultin river where there are also sites known as Carn Liath and Buaile na Fala, are clearly located. '*Dun-Derig*' and '*Dun-David*' are represented now by Dun Dearg near Valtos on the east coast of Trotternish two or three miles south of Staffin, and, according to the Inventory, by the site of the ruined Duntulm Castle, though it is remarked that Dun David was also the name of the site of Dunvegan Castle. Both of these possible locations were obviously well-known to Martin.

The 'little Stone houses, built under Ground' are of course not always easy to find but the one near *Lachsay*, over the hill east of Peingown in Kilmuir, survives and, in spite of its location, might be the same as the 'earth house' described in the Inventory. Stobie's 'Plan of the Parish of Kilmuir and Uigg in Trotterness lying in the Isle of Sky' of 1764 describes the site: 'At A. Tytallm 'The Ruins of a Large House below ground Inhabited of old in times of War.' 'Tytallm' is 'taigh-talamh' (earth-house). According to the Inventory the 'earth-house' at Camustianavaig ('*Camstinvag*') had been 'opened up and filled some years ago'. The stone houses above ground, including those in Portree, Linicro ('*Lincro*') north of Uig, and Culnaknock ('*Culuknock*'), have probably all been plundered for stone and destroyed.

[Inventory p.177 no.568, pp.175-176 no.556; MA – Stobie Plan; Inventory p.185 no. 588]

23. As for peats and other fuels mentioned by Martin the places where peats with sparkling salt petre ('*Flodgery*' – Flodigarry) and coal (Holm, '*Heldersta*' – Halistra near Hallin, '*Mogstat*' – Monkstad) were found are all identifiable. In 1801 trials for coal and some working took place around Uig with some success.

[MA GD221/4442/1/4]

24. Covering a calf with a dead calf's skin is exactly the same as the common practice among sheep, still seen today, of covering an orphan lamb or a twin with a dead lamb's skin to enable it to suck a foster mother. It remains common today for cows, if they have the opportunity, to go to the shore to eat seaweed.

25. Capistal (Thomson: 'Capistal') was near Aird of Sleat on the road from Armadale, and James Macdonald of 'Capstill' has a place in the Macdonald family tree.

[Macdonalds Vol. III p.514]

26. For Skeriness (Skerinish) see n.21 above.

27. The term '*Corky-fyre*' is related to 'corc a' farigh', otherwise 'corc chluasach', signifying a lack of ears or slit-eared.

[Campbell & Thomson pp.56-57.]

28. Cranes were perhaps herons. The young cormorant was widely considered worth the eating until very recently. The 'Bunivochil', otherwise 'Bunabhuachaille', is the great northern diver, once thought very common in the Hebrides both as an adult and when immature. The 'sea pye' is the oystercatcher.

[Gray p.415 (Great northern diver) – see Uist n.27; for the king of otters see Campbell & Thomson pp.63-64]

29. '*Soa-Brettil*' (Munro p.68 'Soabretill') is clearly Soay, lying south of the Cuillin mountains and not far from Glen Brittle which used to be more often called Glen Brettle [see n.45 below] Martin elaborated on 'mertille' in a letter to Edward Lhuyd: 'I think the mertille is not the myrto Brabantia tho it resemble its description as to growth. It is a plant of about 6, 7, or 8 inches long, hath several smal leav's about the following size [drawing]. it hath a blue berry as big as the largest pea, every berry grows seperatly' [Emery p.111].

[Reed; DC Section 2 no.271.]

30. While no specific identification of the serpents on Skye has been made it has been suggested that Martin was describing male and female adders, and, in the case of the 'brown Serpent', the slow worm.

[Currie]

31. The other '*Inferior Isles about* Skie' are all easily identifiable; Oronsay has already been mentioned [n.7. above]; 'Ilan nan Gillin' – Eilean nan Gillen – lies north of Eilean Ban and the Skye bridge near Kyleakin; and west of the low, flat island of Pabbay, near the coast of Scalpay below Scalpay House, is '*Gilliman*', Guillamon Island on the OS map.

32. Martin's references to lime, 'good Stone', caves and so on, in Raasay are quoted in the recent book about that island without comment. It may be that the spring running down the face of a high rock is the waterfall near the southern approach

to Hallaig, but the location of the quarry is open to choice. The notion that the conspicuous hill '*Dun-Cann*' (Dun Caan, Canna) derives its name from a cousin of the King of Denmark is surpassed by the theory put forward by Matheson in exploring the history of the Morrisons.

Quotations related to Brochel Castle are given by MacLeod and the historical note in the Inventory ends a description of the structure, but perhaps the most interesting account is that provided by Alexander Campbell, schoolmaster in Portree in 1794-95. It was stated by Monro in 1549 that there were two castles in Raasay, 'the castell of Kilmaluok and the castell of Brerkdill'. Beside them were 'two fair orcheartis' and not far from the first 'ane paroche kirk callit Kilmaluok'. The nearby settlement was, and still is, known as Clachan, and it is likely that the Castle of Kilmaluag [Blaeu: 'Castel Kilmolnock'] was somewhere close to the site later occupied by Raasay House. Martin's 'pyramid' crosses, and the comments on them by Dr Johnson and James Boswell, are given by MacLeod.

[Macleod; Matheson (1977) pp.65-66; Macleod pp.235-239; Inventory p.180 no.574; OSA pp.186-187; Munro p.70; Macleod pp.31-32, 42; RMS Vol. VI (1593-1608) p.155 no.453]

33. The island of '*Fladda*', said by Martin to lie three leagues north-west of Rona, is evidently not the 'Fladda' next to Raasay but that helping to shelter Staffin Bay and now commonly called Staffin Island, with the 'Isle *Altvig*' [see n.10 above] to the north, and the rock 40 yards long to the north again being Sgeir Eirin. Martin's 'little old chapel' dedicated to St Turos is apparently otherwise unrecorded and remains unknown.

[Blaeu; Thomson]

34. Rev. Robert MacGregor, minister of Kilmuir, wrote in 1840 that the small islands lying around Trotternish were all uninhabited, were used as extensions to their grazing by the tacksmen in north Skye, and, except for 'Fladda-chuain', had nothing remarkable about them. This was to underestimate the interest of these islands. On '*Troda*', or Trodday, the chapel dedicated to St Columba was not the only point of interest. Cattle used to be put there to graze, as MacGregor remarked:

'Even so late as 1770, the dairy-maids who attended a herd of cattle in the Island of Trodda, were in the habit of pouring daily a quantity of milk on a hollow stone for the "Gruagach". Should they neglect to do so, they were sure of feeling the effects of Miss Brownie's wand next day. It is said that the Rev. Donald Macqueen, the minister of this parish, went purposely to Trodda to check that gross superstition. He might then have succeeded for a time in doing so, but it is known that many believed in the Gruagach's existence, long after that Reverend gentleman's death.'

Seton Gordon quoted Dr Johnson's remarks on this Trodda custom.

MacGregor also noted that in former times 'Fladda-chuain' was 'inhabited by a family or two, who had a considerable portion of it under cultivation'. He recorded, too, some religious associations:

'There was a fane, or temple, now in ruins, in the above-mentioned island of Fladda-chuain, supposed to have been built by the Druids, who, according to tradition, went thither once a year to worship and feast. There were nine smooth stones used by them in their religious ceremonies, each about a foot in length. They remained entire, and might still have been seen there had they not been, of late years, stolen as curiosities by some persons unknown. There were three burying-places in this small island, one of which is named to this day Cladh-Mhanaich, that is, the monks' burying-place.'

There is little remaining of the 'temple' or chapel, the blue stone is gone, and the burial grounds are difficult to detect.

[NSA pp.240, 265-266, 275-276; Gordon (1929) pp.205-209, 195-196]

35. Gordon added further information about Fladda-chuain. He said that the monk O Gorgon was buried in Cladh a' Mhanaich, and that around 1870 'there lived in Kilmaluaig a man called Domhnall O' Ghorgon...He was supposed to have been of the same family as the monk, and was the postman between Kilmaluaig and Kilmuir'. In addition, the landing place on the island was called 'Port an Teampuill, the Port of the Temple [chapel], and overlooking the old burying ground is a rock called Creag na Croise, the Rock of the Cross'. There appears to be no sign of the 5 feet high stones.

[MA GD221/4390/1 Rental of Trotternish]

36. The main isle of the group is itself Fladda, while the others include the distinctive 'Bord Cruin[n]', called by Pennant 'Bordh-mor-mhic-leod' and by Gordon 'Bord Mhic-Dhomhnaill', the latter being the more probable as the islands belonged to the Macdonalds of Sleat. In 1730-31 the tenant paid £13.6s.8d for the 'Isle of Fladachan'. It is difficult to reach the table-like top of 'Bord Cruin' as the sides almost all round are vertical cliffs, and it is interesting that Martin called it a fort.

To the south, out from the bay of Duntulm with its narrow Tulm Island, is the rock called An t-Iasgair, Martin's '*Jeskar*', the Fisherman, which is supposed to have been reduced in size when used as a target by passing battleships during the first World War.

Shallow sea water separates the four main Ascrib Islands, historically associated with Geary in Waternish and probably Monro's 'Ellan Askerin' used for 'scheling', fishing and killing seals. For the two islands of 'Timan' see n.8 above.

[Pennant II p.312; Gordon (1929.) pp.196, 187; Munro p.72]

37. The three islands of Isay, Mingay (Martin's '*Mingoy*') and Clett, the last being treated by Martin as coming under the name of 'Mingoy' also, lie south-west of Hallin on the west side of Waternish. All three played a part in the planning of fishery development at Stein and Loch Bay in the 1790s, while Dr Johnson had imagined being owner of Isay when visiting Dunvegan in 1773.

The islands of '*Buia* and *Harlas*', Wiay and Harlosh [Blaeu: 'Via moir' and 'Vya beg' ?], are among those in Loch Bracadale, Wiay being considerably larger than Harlosh Island. Close to the shore next to the bay of Gesto, near Struan, is the conspicuous little hill known as Cnoc Mhartainn [Thomson: Knock Martin] with which a tradition regarding Martin and 'a mapmaker' (John Adair) is associated.

[Pottle & Bennett pp.211-212]

38. '*Killach-stone*' appears to be another rendering of the 'big rock' called 'Kaillach' at the Skye side of Loch Alsh, otherwise called 'Sgeir na Caillich' [see n.8 above].

39. That Sir Donald Macdonald had an orchard at Armadale is more than likely though Martin seems to be the only source for its existence. However Walker's Report on the Hebrides (1764 and 1771) indicated well-established woodland in various Skye locations, including a probable orchard: 'At Armadil in Slait, an old Seat of the Mackdonald Family, there is a Garden of very good Fruit Trees, and in the Plantation around the Place, there are many Ash Trees of as vigorous a

Growth and as large a Size, as are to be seen in any Part of Scotland.'

[Mackay pp.204-205]

40. Martin (p. 180) gives, on one of only a very few occasions, some of his book sources. 'Morisons Hist.' is *Plantarum historiae universalis Oxoniensis* etc. Oxford 1680 by Robert Morison (1620-1682). The work by John Ray (1627-1705) is *Synopsis methodica stirpium Britannicarum* etc. London 1690. Both are botanical works. Mr James Sutherland was keeper of the Edinburgh Botanic Garden.

41. A discharge of 23 June 1733, relating to Talisker, was signed by John Morison, 'Chyrurgion in Sky', probably the same as Martin's John Morison in Talisker, who was perhaps a relative of Donald Morison, 'Chirurgeon in Skinadin' [Skinidin, near Dunvegan], one of a medical family. Donald's son was still in practice in 1754.

[DC Section 3 29/57, Section 1 827 (Obligation 24 November 1693); Bannerman p.122]

42. Giben Hiortaich, 'Giben of *St. Kilda*', was a term used in Ness, Lewis, by those who took young gannets from Sulasgeir and made 'giben', using the oesophagus rather than the stomach. Rev. Kenneth Macaulay, writing about the gannets of St Kilda, described it in some detail:

'The inhabitants of Hirta, have a method of preserving their greese in a kind of bag, made of the stomach of the old Solan Goose caught in March. In their language it is called *Gibain*; and this oily kind of thick substance, manufactured in their way, they use by way of sauce, or instead of butter, among their porridge and flummery. In the adjacent islands they administer this oily substance to their cattle, if seized with violent colds, or obstinate coughs; and it is the general belief, that the application of the *Gibain*, in such cases has a very good effect.'

[Macaulay p.145]

43. St Mary's parish in Trotternish is that of Kilmuir. A witness to a tack of 18 April 1732 was Mr Kenneth Beaton, minister of 'St Marys in Troternish'. Prior to the Reformation part of the parish was known as Kilmaluag, its church being dedicated to St Moluag, but subsequently the area of Kilmuir, with its church dedicated to St Mary, was evidently joined to Kilmaluag and its name used for the combined parts. Uig, once a small parish in itself until at least the Reformation, was later united with Kilmuir and then with Snizort.

[MA GD221/4272/4; OPS Vol.II Pt.I pp.348-349]

44. The matter of being able or unable to 'ease nature' when at sea is also mentioned by Martin in his accounts of the Flannan Isles and of Bute.

[see Martin pp.16, 215]

45. One other record of a 'Macphade' in the parish has been found. This was 'Angus McPhad', tenant in 'Kilmartin' at Staffin in 1718. '*Dongal MackEwan*' remains equally unidentified, though presumably his first name was Dougal and his 'surname' would be a patronymic – 'son of Ewan', as with 'Johne mceowin' at 'Uginish wrach' in 1686. The references to individuals such as Finlay Ross are evidently intended to convey the first-hand knowledge on which this section of Martin's work is based.

[FEP NAS E656/1 Judicial Rental of the Macdonald Estates p.22; DC Section 2 484/10]

46. The 'Village *Bretill*', otherwise a settlement in the lands of what until more recently was called 'Glenbrettle', was commonly treated as part of Rhuandunan; in 1791, for instance, the lands and farm of 'Roudunan', 'Lisol' with its shore, and 'part of Glenbrettil', were set to 'Kenneth McCaskill of Rudunan'. The other part of 'Glenbrettil' was set to Norman McLeod at 'Islandreoch', Glenelg.

[DC Section 2 126]

47. No other record of '*Fergus Kaird*' has yet been found, but in 1686 a 'Finlay keard' was a tenant in Duart near Dunvegan. The only Finlay in Duart three years earlier was 'Finlay mcquien', who might have been the same man, 'keard' or 'Caird' being a nickname meaning 'tinker' rather than a surname. But tenants moved around frequently.

[DC Section 2 484/10 and 485/6]

48. In writing on how children should be educated, and, more particularly, how 'a young Gentleman should be brought up from his Infancy', John Locke said:

'I would also advise his Feet *to be washed* every night in cold Water; and to have his *Shooes* so thin, that they might leak and *let in Water*, when ever he comes near it. Here, I fear, I shall have the Mistriss and Maids too against me; one will think it too filthy, and the other, perhaps, too much pains to make clean his Stockings. But yet truth will have it, that his Health is much more worth than all such considerations and ten-times as much more. And he that considers how Mischievous and Mortal a thing, taking *Wet in the Feet* is to those, who have been bred nicely, will wish he had, with the poor People's Children, gone *Bare-foot*; who, by that means, come to be so reconciled, by Custom, to Wet in their Feet, that they take no more Cold or Harm by it, than if they were wet in their Hands.'

[Locke pp.5-6]

49. Neill Beaton in Skye lived at Lusta, part of the lands of Bay in Waternish. His medical skills have been described among those of the Beatons in general.

[Bannerman p.128]

50. Alexander Nicolson noted that a licence for the institution of a fair at Portree was granted about 1580. The Portree schoolmaster, Alexander Campbell wrote that at 'the latter end of every May and July, is held a well known fair', to which cattle were sent from most of Skye and even from Uist and Harris; but in 1841 there were three fairs held in the parish, in May, July and November, the last 'for hiring servants, and for transacting other country business.'

[Nicolson (1994) p.60; OSA p.202; NSA p.234]

51. The two 'ferries', or ferry routes, were those at Kyleakin and Kylerhea, which are respectively the only two places which could be said to fit the distances given by Martin. The latter is historically the better-known passage, but Nicolson mentioned both: 'Large numbers of horses and black cattle....were exported from Skye by way of the narrows of Kyle Akin, or Kyle Rhea.'

In November 1752 a boat with four of a crew in addition to the owner went from Glenelg to Kyleakin to ferry Macleod of Macleod's horses and had to wait nine days, for which it charged 10s.

[Nicolson (1994) p.190; DC Section 3 20/73]

52. Martin explains the 'Leni-Croich', and without much elaboration his definition appears in Armstrong's dictionary which goes on to describe the 'arrasaid' or 'fearrasaid' also in Martin's words. Dwelly (p.274) describes 'Leine croch' as 'ancient Highland mantle', presumably after Martin.

53. What is known about Somerled and his career has been recently described by John Marsden in the only work devoted to him. Donald was in fact Somerled's grandson, his father being Ranald, but he could certainly be described as the progenitor of the Macdonald families. It was Somerled who was styled 'righ Innse Gall', King of the Isles. The inaccuracies in this passage of Martin's account seem to stem largely from George Buchanan's History.

For Bloody Bay and the fight between John and his son Angus – see Martin p.251; Mull n.3.

Members of the 'Macvurich' (Martin's *'Mack Uurich')* family are the subject of several articles e.g. those by D S Thomson in TGSI Vol.XLIII pp.276-304, Vol. XLVI pp.281-307, Vol. XLIX pp.9-25

Hugh Macdonald's manuscript is probably the history of the Macdonalds, attributed to a Hugh Macdonald, on the basis of Martin's reference. The identity of Hugh remains uncertain.

[J Marsden: Somerled and the Emergence of Gaelic Scotland East Linton 2000; Macphail Vol.I pp.5-72; Bannerman pp.13, 18-19, 83]

54. An early record of the Mackinnons of Strath is that of 1354. They were frequently headed by a Lachlan Mackinnon. Two copies of a rental of 1741 include 'Lauchlan McKinnon' at 'Corichatt[achan] and Tyriches' ('Corichatachans and Tercherie'), with other Mackinnons in most of the Strath parish farms.

[OPS Vol.II pp.344-345; DC Section 5 492/1&2]

55. For the Michaelmas cavalcade and St Michael's Bannock see Uist n.32.

BOOT.

THE Ifle of *Boot* being ten Miles in length, lies on the *Weft-fide* of *Cowal*, from which it is feparated by a narrow Channel; in feveral parts not a Mile broad, the *North-end* of this Ifle is Mountanous and Heathy, being more defign'd for Pafturage, than Cultivation; the Mold is brown, or black, and in fome parts Clayie, the Ground yields a good produce of Oats, Barley, and Peafe: There is but little Wood growing there, yet there is a Coppice at the fide of *Loch-fad*. The Ground is arable from the middle to the *Southward*, the *Hectic-ftone* is to be had in many parts of this Ifle; and there is a Quarry of red ftone near the Town of *Rofa*, by which the Fort there, and the Chappel on its *North-fide* have been built. *Rothfay*, the head Town of the Shire of *Boot* and *Aran*, lies on the *Eaft* Coaft of *Boot*, and is one of the Titles of the Prince of *Scotland*; *King Robert* the Third created his Son Duke of *Rothfay*, and Steward of *Scotland*; and afterwards *Queen Mary* created the *Lord Darnley* Duke of *Rothfay*, before her Marriage with him: This Town is a very ancient Royal *Burrough*, but thinly Peopled, there not being above a hundred Families in it, and they have no forreign Trade: On the *North-fide* of *Rothfay*, there is a very ancient Ruinous Fort

Fort, round in Form, having a thick Wall, and about three Stories high, and Paffages round within the Wall; it is furrounded with a wet Ditch; it has a Gate on the *South*, and a double Gate on the *Eaft*, and a Baftion on each fide the Gate, and without thefe there's a Draw-Bridge, and the Sea flows within 40 Yards of it. The Fort is large enough for exercifing a Battallion of Men, it has a Chappel and feveral little Houfes within; and a large Houfe of four Stories high, fronting the *Eaftern-Gate*. The People here have a Tradition that this Fort was built by King *Rofa*, who is faid to have come to this Ifle before King *Fergus* the Firft. The other Forts are *Down-Owle*, and *Down-Allin*, both on the *Weft* fide.

The Churches here are as follow, *Kilmichel*, *Kil-Blain*, and *Kil-Chattan*, in the *South* Parifh; and Lady *Kirk* in *Rothfay* is the moft *Northerly* Parifh, all the Inhabitants are Proteftants.

THE Natives here are not troubled with any Epedemical Difeafe, the *Small pox* vifits them commonly once every fixth, or feventh Year; the oldeft Man now living in this Ifle is one *Fleming* a Weaver in *Rothfay*, his Neighbours told me that he could never eafe Nature at Sea, who is 90 Years of Age. The Inhabitants generally fpeak the *Englifh* and *Irifh* Tongue, and wear the fame Habit with thofe of the other Iflands; they are very Induftrious

O 4 Fifhers

Fiſhers eſpecially for Herring, for which uſe they are furniſhed with about 80 large Boats, the Tenants pay their Rents with the profit of Herrings, they are to be had any where on the *Weſtern* Coaſt.

THE Principal Heretors here are *Stuart* of *Boot*, who is Hereditary *Sheriff* of this Shire, and hath his Seat in *Roſa. Ballantine* of *Keams*, whoſe Seat is at the Head of the Bay of that Name, and has an Orchard by it. *Stuart* of *Eſcick*, whoſe Seat has a Park and Orchard, and about a Mile to the *South* of *Rothſay*, next lies two Iſles called *Cumbray* the greater, and the leſſer, the former is within a League of *Boot*, this Iſland has a Chappel, and a Well, which the Natives eſteem a *Catholicon* for all Diſeaſes; this Iſle is a Mile in length, but the other Iſle is much leſs in Compaſs, both Iſles are the property of *Montgommery* of *Skelmorly*.

ARRAN

ARRAN.

THE Name of this Iſle is by ſome derived from *Arran*, which in the *Iriſh* Language ſignifies Bread: Others think it comes more probably from *Arjn*, or *Arſyn*, which in their Language is as much, as the Place of the Giant *Fin-Mac-Couls* Slaughter or Execution; for *Aar* ſignifies Slaughter, and ſo they will have *Arin* only the Contraction of *Arrin* or *Fin*; the received Tradition of the great Giant *Fin-Mac-Cowls* Military Valour, which he exerciſed upon the Ancient Natives here, ſeems to favour this Conjecture; this they ſay is evident from the many Stones ſet up in divers Places of the Iſle, as Monuments upon the Graves of Perſons of Note that were kill'd in Battle. This Iſle is twenty four Miles from *South* to *North*, and ſeven Miles from *Eaſt* to *Weſt*. It lies between the Iſle of *Boot*, and *Kyntyre*, in the oppoſite Main-land. The Iſle is high and Mountainous, but ſlopes on each ſide round the Coaſt, and the *Glen* is only made uſe of for Tillage. The Mountains near *Brodick* Bay, are of a conſiderable height, all the Hills generally afford a Good Paſturage, tho' a great part of 'em be covered only with Heath.

THE

THE Mold here is of divers Colours, being black and brown near the Hills, and Clayie and Sandy upon the Coaft.

THE Natives told me that fome Places of the Ifle, affords Fullers-earth. The Coaft on the *Eaft* fide is Rockie near the Shoar ; the Stones on the Coaft for fome Miles beneath *Brodick*, are all of a red Colour, and of thefe the Caftle of *Brodick* is built. The Natives fay that the Mountains near the Caftle of *Brodick* affords Chryftal, and that the Dutchefs of *Hamilton* put fo great a Value on it, as to be at the Charge of cutting a Necklace of it, which the Inhabitants take as a great Honour done them, becaufe they have a great Veneration for her Grace. There is no confiderable Woods here, but a few Coppices, yet that in the *Glen* towards the *Weft* is above a Mile in length. There are Capacious Fields of Arable Ground on each fide *Brodick* Bay, as alfo on the oppofite weftern Coaft. The largeft and beft Field for Pafturage is th t on the *South-weft* fide.

SEVERAL Rivers on each fide this Ifle affords Salmon, particularly the two Rivers on the *Weft* called *Mackir* fide, and the two in *Kirkmichel* and *Brodich* Bay.

THE Air here is temperately Cold and moift, which is in fome meafure qualified by the frefh Breezes that blow from the Hills, but the Natives think a dram of Strong-waters is a good Corrective. THERE

THERE are feveral Caves on the Coaft of this Ifle, thofe on the *Weft* are pretty large, particularly that in *Druim-cruey*, a hundred Men may fit or lie in it, it is contracted gradually from the Floor upwards to the Roof, in the upper-end there is a large piece of a Rock form'd like a Pillar, there's engaven on it a Deer, and underneath it a two-handed Sword ; there is a void fpace on each fide this Pillar.

THE *Southfide* of the Cave has a Horfe-fhoe engraven on it. On each fide the Door, there's a hole cut out, and that they fay was for holding big Trees, on which the Caldrons hang for boyling their Beef and Venifon. The Natives fay that this was the Cave in which *Fin-Mac-Cowl* lodged during the time of his refidence in this Ifle, and that his Guards lay in the leffer Caves, which are near this big one ; there is a little Cave joyning to the largeft, and this they call the Cellar.

THERE is a Cave fome Miles more *Southerly* on the fame Coaft, and they told me that the Minifter Preached in it fometimes, in regard of its being more Centrical than the Parifh Church.

SEVERAL erected Stones are to be feen on each fide this Ifle ; four of thefe are near *Brodich-Bay*, about the diftance of 70 Yards from

from the River, and are ſeven foot high each. The higheſt of theſe Stones that fell under my obſervation was on the *South-ſide* of *Kirkmichel* River, and is above fifteen foot high; there is a Stone Coffin near it which has been fill'd with Humane Bones, until of late that the River waſhed away the Earth, and the Bones that were in the Coffin; *Mac-Loui*, who had ſeen them, ſays they were of no larger ſize than thoſe of our own time. On the *Weſt-ſide* there are three Stones erected in *Baellimianich*, and a fourth at ſome diſtance from theſe, about ſix Foot high each. In the *Moor* on the *Eaſt-ſide Druin-cruey*, there is a Circle of Stones, the Area is about thirty Paces; there is a Stone of ſame ſhape and kind about forty Paces to the *Weſt* of the Circle, the Natives ſay that this Circle was made by the Giant *Fin-Mac-Cowl*, and that to the ſingle Stone *Bran-Fins-Mac-Cowls* Hunting-dog was uſually tied. About half a Mile to the *North-ſide Baelliminich* there are two Stones erected each of them eight Foot high.

THERE is a Circle of Big-ſtones a little to the *South* of *Druin Cruey*, the Area of which is about twelve Paces; there is a broad thin Stone in the middle of this Circle, ſupported by three leſſer Stones, the Ancient Inhabitants are reported to have burnt their Sacrifices on the broad Stone, in time of Heatheniſm.

THERE

THERE is a thin broad Stone tapering towards the top, erected within a quarter of a Mile of the Sea, near *Machir* River, and is nine Foot high, and at ſome little diſtance from the River, there is a large Cavern of Stones.

THERE is an Eminence of about a thouſand Paces in Compaſs on the Sea Coaſt in *Druimcruney* Village, and it is fenced about with a Stone-Wall Of old it was a Sanctuary, and whatever number of Men or Cattle could get within, it was ſecured from the aſſaults of their Enemies, the Place being privileged by Univerſal Conſent.

THE only good Harbour in this Iſle is *Lamlaſh*, which is in *South-eaſt* end of the Iſle of that Name.

THERE is a great fiſhing of Cod, and Whiting, in and about this Bay.

THE whole Iſle is deſign'd by Nature more for Paſturage, than Cultivation; the Hills are generally covered all over with Heath, and produce a mixture of the *Erica-Baccifera*, *Cats-tail* and *Juniper*, all which are very agreeable to the Eye in the Summer. The higheſt Hills of this Iſland are ſeen at a conſiderable diſtance from ſeveral parts of the Continent and *North-weſt* Iſles, and they ſerve inſtead of a Forreſt to maintain the Deer, which are about four hundred

dred in number, and they are carefully kept by a Forreſter, to give ſport to the Duke of *Hamilton*, or any of his Family that go a Hunting there. For if any of the Natives happen to kill a Deer without Licenſe, which is not often granted, he is liable to a Fine of 20*l. Scots* for each Deer. And when they grow too numerous, the Forreſter grants Licenſes for killing a certain number of them, on condition they bring the Skins to himſelf.

THE Cattle here are Horſes and Cows of a middle ſize, and they have alſo Sheep and Goats. This Iſle affords the common Sea and Land Fowls that are to be had in the Weſtern Iſles. The black Cock is not allow'd to be killed here without a Licenſe, the Tranſgreſſors are liable to a Fine.

THE Caſtle of *Brodich* on the North ſide of the Bay of that Name, ſtands on a Plain, from which there is about 400 Paces of a gradual deſcent towards the Sea.

THIS Caſtle is built in a long Form, from South to North there is a Wall of two Stories high that encompaſſes the Caſtle and Tower; the ſpace within the Wall on the South ſide the Caſtle, is capable of muſtring a Battalion of Men.

THE

THE Caſtle is four Stories high, and has a Tower of greater height joined to the North ſide, and that has a Baſtion cloſe to it, to which a lower Baſtion is added. The South and Weſt ſides are ſurrounded with a broad wet Ditch, but the Eaſt and North ſides have a deſcent which will not admit of a wet Ditch. The Gate looks to the Eaſt. This Caſtle is the Duke of *Hamiltons* Seat, when is Grace or any of the Family make their Summer Viſit to this Iſland. The Bayliff or Steward has his Reſidence in this Caſtle, and he has a Deputation to act with full power to Levy the Rents, give Leaſes of the Lands, and hold Courts of Juſtice.

THERE is another Caſtle belonging to the Duke in the North ſide the Iſle, at the head of *Loch Keniſtil*, in which there is an Harbour for Barks and Boats. The Iſle of *Arran* is the Duke of *Hamiltons* Property (a very ſmall part excepted) it lies in the Sheriffdom of *Boot*, and made part of the Dioceſs of *Argyle*.

THE Inhabitants of this Iſland are compoſed of ſeveral Tribes. The moſt ancient Family among them, is by the Natives reckon'd to be *Mack Louis*, which in the ancient Language ſignifies the Son of *Lewis*; they own themſelves to be deſcended of *French* Parentage, their Sirname in Engliſh is *Fullerton*, and their

Title

Title *Kirk Michell*, the Place of their Reſidence. If Tradition be true, this little Family is ſaid to be of 700 years ſtanding. The preſent Poſſeſſor oblig'd me with the ſight of his old and new Charters, by which he is one of the Kings Coroners within this Iſland, and as ſuch, he hath a Halbert peculiar to his Office; he has his right of late from the Family of *Hamilton*, wherein his Title and Perquiſites of Coroner are confirm'd to him and his Heirs. He is oblig'd to have three Men to attend him upon all Publick Emergencies, and he is bound by his Office to purſue all Malefactors, and to deliver them to the Steward, or in his abſence to the next Judge. And if any of the Inhabitants refuſe to pay their Rents at the uſual term, the Coroner is bound to take him Perſonally, or to ſeize his Goods. And if it ſhould happen that the Coroner with his retinue of three Men is not ſufficient to put his Office in execution, then he Summons all the Inhabitants to concurr with him, and immediately they rendezvous to the place, where he fixes his Corners Staff. The Perquiſites due to the Coroner are a Firlet or Buſhel of Oats, and a Lamb from every Village in the Iſle, both which are punctually paid him at the ordinary Terms.

THE Inhabitants of this Iſle are well proportion'd, generally Brown, and ſome of a Black Complection; they enjoy a good ſtate of health, and have a genius for all Callings or Imploy-

Imployments, tho' they have but few Mechanicks; they wear the ſame Habit with thoſe of the neareſt Iſles, and are very Civil; they all ſpeak the *Iriſh Language*, yet the *Engliſh* Tongue prevails on the Eaſt ſide, and ordinarily the Miniſters Preach in it, and in *Iriſh* on the Weſt ſide. Their ordinary aſſeveration is by *Nale*, for I did not hear any Oath in the Iſland.

The Churches in this Iſle are,

KILBRIDE in the South Eaſt, *Kilmore* in the South, *Cabel Ual* a Chapel, *Kilmichel* in the Village of that name, St. *James's* Church at the North end.

THE Natives are all Proteſtants, they obſerve the Feſtivals of *Chriſtmaſs*, *Good-Friday*, and *Eaſter*. I had like to have forgot a valuable Curioſity in this Iſle, which they call *Baul Muluy*. *i. e. Molingus* his Stone Globe; this Saint was Chaplain to *Mack Donald* of the Iſles; his Name is Celebrated here on the account of this Globe, ſo much eſteem'd by the Inhabitants. This Stone for its intrinſick value has been carefully tranſmitted to Poſterity for

P ſeveral

feveral Ages. It is a green Stone much like a Globe in Figure, about the bignefs of a Goofe Egg.

THE Vertues of it is to remove Stiches from the fides of Sick Perfons, by laying it clofe to the Place affected, and if the Patient does not out-live the Diftemper, they fay the Stone removes out of the Bed of its own accord, and *e contra.* The Natives ufe this Stone for Swearing decifive Oaths upon it.

THEY afcribe another extraordinary Vertue to it, and 'tis this; the credulous Vulgar firmly believe that if this Stone is caft among the Front of an Enemy, they will all run away, and that as often as the Enemy rallies, if this Stone is caft among them, they ftill lofe Courage, and retire. They fay that *Mackdonald* of the Ifles carried this Stone about him, and that Victory was always on his fide when he threw it among the Enemy. The Cuftody of this Globe is the peculiar Privilege of a little Family called *Clan-Chattons,* alias *Mack Intofh,* they were ancient Followers of *Mack Donald* of the Ifles. This Stone is now in the Cuftody of *Margaret Millar,* alias *Mack Intofh,* fhe lives in *Baellmianich,* and preferves the Globe with abundance of care; it is wrapped up in fair Linen Cloath, and about that there is a piece of Woollen Cloath, and fhe keeps it ftill lock'd up in her Cheft, when it is not given out to exert its qualities. *ISLESAY.*

ISLESAY.

IS A big Rock, about fix Leagues to the South Weft of *Arran,* it rifes in form of a Sugar-Loaf, but the top is plain, and large enough for drawing up a thoufand Men in Ranks; there is a Frefh Water Lake in the middle of the Plain, the whole Ifle is covered with long Grafs, and is inacceffible, except on the South Weft fide, by a ftair cut out in the Rock; in the middle of it there is a fmall Tower of three Stories high with the top. There is a Frefh Water Spring iffuing out of the fide of this great Rock; below the Entry there is a place where the Fifhers take up their Refidence during their ftay about this Rock in queft of Cod, and Ling; and there is a good Anchorage for their Veffels, very near their Tents.

THIS Rock in the Summer time abounds with variety of Sea Fowl that build and hatch in it. The *Solan Geefe* and *Culturneb* are moft numerous here; the latter are by the Fifhers called *Albanich,* which in the ancient *Irifh* Language fignifies *Scots Men.*

THE Ifle hath a Chappel on the top called *Fiunnay,* and an ancient Pavement, or Caufeway.

P 2 *ISLESAY*

ISELESAY is the Earl of *Caſſil's* Property, the Tenant who Farms it pays him one hundred Merks *Scots* yearly ; the product of the Iſle is Hogs, Fowl, Down, and Fiſh. The Iſle *Avon* above a Mile in Circumference, lies to the S. of *Kintyre Mule*, it hath a Harbour for Barks on the North.

The Iſle GIGAY.

THE Iſle *Gigay*, lies about a League from *Lergie* on the *Weſt-ſide* of *Kyntyre*, it is four Miles in length, and one in breadth, was formerly in the Dioceſs, and is ſtill part of the Sheriffdom of *Argyle*. This Iſle is for the moſt part Arable, but Rockie in other parts ; the Mold is brown, and Clayie inclining to red ; it is good for Paſturage and Cultivation. The Corn growing here is Oats and Barley. The Cattle bred here are Cows, Horſes, and Sheep. There is a Church in this Iſland called *Kil-chattan*, it has an Altar in the Eaſt end, and upon it a Font of Stone which is very large, and hath a ſmall hole in the middle which goes quite through it. There are ſeveral Tomb-ſtones in and about this Church ; the Family of the *Mack Neils*, the principal Poſſeſſors of this Iſle are buried under the Tomb-ſtones on the Eaſt ſide the Church, where there is a Plat of ground ſet apart for them. Moſt of all

all the Tombs have a two-handed Sword engraven on them, and there is one that has the repreſentation of a Man upon it.

NEAR the Weſt ſide the Church there is a Stone of about 16 Foot high, and 4 broad, erected upon the Eminence. About 60 yards diſtance from the Chappel there is a ſquare Stone erected about ten Foot high : at this the ancient Inhabitants bowed, becauſe it was there where they had the firſt view of the Church.

THERE is a Croſs 4 Foot high at a little diſtance, and a Cavern of Stone on each ſide of it.

THIS Iſle affords no Wood of any kind, but a few Buſhes of Juniper on the little Hills. The ſtones upon which the ſcurff *Corkir*, which dies a Crimſon colour, grows here, as alſo thoſe that produce the *Crottil*, which dies a Philamot colour. Some of the Natives told me that they us'd to chew Nettles, and hold them to their Noſtrils to ſtanch bleeding at the Noſe, and that Nettle being applied to the place, would alſo ſtop bleeding at a Vein, or otherwiſe.

THERE is a Well in the North end of this Iſle called *Toubir-more*, i. e. a great Well, because of its effects, for which it is Famous among

P 3

among the Islanders; who together with the Inhabitants use it as a *Catholicon* for Diseases. It's cover'd with Stone and Clay, because the Natives fancy that the stream that flows from it might overflow the Isle; and it is always opened by a *Diroch*, *i. e.* an Inmate, else they think it would not exert its Vertues. They ascribe one very extraordinary effect to it, and 'tis this; That when any Foreign Boats are Wind-bound here (which often happens) the Master of the Boat ordinarily gives the Native that lets the Water run a piece of Money, and they say that immediately afterwards the Wind changes in favour of those that are thus detain'd by contrary Winds. Every Stranger that goes to drink of the water of this Well, is accustomed to leave on its stone Cover a piece of Money, a Needle, Pin, or one of the prettiest varieated Stones they can find.

THE Inhabitants are all Protestants, and speak the *Irish* Tongue generally, there being but few that speak *English*; they are grave and reserv'd in their Conversation, they are accustom'd not to bury on *Friday*; they are Fair or Brown in Complection, and use the same Habit, Diet, &c. that is made use of in the adjacent Continent and Isles. There is only one Inn in this Isle.

THE Isle *Caray* lies a quarter of a Mile South from *Gigay*, it is about a Mile in compass,

pass, affords good Pasturage, and abounds with Connies. There is an Harbour for Barks on the North East end of it. This Island is the Property of *Mack Alister* of *Lergy*, a Family of the *Mackdonalds*.

JURAH.

THE Isle of *Jurah* is by a narrow Channel of about half a Mile broad, separated from *Ila*. The Natives say that *Jurah* is so call'd from *Dih* and *Rah*, two Brethren who are believ'd to have been *Danes*; the Names *Dih* and *Rah* signifying as much as without Grace or Prosperity. Tradition says that these two Brethren fought and killed one another in the Village *Knock Croum*, where there are two stones erected of 7 Foot high each, and under them they say there are Urns with the ashes of the two Brothers; the distance between them is about sixty yards. The Isle is Mountainous along the middle, where there are four Hills of a considerable heighth; the two highest are well known to Sea-faring Men, by the Name of the ***Paps of Jurah***; they are very conspicuous from all quarters of Sea and Land in those Parts.

P 4 THIS

THIS Iſle is twenty four Miles long, and in ſome places ſix or ſeven Miles in breadth; it is the Duke of *Argyle*'s Property, and part of the Sheriffdom of *Argyle*.

THE Mold is brown and grayiſh on the Coaſt, and black in the Hills, which are cover'd with Heath, and ſome Graſs, that proves good Paſturage for their Cattle, which are Horſes, Cows, Sheep, and Goats. There's variety of Land and Water Fowl here. The Hills ordinarily have about three hundred Deer grazing on them, which are not to be hunted by any without the Steward's Licenſe. This Iſle is perhaps the wholſomeſt Plat of ground either in the Iſles or Continent of *Scotland*, as appears from the long life of the Natives, and their ſtate of health, to which the heighth of the hills is believ'd to contribute in a large meaſure, by the freſh breezes of wind that comes from 'em to purifie the Air; whereas *Ila* and *Gigay* on each ſide this Iſle, are much lower, and are not ſo wholſome by far, being liable to ſeveral Diſeaſes that are not here. The Inhabitants obſerve that the Air of this Place is perfectly pure from the middle of *March*, 'till the end or middle of *September*. There is no Epidemical Diſeaſe that prevails here; Fevers are but ſeldom obſerv'd by the Natives, and any kind of Flux is rare; the Gout and Agues are not ſo much as known by them,

them, neither are they liable to Sciatica, Convulſions, Vapours, Palſies, Surfeits, Lethargies, Megrims, Conſumptions, Rickets, Pains of the Stomach, or Coughs, are not frequent here, and none of them are at any time obſerv'd to become Mad. I was told by ſeveral of the Natives, that there was not one Woman died of Child-bearing there theſe 34 years paſt. Blood-letting and Purging are not us'd here.

IF any contract a Cough, they uſe *Brochan* only to remove it. If after a Fever one chance to be taken ill of a Stitch, they take a quantity of *Lady-wrack*, and half as much of *Red-Fog*, and boil them in water; the Patients ſit upon the Veſſel, and receive the Fume, which by experience they find effectual againſt this Diſtemper. *Fevers* and the *Diarhœa*'s are found here only when the Air is Foggy and warm in Winter or Summer.

THE Inhabitants for their Diet make uſe of Beef and Mutton in the Winter and Spring, as alſo of Fiſh, Butter, Cheeſe, and Milk. The Vulgar take *Brochan* frequently for their Diet during the Winter and Spring; and *Brochan* and Bread us'd for the ſpace of two days, reſtores loſt Apetite.

THE Women of all Ranks eat a leſſer quantity of Food than the Men; this and their not wearing any thing ſtrait about them, is believ'd believ'd to contribute much to the health both of the Mothers and Children.

There are ſeveral Fountains of excellent Water in this Iſle, the moſt Clebrated of them is that of the Mountain *Beinbrek* in the *Tarbat*, called *Toubir ni Lechkin*, that is, the Well in a ſtony deſcent; it runs Eaſterly, and they commonly reckon it to be lighter by one half than any other Water in this Iſle; for tho' one drink a great quantity of it at a time, the Belly is not ſwelled or any ways burthened by it. Natives and Strangers find it efficacious againſt Nauſeouſneſs of the Stomach, and the Stone. The River *Niſſa* receives all the water that iſſues from this Well, and this is the reaſon they give why Salmons here are in goodneſs and taſte far above thoſe of any other River whatever. The River of *Crokbreck* affords Salmon alſo, but they are not eſteem'd ſo good as thoſe of the River *Niſſa*.

SEVERAL of the Natives have lived to a great Age, I was told that one of them called *Gillouir Mack Crain* lived to have kept one hundred and eighty *Chriſtmaſſes* in his own houſe; he died about fifty years ago, and there are ſeveral of his acquaintance living to this day, from whom I had this account.

BAILIF

BAILIF *Campbell* lived to the Age of one hundred and ſix years, he died three years ago, he paſſed the thirty three laſt years before his death in this Iſle. *Donald Mac N' Mill*, who lives in the Village of *Killearne* at preſent, is arrived at the age of ninety years.

A Woman of the Iſle of *Scorba* near the North end of this Iſle, lived ſevenſcore years, and enjoy'd the free uſe of her Senſes and Underſtanding all her days; it is now two years ſince ſhe died.

THERE is a large Cave called *King's-Cave*, on the Weſt ſide the *Tarbat*, near the Sea; there is a Well at the entry, which renders it the more convenient for ſuch as may have occaſion to Lodge in it.

ABOUT two Miles further from the *Tarbat*, there is a Cave at *Corpich* which hath an Altar in it; there are many ſmall pieces of pettrified ſubſtance hanging from the Roof of this Cave.

THERE is a Place where Veſſels uſe to Anchor on the Weſt ſide this Iſland, called *Whitfarlan*, about 100 yards North from the Porter's Houſe.

ABOUT

ABOUT Four Leagues South from the North end of this Iſle, lies the Bay *Da'l Taul*, which is about half a Mile in length; there is a Rock on the North ſide the entry, which they ſay is five Fathom deep, and but three Fathom within.

ABOUT a League further to the South on the ſame Coaſt, lies the ſmall Iſles of *Jura*, within which there is a good Anchoring Place, the South entry is the beſt; Iſland *Nin Gowir* muſt be kept on the left hand; it is eaſily diſtinguiſh'd by its bigneſs from the reſt of the Iſles. *Conney Iſle* lies to the North of this Iſland. There are black and white ſpotted Serpents in this Iſle; their head being applied to the Wound, is by the Natives us'd as the beſt Remedy for their Poiſon. Within a Mile of the *Tarbat* there is a Stone erected about eight Foot high. *Loch Tarbat* on the Weſt ſide, runs Eaſterly for about five Miles, but is not an harbour for Veſſels, or leſſer Boats, for it is altogether Rocky.

THE Shoar on the Weſt ſide affords Corral, and Corraline; there is a ſort of *Dulſe* growing on this Coaſt, of a white Colour.

BETWEEN the North end of *Jura*, and the Iſle *Scarba*, lies the Famous and Dangerous Gulph call'd *Cory Vrekan*, about a Mile in breadth,

breadth, it yields an impetuous Current, not to be matched any where about the Iſle of *Britain*. The Sea begins to boil and ferment with the Tide of Flood, and reſembles the boiling of a Pot, and then increaſes gradually, until it appear in many Whirlpools, which form themſelves in ſort of Pyramids, and immediately after ſpout up as high as the Maſt of a little Veſſel, and at the ſame time makes a loud report. Theſe white Waves run two Leagues with the wind before they break; the Sea continues to repeat theſe various motions from the beginning of the Tide of Flood, until it is more than half Flood, and then it decreaſes gradually until it hath ebb'd about half an hour, and continues to boil 'till it is within an hour of low water. This boiling of the Sea is not above a Piſtol ſhot diſtant from the Coaſt of *Scarba Iſle*, where the white Waves meet and ſpout up; they call it the *Kaillach*, *i. e.* an old Hag; and they ſay that when ſhe puts on her *Kerchief*, *i. e.* the whiteſt Waves, it is then reckon'd fatal to approach her. Notwithſtanding of this great Ferment of the Sea, which brings up the leaſt ſhell from the ground, the ſmalleſt Fiſher-Boat may venture to croſs this Gulph at the laſt hour of the Tide of Flood, and at the laſt hour of the Tide of Ebb.

THIS Gulph hath its Name from *Brekan*, ſaid to be Son to the King of *Denmark*, who was

was drowned here, caſt a ſhoar in the North of *Jura*, and buried in a Cave, as appears from the ſtone Tomb and Altar there.

THE Natives told me that about three years ago an *Engliſh* Veſſel happen'd inadvertently to paſs through this Gulph at the time when the Sea began to boil; the whiteneſs of the Waves, and their ſprouting up, was like the breaking of a Sea upon a Rock; they found themſelves attracted irreſiſtably to the white Rock, as they then ſuppoſed it to be; this quickly oblig'd them to conſult their ſafety, and ſo they betook themſelves to the ſmall Boat with all ſpeed, and thought it no ſmall happineſs to Land ſafe in *Jura*, committing the Veſſel under all her Sails to the uncertain Conduct of Tide and Wind; ſhe was driven to the oppoſite Continent of *Knapdale*, where ſhe no ſooner arriv'd, than the Tide and Wind became contrary to one another, and ſo the Veſſel was caſt into a Creek where ſhe was ſafe; and then the Maſter and Crew were by the Natives of this Iſle conducted to her, where they found her as ſafe as they left her, tho' all her Sails were ſtill hoiſted.

THE Natives gave me an account that ſome years ago a Veſſel had brought ſome Rats hither, which increaſed ſo much, that they became very uneaſie to the People, but on a ſuddain

ſuddain they all vaniſh'd, and now there is not one of them in the Iſle.

THERE is a Church here called *Killearn*, the Inhabitants are all Proteſtants, and obſerve the Feſtivals of *Chriſtmas*, *Eaſter*, and *Michaelmaſs*; they do not open a Grave on *Friday*, and bury none on that day, except the Grave has been opened before.

THE Natives here are very well proportioned, being generally black of Complection, and free from bodily imperfections. They ſpeak the *Iriſh* Language, and wear the Plade, Bonnet, &c. as other Iſlanders.

THE Iſle of *Ila* lies to the Weſt of *Jura*, from which it is ſeparated by a narrow Channel, it is twenty four Miles in length from South to North, and eighteen from Eaſt to Weſt; there are ſome little Mountains about the middle on the Eaſt ſide; the Coaſt is for the moſt part heathy, and uneven, and by conſequence not proper for Tillage; the North end is alſo full of Heaths and Hills; the South Weſt and Weſt is pretty well Cultivated, and there is ſix Miles between *Kilrow* on the Weſt, and *Port Eſcock* in the Eaſt, which is arable, and well Inhabited. There's about one thouſand little Hills on this Road, and all abound with Lime-ſtone, among which there is lately diſcovered a Lead-Mine in three different places,

ces, but it has not turn'd to any account as yet. The Corn growing here is Barley, and Oats.

THERE is only one Harbour in this Iſle, called *Loch-Dale*, it lies near the North end, and is of a great length and breadth; but the depth being in the middle, few Veſſels come within half a League of the Land ſide.

THERE are ſeveral Rivers in this Iſle affording Salmon. The Freſh water Lakes are well ſtock'd with Trouts, Eels, and ſome with Salmons, as *Loch Guirm*, which is four Miles in Circumference, and hath ſeveral Forts built on an Iſland that lies in it.

LOCH FINLAGAN about three Miles in Circumference, affords Salmon, Trouts, and Eels; this Lake lies in the Centre of the Iſle. The Iſle *Finlagan*, from which this Lake hath its Name is in it. It s Famous for being once the Court in which the great *Mac Donald* King of the Iſles had his Reſidence, his Houſes, Chappel, *&c.* are now ruinous. His Guards *de Corps* called *Lucht-taeh*, kept Guard on the Lake ſide neareſt to the Iſle; the Walls of their Houſes are ſtill to be ſeen there.

THE High Court of Judicature conſiſting of Fourteen, Sat always here; and there was an Appeal to them from all the Courts in the Iſles;

Iſles; the eleventh ſhare of the Sum in Debate was due to the principal Judge. There was a big Stone of ſeven Foot ſquare, in which there was a deep impreſſion made to receive the Feet of *Mack Donald*, for he was Crown'd King of the Iſles ſtanding in this Stone; and Swore that he would continue his Vaſſals in the poſſeſſion of their Lands, and do exact Juſtice to all his Subjects; and then his Father's Sword was put into his hand. The Biſhop of *Argyle* and 7 Prieſts Anointed him King in preſence of all the heads of the Tribes in the Iſles and Continent, and were his Vaſſals; at which time the Orator rehears'd a Catalogue of his Anceſtors, *&c.*

THERE are ſeveral Forts built in the Iſles that are in freſh water Lakes, as in *Ilan Loch-guirn*, and *Ilan Viceain*; there is a Fort called *Dunnivag* in the South Weſt ſide of the Iſle, and there are ſeveral Caves in different places of it. The largeſt that I ſaw was in the North end, and is called *Uah Vearnag*, it will contain 200 Men to ſtand or ſit in it. There is a Kiln for drying Corn made on the Eaſt ſide of it; and on the other ſide there's a Wall built cloſe to the ſide of the Cave, which was us'd for a Bed-Chamber; it had a fire on the floor, and ſome Chairs about it, and the Bed ſtood cloſe to the Wall. There is a ſtone without the Cave door, about which the Common People make a Tour Sunways.

Q A.

A Mile on the South Weſt ſide of the Cave, is the Celebrated Well call'd *Toubir* in *Knahar*, which in the ancient Language is as much as to ſay, as the Well that ſallied from one Place to another. For it is a receiv'd Tradition among the Vulgar Inhabitants of this Iſle, and the oppoſite Iſle of *Collonſay*, that this Well was firſt in *Collonſay*, until an imprudent Woman happen'd to waſh her hands in it, and that immediately after, the Well being thus abus'd, came in an inſtant to *Ila*, where it is like to continue, and is ever ſince eſteem'd a *Catholicon* for Diſeaſes by the Natives and adjacent Iſlanders, and the great reſort to it is commonly every quarter day.

IT is common with Sick People to make a Vow to come to the Well, and after drinking, they make a Tour Sunways round it, and then leave an Offering of ſome ſmall Token, ſuch as a Pin, Needle, Farthing, or the like, on the ſtone Cover which is above the Well. But if the Patient is not like to recover, they ſend a Proxy to the Well, who acts as above-mention'd, and carries home ſome of the Water to be drank by the Sick Perſon.

THERE is a little Chappel beſide this Well, to which ſuch as had found the benefit of the Water, came back and return'd thanks to God for their Recovery.

THERE

THERE are ſeveral Rivers on each ſide this Iſle that afford Salmon; I was told by the Natives that the *Brion* of *Ila* a Famous Judge, is according to his own deſire, buried ſtanding on the brink of the River *Laggan*, having in his right hand a Spear ſuch as they uſe to dart at the Salmon.

THERE are ſome Iſles on the Coaſt of this *Iſland*, as *Iſland Texa* on the South Weſt about a Mile in Circumference; and *Iſland Ouirſa* a Mile likewiſe in Circumference, with the ſmall *Iſle* called *Nave*.

The Names of the CHURCHES *in this Iſle are as follows.*

KIL *CHOLLIM-KILL*, St. *Columbus* his Church near *Port Eſcock*, *Kil Chovan* in the *Rins* on the Weſt ſide the Iſle. *Kil Chieran* in *Rins*, on the Weſt ſide. *Nerbols* in the *Rins*, St. *Columbus* his Church in *Laggan*, a Chappel in Iſland *Nave*, and *Killhan Alen* North Weſt of *Kidrow*. There is a Croſs ſtanding near St. *Columbas's* or *Porteſcock* ſide, which is ten foot high. There are two Stones ſet up at the Eaſt ſide of *Loch Finlagan*, and they are ſix foot high; all the Inhabitants are Proteſtants, ſome among them obſerve the Feſtivals of *Chriſtmaſs*, and *Goodfryday*. They are well

Q 2 propor-

244 A Defcription of the

proportion'd, and indifferently healthful; the Air here is not near fo good as that of *Jura*, from which it is but a fhort Mile diftant, but *Ila* is lower and more Marfhy, which makes it liable to feveral Difeafes that do not trouble thofe of *Jura*. They generally fpeak the *Irifh* Tongue, all thofe of the beft Rank fpeak *Englifh*; they ufe the fame Habit and Diet with thofe of *Jura*. This Ifle is annexed to the Crown of *Scotland*, Sir *Hugh Campbel* of *Caddel* is the King's Steward there, and has one half of the Ifland. This Ifle is reckon'd the furtheft Weft of all the Ifles in *Britain*; there is a Village on the Weft Coaft of it called *Cul*, *i. e.* the back part, and the Natives fay it was fo called, becaufe the Ancients thought it the back of the World, as being the remoteft part on that fide of it. The Natives of *Ila*, *Collinfay*, and *Jura*, fay that there is an Ifland lying to the South Weft of thefe Ifles, about the diftance of a Days Sailing, for which they have only a bare Tradition. Mr. *Mack Swen*, prefent Minifter in the Ifle *Jura*, gave me the following account of it, which he had from the Mafter of an *Englifh* Veffel that happen'd to Anchor at that little Ifle, and came afterwards to *Jura*, which is thus.

AS I was Sailing fome 30 Leagues to the South Weft of *Ifla*, I was Becalm'd near a little Ifle, where *I* dropt Anchor, and went afhoar. I found

I found it covered all over with long Grafs; there were abundance of Seals lying on the Rocks and on the Shore; there is likewife a multitude of Sea-fowls in it; there is a River in the middle, and on each fide of it, I found great heaps of Fifh-bones of many forts; there are many Planks and Boards, caft up upon the Coaft of the Ifle, and it being all plain, and almoft level with the Sea, I caus'd my Men (being then Idle) to erect a heap of the Wood about two Stories high; and that with a defign to make the Ifland more Confpicuous to Seafaring Men. This Ifle is four *Englifh* Miles in length, and one in breadth: I was about thirteen Hours failing between this Ifle, and *Jura*. Mr. *John Mack Swen* above mentioned, having gone to the Ifle of *Collonfay*. Some few Days after, was told by the Inhabitants that from an Eminence near the Monaftry, in a fair Day, they faw as it were the top of a little Mountain in the *South-weft* Sea, and that they doubted not but it was Land, tho' they never obferv'd it before, Mr. *Mackfwen* was Confirm'd in this Opinion, by the account above mentioned; but when the Summer was over, they never faw this little Hill as they call'd it any more. The reafon of which is fuppos'd to be this, that the high Winds in all probabily, had caft down the pile of Wood, that forty Seamen had erected the preceeding Year, in that Ifland; which by reafon of the defcription above recited, we may aptly enough call the Green Ifland.

Q 3 The

The Iſle of Collonſay.

ABout two Leagues to the North of *Ila*, lies the Iſle *Oronſay*, it is ſeparated from *Collonſay*, only at the Tide of Flood, this *Peninſula* is four Miles in Circumference, being for the moſt part a plain Arable dry Sandy Soil, and is fruitful in Corn and Graſs; it is likewiſe adorn'd with a Church, Chappel, and Monaſtry; they were Built by the famous St. *Columbus*, to whom the Church is Dedicated. There is an Altar in this Church, and there has been a modern Crucifix on it, in which ſeveral precious Stones were fixed, the moſt valuable of theſe, is now in the Cuſtody of Mack. *Duffie*, in black *Raimuſed* Village, and it is us'd as a *Catholicon* for Diſeaſes; There are ſeveral burying Places here & the Tomb-ſtones for the moſt part have a two handed Sword engraven on them. On the *South-ſide* of the Church, within, lies the Tombs of *Mack Duffie* and of the Cadets of his Family, there is a Ship under ſail and a two-handed Sword engraven on the principal Tomb-ſtone, and this Inſcription, *hic jacit Malcolumbus Mac-Duffie de Colonſay*; his Coat of Arms, and colour Staff is fixed in a Stone, through which a hole is made to holdit. There is a Croſs at the *Eaſt* and *Weſt* ſides of this Church, which are now broken, their height was about twelve Foot each, there is a large Croſs on the *Weſt-ſide* of the Church, of an entire Stone very hard, there is a Pedeſtal of three Steps by which they

they aſcend to it, it is 16 Foot high, and a Foot and an half broad; there is a large Crucifix on the *Weſt-ſide* of this Croſs, it has an Inſcription underneath, but not legible, being almoſt wore off by the injury of time; the other ſide has a Tree engraven on it.

ABOUT a quarter of a Mile on the *South-ſide* the Church, there is a Carne, in which there is a Stone Croſs fixed, called *Mac-Duffies* Croſs, for when any of the Heads of this Family werer to be Interr'd, their Corps was laid on this Croſs for ſome Moments, in their Way toward the Church.

ON the *North-ſide* of the Church, there is a ſquare Stone-wall, about two Story high, the Area of it is about fourſcore Paces, and it is joined to the Church Wall; within this Square, there is a leſſer Square of one Story high, and about 60 Paces wide, three ſides of it are built of ſmall Pillars, conſiſting of two thin Stones each, and each Pillar Vaulted above with two thin Stones tapering upwards, There are Inſcriptions on two of the Pillars, but few of the Letters are perfect. There are ſeveral Houſes without the Square, which the Monks liv'd in. There is a Garden at twenty Yards diſtance on the *North-ſide* the Houſes.

THE Natives of *Collonſay*, are accuſtomed after their arrival in *Oronſay* Iſle, to make a

Q 4 Tour

248 *A* Defcription *of the*

Tour Sunways about the Church, before they enter upon any kind of Bufinefs. My Landlord having one of his Family fick of a Fever, asked my Book as a fingular Favour for a few Moments; I was not a little furpriz'd at the honeft Mans requeft, he being illiterate, and when he told me the reafon of it, I was no lefs amazed, for it was to fan the Patients Face with the Leaves of the Book; and this he did at Night: He fought the Book next Morning, and again in the Evening, and then thankd me for fo great a favour; and told me, the fick Perfon was much better by it, and thus I underftood that they had an ancient Cuftom of fanning the Face of the Sick, with the Leaves of the Bible.

THE Ifle *Collonfay* is four Miles in length, from *Eaft* to *Weft*; and above a Mile in breadth: The Mold is brown and fandy on the Coaft, and affords but a very fmall Product, tho' they Plow their Ground three times; the middle is Rockie, and Heathy, which in moft Places is prettily mingled with thick evergreens of *Erica-Baccifera*, *Juniper*, and *Cats-Tail*.

THE Cattle bred here, are Cows, Horfes, and Sheep, all of a low fize. The Inhabitants are generally well Proportion'd, and of a Black Complection, they fpeak only the *Irifh* Tongue, and ufe the Habit, Diet, *&c.* that is us'd in the *Weftern*

Weftern Iflands *of* Scotland, *&c.* 249

Weftern Ifles, they are all Proteftants, and obferve the Feftivals of *Chriftmas*, *Eafter*, and *Good-friday*; but the Women only obferve the Feftival of the Nativity of the Bleffed Virgin. *Kil-ouran* is the principal Church in this Ifle, and the Village in which this Church is, hath its Name from it. There are two Ruinous Chappels, in the *South-fide* of this Ifle. There were two Stone Chefts found lately in *Kilouran* Sands, were compofed of five Stones each, and had Humane Bones in them. There are fome Frefh-water Lakes abounding with Trouts in this Ifle. There are likewife feveral Forts here, one of which is called *Duncoll* it is near the middle of the Ifle, it hath large Stones in it, and the Wall is feven Foot broad.

THE other Fort is called *Dun-Evan*, the Natives have a Tradition among them, of a very little Generation of People, that lived once here, called *Lusbirdan*, the fame with *Pigmies*; this Ifle is the Duke of *Argyle*'s Property.

MULL.

Rothesay Castle

Ardminish, Gigha

At Keills, Jura

Kilchoman Strand, Islay

Cottage at Claggan Bay, Islay

Standing stone, Colonsay

Tombstones on Oronsay

Stone near Balnahard, Colonsay

Bute - Colonsay

Bute

1. Martin does not seem to be certain whether '*Rosa*' and Rothesay were one and the same as he mentions both. He may have come across the former in a manuscript version of Monro's account (1549) or in George Buchanan's History of Scotland, but it has been pointed out that 'Rosay' was the vernacular form recorded after 1397, and around 1700 Kirkwood's list of presbyteries under the Synod of Argyle included 'Rosa'. Today 'Rosa' represents a local pronunciation of Rothesay.

Writing in 1790 Rev. Archibald McLea noted that the town of Rothesay was known in Gaelic as 'Baile a' Mhoide' and the island of Bute as 'Oilean [Eilean] a' Mhoide', while the name of the parish was 'Cill a' bhruic' and the annual fair 'Feil – bhruic'.

[Hewison Vol.I pp.15-19; Kirkwood 3.1.32; OSA p.461. For Rothesay and its castle with circular walls – Hewison Vol.II pp.49, 106 etc., 188 etc.]

2. The quarry source of red sandstone could have been at Ascog, a short distance from Rothesay on the east coast of the island. Woodland has long existed in the neighbourhood of Loch Fad, and with it went coppicing i.e. periodically cutting trees so that they sprouted from the stumps. A possible location for Martin's coppice might have been Barmore wood at the south-west end of Loch Fad and near the Quien Loch (Blaeu: 'Scapsie Loch', Hewison Vol.I p.298 'Scalpsie').

3. The forts or duns Martin mentions, '*Down-Owle*' and '*Down-Allin*' or 'Dun – allerd', are shown on the Blaeu map as 'Doun-ouil' and 'Dunallin'. The former is more usually known as 'Dunagoil', described by Hewison with illustrations (Thomson: 'Fort' by 'Dungoil B[ay]'). Hewison refers to 'Dunallunt', situated on 'Cnoc–an–dune', also on the west coast of the island.

[Hewison Vol.I pp.55-59, p.45]

4. The several chapels or churches mentioned by Martin are described by Hewison. Kilmichael, apparently pronounced by the older 'natives' as 'Kil – muchil', stood on the north-west coast and is what was called a 'primitive edifice', with a burial ground and well nearby. Hewison notes that 'down to the end of last century [1800] several families of Mac-gill-mhichells kept up in Bute the trace of this patronymic'. An entire lengthy chapter, with illustrations, is devoted by him to Martin's '*Kil-blain*', situated in the extreme south of the island east of Dunagoil Bay. 'Kil-blain' evidently includes Martin's representation of the name 'Blane', which was pronounced by Gaelic speakers as 'Blawn'. The chapel of Kilchattan is supposed to have its name from a St Catan rather than having any immediate connection with the Clan Chattan. During the 18th century 'several families in Bute bore the honoured name of Mac-gill-chattan'. The chapel was believed to have been close to St Catan's well on the farm of Kilchattan Beag near Kingarth.

Martin was probably mistaken in placing '*Kilmichel*' in the '*South* Parish' (Kingarth). Chapels are located on the Blaeu map: 'Kilmichael' in Rothesay parish, 'Kilblain' close to the coast south of 'Doun-ouil', 'Kilbride' in Rothesay parish. There is in Glenmore a Kilbride farm but no trace of a chapel or cemetery remains. Another St Bride's chapel was at Rothesay. The Lady Kirk in Rothesay (Blaeu: 'Lady Kirck'), otherwise called St Mary's Chapel, was described at length by Hewison, who pointed out that it was still called 'Cilla' bhruic' in the 18th century. Numerous other chapels, pre-Reformation or later and not mentioned by Martin, are on record in Bute.

[Hewison Vol.I pp.112-114, 161-191. For 'Chattan' names nearby see also Arran and Gigha. Hewison Vol.II pp.232, 235, 237-250, I pp.99-100; OSA p.461]

5. The reference to 'easing nature' occurs elsewhere in Martin's work – e.g. Skye and the Flannan Isles (Lewis).The 'principal heritors' were described by Hewison.

6. As regards Gaelic in Bute, it was still widely spoken at the end of the 18th century: 'The language principally spoken in the parish [Rothesay] is the Gaelic'. 'Most of the natives speak English very well; although, in conversing with one another, they seem to be fond of the Gaelic, their mother tongue, which chiefly prevails among the old people, and may have been an hindrance to the more easy and more ready introduction of new methods of improvements in the parish [Kingarth].' Gaelic was still generally spoken a century later, especially in the north, but by 1950 only 50 islanders could speak it.

[OSA pp.464, 457].

Arran

1. It has been pointed out that the name 'Arran' has long been the subject of debate, and that 'The name pre-dates Gaelic speech'. Balfour notes a tale linking the Feinne with Arran, but this is not quite the same as Martin's 'received Tradition'. Of 'the many Stones set up in divers Places' Fraser records 'Clach an Fhionn', Stone of the Fianna, and the names of at least a dozen others, some of which may be remains of chambered cairns. There are standing stones near the river in Glen Rosa, by the Cnocan Burn at Brodick, and by the Kirkmichael river. Martin's '*Baelliminich*' (p.220; Blaeu: 'Balmeanach') is Ballymeanoch, at the south end of the island. '*Mackir*' is now 'Machrie'.

[Fraser pp.9-12, 113; Balfour Vol.II pp.4-5; OSA p.473; Balfour Vol.I pp.113-125, 149-152. For Brodick Castle, occupied by Sir John de Hastings c.1306 – Balfour Vol.II pp.30 etc.]

2. The cave at '*Druim – cruey*', described by Rev. John Hamilton in the 1790s, was that in which King Robert Bruce is supposed to have taken refuge, and where, according to Martin, '*Fin-Mac-Cowl*' was said to have lodged. Hence it has been known as 'The King's Cave', still with 'the pillar-like buttress' near the entrance which divided the interior. Pennant refers to the series of caves here as 'those of *Fin-mac-cuil*, or *Fingal*'. 'Druim-cruey' or 'Druim Cruaidh', hard ridge, conforms to Fraser's observation that some '*druim* – names have acquired settlement status', and Martin's '*Druim-cruney* Village' must have been nearby although his use of 'village' normally included the extent of associated land. The area of the 'Sanctuary' at Druim-cruey has not been located but as the island is divided more or less vertically into the two parishes and the Kilmorie parish church was at the southern end, one of the caves would certainly be a little more 'Centrical'.

[OSA p.475; Balfour Vol.I pp.213-218; Pennant p.181; Fraser p.45]

3. According to Balfour, Martin provided the Fullarton legend 'in its earliest recorded form'. It is claimed that MacLouis is 'simply Mac-luaidh', son of the fuller, and so a poor attempt at a Gaelic version of Fullerton.

[Balfour Vol.II pp.53-58]

4. Martin's own map of the Western Isles has 'L[och] Renstil' at Loch Ranza, so that 'Loch Kenistil' is probably a misprint. The only castle in the north of Arran seems to be that at Lochranza, perhaps named by Martin after a nearby 'Cean an t-sail', head of salt water.

[Fraser p.112]

5. Two of Martin's five 'churches' are the parishes of Arran with churches at Kilmorie/Kilmory in the south-west and at Kilbride near Lamlash. Another may be the chapel at Kilmichael in Glencloy near Brodick, though there is the possibility of another at Balmichael to the west.

6. The passage on the '*Baul Muluy*', possibly 'the round stone of St Moluag', was quoted by Balfour, with no explanation, as an example of folk medicine.

[Balfour Vol.II pp.308-309]

Ailsa

1. The island now known as Ailsa Craig seems to have been originally called, as by Martin, 'Ailsa' only ('*Islesay*'; cf. Munro pp.46-47 'Ellsay'), the 'Craig' being added much later. Lawson was told by Dr Macleod of Morvern that the Gaelic for Ailsa was 'Ailishair-a-Chuain', Ailsa of the ocean. Though Lawson himself was only able to guess at an English meaning he still understood that there were other Gaelic placenames on the island. Watson noted an early reference to Ailsa as 'Aldasain', and a more recent form, 'Allasa'. He also said that in Gaelic the name was often 'Creag Ealasaid' and 'Ealasaid a' Chuain,' and that the name given to the rock in an Irish tale was 'Carraig Alastair'.

[Lawson p.9; Watson (1926) pp.173, 515; Blaeu: 'Ailza']

2. The 'stair cut out in the Rock' leads up by the 'Tower' or castle as illustrated by Pennant. Lawson quoted Sir James Balfour (c.1580) regarding the buildings on Ailsa: 'In this lylland there is the ruines of ane old Castell and Chapell, possest by the Earls of Cassilis, quo hold the same of the Abbey of Corsereguall.' Pennant found the ruins of a chapel on the beach, presumed by Lawson to be the shore south of the lighthouse, where fishermen apparently camped in their 'tents', i.e. shelters rigged up with sails. Having climbed up as far as the 'castle' Pennant did not venture to the summit though he had heard there was a small chapel there, no doubt Martin's '*Fiunnay*'. The 'Pavement or Causeway' is not now visible but may be submerged under matted vegetation.

[Lawson pp.12, 15; Pennant opp. p.189, pp.190-191]

3. The former presence of 'hogs' may be suggested by the existence of the Swine Cave at the north tip of the island, but Pennant recorded only goats and rabbits. The 'Fresh Water Lake' can only be the Garry Loch lying in a wide crevice above the castle, about 6 feet wide in dry weather and surrounded by sphagnum moss which is water-covered after persistent rain. The loch is anything up to 17 feet or more in depth. There are a few springs on the island; Martin's 'Fresh Water Spring' was probably the well near the castle from which Pennant refreshed himself. The 'coulterneb' was probably the puffin but could have been the much less numerous razorbill. It would not have been the guillemot.

[Pennant pp.190-191; SND Vol.III p.200; Lawson p.14]

4. 'The isle *Avon*' is better known as Sanda, though about 1790 it was said that the island of Sanda was 'still sometimes called Aven' and that there were the remains of 'an old Popish chapel'.

[Blaeu: 'Avon or Sanda'; OSA p.394; Munro p.49: 'this Avoin is ane common place for schippis'.]

Gigha and Cara

1. 'Lergie' was close to the present Tayinloan, Kintyre, and the name was represented until recently in Largie Castle. In Gaelic Largs, Ayrshire, is 'Leargaidh Gall[ta]', and there are three 'Leargaidh' divisions in the south of Arran. 'Leargaid' has been translated as 'place of the green slope'. The ferry route across the channel 'between Lergy and Gigha' is about four miles long.

MacAlister of Lergy/Largie was in fact a Macdonald. Alexander, son of Donald, fourth of Largie, was a brother of John who succeeded his father in the estate. When John died without heirs the estate fell to Alexander's son Hector, called Hector MacAlister of Largie, who died about 1590. Members of the irregular succession continuing into the 17th century retained the MacAlister designation. In 1669 Angus Macdonald of Largie inherited the island of Cara from his father, another Alexander. The Macdonald (MacAlister) of Largie in Martin's time was probably John, son of Angus, who died in 1710.

[Fraser p.87; Macdonalds Vol.III pp380-387. For old Largie Castle Inventory Vol.I pp.160-161 no.312]

2. Rev. William Fraser, interim minister of the parish of Gigha and Cara in 1792, wrote: 'The common burying place in the island [Gigha] is called Cill Chattan…Here are the ruins of an old chapel, 33 feet long, 14 broad'. [Blaeu: 'Kilchat']. The stone font at the east end, 'perforated in the centre', was still present but positioned 'in the sole' of 'a long narrow window'; and near the ruins, in the middle of *Achadh-a-Charra*, was 'a beautiful plain stone', 14 feet high and presumably Martin's 16 feet high monolith. The minister also noted another stone, and 'a cross which fell some years since' and was broken. Some 40 years later it was remarked that the ruined walls of the old church or chapel, with the stone font, were about a mile from the new parish church.

[OSA pp.432-433; NSA pp.400-440; Inventory Vol.I pp.111-112 no.276. The Macneil tombstones still exist in Gigha, presumably those paving the floor of the chapel of Kilchattan. Inventory Vol.I p.112 no.276]

On Cara there was also a chapel, marked but not named on the Blaeu map. It stood close to the tacksman's house: 'Adjoining to the house there is an old chapel, (26 feet long, and proportionally broad) with a Gothick arched door on the north side. This was formerly a burying place, and is now converted into a *kitchen*.' Munro (p.49) refers to 'ane little Ile callit *Caray* with ane chapel in it'.

[OSA p.435; Inventory Vol.I pp.106-107 no.268, p.189 no.327]

3. Martin's '*Toubir-more*' is still known to people in Gigha and spoken of for its healing powers. It seems to have been known as 'Tobar-rath Bhuathaig', the 'Lucky well of Beathag'. The opening and closing of the well, with its cover of stones and its useful effects upon the wind, were described a century after Martin's account. The 'diroch' was evidently one of the island who had the right and special knowledge to open and maintain the well. Once opened the well was cleaned with a wooden dish or clam shell, and then in order to produce the required wind water was thrown in the necessary direction 'with a certain form of words, which the person repeated every time he threw the water'. But by the 1790s the practice was virtually given up and forgotten. 'This ceremony of *cleaning the well*, as it is called, is now seldom or never performed; though still there are two old women, of the names Galbreath and Graham,

who are said to have the secret, but who have cause to lament the *infidelity of the age*, as they derive little emolument from their profession.'

[OSA p.428]

4. Some straggling juniper bushes are still to be found on the island. The 'scurff *Corkir*' is the cudbear-lichen which can be used to make a purplish-red dye. 'Scur' or 'scurf' is lichen, while 'corkir', 'corcar' or 'corcur', have to do with purple or crimson (dye). Armstrong (p.144) notes: 'What the Highlands call *corcur* is a white mossy scurf adhering to large stones, and with which they make a pretty crimson dye. It is first well dried in the sun, then pulverized and steeped, commonly, in urine, and the vessel made air-tight. In this state it is suffered to remain for three weeks, when it is fit to be boiled in the yarn which it is to colour.'

5. Gaelic remained the ordinary language of 'the common people' in Gigha for many years, although English was beginning to make inroads by 1790, at which time 'several speak it well enough to transact business'. Today there are still 5 or 6 native Gaelic speakers.

[OSA p.441]

Jura

1. As 'Bailif *Campbell*' (Martin p.235), according to his tombstone, died in 1695 and Martin referred to him as dying 'three years ago', it seems that Martin was in Jura in 1698 (one of the few dateable visits to particular islands), which means that he could have travelled there with John Adair, even though he evidently went from Jura to Colonsay in a local boat.

2. Nearest to Gigha, wrote Monro (1549) not quite accurately, 'layis *Diuray* ane uther fine forrest for deiris'. Martin refers to about 300 deer on the hills. The former also mentions the custom of driving deer by 'tynchellis' through the gaps at the narrowest point of the island and then driving them back through the other way so that 'infinit deir' were killed. The word 'tinchell' may be derived from 'timchioll', around, and be explained as a practice whereby deer were driven into some kind of enclosure. The explanation of the placename 'Jura' meaning 'deer island' is more probable than the story of the brothers Dih and Rah.

[Munro pp.49-50]

3. The stones at '*Knock Cronm*' [Blaeu: 'Knockroim'; Thomson: 'Knockrom'], where Dih and Rah were traditionally said to be buried, actually number three.

[Inventory Vol.5 p.69 no.109]

4. '*Brochan*' is a form of gruel or porridge.

5. The 'four Hills of a considerable heighth' are (from north to south) Corra Bheinn (1867 feet), Beinn Shiantaidh (2477), Beinn an Oir (2571), and Beinn a Chaolais (2407). Martin's '*Beinbrek*', i.e. Beinn Bhreac, may be the hill of this name sloping up from the south shore of Loch Tarbert or another Beinn Bhreac much further north at the head of Gleann Grundale above Ardlussa. While the former fits more readily Martin's location 'in the *Tarbat*', '*Toubir ni Lechkin*', Tobar na Leacan, is usually considered to be Tobar Leac nam Fiann on a slope in northern Jura near the small Loch nan Caorach

[Inventory Vol.5 p.262 no 395].

Excavations at the latter site produced flints, clay pipe fragments, and other offerings which suggested long human association [Mercer p.191]. Since, according to Martin, the water flowing from the well ran into the river '*Nissa*', and since it has been surmised that 'Nissa' is the river Lussa, it is readily assumed that 'Toubir ni Leachkin' is 'Tobar Leac nam Fiann'.

6. The bending river Abhainn a' Chnuic Bhric, flowing north-west into a loch and then southwards to Inver, is Martin's '*River of Crokbreck*', and still holds salmon in season.

7. However unlikely it may be that Gillouir MacCrain lived to be 180 he was nevertheless one of the long-lived MacCrain[e]s of Caigenhouse, a little north of Craighouse, on the east coast of Jura. Some of them lived into the 20th century, although according to Donald Budge (1960) 'There are no longer people of the name Maccrain in Jura'. In the parish register of deaths, Mary McCraine, known as Mairi Ribeach, died at Lussagiven in 1855 aged 118. Gillouir is supposed to have died in 1671. 'Bailif' Duncan Campbell, first of Jura, was appointed bailie of the island in 1661. Born in 1596, he lived at Sannaig where he succeeded Macdonalds and died aged 99 in 1695. It seems to be impossible now to identify '*Donald Mac N'Mill*' (Macmillan – once a common name in Jura), but the village where he lived, '*Killearne*', must be the former 'Killearnadale' [Munro p.50 'Kilernadill'; Blaeu: 'Kilaridil'] now called Keils, where a chapel or church stood within the graveyard. Gillouir MacCrain was buried 'on the west side of the old south-west gate of Kilearnadil churchyard.'

[Budge pp.165, 177-179; Youngson pp.420, 510, 539, 126-127, 76-77]

8. The west coast of Jura, especially from Loch Tarbert northwards, is remarkable for the series of raised beaches and caves. The King's Cave or Uamh Righ (cf. King's Cave, Arran) is perhaps the best-known, partly as a consequence of excavation there in 1971. It is on the north shore of Loch Tarbert, and its Christian associations are evident in the numerous simple crosses on the walls. A few caves served as a 'corpach' or 'resting place for the dead' on their way to Iona. One of them was at 'Rhuintalen' (OS Rudh' an t-Sailein, Ruantallain) on the north side of the mouth of Loch Tarbert; another, 'called the corpach of I Columkill' [Iona], perhaps that mentioned by Budge as Uamh Muinntir I, cave of the Iona people, was said to be at Corpach Bay below Cnoc na Corpaich. The largest of all the caves was said by Budge to be called 'Uamh – Ghlamaich', the 'Uaghlamaich' decribed by Rev. Kennedy in 1843.

[Mercer p.108; Tolan-Smith pp.7-8; NSA p.535; Budge p.6]

9. The anchorage of 'Whitfarlan' (Whitefarland Bay at Inver) is in the narrow Sound of Islay, just over a mile north of the Feolin – Port Askaig ferry route. Another 'Whitefareland' is just north of Imachar on the west coast of Arran.

The bay '*Da'l Yaul*' remains unidentified unless it be Lowlandman's Bay, north of Small Isles Bay. The small isles themselves include 'Eilean na Gobhar' ('*Nin Gowir*') – Isle of Goats, and Eilean nan Coinein ('*Conney Isle*') – Isle of Rabbits. Many accounts have been given of '*Cory Vrekan*' [e.g. Mercer pp.4, 11; Youngson pp.172-175; Budge pp.1-5]

10. For the opening of a grave on a Friday - cf. Martin p.230 (Gigha): 'they are accustom'd not to bury on Friday'. In recent times the brown rat has been common on Jura, as are adders – possibly Martin's serpents.

Islay

1. The road between '*Port Escock*' (Port Askaig) and '*Kilrow*' divides at Bridgend, the site of the old mediaeval church and burial ground being within the grounds of Islay House. This church of 'Kilrow' or 'Kilarrow' was 'the parish church of St Maelrubha', and the presence of numerous grave slabs and parts of crosses probably confirms this identification, though the neighbouring beach with the outflow of the river Sorn is named on the OS map 'Traigh Cill an Rudha'. The later, 18th century Kilarrow parish church is at Bowmore. The occurrence of the name as 'Kilmorow' in 1500 is given as an example of the dedication to St Maolrubha by Watson.

[Inventory Vol. 5 pp.184-189; Watson (1926) p.288]

2. Monro (1549) refers to 'mekle leid orir' (much lead ore) in Islay, and his placename 'Moychaolis' may now be represented by Mulreesh, nearly three miles west of Port Askaig, where the remains of much later lead workings are evident. The presence of limestone noted by Martin encouraged lime quarrying and burning, chiefly for agricultural use, and a number of 19th century kilns can still be seen.

[Munro p.55; Storrie pp.17-18; Inventory Vol.5 p.45]

3. Wherever he went Martin noted harbours. In Islay his '*Loch-Dale*' is the great inlet from the south-west, Loch Indaal (cf. Thomson: 'Loch na Daal', now Loch na Dal, near Isle Ornsay in Skye).

4. Martin also commented on inland lochs such as '*Loch Guirm*' (Loch Gorm) near Kilchoman, the largest sheet of fresh water in Islay. On an island in the loch are the ruins of a castle first recorded by Monro (1549), but the visible remains probably date from around 1600, and there are later additions that may have suggested to Martin the 'several Forts' built on one island. The island was chiefly in the possession of the Macdonalds of Dunivaig and the Glens in the late 16th century but was occasionally 'usurped' by MacLean of Duart.

The interest of Loch Finlaggan lies largely in the island, Eilean Mor, 'ane fair Ile in fresh water Loch', where the Lords of the Isles had a stronghold and near which the Council of the Isles, Martin's 'High Court of Judicature', met on the smaller neighbouring island known as 'Eilean na Comhairle'. Martin's '*Lucht-taeh*' (bodyguard) is luchd-taighe (people of the house).

The island named by Martin as 'Ilan Viceain' (Blaeu: 'Elan na kean') is in the small Loch Lossit, south-east of Ballygrant.

[Munro p.56; Inventory Vol. 5 pp.282-283 no.406; Munro p.56, Appendix 1 pp.95-110; Inventory Vol. 5 pp.275-281 no.404, pp.153-154 no.304]

5. The fort or castle of '*Dunnivag*' (Dunivaig) is well recorded and fully described. It stands on the east side of Lagavulin Bay in the south of Islay.

[Inventory Vol 5 pp.268-275 no.403]

6. The cave called '*Uah Vearnag*' seems to have been that noted by Pennant on his way from Islay to Oronsay: 'Leave, on the *Ilay* coast, near the mouth of the *Sound*, the celebrated cave of Uamh-Fhearnaig, or *Uam*[h]*-mhor*. Fourteen or fifteen families retire to it during the fine season, as their sheelins, or Summer residence; and three families reside in it the whole year.' This cave is at the mouth of the stream descending from the Coir' Odhar about 2 miles west of the Rudh' a Mhail lighthouse. It strikes as unusually warm within and has the remains of bench 'beds'. The capacity of Martin's '*Uah Vearnag*' to hold so many men, in addition to the actual name, would

seem to match Pennant's description, but there seems to be no evidence of either a well or a little chapel nearby. If the cave had been a possible 'Uamh nam Fear' in the north-west corner of the island, the well '*Tonbir in Knahar*' could be the so-called Tobar Haco, with a burial ground nearby or with the chapel or burial ground being Cill Ronain near Sanaigmore. The 'tour sunways' round both cave and well is an obvious example of moving 'deasail' around places or objects.

[Pennant p.234; Inventory Vol.5 p.167 no.343]

7. The chapel and burial ground near the mouth of the river Laggan at Laggan Bay have been eroded by the river water and if 'the *Brion* of *Ila*' was buried here his remains are likely to have been washed away also. The '*Brion*' was probably the brieve of Islay. The Gaelic charter by Donald, Lord of the Isles, to Brian Vicar MacKay and his heirs, of 6 May 1408, was witnessed by Patrick Mc a Bhruin; the name is said to be a version of 'Macbrehon' or 'Mac a' bhrithinn', son of the judge (brieve), and later anglicised as Brown. In 1510 the death of 'Sir John Breif' was recorded, and in 1618 a family named 'Breghoun' was living in the area of Laggan. The members included Patrick Breghoun, his son Donald, and others called 'McBreghoun'. It is possible that this Patrick was the 'Britheamh Ileach' (brieve of Islay) of the time, and perhaps 'the *Brion* of *Ila*' to whom Martin referred.

[Smith pp.18-19 no.3, 364, 443]

8. In 1793 there was still 'a salmon fishing' in the river Laggan.

[OSA p.409]

9. The three islands named by Martin, *Texa*, *Ouirsa* (Orsay, off Portnahaven at the point of the Rinns), and *Nave* off Ardnave Point in the north, are the largest on the Islay coast. Each of them has the remains of a chapel and burial ground. Watson referred to 'Neave or Cooms Island' off the north coast of Sutherland, suggesting that the name indicated a sanctuary or a piece of church land with a chapel, and said that it was 'the only one on an island'; but Nave Island of Islay seems to be another instance. Sir James Turner described Orsay as 'A litle skurvie ile in the end of Yla'. 'Nave was noticed by Monro: 'Narrest this lyis *Ellannefe* on the north coist of Ila besides the enteres of Loch Grinord foirsaid, with ane Kirk in it.'

[Inventory Vol.5 pp.259-261 no.391, 254-256 no.387, 225-228 no.383; Watson (1926) pp.249-250; Smith p.400; Munro p.60]

10. Martin's list of the churches of Islay is exceptionally clear. '*Kil Chollim-Kill*' near Port Askaig represents the chapel and burial ground at Kiells a mile or so south-west of Port Askaig. '*Kil Chovan* in the *Rins*' must have been located in its district by Martin in order to distinguish the old church of 'Cill Chomain' there from the chapel of 'Cill Chomhan' in the extreme south of the island. The punctuation of the next stage of the list, '*Kil Chieran* in *Rins*, on the West side *Nerbols* in the *Rins*' opens the possibility of there being two chapels or churches, one at Kilchiaran on the west side, the other close to the farm of Nereabolls on the slope above Loch Indaal. The numerous placenames in Islay ending in '-bus' or '-bolls' (e.g. Kinnabus, Coillabus, Cornabus, Grobolls, Lyrabus etc.) are apparently of Norse origin, the final syllable deriving from *bolstadr*, a farmstead. The chapel dedicated to St Columba (Martin's 'St. *Columbus* his Church in *Laggan*') has already been mentioned as having been destroyed by river erosion. The last named church, 'Killhan Alen' (Cill an Ailein) was situated just inland from the dunes at the back of Traigh Bail' Aonghais, but there are no visible remains. The cross near St Columba's

chapel, Port Askaig, said by Martin to be 10 feet high, is probably that now described as a cross-shaft 1.8 metres high.

[Inventory Vol. 5 pp.161-163 nos.327, 330; Nicolaisen p.94]

11. The standing stones 'set up at the East side of *Loch-Finlagan*' could have been at the south-west end of the loch where the single stone marked on earlier OS maps and once standing at 1.8 metres in height has now fallen. If there were originally two stones here they might have conformed to Martin's description almost as well as the single stone west of Finlaggan farmhouse although the latter could perhaps be seen more easily as lying to the east of the loch.

[Inventory Vol. 5 pp.68-69 nos.105, 97]

12. Sir Hugh Campbell of Cawdor (Calder, Martin's '*Caddel*'), as owner of much of the island, made arrangements for building what was to become Islay House at Kilarrow in April 1677. He died in 1716. The 'Village on the West Coast' called Cul is presumably represented now by Coul near Machir and Kilchoman.

There remains the mysterious 'little Isle' which 'we may aptly enough call the Green Island' and on which the master of an English vessel caused to be built a heap of timber 'two Stories high' in order to occupy his crew of forty seamen. Martin's account comes from Rev. John MacSween, 'prelatorial incumbent in Gigha, Jura and Colonsay', who is the subject of a whole chapter in Peter Youngson's book on Jura. If it existed at all the island is unlikely to have been Rathlin off the coast of northern Ireland.

[Storrie pp.55-69; Youngson pp.183-195]

Colonsay

1. 'Oronsay' is a common placename throughout the Hebrides. Of Norse origin it signifies an island separated from other land only by high tides. As regards the Oronsay beside Colonsay Pennant gives a tradition that Oran, friend of St Columba, 'had the honor of giving name to the island'. The Augustinian priory on this Oronsay, dedicated to St Columba (Martin's 'St. *Columbus*'), together with its funerary and other relics, have been described in detail. The priory was founded by John, first Lord of the Isles, between 1325 and 1353, and there seems to be no evidence to suggest that there was an earlier foundation dating from St Columba's lifetime. The altar survives, and the existence of 'a modern Crucifix.. in which several precious Stones were fixed' has been attributed to the presence in 1624 of two Franciscan missionaries seeking to revive the Catholic faith in the area.

[See Skye n.7; Inventory Vol. 5 pp.230-254 no.386]

2. It seems likely that 'black *Raimused* Village' is represented by Balarumindubh, a farm just over a mile south of Scalasaig on Colonsay and not far from Carragh Mhic a Phi. The MacDuffie (MacPhee) in 'black *Raimused*' was perhaps a tenant who claimed, possibly with justification, descent from the last of the MacPhees or MacDuffies of Colonsay, Malcolm, who was said to have been taken in 1623 to Pairc na h-Eaglais at Balaruminmor, placed against the great standing stone, and shot. The graveslabs at Oronsay may include a now illegible tombstone read by Martin as that of '*Malcolumbus Mac-Duffie*', but it has been pointed out that Martin may equally well have misread the inscription commemorating Murchardus MacDuffie.

There appear to be no remains of '*Mac-Duffies* Cross' which was fixed into a cairn supposed to have been at the south-west edge of a field called 'Pairc na Croise'. Yet another 'tour sunways' (deasail) took place round the church buildings when Colonsay people visited Oronsay.

[Inventory Vol.5 p.158 no.317; Loder pp.131-132; Inventory Vol.5 pp.246, 248 no.386, pp.224 no.381, 242 no.386 (inscriptions on the cloister pillars)]

3. In the context 'my Book' suggests the Bible.

4. Martin says that '*Kil-ouran*' was 'the principal Church in this Isle' (Colonsay), and according to Rev. Francis Stewart, writing around 1793 and in line with tradition, Oron, an early saint, 'had his cell in Colonsay, on the farm in which the present proprietor's house stands'. In 1844 Rev. Alexander Kennedy remarked that the Kiloran mansion house was built in 1722 upon 'the site of the old Culdee establishment there', whereas Loder states that it stood on the site 'occupied by part of the cemetery of Kiloran Abbey'. The placename 'Kiloran' indicates the former presence of some ecclesiastical foundation, perhaps more than a chapel, in the neighbourhood of the mansion, but the account of the mediaeval church at Lower Kilchattan calls it the old parish church and makes no mention of any early religious building at Kiloran.

Martin also refers to 'two Stone Chests' found in the Kiloran sands, comparable perhaps to the viking burial discovered there in the sand dunes in 1882, and to two ruinous chapels in the south of the island. There were apparently at least three such chapels, Cill Choinnich towards Ardskenish, of which nothing remains, Teampull a Ghlinne on the road to Oronsay, and the third at the burial ground near Balaruminmor.

[OSA p.378; NSA p.545; Loder pp.68, 149; Grieve Vol.II pp.157, 231-239; Inventory Vol.5 pp.193-194 no.364, pp.150-151 no.298; Mercer p.89]

5. Of the two duns that Martin mentions '*Duncoll*' is Dun Cholla near Balaruminmor, with its 'unusually large and well coursed outer facing stones' still present, and '*Dun -Evan*' is Dun Eibhinn or Dun Eibhne west of Scalasaig. The latter seems to have been occupied by a Malcolm MacDuffie, named in an inscription on an early 16th century graveslab at Iona as 'Lord of Dunevin in Colonsay'. Whether pigmies, known as 'Lusbirdan', ever occupied it remains a matter of tradition (cf. Luchruban in Lewis).

[Inventory Vol.5 pp.89-90 nos.147, 149]

MULL.

THE Isle of *Mull*, lies on the West Coast opposite to *Lochaber*, *Swoonard*, and *Moy-dort*. It is divided from these by a narrow Channel, not exceeding half a League in breadth; the Isle is twenty four Miles long, from *South* to *North*, and as many in breadth from *East* to *West*. A *South-east* Moon causes high Tide here. This Isle is in the Sheriffdom of *Argyle*; the Air here is temperately Cold and moist; the fresh Breezes that blow from the Mountains, do in some measure qualifie it; the Natives are accustomed to take a large Dose of *Aqua Vitæ*, as a Corrective when the Season is very moist, and then they are very careful to chew a piece of *Charmel* Root, finding it to be *Aromatick*; especially, when they intend to have a drinking bout, for they say this in some measure prevents Drunkenness.

THE Mold is generally black, and brown, both in the Hills and Valleys, and in some parts a Clay of different Colours. The Heaths afford abundance of Turff, and Peats, which serve the Natives for good Fewel. There is a great ridge of Mountains about the middle of the Isle, one of them very high, and therefore called *Bein Vore*, i. e. a great Mountain. It is to be seen from all the western Isles, and a considerable

considerable part of the Continent. Both Mountains and Valleys afford good Pasturage for all sorts of Cattle, as Sheep, Goats, and Deer, which herd among the Hills and Bushes. The Horses are but of a low size, yet very sprightly; their black Cattle are likewise low in size, but their flesh is very delicious and fine. There's abundance of Wild Fowl in the Hills and Valleys; and among 'em the black Cock, heath Hen, Tarmagan, and very fine Hawks. The Sea Coast affords all such Fowl as are to be had in the Western Isles. The Corn growing here is only Barley and Oats. There's great variety of Plants in the Hills and Valleys, but there is no Wood here, except a few Coppices on the Coast. There are some Bays, and Places for Anchorage about the Isle. The Bay of *Duart* on the East side, and to the North of the Castle of that Name, is reckoned a safe Anchoring place, and frequented by Strangers. *Lochbuy* on the opposite West side, is but an indifferent Harbour, yet Vessels go into it for Herring.

THE Coast on the West abounds with Rocks for two Leagues West and South West. The *Bloody Bay* is overagainst the North end of Island *Columkil*, and only fit for Vessels of about an hundred Tun.

SOME few Miles further to the North East is *Loch Levin*, the entry lies to the Westward, and

and goes twelve Miles Easterly, there are Herrings to be had in it sometimes, and it abounds with Oysters, Cockles, Muscles, Clams, &c.

LOCH-LAY lies on the South side of *Loch Levin*, it is proper only for small Vessels, Herring are to be had in it sometimes, and it abounds with variety of Shell-Fish; the small Isles called the white Isle, and Isle of Kids are within this Bay. To the North of *Loch Levin*, lies *Loch Scafford*, it enters South West, and runs North East; within it lies the Isles *Eorsa*, and *Inchkenneth*, both which are reputed very Fruitful in Cattle, and Corn.

THERE is a little Chappel in this Isle, in which many of the Inhabitants of all Ranks are buried. Upon the North side of *Loch Scafford* lies the Isle of *Vevay*, it's three Miles in Circumference, and encompassed with Rocks and Shelves, but Fruitful in Corn, Grass, &c.

TO the West of *Ulva*, lies the Isle *Gometra*, a Mile in Circumference, and Fruitful, in proportion to the other Isles.

About four Miles further lie the small Isles call'd *Kairnburg-More*; and *Kernbug-Beg*, they are naturally very strong, fac'd all round with a Rock, having a narrow entry, and a violent Current of a Tide on each side, so that they are

are almost impregnable. A very few Men are able to defend these two Forts against a thousand. There is a small Garrison of the Standing Forces in them at present.

TO the South of these Forts lie the small Isles of *Fladday*, *Lungay*, *Back*, and the *Call* of the Back; Cod and Ling are to be had plentifully about all these Islands.

NEAR to the North East end of *Mull*, lies the Isle *Calve*, it is above two Miles in compass, has a Coppice, and affords good Pasturage for all kind of Cattle. Between this Isle, and the Isle of *Mull*, there is a capacious and excellent Bay, called *Tonbir Mory*, *i. e.* the Virgin *Maries* Well, because the water of a Well of that Name, which is said to be Medicinal, runs into the Bay.

ONE of the Ships of the *Spanish Armada*, called the *Florida*, perished in this Bay, having been blown up by one *Smallet* of *Dunbarton*, in the year 1688. There was a great Sum of Gold and Money on board the Ship, which disposed the Earl of *Argyle*, and some English-men to attempt the recovery of it; but how far the latter succeeded in this Enterprize, is not generally well known; only that some pieces of Gold, and Money, and a golden Chain was taken out of her. I have seen some fine brass Cannon, some Pieces of Eight, Teeth, Beads

Beads and Pins that had been taken out of that Ship. Several of the Inhabitants of *Mull* told me that they had converſed with their Relations that were living at the Harbour when this Ship was blown up, and they gave an account of an admirable Providence that appear'd in the preſervation of one Doctor *Beaton*, (the Famous Phyſician of *Mull*,) who was on board the Ship when ſhe blew up, and was then ſitting on the upper Deck, which was blown up entire, and thrown a good way off, yet the Doctor was ſaved, and liv'd ſeveral years after.

THE black and white *Indian* Nuts are found on the Weſt ſide of this Iſle; the Natives pulverize the black Kernel or the black Nut, and drink it in boyl'd Milk for Curing the *Diarhœa*.

THERE are ſeveral Rivers in the Iſle that afford *Salmon*, and ſome Rivers abound with the black *Muſcle* that breeds Pearl. There are alſo ſome Freſh water Lakes that have Trouts, and Eels. The whole Iſle is very well water'd with many Springs and Fountains. They told me of a Spring in the ſouth ſide of the Mountain *Bein Vore*, that has a yellow colour'd ſtone in the bottom, which doth not burn, or become hot, tho' it ſhould be kept in the Fire for a whole day together.

THE

THE *Amphibia* in this Iſle are *Seals*, *Otters*, *Vipers*, of the ſame kind as thoſe deſcribed in the Iſle of *Skie*, and the Natives uſe the ſame Cures for the biting of *Vipers*. *Foxes* abound in this Iſle, and do much hurt among the Lambs, and Kids.

THERE are three Caſtles in the Iſle; to wit, the Caſtle of *Duart*, ſcituated on the Eaſt, built upon a Rock, the Eaſt ſide is ſurrounded by the Sea. This was the Seat of Sir *John Mack Lean*, Head of the Ancient Family of the *Mack Leans*; and is now together with the Eſtate, which was the major part of the Iſland, become the Duke of *Argyle's* Property by the Forfeiture of Sir *John*.

SOME Miles further on the Weſt Coaſt, ſtands the Caſtle of *Moy*, at the head of *Lochbuy*, and is the Seat of *Mack Lean* of *Lochbuy*.

THERE is an old Caſtle at *Aros* in the middle of the Iſland, now in ruines. There are ſome old Forts here called *Dunns*, ſuppos'd to have been built by the Danes. There are two Pariſh Churches in the Iſle, *viz. Killinchen-Benorth*, *Loch-Levin*, and a little Chappel, call'd *Kilwichk-Ewin* at the Lake above *Loch-Lay*, each Pariſh hath a Miniſter. The Inhabitants are all Proteſtants, except two or three, who are Roman Catholicks; they obſerve the Feſtivals

Feſtivals of *Chriſtmas*, *Eaſter*, *Good-Friday*, and *St. Michael's*. They ſpeak the *Iriſh* Language generally, but thoſe of the beſt Rank ſpeak *Engliſh*; they wear the ſame Habit as the reſt of the *Iſlanders*.

JONA.

THIS *Iſle* in the *Iriſh* Language is called *I. Colmkil*, *i. e.* the *Iſthmus* of *Columbus* the Clergy-Man. *Colum* was his proper Name, and the addition of *Kil*, which ſignifies a Church, was added by the *Iſlanders* by way of excellence; for there were few Churches then in the remote and leſſer *Iſles*.

THE Natives have a Tradition among them, that one of the Clergy-Men who accompanied *Columbus* in his Voyage thither, having at a good diſtance eſpied the *Iſle*, and cry'd joyfully to *Columbus* in the *Iriſh* Language, *Chi mi i*, i. e. I ſee her; meaning thereby, the Countrey of which they had been in queſt. That *Columbus* then anſwer'd, It ſhall be from henceforth called *T*.

THE *Iſle* is two Miles long from South to North, and one in breadth, from Eaſt to Weſt. The

The Eaſt ſide is all arable and plain, Fruitful in Corn and Graſs; the Weſt ſide is high and Rocky.

THIS *Iſle* was anciently a Seminary of Learning, Famous for the ſevere Diſcipline and Sanctity of *Columbus*. He built two Churches, and two Monaſteries in it, one for Men, the other for Women; which were Endowed by the Kings of *Scotland*, and of the *Iſles*; ſo that the Revenues of the Church then amounted to 4000 Merks *per Ann.* *Jona* was the Biſhop of the *Iſle's* Cathedral, after the *Scots* loſt the *Iſle of Man*, in which King *Cratilinth* erected a Church to the honour of our Saviour, called *Fanum Sodorenſe*. Hence it was that the Biſhop of the *Iſles* was ſtiled *Epiſcopus Sodorenſis*. The Vicar of *Jona* was Parſon of *Soroby* in *Tyre-iy*, and Dean of the *Iſles*. St. *Maries* Church here is built in form of a Croſs, the Choir 20 yards long, the *Cupulo* 21 Foot ſquare, the body of the Church of equal length with the Choir, and the two croſs Iles half that length. There are two Chappels on each ſide of the Choir, the entry to them opens with large Pillars neatly Carv'd in *Baſſo Relievo*; the Steeple is pretty large, the Doors, Windows, *&c.* are curiouſly Carv'd; the Altar is large, and of as fine Marble as any I ever ſaw. There are ſeveral Abbots buried within the Church; *Mack Ilikenich* his Statue is done in black Marble, as big as the Life, in an Epiſcopal Habit, with a

R Mitre,

Mitre, Crosier, Ring, and Stones along the Breast, *&c.* The rest of the Abbots are done after the same manner; the Inscription of one Tomb is as follows,

Hic Jacet Joannes Mack Fingone, Abbas de Oui, *qui Obijt Anno Domini Milesimo Quingentesimo.*

BISHOP *Knox*, and several Persons of distinction, as *Mack Leod* of *Harries*, have also been buried here.

THERE'S the Ruines of a Cloyster behind the Church, as also of a Library, and under it a large Room; the Natives say it was a Place for Publick Disputations.

THERE is a heap of Stones without the Church, under which *Mackean* of *Ardminurchin* lies buried. There is an empty piece of ground between the Church and the Gardens, in which Murderers, and Children that died before Baptism were buried. Near to the West end of the Church in a little Cell lies *Columbus* his Tomb, but without Inscription; this gave me occasion to cite the *Distich*, asserting that *Columbus* was buried in *Ireland*; at which the Natives of *Jona* seem'd very much displeas'd, and affirm'd that the *Irish* who said so were impudent Liars; that *Columbus* was once buried in this Place, and that none ever came

came from *Ireland* since to carry away his Corps, which had they attempted, would have prov'd equally vain and presumptuous.

NEAR St. *Columbus*'s Tomb, is St. *Martin*'s Cross, an entire Stone of eight foot high; it is a very hard and red stone, with a mixture of grey in it. On the West side of the Cross is engraven a large Crucifix, and on the East a Tree; it stands on a Pedestal of the same kind of stone. At a little further distance is *Dun Ni Manich*, i. e. *Monks Fort*, built of Stone and Lime, in form of a Bastion, pretty high. From this Eminence the Monks had a view of all the Families in the *Isle*, and at the same time enjoy'd the free Air. A little further to the West lie the Black stones, which are so call'd, not from their Colour, for that is gray, but from the effects that Tradition say ensued upon Perjury, if any one became guilty of it after swearing on these Stones in the usual manner, for an Oath made on them was decisive in all Controversies.

MACK DONALD King of the *Isles* deliver'd the Rights of their Lands to his Vassals in the Isles and Continent, with up-lifted hands, and bended knees on the black Stones; and in this posture, before many Witnesses, he solemnly Swore that he would never recall those Rights which he then granted, and this was instead of his great Seal. Hence it is that

R 2 when

when one was certain of what he affirm'd, he faid poffitively, I have freedom to Swear this Matter upon the black ftones.

ON the *South* fide the Gate without the Church is the Taylors Houfe, for they only wrought in it. The Natives fay that in the time of a Plague, the outer Gate was quite fhut up, and that all Provifions was thrown in through a hole in the Gate for that purpofe.

AT fome diftance South from *St. Maries*, is *St. Ouran*'s Church, commonly call'd *Reliqui Ouran*, the *Saint* of that Name is buried within it.

THE Laird of *Mack Kinnon* has a Tomb within this Church, which is the ftatelieft Tomb in the Ifle. On the wall above the Tomb there is a Crucifix engraven, having the Arms of the Family underneath; *viz.* a Boars Head, with a couple of Sheeps bones in its jaws. The Tomb-ftone has a Statue as big as the Life, all in Armour, and upon it a Ship under Sail, a Lion at the Head, and another at the Feet. The Infcription on the Tomb is thus: *Hic eft Abas Lachlani, Mack Fingone, & ejus Filius Abbatis de I. Ætatis in Dno* M° cccc *Ann.*

THERE are other Perfons of Diftinction in the Church, all done in Armour.

ON

ON the South fide of the Church mention'd above, is the Burial Place in which the Kings and Chiefs of Tribes are Buried, and over them a Shrine; there was an Infcription giving an account of each particular Tomb, but Time has worn them off. The middlemoft had written on it, *The Tombs of the Kings of Scotland*; of which forty eight lie there.

UPON that on the right hand, was written *The Tombs of the Kings of Ireland*, of which four were buried here.

AND upon that on the left hand was written *The Kings of Norway*, of which eight were buried here.

ON the right hand within the entry to the Church-yard, there is a Tomb-ftone now overgrown with Earth, and upon it there's written, *Hic Jacet Joannes Turnbull, quondam Epifcopus Canterburienfis.* This I deliver upon the Authority of Mr. *Jo. Mack Swen*, Minifter of *Jura*, who fays he read it.

NEXT to the King's, is the Tomb-ftone of *Mack Donald* of *Ila*; the Arms a Ship with hoifted Sails, a Standard, four Lions, and a Tree; the Infcription, *Hic Jacet Corpus Angufii Mack Donuill de Ile.*

R 3 IN

IN the Weſt end is the Tombs of *Gilbrid* and *Paul Sporran*, Ancient Tribes of the *Mack Donalds*.

THE Families of *Mack-Lean* of *Duart*, *Lochbuy*, and *Coll*. lie next all in Armour, as big as the Life.

MACK ALISTER, a Tribe of the *Mack Donalds*, *Mack Ouery* of *Ulvay*, are both done as above.

THERE is a heap of Stones on which they us'd to lay the Corps while they dug the Grave. There is a Stone likewiſe erected here, concerning which the credulous Natives ſay, That whoſoever reaches out his Arm along the Stone three times, in the Name of the *Father*, *Son*, and *Holy Ghoſt*, will never err in Steering the Helm of a Veſſel.

ONE Tomb hath a Clergy-Man, with this Inſcription upon it: *Sancta, &c.*

ABOUT a quarter of a Mile further South is the Church *Ronad*, in which ſeveral *Prioreſſes* are buried; one of the Inſcriptions is, *Hic jacet Dna. Anna Terleti, Filia quandam Prioriſſa de Jona, quæ obijt Anno Mo Chriſti, Animam Abrahamo Commendamus.*

THE

Another Inſcription is; *Behag Nijn Sorle vic Il vrid Prioriſſa*; i. e. *Bathia* Daughter to *Somerled*, Son of *Gilbert*, Prioreſs.

WITHOUT the Nunnery there is ſuch another Square as that beſide the Monaſtery for Men. The two Pavements which are of a hard red Stone are yet entire; in the middle of the longeſt Pavement there is a large Croſs, like to that mention'd above, and is called *Mack-Leans* Croſs. There are 9 Places on the Eaſt ſide the Iſle, called Ports for Landing.

THE Dock which was dug out of Port *Churich*, is on the ſhoar, to preſerve *Columbus*'s Boat called *Curich*, which was made of ribs of Wood, and the out ſide cover'd with Hides; the Boat was long, and ſharp pointed at both ends; *Columbus* is ſaid to have tranſported 18 Church-men in this Boat to *Jona*.

THERE are many pretty variegated Stones in the ſhoar below the Dock, they ripen to a green colour, and are then proper for Carving. The Natives ſay theſe ſtones are Fortunate, but only for ſome particular thing, which the Perſon thinks fit to name, in excluſion of every thing elſe.

There was a Tribe here call'd *Clan vic n'oſter*, from *Oſtiarii*, for they are ſaid to have been

R 4 Porters.

Porters. The Tradition of these is, that before *Columbus* died, thirty of this Family lived then in *Jona*, and that upon some provocation, *Columbus* entail'd a Curse upon them; which was, That they might all perish to the Number of five, and that they might never exceed that Number, to which they were accordingly reduc'd; and ever since, when any Woman of the Family was in Labour, both she, and the other four were afraid of death; for if the Child that was to be then born, did not die, they say one of the five was sure to die; and this they affirm to have been verified on every such occasion successively to this day. I found one only of this Tribe living in the Isle, and both he and the Natives of this and of all the Western Isles, unanimously declare, that this observation never fail'd, and all this little Family is now extinct, except this one poor Man.

THE Life of *Columbus* written in the *Irish* Character, is in the Custody of *John Mack Neil*, in the Isle of *Barray*; another Copy of it is kept by *Mack-Donald* of *Benbecula*.

THE Inhabitants have a Tradition, that *Columbus* suffer'd no Women to stay in the Isle except the Nuns; and that all the Tradesmen who wrought in it, were oblig'd to keep their Wives and Daughters in the opposite little Isle, called on that account *Womens-Isle*. They say likewise,

likewise, that it was to keep Women out of the Isle, that he would not suffer Cows, Sheep or Goats to be brought to it.

BEDA in his *Ecclesiastical History*, Lib. 3. Cap. 4. gives this account of him. In the year of our Lord, 565. (at the time that *Justin* the younger succeeded *Justinian* in the Government of the *Roman* Empire) the Famous *Columba* a Presbyter and Abbot, but in Habit and Life a Monk; came from *Ireland* to *Britain* to Preach the word of God to the Northern Provinces of the *Picts*, that is, to those who by high and rugged Mountains are separated from the southern Provinces. For the southern *Picts* who have their habitation on this side the same hills, had as they affirm themselves, renounc'd Idolatry, and receiv'd the Faith a long time before, by the Preaching of *Ninian* the Bishop, a most Reverend and Holy Man, of the Countrey of the *Brittons*, who was regularly Educated at *Rome*, in the Mysteries of Truth.

IN the ninth year of *Meilochen* Son to *Pridius* King of *Picts*, a most powerful King, *Columbus* by his Preaching and Example, Converted that Nation to the Faith of Christ. Upon this account they gave him the Isle above-mention'd, (which he calls *Hii*, *Book* 3. *Cap.* 3.) to erect a Monastery in which his Successors possess to this day, and where he he himself was buried, in the seventy seventy year of his Age, and the thirty second after his going to *Britain* to preach the Gospel. He built a Noble Monastery in *Ireland*, before his coming to *Britain*, from both which Monasteries he and his Disciples Founded several other Monasteries in *Britain* and *Ireland*; among all which, the Monastery of the Island in which his Body is interr'd, has the preheminence. The Isle has a Rector, who is always a Presbyter Abbot, to whose Jurisdiction the whole Province, and the Bishops themselves ought to be subject, tho' the thing be unusual, according to the Example of that first Doctor, who was not a Bishop, but a Presbyter and Monk; and of whose Life and Doctrine some things are said to be wrote by his Disciples. But whatever he was, this is certain, that he left Successors eminent for their great Chastity, Divine Love, and regular Institution.

THIS Monastery furnished Bishops to several Dioceses of *England* and *Scotland*; and amongst others, *Aidanus*, who was sent from thence, and was Bishop of *Lindisfairn*, now *Holy-Island*.

The

The Isle of Tire-iy, *is so call'd, from* Tire *a Country, and* iy *an Isthmus; the Rocks in the Narrow Channel seem to favour the Etymology.*

THIS Isle lies about eight Leagues to the West of *Jona*, or *I. Colm-Kil*, the Land is low and Moorish, but there are two little Hills on the South West side; the Mold is generally brown, and for the most part Sandy. The Western side is Rocky for about three Leagues; the Isle affords no convenient Harbour for Ships, but has been always valued for its extraordinary Fruitfulness in Corn, yet being Till'd every year, it is become less Fruitful than formerly. There is a plain piece of ground about six Miles in compass on the East Coast, called the *Rive*, the Grass is seldom suffer'd to grow the length of half an inch, being only kept as a Common, yet is believ'd to excell any parcel of Land of its extent in the Isles, or opposite Continent; there are small Channels in it, through which the Tide of Flood comes in, and it sometimes overflows the whole.

THE Isle is four Miles in length from the South East, to the North West; the Natives for the most part live on Barley-Bread, Butter, Milk, Cheese, Fish, and some eat the Roots of of Silver-weed; there are but few that eat any Flesh, and the Servants use Water-Gruel often with their bread. In plentiful years the Natives drink Ale generally. There are three Alehouses in the Isle, the Brewers preserve their Ale in large Earthen Vessels, and say they are much better for this purpose than those of Wood; some of them contain twelve English Gallons. Their Measure for Drink is a third part larger than any I could observe in any other part of *Scotland.* The Ale that I had in the Inn being too Weak, I told my Host of it, who promis'd to make it better; for this end he took a *Heckrick Stone,* and having made it red hot in the fire, he quench'd it in the Ale. The Company and I were satisfied that the drink was a little more brisk, and I told him that if he could add some more life to our Ale, he would extreamly oblige the Company. This he frankly undertook, and to effect it, toasted a Barley Cake, and having broke it in pieces he put it into the dish with the Ale; and this Experiment we found as effectual as the first. I enquir'd of him if he had any more Art to revive our Ale, and then he would make it pretty good; he answer'd, that he knew of nothing else but a Malt-Cake, which he had not then ready, and so we were oblig'd to content our selves with what pains had been already us'd to revive our drink. The Natives preserve their Yest by an Oaken Wyth which they twist and put into it, and for future use, keep

keep it in Barley-Straw. The Cows and Horses are of a very low size in this Isle, being in the Winter and Spring time often reduc'd to eat Sea-Ware. The Cows give plenty of Milk, when they have enough of fresh Sea-Ware to feed on it fattens them; the Horses pace naturally, and are very sprightly tho' little. The ground abounds with Flint-stone; the Natives tell me they find pieces of Sulphur in several places. The West Winds drive the ordinary *Indian* Nuts to the shoar of this Isle, and the Natives use them as above, for removing the *Diarrhæa*; and the water of the Well called *Toubir,* in *Donich,* is by the Natives drunk as a *Catholicon* for Diseases.

SOME Years ago, about one hundred and sixty little Whales, the biggest not exceeding twenty foot long, run themselves ashoar in this Isle, very seasonably, in time of scarcity, for the Natives did eat them all; and told me that the Sea-Pork, *i. e.* the Whale, is both wholsom, and very nourishing Meat. There is a Fresh-water Lake in the middle of the Isle, on the East side of which there is an old Castle, now in Ruines. The Isle being low and Moorish, is unwholsome, and makes the Natives subject to the Ague. The Inhabitants living in the South East parts, are for the most part Bald, and have but very thin hair on their heads. There is a Cave in the South West, which the Natives are accustom'd to watch in the

the Night, and then take many Cormorants in it. There are ſeveral Forts in the Iſle, one in the middle of it, and *Dun Taelk* in *Baelly-Petris*, they are in form the ſame with thoſe in the Northern Iſles. There are ſeveral great and ſmall Circles of Stone in this Iſle. The Inhabitants are all Proteſtants, they obſerve the Feſtivals of *Chriſtmas*, *Good-Friday*, *Eaſter*, and St. *Michael*'s Day. Upon the latter there is a general Cavalcade, at which all the Inhabitants Rendezvous. They ſpeak the *Iriſh* Tongue, and wear the Highland Dreſs. This Iſle is the Duke of *Argyle*'s Property, it being one of the Iſles lately poſſeſs'd by the Laird of *Mack-Lean*; the Pariſh Church in the Iſle is called *Soroby*, and is a Parſonage.

The

The Iſle of COLL.

THIS Iſle lies about half a League to the Eaſt and North Eaſt of *Tyr-iy*, from which it hath been ſevered by the Sea. It is ten Miles in length, and three in breadth; it is generally compos'd of little Rocky Hills, cover'd with Heath. The Northſide is much plainer, and arable ground, affording Barley and Oats; the Inhabitants always feed on the latter, and thoſe of *Tyr-iy* on the former. The Iſle of *Coll* produces more Boys than Girls, and the Iſle of *Tyr-iy* more Girls than Boys; as if Nature intended both theſe Iſles for mutual Alliances, without being at the trouble of going to the adjacent Iſles or Continent to be matched. The Pariſh Book in which the number of the Baptized is to be ſeen, confirms this obſervation.

THERE are ſeveral Rivers in this Iſle that afford Salmon. There is a Freſh-water Lake in the South Eaſt ſide, which hath Trouts, and Eels. Within a quarter of a Mile lies a little Caſtle, the Seat of *Mack-Lean* of *Coll*, the Proprietor of the Iſle, he and all the Inhabitants are Proteſtants; they obſerve the Feſtivals of *Chriſtmaſs*, *Good-Friday*, *Eaſter*, and *St. Michael*, at the latter they have a general Cavalcade. all the Inhabitants ſpeak the *Iriſh*

Tongue,

Tongue, (a few excepted) and wear the Habit us'd by the reft of the Iflanders. This Ifle is much wholfomer than that of *Tir-iy.* I faw a Gentleman of *Mack-Lean* of *Coll's* Family here, Aged eighty five, who walked up and down the Fields daily.

COD and Ling abound on the Coaft of this Ifle, and are of a larger fize here, than in the adjacent Ifles or Continent.

ON the South Eaft Coaft of this Ifle, lie the train of Rocks, call'd the *Carn of Coll*; they reach about half a League from the Shoar, and are remarkable for their Fatality to Sea-faring Men, of which there are feveral late inftances. There is no Venomous Creature in this Ifland, or that of *Tyr-iy.*

The

RUM.

THIS Ifle lies about four Leagues South from *Skie*; it is Mountaneous and heathy, but the Coaft is Arable and Fruitful. The Ifle is five Miles long from S. to N. and three from E. to W. the North end produces fome Wood. The Rivers on each fide afford Salmon. There is plenty of Land and Sea-Fowl, fome of the latter, efpecially the *Puffin* build in the Hills as much as in the Rocks on the Coaft, in which there are abundance of Caves; the Rock facing the Weft fide is Red, and that on the Eaft fide Grey. The Mountains have fome hundred of Deer grazing in them. The Natives gave me an account of a ftrange Obfervation which they fay proves Fatal to the Pofterity of *Lachlin,* a *Cadet* of *Mack-Lean* of *Coll's* Family; That if any of them fhoot at a Deer on the Mountain *Finchra,* he dies fuddainly, or contracts fome violent Diftemper, which foon puts a period to his Life. They told me fome Inftances to this purpofe; whatever may be in it, there is none of the Tribe above named, will ever offer to fhoot the Deer in that Mountain.

THE Bay *Loch-Scresord* on the Eaft fide is not fit for Anchoring, except without the Entry.

S THERE

THERE is a Chappel in this Iſle, the Natives are Proteſtants, *Mack Lean of Coll* is proprietor, and the Language and Habit the ſame with the Northern Iſles.

Iſle MUCK.

IT lies a little to the South-weſt of Rum, being 4 miles in Circumference, all ſorrounded with a Rock, it is fruitful in Corn and Graſs: the Hawks in the Rocks here are reputed to be very good. The Cattle, Fowls, and Amphibia of this Iſland, are the ſame as in other Iſles, the Natives ſpeak the *Iriſh* Tongue only, and uſe the Habit wore by their Neighbours.

Iſle CANNAY.

THIS Iſle lies about half a mile off *Rum*, it is 2 miles from South to North, and one from Eaſt to Weſt. It is for the moſt part ſurrounded with a high Rock, and the whole fruitful in Corn and Graſs; The South end hath plenty of Cod and Ling.

There is a hill in the North end which diſorders the Needle in the Compaſs, I laid the Compaſs on the ſtony ground near it, and the Needle went often round with great ſwiftneſs, and inſtead of ſettling towards the North, as uſual, it ſettled here due Eaſt. The Stones in the ſurface of the Earth are black, and the Rock below facing the Sea is red; ſome affirm that the Needle of a Ships Compaſs Sailing by the Hill is diſordered by the force of the Magnet in this Rock, but of this I have no certainty.

THE Natives call this Iſle by the name *Tarſin* at Sea, the Rock *Heisker*, on the South end abounds with wild Geeſe in *Auguſt*, and then they caſt their quills. The Church in this Iſle is dedicated to St. *Columbus*. All the Natives are Roman Catholicks, they uſe the Language and Habit, of the other Iſles. *Allan Mac donald* is Proprietor. There is good Anchorage on the N. E. of this Iſle.

A Defcription of the Ifle of EGG.

THIS Ifle lies to the South of *Skie* about four Leagues, it is three miles in Length a mile and a half in breadth, and about Nine in Circumference. It is all Rockie and Mountanous from the middle towards the Weft ; the Eaft fide is plainer, and more arable ; the whole is indifferent good for pafturage and Cultivation; there is a Mountain in the South end, and on the top of it there is a high Rock called *Skur Egg*; about an hundred and fifty paces in Circumference and has a frefh water Lake in the Middle of it ; there is no accefs to this Rock but by one paffage, which makes it a natural Fort. There is a Harbour on the South Eaft fide this Ifle, which may be entered into by either fide the fmall Ifle without it. There is a very big Cave on the South Weft fide of this Ifle, capable of containing feveral hundreds of People. The Coaft guarding the North Weft is a foft Quarry of white Stone, having fome Caves in it. There is a Well in the Village called *Fivepennies*, reputed efficacious againft feveral Diftempers ; the Natives told me that it never fails to Cure any Perfon of their firft Difeafe, only by drinking a quantity of it for the fpace of two or three days ; and that if a Stranger lie at this Well in the Night time,

time, it will procure a deformity in fome part of his Body, but has no fuch effect on a Native ; and this they fay hath been frequently experimented.

THERE is a heap of Stones here, called *Martin Deffil*, *i. e.* a Place Confecrated to the Saint of that Name, about which the Natives oblige themfelves to make a Tour round Sunways.

THERE is another heap of Stones, which they fay was Confecrated to the Virgin *Mary*.

IN the Village on the South Coaft of this Ifle there is a Well, call'd St. *Kathrine*'s Well, the Natives have it in great efteem, and believe it to be a *Catholicon* for Difeafes. They told me that it had been fuch ever fince it was Confecrated by one Father *Hugh*, a Popifh Prieft, in the following manner. He obliged all the Inhabitants to come to this Well, and then imploy'd them to bring together a great heap of Stones at the head of the Spring, by way of Pennance; this being done, he faid Mafs at the Well, and then Confecrated it ; he gave each of the Inhabitants a piece of wax Candle, which they lighted, and all of them made the *Deffil*, of going round the Well Sunways, the Prieft leading them ; and from that time it was

S 3 accounted

accounted unlawful to boil any Meat with the Water of this Well.

THE Natives observe St. *Kathrine*'s Anniversary, all of them come to the Well, and having drank a draught of it, they make the *Dessil* round it Sunways; this is always perform'd on the 15th day of *April*. The Inhabitants of this Isle are well proportion'd, they speak the *Irish* Tongue only, and wear the Habit of the Islanders; they are all Roman Catholicks, except one Woman, that is a Protestant.

THERE is a Church here on the East side the Isle, Dedicated to *St. Donnan*, whose Anniversary they observe.

ABOUT thirty yards from the Church there is a Sepulchral Urn under ground; it is a big Stone hewn to the bottom, about four foot deep, and the Diameter of it is about the same breadth; I caus'd 'em to dig the ground above it, and we found a flat thin Stone covering the Urn; it was almost full of Humane Bones, but no Head among them, and they were fair and dry. I enquir'd of the Natives what was become of the Heads, and they could not tell; but one of them said, perhaps their Heads had been cut off with a two-handed Sword, and taken away by the Enemy. Some few paces to the North of the Urn there is

is a narrow stone passage under ground, but how far it reaches, they could give me no account.

THE Natives dare not call this Isle by its ordinary Name of *Egg*, when they are at Sea, but Island *Nim-Ban-More*, *i. e.* the Isle of big Women. *St. Donnan*'s Well, which is in the South West end, is in great esteem by the Natives, for *St. Donnan* is the Celebrated Tutelar of this Isle. The Natives do not allow Protestants to come to their Burial.

THE Proprietors of the Isle are *Allan Mack-Donald* of *Moydort*, and *Allan Mack-Donald* of *Moron*.

S 4 Saint

Port Ban, Iona

Bailephuil, Tiree, in former days

At Coroghon, Canna

Remains of the early nunnery, Canna

Laig Bay, Eigg

Ruins at Fivepennies, Eigg

Ruins at Harris, Rum

Fionchra, Rum

Mull – Eigg

Mull

1. Though at some distance from Lochaber Mull has the district of Morvern, with Kingairloch and Sunart ('*Swoonard*'), across the Sound of Mull to the east, and Ardnamurchan, which could be considered part of Moidart, to the north. Situated in its westerly position in the island and being markedly higher than surrounding hills, Ben More ('*Bein Vore*' – Beinn Mhor) can indeed be made out from many though not all of the Hebrides as well as from western parts of the mainland.

2. The bird species of the interior included blackcock, grouse ('heath Hen') and ptarmigan; Graham, writing in the period 1852-1870, said that blackcock then flourished in the south-west of Mull 'much more abundantly' than the red grouse which was also present, and that ptarmigan were on Ben More. What Martin meant by hawks may have covered a broader category of birds of prey including eagle, kestrel, merlin, peregrine, sparrowhawk, and possibly hen harrier, all of which Graham noted on Mull.

[Graham pp.229, 209-213]

3. Loch Buie ('*Lochbuy*') is more accurately on the south coast of Mull, and Bloody Bay, where the 'great sea fight' between John Lord of the Isles and his son Angus took place about 1481, is generally located towards Ardmore Point north-west of Tobermory rather than, as Martin places it, close to Iona. Martin's '*Loch Levin*' (Blaeu: 'Loch Leffan') has become Loch Scridain, the latter name being possibly borrowed from a place called Scridain (Blaeu: 'Skridan') more or less east of Pennyghael and perhaps up the Coladoir river (Blaeu: 'Glen Kollodyr'). Loch na Lathaich ('*Loch-Lay*'; Blaeu: 'Loch Laen') is on the south side of the entrance to Loch Scridain and has within it Eilean Bain ('white Isle') but no obvious 'Isle of Kids' unless it be the 'I. na escheron' (eiserean – shellfish, scallop) of Thomson's map against the east shore of the bay near Eorabus. The present Loch na Keal (Watson: 'Loch of the Churches') is Martin's '*Loch Scafford*' (Blaeu: 'Loch Scaffort'), the latter probably being a form of the original Norse name. Within this loch, as Martin says, are the islands called Eorsa and Inch Kenneth.

[OSA p.328, NSA pp.355-356; Munro p.61 ('Loch Leafan', 'Loch Laois', 'Loch Stafart'); OSA p.291 'Lochlahich'; Watson (1926) p.276; Inventory Vol.3 pp.138-142 for a history of the chapel on Inch Kenneth]

4. The two small islands called Cairn na Burgh More and Cairn na Burgh Beg ('*Kairnburg-More*' and '*Kernbug-Beg*') form the north-eastern extremity of the Treshnish Isles lying out north-west of Gometra and Ulva. The fortifications on each are described as parts of one castle. The small isles 'to the south' of Cairn na Burgh More including Fladda, Langa, Bac Mor and Bac Beag, are the other islands in the Treshnish group.

[Inventory Vol.3 pp.184-190 no.335]

5. Calve Island ('Isle *Calve*') partly encloses the bay of Tobermory ('*Tonbir Mory*') a place in Martin's day known only for its harbour and its well, Tober Mhoire, rather than as a settlement. The traditional site of the well is said to have been south of the mediaeval chapel, the remains of which are in the large burial ground, though a commemorative pillar erected

in 1902 east of the chapel is also supposed to mark the site. The sunken ship from the Spanish Armada is today one of the best known features of the bay of Tobermory; early attempts to salvage the remains of it were described in 1843 by Rev. McArthur. Both Martin and McArthur refer to the ship as the *Florida*, but more recently the name has been given as *Florencia*. One of the most interesting aspects of the sinking was the remarkable survival or 'preservation', reported by Martin, of 'one Doctor *Beaton* (the Famous Physician of *Mull*)', who was apparently thrown a considerable distance when the upper deck, on which he was sitting, was 'blown up entire'. This was probably Malcolm Beaton, son of Andrew, and like his father principal physician to the MacLeans of Duart. This Beaton family held the lands of Pennycross on the south side of Loch Scridain near Pennyghael, where a cross called 'Crois an Ollaimh' stands on the north side of the road to Bunessan.

[Inventory Vol.3 pp.163-165; NSA p.255; MacNab p.95; Bannerman pp.26-27; for the '*Indian* Nuts' see Lewis n.26]

6. The foxes that were abundant in 1700 have been supposed to have disappeared from the island by 1800, but according to Rev. Duncan Clerk, minister of Torosay, the foxes were present in 1790 and were gone from his parish when he was writing in 1843 – 'now there is not one'.

[MacNab p.55; NSA p.283; OSA pp.344, 298]

7. Martin mentions three castles although there was a fourth, Dun Ara, of which there seems to be little history and which in any case he may have included among the 'old Forts...called *Dunns*' also on the island. Accounts of the three castles, Aros, Duart and Moy, are readily available.

[Inventory Vol.3 pp.200-202 no.340, pp.173-177 no.333, 191-200 no.339, 217-227 no.346 respectively]

8. Martin refers to two parish churches, but at one time there were possibly up to fourteen mediaeval parish churches, including Kilmore or Kilcolmkill at Dervaig, Kilfinichen, Killean (Torosay), Kilninian, Kilpatrick, Kilvickeon (near Bunessan), Pennygown, St Mary's (Carsaig), St Mary's (Tobermory), Inch Kenneth, Crackaig, Ulva, Cill an Ailein, Laggan. Rev. Dugal Campbell of Kilfinichen and Kilviceuen parish, outlined a history of their fate by Martin's time:

> 'The several parishes into which the island of Mull was divided in times of Popery, were all united at the Reformation, and called the parish of Mull...About the time of the Revolution, all that part of Mull N. of the Tarbart or Isthmus at Aross was erected into a parish called the parish of Kilninian. The rest of the island of Mull continued to be one parish for upwards of 40 years after this period, and was called the parish of Ross. But being too extensive a charge, a new parish was erected, called the parish of Torasay. What remained was in writings called the parish of Kilfinichen and Kilviceuen, from two places of worship, the one in Airdmeanach, called Kilfinichen, and the other in Ross, called Kilviceuen.'

Loch na Keal divided Kilfinichen from Kilninian. The parish of Kilninian, later known as the parish of Kilninian and Kilmore, included the Treshnish islands, Ulva, Gometra and Staffa. The chapelof Kilfinichen stood to the north side and not far from the head of Loch Scridain, while that of Kilvickean ('little Chappel, called *Kilwichk-Ewin*') was to the south of Loch Assapol, 'the Lake above *Loch-Lay*'. Curiously Martin omitted mention of the parish and church of Kilninian, united with Kilmore in 1628.

In the printed text the words '*Killinchen-Benorth, Loch Levin*' misrepresent what must have been Martin's original 'Killinchen benorth Loch Levin'. Martin seems to have had the impression that the church at Kilfinichen was either in size or role more significant at his time than the 'little chapel' of Kilvickeon.

[OSA pp.281-282; Inventory Vol.3 pp.145-146 no.296, pp.152-153 no.308, pp.150-151 no.305]

Iona

1. The significance of the name, Irish or Gaelic 'I' for Iona, was considered at length by Watson, who concluded that it denoted something like 'Yew-tree island'; but there are other theories, including the tradition recorded by Martin. Carmichael held the view that 'I' was simply a 'mal-pronunciation of Aoi', 'Aoi' being an isthmus.

[Watson (1926) pp.87-90; Carmichael: 'Grazing and Agrestic Customs of the Outer Hebrides'-in Report of the Napier Commission Edinburgh 1884 Appendix A p.464 no.xcix]

2. It is possible to agree in general with Martin's brief description of the island landscape except that the middle part of the west coast is machair, low, sandy, and no doubt 'Fruitful in Corn and Grass'.

3. Martin's account of Iona's monastic remains, lacking the benefit of modern archaeological investigations and surveys, is a blend of observation, tradition, and reading of a few earlier writers such as Monro and Bede. The reference to a life of St Columba, 'written in the *Irish* Character', does not indicate that Martin himself actually saw or read it, but clearly John MacNeil in Barra was the guardian of it in Martin's lifetime, as was Donald MacDonald of Benbecula, a 'strict Roman Catholic', of another copy.

[Macdonalds Vol.II p.349, Vol.III p.279]

4. The tomb of '*Mack Ilikenich*' is thought to be that of an abbot of Iona (1421-c.1465) called Dominic, son of Gille-Coinnich; the inscriptions on other graveslabs, including those of Abbot John MacFingone (MacKinnon), John MacIan of Ardnamurchan ('*Mackean of Ardminurchin*'), and Angus MacDonald of Islay, are comparatively well recorded, but some tombstones seen by Martin disappeared many years ago, as for instance that of '*Behag Nin Sorle vic Il vrid*', Bethoc daughter of Somerled son of Gilbride, which survived until the early 19th century. For the most part Martin's description of the Iona antiquities may simply be compared with that in the Inventory. The black stones, upon which, according to Martin, the Lords of the Isles were expected to kneel when making grants of property, were apparently reduced to one which was destroyed 'by a local lunatic' about 1820. 'Church *Ronad*', St Ronan's Church, is believed to have been the mediaeval parish church of Iona and in a restored state serves as a museum. Presumably the church gave rise to the name 'St Ronan's Bay' nearby. There are at least six 'Port' placenames on the *west* side of the island.

[Inventory Vol.4; Vol.4 pp.138, 233, pp.251-252 no.13]

5. Of the few other 'curiosities' of Iona mentioned by Martin the stones which 'ripen to a green colour' and were found at Port na Curaich were presumably broken pieces of Iona marble which is 'white in colour, streaked and mottled with yellowish-green serpentine', and which was being worked in 1693 when it was noted that the late Earl of Argyll 'caused polish a piece at London aboundantly beautifull'. As for the clan of porters, the word 'oster' is no doubt the Gaelic 'osdair' ('ostair'), an innkeeper, which may give a slightly different meaning to Martin's phrase. There seems to be no knowledge of the

ultimate fate of the 'tribe' beyond the 'one poor man' met by Martin.

[Inventory Vol.4 p.254 no.16; D. Viner: The Iona Marble Quarry 2nd edit. Iona 1992]

6. Returning to the subject of Columba, as he was evidently inclined to do, Martin recorded the tradition that no women were allowed on Iona except nuns, and that wives and daughters had to be kept in 'the opposite little Isle, called on that account *Womens-Isle'*. This was Eilean nam Ban, on the Mull side of the Sound of Iona (Blaeu: 'Yl. na Ban'; Pennant opp. p.261 'Imbaa'). Martin treated Iona like many a tourist after him, as if Columba and the monastic settlement were almost the only points of interest on the island.

Tiree

1. Martin's view on the origin of the island's name was not shared by Watson who found the latter part of the ancient form 'Tir-iath', the land of Eth, inexplicable. Rev. McColl, parish minister in 1792, suggested that 'Tiry or Tir-I seems to import the country belonging to I. or Iona'; but fifty years later Rev. MacLean, of the same parish, was more cautious and had no more than a preference for an alternative: 'the name is derived from *Tir-reidh*, (pronounced *Tir-re),* signifying *the flat or level land*'. Another derivation rejected by Watson was an Old Irish 'ith', meaning corn, though this was attractive 'in view of Tiree's proverbial richness in barley'. There was good reason too for McColl's theory since the island was at an early stage closely linked to Iona.

[Watson pp.85-86. OSA p.255; NSA p.195]

2. What Martin called 'the *Rive*' was described at some length under its modern name by Rev. McColl, who began:

'There is a plain, called the Reef, near the center of Tiry, reckoned by travellers a very great curiosity. It is almost a pentagon of 1200 Scotch acres, with a sandy bottom mostly covered with black earth ten inches deep, a beautiful carpet variegated with flowers. It seems to have been gained from the sea; the work of ages.'

Both Martin and McColl refer to channels, one at least called 'Faothail', the usual Gaelic term for a fordable channel along which the tide flows.

[OSA p.261 n.]

3. Probably it was Tiree's richness in corn that encouraged the establishment of three ale-houses on the island and the use of an extra-large measure. Rev. McColl reported 'only three licensed small stills, and four public houses at the ferries and harbours in both isles', and in 1840 there were 'two licensed inns in Tiree, and one in Coll', as well as the recent emergence of 'several low illicit tippling-houses'. The latter had a 'pernicious effect on the morals of the people', especially of the lighthouse workers at Hynish 'who have generally some money at command, and might be expected to be profitable customers'. Martin appears to have lodged in an inn, but where this was he does not say.

[OSA p.275; NSA p.218]

4. As always, except on Iona, Martin took note of curing wells, caves, fortifications and unusual events in Tiree. The well he called '*Tonbir,* in *Donich*' (Tobar an Domhnaich – the Lord's well) was said by J.G. Campbell to be in Balmeanach, in the west of Tiree. The 'Fresh-water Lake in the middle of the Isle' was Loch an Eilean between Heylipoll and Crossapoll (Blaeu: 'Castel Loch Hyrbol', 'L[och] Hylebol'). The castle on the east side, originally on an island, was probably in ruins in the 1680s

following a siege by the ninth Earl of Argyll in 1678-1679. Of the earlier antiquities, the fort in the middle of Tiree was probably Dun Ceann a Bhaigh, while that Martin called '*Dun Taelk* in *Baelly Petris*' must have been one of the two duns in the vicinity of Balephetrish. Two of the stone circles were at Hough, and there were standing stones at Balinoe, Barrapoll and Caolas.

[Campbell (1902) p.292; Inventory Vol.3 p.170 no.328, p.208 no.344; OSA p.264; Inventory Vol.3 p.107 no.202; Beveridge (1903) p.104n; Inventory Vol.3 p.75 no.130, pp.96-97 no.173, p.65 nos.89 and 91, p.66 no.96]

5. The cave of cormorants was probably in the cliffs of Ceann a Mhara where McColl noted 'a great number of large natural caves, frequented, in time of hatching, by innumerable flocks of sea-fowls'.

For the 'general Cavalcade' in Tiree and Coll see Uist n.32.

Given Tiree's association with Iona it is surprising that Martin made no comment on any of almost a dozen ecclesiastic sites in the island, except for a brief mention of Soroby.

[OSA pp.262, 256; Inventory Vol.3 pp.166-170 no.327]

Coll

1. The 'Parish Book', a register of baptisms seen by Martin, is not with other registers from Coll and Tiree in General Register House. These begin in 1766 (Tiree) and 1776 (Coll).

2. Monro said that Coll had 'ane castell and ane paroch kirk'. The former, Martin's 'little Castle', was indeed the seat of MacLean of Coll, known as Breachacha Castle. It has been suggested that the mediaeval parish church stood at Crossapoll in the south-west corner of the island, but later opinion places it in the burial ground of Killunaig (Blaeu: 'Kilynaig') on the north-west coast. The 'train of rocks called the Carn of Coll' is the Cairns of Coll, at the *north-east* tip of the little islands off the coast near Sorisdale. Blaeu names these rocks as 'Ylen Charn', 'Yl. Moir Karn'.

[Inventory Vol.3 pp.177-184 no.334, p.137 no.202, pp.148-149 no.301]

Rum

1. Martin is at times rather vague in his identification or description of birds. His reference to the 'puffin' as building in the hills raises a number of possibilities. The use of the word 'puffin' would in this case seem to be appropriate for the manx shearwater which nests ('builds') 'in the Hills'. Martin may have derived 'puffin' from the Latin name for the shearwater *Puffinus Puffinus* (Harvie-Brown p.200 *Puffinus anglorum)*, but he could hardly have heard it from islanders who would normally refer to the species as 'fachach'. On the other hand 'puffin' might have been used to refer to the shearwater by a Gaelic speaker using English, as 'fachach', according to Dwelly (p.400), can also mean puffin. Having been to St Kilda Martin should have known the difference between the species, though both nest in holes in the ground or recesses among rocks. Rev. Donald McLean, minister of the Small Isles parish in 1794, renewed the confusion.

[Harvie-Brown & Buckley (1892) p.200; OSA p.234]

2. The story about deer on the hill in the west of Rum called Fionchra (Martin's '*Finchra*') received a comment from John Love who pointed out that a corrie on Fionchra was especially favoured by hinds giving birth, with the implications that the threat hanging over certain MacLeans descended from the Laird of Coll was used as a means of preventing deer, especially perhaps the hinds, from being shot in that area.

[Love p.64]

3. Two points made by Martin have been questioned by Love. Loch Scresort ('*Loch Scresord*') the former said, was 'not fit for Anchoring', although this was qualified by 'except without the Entry'. And Martin claimed that the inhabitants of Rum were Protestants, whereas it seems that around 1700 they were still very much Catholics. Papers of 1728 and 1729 certainly indicate that a high proportion of Rum inhabitants were Catholic at that time. The whole short account of Rum gives the impression that Martin sailed round it without landing, except perhaps briefly at a spot where the 'natives' could tell him the story about Fionchra. There is little detail in his description, which refers to a chapel but says nothing of its location, though it was most probably at Kilmory. Nothing was said either about the 'tynchellis', converging stone walls eventually forming an enclosure into which hunted deer were driven.

[Love p.64; NAS CH1/5/52 pp.344, 455; Munro pp.66-67; OSA p.233; Love pp.109-112]

Muck and Canna

1. Martin's paragraph on '*Isle Muck*' requires no comment, other than to note that, like Rum, the island was owned by the MacLeans of Coll.

2. Martin landed on Canna, apparently with the intention of testing a compass at what is now familiarly called Compass Hill but once was known in Gaelic as 'Sgur-dhearg'. J.L Campbell referred to 'Cnoc a' Chombaist', possibly his own translation from the English.

[Pennant p.276; Campbell (1984) p.245]

3.The small island of Heisgeir, which was apparently also known as Heisgeir nan Cuiseag, Heisgeir of the rushes, is six miles south from the western end of Canna. The proprietor of both Heisgeir and Canna, Allan Macdonald, had succeeded his father, Donald Dubh of Clanranald, in 1686.

[Campbell (1984) p.108]

Eigg

1. The last of the Small Isles as described by Martin is Eigg ('Egg'), like Canna and the others, a Catholic island around 1700. The high and distinctive '*Skur Egg*' (OSA p.245 'Scure Eigg') appeared on earlier OS maps as An Sgurr.

2. Several names and places given by Martin are difficult to locate. Near the northern end of the island beyond Cleadale were the lands and settlement of Five Pennies, still occupied in the mid nineteenth century. The 'Village' was called Five Pennies, not the well, though the latter is still known and distinguished for its surrounding growth of watercress. 'Sandavore' and 'Sandaveg' near Galmisdale consisted of five and four pennylands respectively. The curious name of a heap of stones possibly at Five Pennies, '*Martin Dessil*', evidently includes the word 'deasail', as Martin himself indicates, but the location and purpose of the heap, if consecrated to St Martin are no better known than those of another heap consecrated to the Virgin Mary. There seems to be no recollection of the stone heaps.

[Robertson p.202 – for story referring to 'Tuathanach nan Cuig Peighinn'; Robertson p.208; Thomson]

3.The 'Village' in which was 'St. Katherine's Well' was Galmisdale; again the 'making' of the '*Dessil*' as Martin has it was a distinguishing feature. This well was situated by the way out of Galmisdale to Grulin just past the farmhouse and to the left of the road. Although obscured now its location is still known.

4.The association of St Donnan with Eigg is well known and is preserved in the placename Kildonnan. The saint himself appears in a number of traditions. Martin's 'sepulchral urn' underground near the church was further decribed by Rev. McLean in 1794:

'There are no barrows or tumuli in the parish, except one in Eigg, on the farm or of Kiell Donnain, near an old Popish chapel, from which it lies at the distance of about 80 yards. It is said to be the burial place of Donnan, the tutelary-saint of Eigg; and it lies in a field of arable ground, and the thin flag covering the sepulchral urn, in which Donnan's remains had been deposited, was some years ago exposed by the plough; upon which the urn, being a large round hollow stone, was taken up and examined, and found to contain a number of bones, but no scull appeared among them. It was again buried, at a distance of a few yards from the place where it formerly lay.'

[Robertson pp.193-210; Inventory pp.220-221 nos.688, 689; OSA pp.244-245]

5. Allan Macdonald of Moron (Morar) was fifth in descent from the first of the family, also Allan, son of Clanranald. The first Allan's estate included 9 merklands in Eigg. Allan Macdonald of Moidart ('*Moydort*') was the second son of Donald Macdonald, the eldest son being known as [John] Moidartach. The two Allans were related through their Clanranald ancestry and by the marriage of Allan of Morar to Marion, sister of Allan of Moidart.

[Macdonalds: III p.251, pp.232-233]

6. In his account of Canna Martin wrote: 'The Natives call this Isle by the name *Tarsin* at Sea.' He then added a similar sentence about Eigg: 'The Natives dare not call this isle by its ordinary Name of *Egg* when they are at Sea, but Island *Nim-Ban-More, i.e.* the Isle of big Women.' Almost a century later Rev. McLean developed this further:

'Tradition says, that of old the islands forming this parish, had names sometimes given them different from those which they now bear: Thus Eigg was called *Eillan nan Banmore*, (the Island of the Great Women); Rum was called *Rioghachd na Forraiste Fiadhaich*, (the Kingdom of the Wild Forrest); Canna was called *An t-eillan tarssuin*, (the Island lying across); and Isle Muck, *Tirr Chrainne*, (the Sow's Island). But these may be supposed poetical names, given by the Gaelic bards; and the superstitious are said to have used them, and them only, when at sea, and bound for these islands.'

[OSA p.241]

7. The 'very big Cave on the South West side of this Isle' which was capable of holding 'several hundreds of People' could have been either '*Uamha Chrabhuidh* (the Cave of Devotion) in which the Roman Catholic inhabitants were wont to attend mass in time of the Reformation', or a little to the east 'Uamha Fhrainc, (the Cave of Francis)' famed for a massacre. The former still had an altar in 1794. Unusually for him, Martin does not refer to the tale of the massacre.

[OSA pp.245-246]

Saint KILDA, or HIRT.

THE firft of thefe Names is taken from one *Kilder*, who lived here, and from him the large Well *Tonbir-Kilda* has alfo its Name. *Hirta* is taken from the *Irifh Ier*, which in that Language fignifies *Weft*; this Ifle lies directly oppofite to the Ifles of *N. Uift*, *Harries*, &c. It is reckoned 18 Leagues from the former, and 20 from *Harries*. This Ifle is by *Peter Goas* in a Map he made of it at *Roterdam*, called St. *Kilder*; it is the remoteft of all the *Scots North-weft* Ifles: It is about two Miles in length, and one in breadth; it is faced all round with a fteep Rock, except the Bay on the *South-eaft*, which is not a Harbour fit for any Veffel, tho' in the time of a Calm one may Land upon the Rock, and get up into the Ifland with a little climbing. The Land rifes pretty high in the middle, and there is one Mountain higher than any other part of the Ifland. There are feveral Fountains of good Water on each fide this Ifle. The Corn produced here is Oats and Barley, the latter is the largeft in the weftern Ifles.

THE Horfes and Cows here, are of a lower fize than in the adjacent Ifles, but the Sheep differ only in the bignefs of their Horns, which are very long.

THERE

THERE is an ancient Fort, on the *South-end* of the Bay, called *Dun-fir Volg*, i. e. the Fort of the *Volfcij*, this is the fenfe put upon the word by the *Antiquaries* of the oppofite Ifles of *Uift*.

THE Ifle *Soa*, is near half a Mile diftant from the *Weft-fide* of St. *Kilda*, it is a Mile in circumference, very high, and fteep all round. *Borera* lies above two Leagues N. of St. *Kilda*, it is near a Mile in circumference, the moft of it furrounded with a high Rock, the largeft and the two leffer Ifles are good for Pafturage, and abound with a Prodigious number of Sea-fowl, from *March*, till *September*, the *Solan* Geefe are very numerous here, in fo much that the Inhabitants commonly keep yearly above twenty thoufand Young and Old in their little Stone Houfes, of which there are fome hundreds for preferving their Fowls, Eggs, &c. They ufe no Salt for preferving their Fowl, the Eggs of the Sea Wild-fowl, are preferved fome Months in the Afhes of Peats, and are aftringent to fuch as be not accuftomed to eat them.

THE *Solan* Goofe, is in fize fomewhat lefs than a Land Goofe; and of a white Colour except the tips of the Wings, which are Black, and the top of their Head, which is Yellow; their Bill is long, fmall pointed, and very hard, and pierces an Inch deep into Wood, in their defcent ſcent after a Fiſh laid on a Board, as ſome uſe to catch 'em. When they ſleep, they put their Head under their Wings, but one of them keeps Watch, and if that be ſurpriz'd by the Fowler, (which often happens,) all the reſt are then eaſily caught, by the Neck, one after another; but if the Sentinel gives warning by crying loud, then all the Flock make their eſcape. When this Fowl fiſhes for Herring, it flies about ſixty Yards high, and then deſcends perpendicularly into the Sea, but after all other Fiſh it deſcends a ſquint, the reaſon for this manner of purſuing the Herring, is becauſe they are in greater Shoals than any other Fiſh whatſoever.

THERE is a barren Tribe of *Solan* Geeſe, that keep always together, and never mix among the reſt that build and hatch. The *Solan* Geeſe come to thoſe Iſlands in *March*, taking the advantage of a *South-weſt* Wind, before their coming, they ſend a few of their Number, as Harbingers before them, and when they have made a Tour round the Iſles, they return immediately to their Company, and in a few days after the whole Flock comes together, and ſtays till *September*; the Natives make a Pudding of the fat of this Fowl, in the Stomack of it, and boyl it in their Water-gruel, which they call *Brochan*, they drink it likewiſe for removing the Cough: It is by daily Experience found to be an excellent vulnerary.

THE

THE Inhabitants eat the *Solan* Gooſe Egg raw, and by Experience find it to be a good Pectoral. The *Solan* Geeſe are daily making up their Neſts from *March* till *September*, they make 'em in the Shelves of high Rocks, they Fiſh, Hatch, and make their Neſts by turns, and they amaſs for this end a great heap of Graſs, and ſuch other things as they catch floating on the Water; the Steward of St. *Kilda*, told me that they had found a Red Coat in a Neſt, a Braſs Sun-dial, and an Arrow, and ſome *Molucca* Beans in another Neſt. This *Solan* Gooſe is believed to be the ſharpeſt ſighted of all Sea-fowls, it preſerves five or ſix Herrings in its Gorget entire, and carries them to the Neſt, where it ſpews them out to ſerve as Food to the Young ones; they are obſerved to go a fiſhing to ſeveral Iſles that lie about thirty Leagues diſtant, and carry the Fiſh in their Gorget all that way, and this is confirm'd by the Engliſh Hooks, which are found ſticking to the Fiſh-Bones in their Neſts, for the Natives have no ſuch Hooks among them.

THEY have another Bird here call'd *Fulmar*, it is a Grey Fowl, about the ſize of a *Moor* Hen, it has a ſtrong Bill with wide Noſtrils, as often as it goes to Sea, it is a certain ſigne of a Weſtern Wind, for it ſits always on the Rock, when the Wind is to blow from any other Quarter. This Fowl the Natives ſay, picks its Food out of of live Whales, and that it eats Sorrel, for both thoſe ſorts of Food are found in its Neſt. When any one approaches the *Fulmar*, it ſpouts out at its Bill, about a Quart of pure Oyl, the Natives ſurprize the Fowl, and preſerve the Oyl, and burn it in their Lamps, it is good againſt *Rheumatick* Pains and Aches in the Bones, the Inhabitants of the adjacent Iſles, value it as a *Catholicon* for Diſeaſes; ſome take it for a Vomit, others for a Purge. It has been ſucceſsfully us'd againſt *Rheumatick* Pains in *Edinburgh*, and *London*; in the latter it has been lately us'd to aſſwage the ſwelling of a ſtrained Foot, a Cheek ſwell'd with the Tooth-ach, and for diſcuſſing a hard Boil, and proved ſucceſsful in all the three caſes.

THERE is plenty of Cod, and Ling, of a great ſize, round this Iſle, the Improvement of which might be of great Advantage.

THE Inhabitants are about two hundred in Number, and are well proportioned, they ſpeak the *Iriſh* Language only; their Habit is much like that us'd in the adjacent Iſles, but coarſer: They are not ſubject to many Diſeaſes; they contract a Cough, as often as any Strangers land and ſtay for any time among them, and it continues for ſome eight or ten days; they ſay the very Infants on the Breaſt are infected by it. The Men are ſtronger than the Inhabitants of the oppoſite weſtern Iſles; they

they feed much on Fowl, eſpecially the *Solan* Geeſe, *Puffin*, and *Fulmar*, eating no Salt with them. This is believed to be the cauſe of a Leproſie, that is broke out among them of late; one of them that was become Corpulent, and had his throat almoſt ſhut up, being advis'd by me to take Salt with his Meat, to exerciſe himſelf more in the Fields than he had done of late, to forbear eating of fat Fowl, and the fat Pudding call'd *Giben*, and to eat Sorrel, was very much concern'd, becauſe all this was very diſagreeable; and my adviſing him to eat Sorrel, was perfectly a ſurprize to him: But when I bid him conſider how the fat *Fulmar* eat this Plant, he was at laſt diſpoſed to take my Advice; and by this means alone in few days after, his Voice was much clearer, his Appetite recovered, and he was in a fair way of recovery. Twelve of theſe Lepers died the Year after of this Diſtemper, and were in the ſame Condition with this Man.

BOTH Sexes have a Genius for Poeſie, and compoſe entertaining Verſes and Songs, in their own Language which is very Emphatical. Some Years ago, about twenty of their Number happened to be confined in the Rock *Stack N'armin* for ſeveral days together, without any kind of Food; the Seaſon then not favouring their Endeavours, to return home; one of their Number plucked all their Knives out of the Hafts, wrought a Hook out of each, and then beat them

them out to their former length; he had a Stone for an Anvil, and a Dagger for a Hammer and File; and with thefe rude Hooks, and a few forry Fifhing-lines, they purchafed Fifh for their Maintenance,during their confinement for feveral Days in the Rock. All the Men in the Ifle, having gone to the Ifle *Boreray* for purchafe, the Rope that faftened their Boat, happened to break, and by this unlucky accident, the Boat was quite loft; and the Poor People confined in the Ifle, from the middle of *March*, till the latter end of *May*; without fo much as a cruft of Bread, but they had Sheep, Fowl and Fifh in abundance. They were at a lofs, how to acquaint their Wives and Friends, that all of them were alive; but to effect this, they kindled as many Fires on the top of an Eminence, as there was Men in Number; this was no fooner feen, and the Fires counted than the Women underftood the fignal, and were fo overjoyed at this unexpected News, that they fell to labour the Ground with the Foot-fpade, a fatigue they had never been accuftomed to; and that Years product of Corn, was the moft plentiful that they bad for many Years before. After the Stewards arrival in the Ifle, about the end of *May*, he fent his Galley to bring home all the Men confined in the Ifle, to their fo much longed for St. *Kilda*; where the mutual Joy between them and their Wives, and other Relations was extraordinary.

THE

THE Inhabitants are of the reformed Religion, they affemble in the Church-yard, on the Lord's day, and in the Morning they fay the Lord's Prayer, Creed, and ten Commandments: They work at no Imployment till Monday, neither will they allow a Stranger to work fooner. The Officer, or Stewards Deputy Commonly, and fometimes any of their Neighbours baptize their Children foon after they are born; and in the following form; *A. I.* I baptize you to your Father and Mother, in the Name of the Father, Son, and Holy Ghoft. They marry early and publickly, all the Natives of both Sexes being prefent, the Officer who performs the Marriage tenders a Crucifix to the married Couple, who lay their right hands on it, and then the Marriage is ratified.

THEY obferve the Feftivals of *Chriftmas, Eafter, Good-friday*, and that of *All-Saints*, upon the latter they bake a large Cake, in form of a Triangle, furrowed round, and it muft be all eaten that Night. They are Hofpitable, and Charitable to Strangers, as well as the Poor belonging to themfelves, for whom all the Families contribute a Proportion monthly, and at every Feftival, each Family fends them a piece of Mutton or Beef.

THEY

THEY fwear decifive Oaths by the Crucifix, and this puts an end to any Controverfie, for there is not one Inftance, or the leaft fufpicion of Perjury among them. The Crucifix is of Brafs, and about nine inches in length, it lies upon the Altar, but they pay no Religious Worfhip to it. One of the Inhabitants was fo fincere, that (rather than forfwear himfelf on the Crucifix) he confefs'd a Capital Crime before the Minifter, and my felf. They never Swear, or Steal, neither do they take Gods Name in vain at any time, they are free from Whoredom and Adultery, and of thofe other Immoralities that abound fo much every where elfe.

ONE of the Inhabitants called *Roderick*, a Fellow that could not Read, obtruded a falfe Religion upon the credulous People, which he pretended to have receiv'd from *St. John* the Baptift. It is Remarkable, that in his Rapfodies, which he called Prayers, he had the word *Eli*, and to this purpofe, *Eli* is our Preferver. There is a little Hill, upon which he fays *John* the Baptift deliver'd Sermons and Prayers to him; this he call'd *John's-Bufh*, and made the People believe it was fo Sacred, that if either Cow or Sheep did tafte of its grafs, they were to be killed immediately after, and the Owners were to eat them, but never without the Company of the Impoftor. He made them likewife believe

believe that each of them had a Tutelar Saint in Heaven to intercede for them, and the Anniverfary of every one of thofe was to be neceffarily obferv'd, by having a fplendid Treat, at which the Impoftor was always the principal Perfon. He taught the Women a Devout Hymn, which he faid he had from the Virgin *Mary*; he made them believe that it fecur'd any Woman from Mifcarriage that could repeat it by heart, and each of them paid the Impoftor a Sheep for it.

UPON Mr. *Campbel's* Arrival and mine in *St. Kilda*, *Roderick* made a Publick Recantation of his Impofture; and being then by us brought to the Ifle of *Harries*, and afterwards to the Ifle of *Skie*, he has made Publick Confeffion in feveral Churches of his Converfe with the Devil, and not *John* the Baptift, as he pretended, and feems to be very penitent. He is now in *Skie* Ifle, from whence he is never to return to his Native Country. His Neighbours are heartily glad to be rid of fuch a Villain, and are now happily deliver'd from the Errors he impofed upon them. The Ifle is the Laird of *Mack-Leod's* Property, he is Head of one of the moft ancient Tribes in the Ifles; he beftows the Ifle upon a *Cadet* of his Name, whofe Fortune is low, to maintain his Family, and he is called Steward of it; he vifits the Ifle once every Summer, to demand the Rents, *viz.* Down, Wooll, Butter, Cheefe, Cows, Horfes,

T

ſes, Fowl, Oil, and Barley. The Stewards Deputy is one of the Natives, and ſtays always upon the place; he has free Lands, and an Omer of Barley from each Family; and has the honour of being the firſt and laſt in their Boat, as they go and come to the leſſer Iſles or Rocks. The ancient meaſure of Omer and Cubit continues to be us'd in this Iſle. They have neither Gold nor Silver, but Barter among themſelves and the Stewards Men for what they want. Some years ago the Steward determin'd to exact a Sheep from every Family in the Iſle, the number amounting to twenty ſeven; and for this he put them in mind of a late Precedent, of their having given the like number to his Predeceſſor. But they anſwer'd, that what they gave then, was voluntary, and upon an extraordinary occaſion of his being Wind-bound in the Iſle, and that this was not to be a Cuſtom afterwards. However the Steward ſent his Brother, and with him a competent number of Men to take the Sheep from them by force, but the Natives arming themſelves with their Daggers, and Fiſhing-Rods, attack'd the Stewards Brother, giving him ſome blows on the head, and forc'd him and his Party to retire, and told him that they would pay no new Taxes; and by this ſtout reſiſtance, they preſerv'd their Freedom from ſuch impoſition.

THE Inhabitants live contentedly together in a little Village on the Eaſt ſide St. *Kilda*, which

which they commonly call the Country; and the Iſle *Boreray*, which is little more than two Leagues diſtant from them they call the Northern Country. The diſtance between their Houſes is by them called the High-ſtreet; their Houſes are low built of Stone, and a cement of dry Earth; they have Couples and Ribs of Wood cover'd with thin earthen Turff, thatch'd over theſe with Straw, and the Roof ſecur'd on each ſide with double ropes of Straw or Heath, pois'd at the end with many Stones; their Beds are commonly made in the Wall of their Houſes, and they lie on Straw, but never on Feathers or Down, tho' they have them in greater plenty than all the Weſtern Iſles beſides. The Reaſon for making their Bed-room in the Walls of their Houſes, is to make room for their Cows, which they take in during the Winter and Spring.

THEY are very exact in their Properties, and divide both the Fiſhing as well as Fowling Rocks with as great niceneſs as they do their Corn and Graſs; one will not allow his Neighbour to ſit and Fiſh on his Seat, for this being a part of his Poſſeſſion, he will take care that no encroachment be made upon the leaſt part of it, and this with a particular regard to their Succeſſors, that they may loſe no Privilege depending upon any parcel of their Farm. They have but one Boat in the Iſle, and every Man hath a ſhare in it, proportionably to the Acres

T 2 of

292 A Deſcription of the

of Ground for which they pay Rent. They are ſtout Rowers, and will tug at the Oar for a long time, without any intermiſſion. When they Sail they uſe no Compaſs, but take their meaſures from the Sun, Moon, or Stars; and they rely much on the courſe of the various Flocks of Sea-Fowl, and this laſt is their ſureſt Directory. When they go to the leſſer Iſles and Rocks to bring home Sheep, or any other Purchaſe, they carry an iron Pot with them, and each Family furniſhes one by turns, and the Owner on ſuch Occaſions, has a ſmall Tax paid him by all the Families in the Iſle, which is by them call'd the Pot-penny.

THERE was another Tax payed by each Family to one of the Natives, as often as they kindled a Fire in any of the leſſer Iſles or Rocks, and that for the uſe of his Steel and Flint; and this was by them call'd the Fire-penny.

THIS Tax was very advantageous to the Proprietor, but very uneaſie to the Commonwealth, who could not be furniſh'd with Fire on theſe Occaſions any other way. But I told them that the Chryſtal growing in the Rock on the ſhoar would yield Fire if ſtruck with the back of a Knife, and of this I ſhew'd them an Experiment; which when they ſaw, was a very ſurprizing, and to them a profitable Diſcovery in their eſteem, being ſuch as could be had by every Man in the Iſle; and at the

Weſtern Iſlands of Scotland, &c. 293

the ſame time deliver'd them from an endleſs Charge; but it was very diſobliging to the poor Man who loſt his Tax by it.

THE Inhabitants of *St. Kilda* excel all thoſe I ever ſaw in climbing Rocks; they told me that ſome years ago their Boat was ſplit to pieces upon the Weſt ſide of *Boreray* Iſle, and they were forc'd to lay hold on a bare Rock, which was ſteep, and above twenty Fathom high; notwithſtanding this difficulty, ſome of them climb'd up to the top, and from thence let down a Rope, and Plads, and ſo drew up all the Boats Crew, tho' the climbing this Rock would ſeem impoſſible to any other except themſelves.

THIS little Commonwealth hath two Ropes of about twenty four Fathoms length each, for climbing the Rocks, which they do by turns; the Ropes are ſecur'd all round with Cows Hides ſalted for the uſe, and which preſerves them from being cut by the edge of the Rocks. By the aſſiſtance of theſe Ropes they purchaſe a great number of Eggs and Fowl; I have ſeen them bring home in a Morning twenty nine large Baskets all full of Eggs; the leaſt of the Baskets contain'd four hundred big Eggs, and the reſt eight hundred and above of leſſer Eggs. They had with them at the ſame time about two thouſand Sea-Fowl, and ſome Fiſh, together with ſome Limpets, call'd *Patella*, the

T 3

the biggest I ever saw. They catch many Fowls likewise, by laying their Gins which are made of Horse-hair, having a Noose at the distance of two Foot each; the ends of the Rope at which the Noose hangs are secur'd by a Stone.

THE Natives gave me an account of a very extraordinary Risque which one of them ran as laying his Gins, which was thus. As he was walking barefoot along the Rock where he had fixed his Gin, he happen'd to put his Toe in a Noose, and immediately fell down the Rock, but hung by the Toe, the Gin being strong enough to hold him, and the Stones that secur'd it on each end being heavy, the poor Man continu'd hanging thus for the space of a Night on a Rock twenty Fathom height above the Sea, until one of his Neighbours hearing him cry, came to his rescue, drew him up by the Feet, and so sav'd him.

THESE Poor People do sometimes fall down as they climb the Rocks, and perish: Their Wives on such occasions make doleful Songs, which they call Lamentations. The chief Topicks are their Courage, their Dexterity in Climbing, and their great affection which they shewed to their Wives and Children.

IT

IT is ordinary with a Fowler after he has got his Purchase of Fowls, to pluck the Fatest, and carry it home to his Wife as a mark of his Affection, and this is called the Rock-Fowl.

THE Batchellors do in like manner carry this Rock-Fowl to their Sweet-hearts, and it is the greatest Present they can make, considering the danger they run in acquiring it.

THE Richest Man in the Isle has not above eight Cows, eighty Sheep, and two or three Horses. If a Native here have but a few Cattle, he will Marry a Woman tho' she have no other Portion from her Friends but a Pound of Horse-hair, to make a Gin to catch Fowls.

THE Horses here are very low of stature, and employ'd only to carry home their Peats and Turff, which is their Fuel. The Inhabitants ride their Horses(which were but eighteen in all) at the Anniversary Cavalcade of *All Saints*; this they never fail to observe. They begin at the shoar, and ride as far as the Houses; they use no Saddles of any kind, nor Bridle, except a Rope of Straw which manages the Horses head; and when they have all taken the Horses by turns, the Show is over for that time.

T 4 THIS

THIS Ifle produces the fineft Hawks in the Weftern Ifles, for they go many Leagues for their Prey, there being no Land-Fowl in St. *Kilda* proper for them to eat, except Pigeons, and Plovers.

ONE of the Inhabitants of St. *Kilda* being fome time ago Wind bound in the Ifle of *Harries*, was prevail'd on by fome of them that Traded to *Glafgow* to go thither with them. He was aftonifh'd at the length of the Voyage, and of the great Kingdoms as he thought 'em, that is Ifles by which they Sail'd; the largeft in his way did not exceed twenty four Miles in length, but he confider'd how much they exceeded his own little Native Country.

UPON his Arrival at *Glafcow*, he was like one that had dropt from the Clouds into a new World; whofe Language, Habit, &c. were in all refpects new to him; he never imagin'd that fuch big Houfes of Stone were made with hands; and for the Pavements of the Streets, he thought it muft needs be altogether Natural; for he could not believe that Men would be at the pains to beat ftones into the ground to walk upon. He ftood dumb at the door of his Lodging with the greateft admiration; and when he faw a Coach and two Horfes, he thought it to be a little Houfe they were drawing at their Tail, with Men in it; but he condemn'd

condemn'd the Coach-man for a Fool to fit fo uneafie, for he thought it fafer to fit on the horfes back. The Mechanifm of the Coach-Wheel, and its running about, was the greateft of all his Wonders.

WHEN he went through the Streets, he defired to have one to lead him by the hand. *Thomas Rofs* a Merchant, and others, that took the diverfion to carry him through the Town, ask'd his Opinion of the high Church? He anfwer'd, that it was a large Rock, yet there were fome in *St. Kilda* much higher, but that thefe were the beft Caves he ever faw; for that was the Idea which he conceiv'd of the Pillars and Arches upon which the Church ftands. When they carried him into the Church, he was yet more furpriz'd, and held up his hands with admiration, wondring how it was poffible for Men to build fuch a prodigious Fabrick, which he fuppos'd to be the largeft in the Univerfe. He could not imagine what the Pews were defign'd for, and he fancied the People that wore Masks (not knowing whether they were Men or Women,) had been guilty of fome ill thing, for which they dar'd not fhew their faces. He was amazed at Womens wearing Patches, and fancied them to have been Blifters. Pendants feem'd to him the moft ridiculous of all things; he condemn'd Perriwigs mightily, and much more the Powder us'd in them; in fine, he condemn'd all things

things as ſuperfluous, he ſaw not in his own Country. He look'd with amazement on every thing that was new to him. When he heard the Church Bells ring he was under a mighty conſternation, as if the Fabrick of the World had been in great diſorder. He did not think there had been ſo many People in the World, as in the City of *Glaſcow* ; and it was a great Myſtery to him to think what they could all deſign by living ſo many in one place. He wondred how they could all be furniſh'd with Proviſion, and when he ſaw big Loaves, he could not tell whether they were Bread, Stone, or Wood. He was amaz'd to think how they could be provided with Ale, for he never ſaw any there that drank Water. He wondred how they made them fine Cloaths, and to ſee Stockings made without being firſt cut, and afterwards ſewn, was no ſmall wonder to him. He thought it fooliſh in Women to wear thin Silks, as being a very improper habit for ſuch as pretended to any ſort of Employment. When he ſaw the Womens Feet, he judged them to be of another ſhape than thoſe of the Men, becauſe of the different ſhape of their Shooes. He did not approve of the heels of Shooes worn by Men or Women ; and when he obſerv'd Horſes with ſhooes on their feet, and faſtned with Iron Nails, he could not forbear laughing, and thought it the moſt ridiculous thing that ever fell under his obſervation. He long'd to ſee his Native Country again, and

and paſſionately wiſh'd it were bleſſed with Ale, Brandy, Tobacco and Iron, as *Glaſcow* was.

THERE's a Couple of Large Eagles who have their Neſt on the North end of the Iſle ; the Inhabitants told me that they commonly make their Purchaſe in the adjacent Iſles and Continent, and never take ſo much as a Lamb or Hen from the Place of their Abode, where they propagate their kind. I forgot to give an account of a ſingular Providence that happen'd to a Native of the Iſle of *Skie*, called *Neil*, who when an Infant was left by his Mother in the Field, not far from the Houſes on the North ſide *Loch Portrie*; an Eagle came in the mean time, and carried him away in its Tallons as far as the ſouth ſide of the *Loch*, and there laying him on the ground, ſome People that were herding Sheep there perceiv'd it, and hearing the Infant cry, ran immediately to its reſcue; and by good Providence found him untouch'd by the Eagle, and carried him home to his Mother. He is ſtill living in that Pariſh, and by reaſon of this Accident, is diſtinguiſh'd among his Neighbours by the Sirname of *Eagle*.

An

St Kilda

On Dun, St Kilda

St Kilda or Hirt

1.Martin had already written and had published his first book A Late Voyage to St Kilda (1698) following a visit to the island group in 1697. A very useful companion to the contents of this section is M. Harman: An Isle Called Hirte Waternish 1997.

2.The size of the population and the occurrence of 'leprosy' have both been questioned and reconsidered [Harman pp.124-129].

3.The triangular cake at 'All Saints' is that forming part of the Michaelmas celebrations in various islands [see Uist n.32].

4.The treatment of Roderick the 'impostor' serves to illustrate Martin's protestant approach in general. Roderick himself is made to appear one of the 'curiosities' which Martin was looking for.

5.The custom of calling the main island 'the country' and Boreray 'the northern country' can be compared to a similar practice in the Flannan Isles within living memory.

6.'When they sail they use no Compass' (Martin p.292) – in some later editions 'Sail' is misprinted 'fail'.

7. For the 'anniversary cavalcade' see n.3 above.

8.The account of the St Kilda native in Glasgow is similar to, though far longer than, that of a Rona inhabitant at Coul in Easter Ross. It is possible that the visitor's guide in Glasgow, Thomas Ross, was the person of the same name who was schoolmaster at Dunvegan in 1693 and probably related to James Ross, 'Chirurgeon in Husabost' in Skye (DC Section 3 8/14/9). Presumably Martin heard of the Glasgow experience from the St Kilda man himself.

9.The whole of this description of St Kilda seems to consist of hastily recollected topics deriving from the author's visit there nearly five years earlier. Thus within one paragraph he moves exceptionally abruptly from one to another quite different subject for no apparent reason.

An Account of the Second Sight, in Irish call'd Taifh.

THE *Second Sight* is a fingular Faculty of Seeing, an otherwife invifible Object, without any previous Means us'd by the Perfon that fees it for that end; the Vifion makes fuch a lively impreffion upon the Seer, that they neither fee nor think of any thing elfe, except the Vifion, as long as it continues; and then they appear Penfive, or Jovial, according to the Object which was reprefented to them.

AT the fight of a Vifion the Eye-lids of the Perfon are erected, and the Eyes continue ftaring until the Object vanifh. This is obvious to others who are by, when the Perfons happen to fee a Vifion, and occur'd more than once to my own Obfervation, and to others that were with me.

THERE is one in *Skie*, of whom his Acquaintance obferved, that when he fees a Vifion, the inner part of his Eye-lids turn fo far upwards, that after the Object difappears, he muft draw them down with his Fingers, and fometimes employs others to draw them down, which he finds to be the much eafier way.

THIS

THIS Faculty of the *Second Sight* does not Lineally defcend in a Family, as fome imagine, for I know feveral Parents who are endowed with it, but their Children not, *& vice verfa*: Neither is it acquir'd by any previous Compact. And after a ftrict Enquiry, I could never learn from any among them, that this Faculty was communicable any way whatfoever.

THE Seer knows neither the Object, time nor place of a Vifion before it appears, and the fame Object is often feen by different Perfons, living at a confiderable diftance from one another. The true way of judging as to the time and circumftance of an Object, is by obfervation; for feveral Perfons of Judgment without this Faculty, are more capable to judge of the defign of a Vifion, than a Novice that is a Seer. If an Object appear in the Day or Night, it will come to pafs fooner or later accordingly.

IF an Object is feen early in a Morning (which is not frequent) it will be accomplifh'd in a few hours afterwards. If at Noon, it will commonly be accomplifh'd that very day. If in the Evening, perhaps that Night, if after Candles be lighted, it will be accomplifh'd that Night; the latter always in accomplifhment, by Weeks, Months, and fometimes Years, according

cording to the time of Night the Vifion is feen.

WHEN a Shroud is perceiv'd about one, it is a fure Prognoftick of Death, the time is judged according to the height of it about the Perfon; for if it is not feen above the middle, death is not to be expected for the fpace of a year, and perhaps fome Months longer; and as it is frequently feen to afcend higher towards the head, Death is concluded to be at hand within a few days, if not hours, as daily experience confirms. Examples of this kind were fhewn me, when the Perfons of whom the obfervations then made enjoy'd perfect health.

ONE Inftance was lately foretold by a Seer that was a Novice, concerning the death of one of my Acquaintance; this was communicated to a few only, and with great confidence, I being one of the number, did not in the leaft regard it, until the death of the Perfon about the time foretold, did confirm me of the certainty of the Prediction. The Novice mention'd above, is now a skilful Seer, as appears from many late inftances; he lives in the Parifh of St. *Maries*, the moft Northern in *Skie*.

IF a Woman is feen ftanding at a Man's left hand, it is a prefage that fhe will be his Wife, whether they be Married to others, or unmarried at the time of the Apparition.

IF

IF two or three Women are feen at once ftanding near a Mans left hand, fhe that is next him will undoubtedly be his Wife firft, and fo on, whether all three, or the Man be fingle or married at the time of the Vifion or not, of which there are feveral late Inftances among thofe of my Acquaintance. It is an ordinary thing for them to fee a Man that is to come to the Houfe fhortly after; and if he is not of the Seers Acquaintance, yet he gives fuch a lively defcription of his Stature, Complection, Habit, *&c.* that upon his Arrival he anfwers the Character given him in all refpects.

IF the Perfon fo appearing be one of the Seer's Acquaintance, he will tell his Name, as well as other Particulars; and he can tell by his Countenance whether he comes in a good or bad humour.

I have been feen thus my felf by Seers of both Sexes at fome hundred miles diftance; fome that faw me in this manner, had never feen me Perfonally, and it happened according to their Vifions, without any previous defign of mine to go to thofe Places, my coming there being purely accidental.

IT is ordinary with them to fee Houfes, Gardens and Trees, in Places void of all three; and

and this in procefs of time ufes to be accomplifhed, as at *Mogftot* in the Ifle of *Skie*, where there were but a few forry Cow-houfes thatched with Straw, yet in a few years after, the Vifion which appear'd often was accomplifh'd, by the building of feveral good Houfes on the very fpot reprefented to the Seers, and by the Planting of Orchards there.

TO fee a fpark of fire fall upon ones Arm or Breaft, is a forerunner of a dead Child to be feen in the arms of thofe Perfons, of which there are feveral frefh Inftances.

TO fee a Seat empty at the time of ones fitting in it, is a prefage of that Perfons death quickly after.

WHEN a Novice, or one that has lately obtain'd the *Second Sight*, fees a Vifion in the Night time without doors, and comes near a fire, he prefently falls into a fwoon.

SOME find themfelves as it were in a croud of People, having a Corpfe which they carry along with them, and after fuch Vifions the Seers come in fweating, and defcribe the People that appear'd; if there be any of their Acquaintance among 'em, they give an account of their Names, as alfo of the Bearers, but they know nothing concerning the Corps.

ALL

ALL thofe who have the *Second Sight* do not always fee thefe Vifions at once, tho' they be together at the time. But if one who has this Faculty, defignedly touch his Fellow Seer at the inftant of a Vifions appearing, then the fecond fees it as well as the firft, and this is fometimes difcern'd by thofe that are near them on fuch occafions.

THERE is a way of foretelling Death by a Cry that they call *Taisk*, which fome call a *Wrath* in the Low-land.

THEY hear a loud Cry without doors, exactly refembling the voice of fome particular Perfon, whofe death is foretold by it. The laft inftance given me of this kind was in the Village *Rigg*, in *Skie* Ifle.

FIVE Women were fitting together in the fame Room, and all of them heard a loud Cry paffing by the Window; they thought it plainly to be the voice of a Maid who was one of the Number, fhe blufhed at the time, tho' not fenfible of her fo doing, contracted a Feaver next day, and died that Week.

THINGS alfo are foretold by *Smelling*, fometimes as follows. Fifh or Flefh is frequently fmelled in a fire, when at the fame time neither of the two are in the Houfe, or

U in

in any probability like to be had in it for ſome Weeks or Months, for they ſeldom eat Fleſh, and tho' the Sea be near them, yet they catch Fiſh but ſeldom, in the Winter and Spring. This *Smell* ſeveral Perſons have who are not endued with the *Second Sight*, and it is always accompliſh'd ſoon after.

Children, Horſes and Cows ſee the *Second Sight*, as well as Men and Women advanced in years.

THAT Children ſee it is plain, from their crying aloud at the very inſtant that a Corpſe or any other Viſion appears to an ordinary Seer. I was preſent in a Houſe where a Child cried out of a ſuddain, and being ask'd the reaſon of it, he anſwer'd that he had ſeen a great white thing lying on the Board which was in the Corner; but he was not believ'd, until a Seer who was preſent told them that the Child was in the right; for, ſaid he, I ſaw a Corpſe and the ſhroud about it, and the Board will be us'd as part of a Coffin, or ſome way imployed about a Corpſe; and accordingly, it was made into a Coffin, for one who was in perfect health at the time of the Viſion.

THAT Horſes ſee it is likewiſe plain, from their violent and ſudden ſtarting, when the Rider or Seer in Company with him ſees a Viſion of any kind, Night, or Day. It is obſervable

ſervable of the Horſe, that he will not go forward that way, until he be lead about at ſome diſtance from the common Road, and then he is in a ſweat.

A Horſe faſtned by the common Road on the ſide of *Loch-Skerineſs* in *Skie*, did break his Rope at Noon day, and run up and down without the leaſt viſible cauſe. But two of the Neighbourhood that happen'd to be at a little diſtance, and in view of the Horſe, did at the ſame time ſee a conſiderable number of Men about a Corpſe, directing their courſe to the Church of *Sniſort*; and this was accompliſh'd within a few days after, by the Death of a Gentlewoman who lived thirteen Miles from that Church, and came from another Pariſh, from whence very few come to *Sniſort* to be Buried.

THAT Cows ſee the *Second Sight*, appears from this; that when a Woman is Milking a Cow, and then happens to ſee the *Second Sight*, the Cow runs away in a great fright at the ſame time, and will not be pacified for ſome time after.

BEFORE I mention more particulars diſcover'd by the *Second Sight*, it may not be amiſs to anſwer the Objections that have lately been made againſt the reality of it.

U 2 *Object.*

Object. 1. Theſe Seers are Viſionary and Melancholy People, and fancy they ſee things that do not appear to them, or any body elſe.

Anſwer. The People of theſe Iſles, and particularly the Seers, are very temperate, and their Diet is ſimple, and moderate, in quantity and quality, ſo that their Brains are not in all probability diſordered by undigeſted Fumes of Meat or Drink. Both Sexes are free from Hyſterick Fits, Convulſions, and ſeveral other Diſtempers of that ſort; there's no Madmen among them, nor any inſtance of ſelf-murther. It is obſerv'd among 'em, that a Man Drunk never ſees the *Second Sight*; and he that is a Viſionary would diſcover himſelf in other things as well as in that, and ſuch as ſee it, are not judged to be Viſionarys by any of their Friends or Acquaintance.

Object. 2. There is none among the Learn'd able to oblige the World with a ſatisfying account of thoſe Viſions, therefore it is not to be believed.

Anſwer. If every thing for which the Learned are not able to give a ſatisfying account be condemn'd as impoſſible, we may find many other things generally believed, that muſt be rejected as falſe by this Rule. For inſtance, Yawning, & its influence; & that the Load-ſtone attracts Iron, and yet theſe are true as well as harmleſs, tho' we can give no ſatisfying account of their Cauſes. And if we know ſo little of Natural Cauſes, how much leſs can we pretend to things that are ſupernatural.

Object. 3. The Seers are Impoſtors, and the People who believe them, are credulous, and eaſily impoſed upon.

Anſwer. The Seers are generally illiterate, and well-meaning People, and altogether void of deſign, nor could I ever learn that any of them made the leaſt gain by it, neither is it reputable among 'em to have that Faculty; beſides the People of the Iſles are not ſo credulous as to believe implicitely, before the thing foretold is accompliſhed, but when it actually comes to paſs afterwards, it is not in their power to deny it, without offering violence to their Senſes and Reaſon. Beſides, if the Seers were deceivers, can it be reaſonable to imagine, that all the Iſlanders who have not the *Second Sight*, ſhould combine together, and offer violence to their Underſtandings and Senſes, to force themſelves to believe a Lye from Age to Age. There are ſeveral Perſons among them, whoſe Birth and Education raiſe them above the ſuſpicion of concurring with an Impoſture, meerly to gratifie an illiterate and contemptible ſort of Perſons; nor can a reaſonable Man believe that

U 3

that Children, Horfes and Cows could be pre-ingaged in a Combination to perfwade the World of the reality of the *Second Sight*.

SUCH as deny thofe Vifions, give their affent to feveral ftrange paffages in Hiftory, upon the Authority of Hiftorians that lived feveral Centuries before our time, and yet they deny the People of this Generation the liberty to believe their intimate Friends and Acquaintance, Men of probity and unqueftionable Reputation, and of whofe veracity they have greater certainty, than we can have of any ancient Hiftorian.

EVERY Vifion that is feen comes exactly to pafs, according to the true Rules of Obfervation, tho' Novices and heedlefs Perfons do not always judge by thofe Rules. I remember the Seers return'd me this Anfwer to my Objection, and gave feveral Inftances to that purpofe, whereof the following is one.

A Boy of my acquaintance was often furpriz'd at the fight of a Coffin clofe by his fhoulder, which put him into a fright, and made him to believe it was a forerunner of his own Death, and this his Neighbours alfo judged to be the meaning of that Vifion; but a Seer that lived in the Village *Knockow*, where the Boy was then a Servant, told them that they were

were under a great miftake, and defired the Boy to lay hold of the firft opportunity that offered; and when he went to a Burial, to remember to act as a Bearer for fome moments, and this he did accordingly, within a few days after, when one of his Acquaintance died; and from that time forward he was never troubled with feeing a Coffin at his fhoulder, tho' he has feen many at a diftance that concerned others. He is now reckoned one of the exacteft Seers in the Parifh of St. *Maries* in *Skie*, where he lives.

THERE is another inftance of a Woman in *Skie*, who frequently faw a Vifion reprefenting a Woman having a Shroud about her up to the middle, but always appear'd with her back towards her, and the Habit in which it feem'd to be drefs'd refembled her own; this was a Myftery for fome time, until the Woman try'd an Experiment to fatisfie her Curiofity, which was to drefs her felf contrary to the ufual way, that is, fhe put that part of her Cloaths behind, which was always before, fancying that the Vifion at the next appearing would be the eafier diftinguifhed, and it fell out accordingly, for the Vifion foon after prefented its felf with its face and drefs looking towards the Woman, and it prov'd to refemble her felf in all points, and fhe died in a little time after.

U 4 THERE

THERE are Visions seen by several Persons, in whose days they are not accomplished, and this is one of the reasons, why some things have been seen that are said never to come to pass, and there are also several Visions seen which are not understood until they be accomplished.

THE *second Sight* is not a late discovery seen by one or two in a Corner, or a remote Isle, but it is seen by many Persons of both Sexes in several Isles, seperated above forty or fifty Leagues from one another, the Inhabitants of many of these Isles, never had the least converse by Word or Writing; and this faculty of seeing Visions, having continued as we are informed by Tradition, ever since the Plantation of these Isles, without being disproved by the nicest Sceptick, after the strictest enquiry seems to be a clear proof of its reality.

IT is observable, that it was much more common twenty Years ago than at present, for one in ten do not see it now, that saw it then.

THE *second sight* is not confined to the western Isles alone, for I have an account that it is likewise seen in several parts of *Holland*, but particularly in *Bommel*, by a Woman, for which she is courted by some, and dreaded by others. She sees a Smoak about ones Face, which is a forerunner of the death of a Person so

so seen, and she did actually foretel the death of several that lived there; she was living in that Town this last Winter.

THE Corps-candles, or Dead-mens Lights in *Wales*, which are certain Prognosticks of Death are well known and attested.

THE *second sight* is likewise seen in the Isle of Man, as appears by this Instance; *Captain Leaths* the Chief Magistrate of *Belfast*, in his Voyage 1690, lost thirteen Men by a violent Storm, and upon his landing in the Isle of *Man*, an ancient Man Clerk to a Parish there, told him immediately that he had lost thirteen Men, the Captain enquiring how he came to the knowledge of that, he answered, that it was by thirteen Lights which he had seen come into the Church-Yard, as Mr. *Sacheverel* tells us, in his late Description of the Isle of *Man*.

IT were ridiculous to suppose a Combination between the People of the western Isles of *Scotland*, *Holland*, *Wales*, and the Isle of *Man*, since they are separated by long Seas, and are People of different Languages, Governments, and Interests: They have no Correspondence between them, and it is probable, that those inhabiting the North West Isles have never yet heard that any such Visions are seen in *Holland*, *Wales*, or the Isle of *Man*.

FOUR

FOUR Men of the Village *Flodgery* in *Skie*, being at Supper, one of them did ſuddenly let fall his Knife on the Table, and looked with an angry Countenance, the Company obſerving it, enquired his Reaſon, but he return'd them no anſwer until they had ſupp'd, and then he told them that when he let fall his Knife, he ſaw a Corps with the Shroud about it laid on the Table, which ſurpriz'd him, and that a little time would accompliſh the Viſion. It fell out accordingly, for in a few days after one of the Family died, and happen'd to be laid on that very Table, this was told me by the Maſter of the Family.

Daniel Stewart an Inhabitant of *Hole* in the North Pariſh of St. *Maries* in the Iſle of *Skie*, ſaw at Noon-day five Men on Horſe-back riding Northward, he ran to meet them, and when he came to the Road, he could ſee none of them, which was very ſurprizing to him, & he told it his Neighbours, the very next day he ſaw the ſame number of Men and Horſe, coming along the Road, but was not ſo ready to meet them as before, until he heard them ſpeak, and then he found them to be thoſe that he had ſeen the day before in a Viſion, this was the only Viſion of the kind he had ever ſeen in his Life. The Company he ſaw was Sir *Donald Mac Donald* and his retinue, who at the time of the Viſion was at *Armidil*, near forty Miles South from the place where the Man lived.

A Woman of *Stornbay* in *Lewis*, had a Maid who ſaw Viſions, and often fell into a Swoon; her

her Miſtris was very much concern'd about her, but could not find out any means to prevent her, ſeeing thoſe things at laſt ſhe reſolved to pour ſome of the Water us'd in Baptiſm on her Maids Face, believing this would prevent her ſeeing any more Sights of this kind, and accordingly ſhe carried her Maid with her, next Lord's Day, and both of 'em ſat near the Baſin in which the Water ſtood, and after Baptiſm before the Miniſter had concluded the laſt Prayer, ſhe put her hand in the Baſin, took up as much Water as ſhe could, and threw it on the Maids Face, at which ſtrange action the Miniſter and the Congregation were equally ſurpriz'd; after Prayer the Miniſter enquir'd of the Woman the meaning of ſuch an unbecoming and diſtracted action, ſhe told him it was to prevent her Maids ſeeing Viſions; and it fell out accordingly, for from that time ſhe never once more ſaw a Viſion of any kind. This account was given me by Mr. *Moriſon*, Miniſter of the Place, before ſeveral of his Pariſhioners who knew the truth of it, I ſubmit the matter of fact to the cenſure of the Learned, but for my own part, think it to have been one of Satans Devices, to make credulous People have an eſteem for Holy Water.

John Moriſon of *Bragir* in *Lewis*, a Perſon of unqueſtionable Sincerity and Reputation, told me, that within a Mile of his Houſe a Girl of twelve Years Old, was troubled at the frequent ſight of a Viſion reſembling her ſelf, in Stature, Com-

Complexion, Dreſs, *&c.* and ſeem'd to ſtand or ſit and to be always Imployed as the Girl was; this prov'd a great trouble to her, her Parents being much concern'd about it, conſulted the ſaid *John Moriſon*, who enquired if the Girl was inſtructed in the Principles of her Religion, and finding ſhe was not, he bid them teach her the Creed, ten Commandments, and the Lord's Prayer, and that ſhe ſhould ſay the latter daily after her Prayers. Mr. *Moriſon* and his Family joyn'd in Prayer in the Girls behalf, begging that God of his goodneſs would be pleas'd to deliver her from the trouble of ſuch a Viſion, after which and the Girl's complying with the advice as above, ſhe never ſaw it any more.

A Man living three Miles to the North of the ſaid *John Moriſon*, is much haunted by a Spirit, appearing in all Points like to himſelf; and he asks many impertinent Queſtions of the Man when in the Fields, but ſpeaks not a word to him at home, tho' he ſeldom miſſes to appear to him every night in the Houſe, but to no other Perſon. He told this to one of his Neighbours, who adviſ'd him to caſt a live Coal at the face of the Viſion the next time he appear'd; the Man did ſo next night, and all the Family ſaw the action; but the following day the ſame Spirit appear'd to him in the Fields, and beat him ſeverely, ſo as to oblige him to keep his Bed for the ſpace of fourteen days

days after. Mr. *Moriſon* Miniſter of the Pariſh, and ſeveral of his Friends came to ſee the Man, and join'd in Prayer that he might be freed from this trouble, but he was ſtill haunted by that Spirit a year after I left *Lewis*.

A Man in *Knockow*, in the Pariſh of St. *Maries*, the Northermoſt in *Skie*, being in perfect health, and ſitting with his Fellow Servants at Night, was on a ſuddain taken ill, dropt from his Seat backward, and then fell a Vomiting, at which all the Family were much concern'd, he having never been ſubject to the like before, but he came to himſelf ſoon after, and had no ſort of pain about him. One of the Family who was accuſtomed to ſee the *Second Sight*, told them that the Mans ilneſs proceeded from a very ſtrange Cauſe, which was thus. An ill natur'd Woman (naming her by her Name) who lives in the next adjacent Village of *Bornſkittag*, came before him in a very furious and angry manner, her Countenance full of Paſſion, and her Mouth full of Reproaches, and threatned him with her head and hands, until he fell over as you have ſeen him. This Woman had a fancy for the Man, but was like to meet with a diſappointment as to his Marrying her. This Inſtance was told me by the Maſter of the Family, and others who were preſent when it happen'd.

ONE

ONE that liv'd in St. *Maries* on the West side of the Isle of *Skie*, told Mr. *Mack Pherson* the Minister, and others, that he saw a Vision of a Corpse coming towards the Church, not by the common Road, but by a more rugged Way, which rendred the thing incredible, and occasion'd his Neighbours to call him a Fool; but he bid them have patience, and they would see the truth of what he asserted in a short time, and it fell out accordingly; for one of the Neighbourhood died, and his Corpse was carried along the same unaccustomed Way, the common Road being at that time filled with a deep Snow. This Account was given me by the Minister, and others living there.

Mr. *Mack Pherson*'s Servant foretold that a Kiln should take fire, and being some time after reprov'd by his Master for talking so foolishly of the *Second Sight*, he answer'd that he could not help his seeing such things as presented themselves to his view in a very lively manner; adding further, I have just now seen that Boy sitting by the fire, with his face red, as if the blood had been running down his forehead, and I could not avoid seeing this, and as for the accomplishment of it within forty eight hours there is no doubt, says he, it having appear'd in the day time. The Minister became very angry at his Man, and charg d him never to speak one word more of the *Second Sight*, or

or if he could not hold his tongue, to provide himself another Master; telling him he was an unhappy Fellow who studied to abuse Credulous People with false Predictions. There was no more said on this Subject until the next day, that the Boy of whom the Seer spoke came in, having his face all cover'd with blood, which happen'd by his falling on a heap of Stones. This Account was given me by the Minister, and others of his Family.

DANIEL DOW, alias *Black*, an Inhabitant of *Bornskittag*, was frequently troubled at the sight of a Man threatning to give him a Blow; he knew no Man resembling this Vision; but the Stature, Complection and Habit were so impress'd on his Mind, that he said he could distinguish him from any other, if he should happen to see him. About a year after the Vision appear'd first to him, his Master sent him to *Kyle Raes*, above thirty Miles further South East, where he was no sooner arriv'd, than he distinguished the Man who had so often appear'd to him at home, and within a few hours after, they happen'd to quarrel, and came to blows, so as one of them (I forgot which) was wounded in the head. This was told me by the Seers Master, and others who live in the place; The Man himself has his Residence there, and is one of the precisest Seers in the Isles.

Sir

Sir *Normand Mack Leod*, and ſome others playing at Tables, at a Game called in *Iriſh Falmer-more*, wherein there are three of a ſide, and each of them throw the Dice by turns, there happen'd to be one difficult Point in the diſpoſing of one of the Table men; this oblig'd the Gameſter to deliberate before he was to change his Man, ſince upon the diſpoſing of it, the winning or loſing of the Game depended; at laſt the Butler who ſtood behind adviſed the Player where to place his Man, with which he complied, and won the Game; this being thought extraordinary, and Sir *Normand* hearing one whiſper him in the ear, ask'd who adviſ'd him ſo skilfully? he anſwer'd it was the Butler, but this ſeem'd more ſtrange, for he could not play at Tables. Upon this, Sir *Normand* ask'd him how long it was ſince he had learnt to Play? and the Fellow own'd that he never play'd in his life, but that he ſaw the Spirit *Browny* reaching his arm over the Players head, and touched the Part with his finger, on the Point where the Table-man was to be plac'd. This was told me by Sir *Normand* and others who happen'd to be preſent at the time.

DANIEL DOW above-named, foretold the death of a young Woman in *Minginis*, within leſs than twenty four hours before the time, and accordingly ſhe died ſuddenly in the Fields, tho'

at the time of the Prediction ſhe was in perfect health; but the Shroud appearing cloſe about her head, was the ground of his confidence, that her death was at hand.

THE ſame *Daniel Dow* foretold the death of a Child in his Maſters arms, by ſeeing a ſpark of fire fall on his left arm; and this was likewiſe accompliſh'd ſoon after the Prediction.

SOME of the Inhabitants of *Harries* Sailing round the Iſle of *Skie*, with a deſign to go to the oppoſite main Land, were ſtrangely ſurpriz'd with an Apparition of two Men hanging down by the Ropes that ſecur'd the Maſt, but could not conjecture what it meant. They purſued their Voyage, but the Wind turn'd contrary, and ſo forc'd them into *Broadford* in the Iſle of *Skie*, where they found Sir *Donald Mack Donald* keeping a Sheriffs Court, and two Criminals receiving Sentence of death there, the Ropes andMaſt of that very Boat were made uſe of to hang thoſe Criminals. This was told me by ſeveral, who had this Inſtance from the Boats Crew.

SEVERAL Perſons living in a certain Family, told me that they had frequently ſeen two Men ſtanding at a young Gentlewomans left hand, who was their Maſters Daughter; they told the Mens Names, and being her Equals, it was not doubted but ſhe would be

X Married

Married to one of them; and perhaps to the other, after the death of the firſt. Some time after a third Man appear'd, and he ſeem'd always to ſtand neareſt to her of the three, but the Seers did not know him, tho' they could deſcribe him exactly. And within ſome Months after, this Man who was ſeen laſt, did actually come to the Houſe, and fulfilled the Deſcription given of him by thoſe who never ſaw him but in a Viſion, and he married the Woman ſhortly after. They live in the Iſle of *Skie*, both they and others confirmed the truth of this Inſtance when I ſaw them.

MACK LEODS Porter paſſing by a Galley that lay in the Dock, ſaw her filled with Men, having a Corps, and near to it he ſaw ſeveral of *Mack Leod*'s Relations; this did in a manner perſwade him that his Maſter was to die ſoon after, and that he was to be the Corps which was to be tranſported in the Galley: Some Months after the Viſion was ſeen, *Mack Leod* with ſeveral of his Relations and others went to the Iſle of *Mull*, where ſome days after *Mack Lean* of *Torlosk* happen'd to die, and his Corps was tranſported in the Galley to his Burial Place, and *Mack Leod*'s Relations were on board to attend the Funeral, while *Mack Leod* ſtaid aſhore, and went along with the Corps, after their Landing.

Mr.

Mr. *Dougal Mack Pherſon*, Miniſter of Saint *Maries* on the Weſt ſide of *Skie*, having his Servants in the Kiln drying Corn, the Kiln happen'd to take fire, but was ſoon extinguiſh'd. And within a few Months after, one of the Miniſters Servants told him that the Kiln would be on fire again ſhortly; at which he grew very angry with his Man, threatning to beat him if he ſhould preſume to Propheſie miſchief by that lying way of the *Second Sight*. Notwithſtanding this, the Man aſſerted poſitively and with great aſſurance that the Kiln would certainly take fire, let them uſe all the precautions they could. Upon this, Mr. *Mack Pherſon* had the Curioſity to enquire of his Man if he could gueſs within what ſpace of time the Kiln would take fire? he told him before *Hallowtide*. Upon which, Mr. *Mack Pherſon* call'd for the Key of the Kiln, and told his Man that he would take care of the Kiln until the limited day was expir'd, for none ſhall enter it ſooner, and by this Means I ſhall make the Devil if he is the Author of ſuch Lies, and you both Liars. For this end he kept the key of the Kiln in his Preſs until the time was over, and then deliver'd the key to the Servants, concluding his Man to be a Fool and a Cheat. Then the Servants went to dry Corn in the Kiln, and were charg'd to have a ſpecial care of the fire, yet in a little time after the Kiln took fire, and it was all in a flame,

X 2 accord-

according to the Prediction, tho' the Man miftook the time. He told his Mafter, that within a few moments after the fire of the Kiln had been firft extinguifhed, he faw it all in a flame again ; and this appearing to him in the day time, it would come to pafs the fooner.

John Mack Normand, and *Daniel Mack Ewin*, Travelling along the Road, two Miles to the North of *Snifort* Church, faw a body of Men coming from the North, as if they had a Corps with 'em to be buried in *Snifort* ; this determin'd them to advance towards the River, which was then a little before them, and having waited at the Ford, thinking to meet thofe that they expected with the Funeral, were altogether difappointed ; for after taking a view of the ground all round them, they difcover'd that it was only a Vifion. This was very furprizing to them both, for they never faw any thing by way of the *Second Sight* before or after that time. This they told their Neighbours when they came home, and it happen'd that about two or three Weeks after a Corps came along that Road, from another Parifh, from which few or none are brought to *Snifort*, except Perfons of diftinction ; fo that this Vifion was exactly accomplifhed.

A

A Gentleman who is a Native of *Skie*, did when a Boy, difoblige a Seer in the Ifle of *Rafay*, and upbraid him for his uglinefs, as being black by Name, and Nature. At laft the Seer told him very angrily, my Child, if I am Black, you'll be Red e're long. The Mafter of the Family chid him for this, and bid him give over his Foolifh Predictions, fince no body believ'd them ; but next Morning the Boy being at Play near the Houfes, fell on a ftone, and wounded himfelf in the Forehead, fo deep, that to this day there's a hollow Scar in that part of it.

JAMES BEATON Surgeon, in the Ifle of *North Vift*, told me that being in the Ifle of *Mull*, a Seer told him confidently that he was fhortly to have a bloody Forehead, but he difregarded it, and call'd the Seer a Fool. However this *James* being called by fome of the *Mackleans* to go along with them to attack a Veffel belonging to the Earl of *Argyle*, who was then coming to poffefs *Mull* by force, they attak'd the Veffel, and one of the *Mack-Leans* being Wounded, the faid *James* while dreffing the Wound, happen'd to rub his Forehead, and then fome of his Patients blood ftuck to his face, which accomplifh'd the Vifion.

MY Lord Vifcount *Tarbat*, one of Her Majefties Secretaries of State in *Scotland*, Travelling in the Shire of *Rofs*, in the North of *Scotland*, came

X 3 into

into a Houſe and ſat down in an Arm'd Chair, one of his Retinue who had the faculty of ſeeing the *Second Sight*, ſpoke to ſome of my Lord's Company, deſiring them to perſwade him to leave the Houſe, for ſaid he, there is a great misfortune will attend ſome body in it, and that within a few Hours. This was told my Lord, but he did not regard it; the Seer did ſoon after renew his Intreaty, with much eagerneſs, begging that my Lord might remove out of that unhappy Chair, but had no other anſwer than to be expoſed for a Fool. Some Hours after my Lord remov'd, and purſued his Journey, but was not gone many Hours vvhen a Trooper riding upon Ice, near the Houſe vvhence my Lord remov'd, fell and broke his Thigh, and being aftervvards brought into that Houſe, vvas laid in the Armed Chair, vvhere his Wound vvas dreſs'd, vvhich accompliſhed the Viſion. I heard this Inſtance from ſeveral Hands, and had it ſince confirmed by my Lord himſelf.

A Man in the Pariſh of St. *Maries*, in the Barrony of *Troterneſs* in *Skie*, called *Lachlin*, lay ſick for the ſpace of ſome Months, decaying daily, in ſo much that all his Relations and acquaintance deſpaired of his recovery: One of the Pariſhioners called *Archibald Mack Donald*, being reputed famous for his Skill in foretelling things to come, by the *Second Sight*, aſſerted poſſitively that the Sick Man would never die in

in the Houſe where he then lay; this being thought very improbable, all the Neighbours condemn'd *Archibald* as a fooliſh Prophet, upon which, he paſſionately affirmed, that if ever that Sick Man dies in the Houſe where he now lies, I ſhall from henceforth renounce my part of Heaven: Adding withal the Sick Man was to be carried alive out of the Houſe in which he then lay, but that he would never return to it a live, and then he nam'd the Perſons that ſhould carry out the Sick Man alive. The Man having lived ſome Weeks longer than his Friends imagin'd, and proving uneaſie, and troubleſome to all the Family, they conſidered that *Archibald* had reaſon for his peremptory aſſertion, and therefore they reſolved to carry him to a Houſe joyning to that in which he then lay, but the Poor Man would by no means give his conſent to be removed from a Place where he believed he ſhould never die; ſo much did he rely on the words of *Archibald*, of whoſe Skill he had ſeen many demonſtrations. But at laſt his Friends being fatigu'd day and night with the Sick Man's uneaſineſs, they carried him againſt his Inclination, to another little Houſe, which was only ſeperated by an Entry from that in which he lay, and their Feet were ſcarce within the Threſhold, when the Sick Man gave up the Ghoſt; and it was remarkable that the two Neighbours, which *Archibald* named would carry him out, were actually the Perſons that did ſo. At the time of the Prediction, *Archibald*

X 4 ſaw

faw him carried out as above, and when he was within the Door of the other Houfe, he faw him all white, and the Shroud being about him, occafioned his confidence as above mention'd; this is matter of fact, which Mr. *Daniel Nicolfon* Minifter of the Parifh, and a confiderable Number of the Parifhioners, are able to vouch for, and ready to atteft, if occafion requires.

THE fame *Archibald Macdonald*, happen'd to be in the Village *Knockow* one Night, and before Supper, told the Family that he had juft then feen the ftrangeft thing he ever faw in his Life; to wit, a Man with an ugly long Cap, always fhaking his Head, but that the ftrangeft of all, was a little kind of a Harp which he had, with four Strings only, and that it had two Harts Horns fixed in the Front of it; all that heard this odd Vifion fell a laughing at *Archibald*, telling him that he was dreaming, or had not his Wits about him, fince he pretended to fee a thing that had no being, and was not fo much as heard of in any part of the World. All this could not alter *Archibalds* Opinion, who told them that they muft excufe him, if he laugh'd at them after the accomplifhment of the Vifion. *Archibald* return'd to his own Houfe, and within three or four days after, a Man with the Cap, Harp, &c. came to the Houfe, and the Harp, String, Horns, and Cap, anfwered the Defcription of them at firft view, he fhook his Head

when he plai'd, for he had two Bells fixed to his Cap; this Harper was a Poor Man, and made himfelf a Buffoon for his Bread, and was never before feen in thofe parts, for at the time of the Prediction, he was in the Ifle of *Barray*; which is above twenty Leagues diftant from that part of *Skie*. This Story is vouched by Mr. *Daniel Martin*, and all his Family, and fuch as were then prefent, and live in the Village where this happen'd.

Mr. *Daniel Nicolfon* Minifter of St. *Maries* in *Skie*, the Parifh in which *Archibald Macdonald* liv'd, told me that one Sunday after Sermon at the Chappel *Uge*, he took occafion to enquire of *Archibald*, if he ftill retain'd that unhappy faculty of feeing the *Second Sight*, and he wifhed him to lay it afide, if poffible, for faid he, it is no true Character of a Good Man. *Archibald* was highly difpleas'd, and anfwered, That he hop'd he was no more unhappy than his Neighbours, for feeing what they could not perceive; adding, I had, fays he, as ferious Thoughts as my Neighbours, in time of hearing a Sermon to day, and even then I faw a Corps laid on the Ground clofe to the Pulpit, and I affure you it will be accomplifhed fhortly, for it was in the day time. Mr. *Nicolfon* and feveral Parifhioners then prefent, endeavoured to difwade *Archibald* from this Difcourfe; but he ftill afferted that it would quickly come to pafs, and that all his other Predictions of this kind had ever been accomplifhed. There

There was none in the Pariſh then Sick, and few are buried at that little Chappel, nay ſometimes not one in a Year is buried there. Yet when Mr. *Nicolſon* return'd to preach in the ſaid Chappel, two or three Weeks after, he found one buried in the very ſpot, nam'd by *Archibald*; this Story is vouched by Mr. *Nicolſon*, and ſeveral of the Pariſhioners ſtill living.

Mr. *Daniel Nicolſon* above mentioned, being a Widower at the age of 44, this *Archibald* ſaw in a Viſion, a Young Gentlewoman, in a good Dreſs, frequently ſtanding at Mr. *Nicolſon*'s right hand, and this he often told the Pariſhioners poſitively; and gave an account of her Complection, Stature, Habit, and that ſhe would in time be Mr. *Nicolſon*'s Wife; this being told the Miniſter by ſeveral of 'em, he deſired them to have no regard to what that fooliſh Dreamer had ſaid, for ſaid he, it is twenty to one if ever I marry again. *Archibald* happened to ſee Mr. *Nicolſon* ſoon after this ſlighting Expreſſion, however he perſiſted ſtill in his Opinion, and ſaid confidently that Mr. *Nicolſon* would certainly marry, and that the Woman would in all points make up the Character he gave of her, for he ſaw her as often as he ſaw Mr. *Nicolſon*. This Story was told me above a Year before the accompliſhment of it, and Mr. *Nicolſon* ſome two or three Years after *Archibald*'s Prediction, went to a Synod in *Boot*, where he had the firſt opportunity of ſeeing one

one Mrs. *Moriſon*, and from that Moment fancied her, and afterwards married her; ſhe was no ſooner ſeen in the Iſle of *Skie*, than the Natives who had never ſeen her before, were ſatisfied that ſhe did compleatly anſwer the Character given of her, &c. by *Archibald*.

ONE who had been accuſtomed to ſee the *Second Sight*, in the Iſle of *Egg*, which lies about three or four Leagues to the South Weſt part of the Iſle of *Skie*, told his Neighbours that he had frequently ſeen, an Apparition of a Man in a Red Coat lin'd with Blue, and having on his Head a ſtrange ſort of Blue Cap, with a very high Cock on the fore part of it, and that the Man who there appeared, was kiſſing a comely Maid, in the Village where the Seer dwelt; and therefore declar'd that a Man in ſuch a dreſs would certainly debauch or marry ſuch a Young Woman; this unuſual Viſion did much expoſe the Seer, for all the Inhabitants treated him as a Fool, tho' he had on ſeveral other occaſions foretold things that afterwards were accompliſhed, this they thought one of the moſt unlikelieſt things to be accompliſhed, that could have entred into any Mans Head; this Story was then diſcours'd of in the Iſle of *Skie*, and all that heard it laugh'd at it, it being a rarity to ſee any Forreigner in *Egg*, and the Young Woman had no Thoughts of going any where elſe; this Story was told me at *Edinburgh*, by *Normand Mac Leod* of *Graban*, in *September* 1688, he he being just then come from the Isle of *Skie*; and there were present the *Laird* of *Mac Leod*, and Mr. *Alexander Mac Leod* Advocate, and others.

ABOUT a Year and a half after the late Revolution, Major *Ferguson*, now Colonel of one of her Majesties Regiments of Foot, was then sent by the Government with six hundred Men, and some Friggots to reduce the Islanders that had appeared for *K. J.* and perhaps the small Isle of *Egg*, had never been regarded tho' some of the Inhabitants had been at the Battle of *Kelicranky*, but by a meer Accident, which determin'd Major *Ferguson* to go to the Isle of *Egg*, which was this. A Boats Crew of the Isle of *Egg*, happen'd to be in the Isle of *Skie*, and kill'd one of Major *Fergusons* Soldiers there; upon Notice of which, the Major directed his Course to the Isle of *Egg*, where he was sufficiently reveng'd of the Natives; and at the same time, the Maid above mentioned being very handsome, was then forcibly carried on Board one of the Vessels, by some of the Soldiers where she was kept above twenty four Hours, and ravish'd, and bruitishly rob'd at the same time of her fine Head of Hair; she is since married in the Isle, and in Good Reputation; her Misfortune being pitied and not rekon'd her Crime.

Sr. *Normand Mack Leod*, who has his residence in the Isle of *Bernera*, vvhich lyes betvveen the Isle of N. *Uist* and *Harries*, vvent to the

the Isle of *Skie* about Business, without appointing any time for his return; his Servants in his absence, being all together in the large Hall at Night, one of them who had been accustomed to see the *Second Sight*, told the rest they must remove, for they would have abundance of other Company in the Hall that Night. One of his Fellow Servants answer'd that there was very little appearance of that, and if he had seen any Vision of Company, it was not like to be accomplish'd this Night: But the Seer insisted upon it that it was; they continued to argue the improbability of it, because of the darkness of the Night, and the danger of coming through the Rocks that lie round the Isle; but within an hour after, one of Sir *Normands* Men came to the House, bidding them provide Lights, &c. for his Master had newly Landed, and thus the Prediction was immediately accomplished.

Sir *Normand* hearing of it, call'd for the Seer, and examin'd him about it; he answer'd, that he had seen the Spirit call'd *Browny* in Humane Shape, come several times, and make a shew of carrying an old Woman that sat by the fire to the door, and at last seem'd to carry her out by neck and heels, which made him laugh heartily, and gave occasion to the rest to conclude he was mad to laugh so without any reason. This Instance was told me by Sir *Normand* himself.

FOUR

FOUR Men from the Ifle of *Skie* and *Harries*, having gone to *Barbadoes*, ftay'd there for fourteen years; and tho' they had wont to fee the *Second Sight* in their Native Countrey, they never faw it in *Barbadoes*, but upon their return to *England*, the firft Night after their Landing they faw the *Second Sight*, as was told me by feveral of their Acquaintance.

JOHN MORISON who lives in *Bernera* of *Harries*, wears the Plant call'd *Fuga Demonum* few'd in the neck of his Coat, to prevent his feeing of Vifions, and fays he never faw any fince he firft carried that Plant about him. He fuffer'd me to feel the Plant in the neck of his Coat, but would by no means let me open the Seam, tho' I offer'd him a Reward to let me do it.

A Spirit by the Countrey People call'd *Browny*, was frequently feen in all the moft Confiderable Families in the Ifles and North of *Scotland*, in the fhape of a tall Man, but within thefe twenty or thirty years paft, he is feen but rarely.

THERE were Spirits alfo that appear'd in the Shape of Women, Horfes, Swine, Cats, and fome like fiery Balls, which would follow Men in the Fields; but there has been but few Inftances of thefe for forty years paft.

THESE

THESE Spirits us'd alfo to form Sounds in the Air, refembling thofe of a Harp, Pipe, Crowing of a Cock, and of the grinding of Querns; and fometimes they have heard Voices in the Air by Night, finging Irifh Songs; the words of which Songs fome of my Acquaintance ftill retain. One of 'em refembled the Voice of a Woman who had died fome time before, and the Song related to her State in the other World. Thefe Accounts I had from Perfons of as great Integrity as any are in the World.

A Brief

A Brief Account of the Advantages the Ifles afford by Sea and Land, and particularly for a Fifhing Trade.

THE North Weft Ifles are of all other moft capable of Improvement by Sea and Land; yet by reafon of their diftance from Trading Towns, and becaufe of their Language which is *Irifh*, the Inhabitants have never had any opportunity to Trade at Home or Abroad, or to acquire Mechanical Arts, and other Sciences, fo that they are ftill left to act by the force of their Natural Genius, and what they could learn by obfervation. They have not yet arriv'd to a competent knowledge in Agriculture, for which caufe many Tracts of rich Ground lie neglected, or at leaft but meanly improv'd, in proportion to what they might be. This is the more to be regreetd, becaufe the People are as capable to acquire Arts or Sciences as any other in *Europe*. If two or more Perfons skill'd in Agriculture were fent from the Low-lands, to each Parifh in the Ifles, they would foon enable the Natives to furnifh themfelves with fuch plenty of Corn, as would maintain all their Poor and Idle People; many of which, for want of Subfiftence at home, are forc'd to feek their Livelihood in Foreign Countries, to the great lofs as well as difho-nour

nour of the Nation. This would enable them alfo to Furnifh the oppofite barren Parts of the Continent with Bread; and fo much the more that in plentiful years they afford them good quantities of Corn in this Infant State of their Agriculture. They have many large parcels of Ground never yet Manur'd, which if Cultivated, would maintain double the number of the prefent Inhabitants, and increafe and preferve their Cattle; many of which for want of Hay or Straw, die in the Winter, and Spring; fo that I have known particular Perfons lofe above one hundred Cows at a time, meerly by want of Fodder.

THIS is fo much the more inexcufable, becaufe the ground in the Weftern Ifles is naturally richer in feveral refpects than in many other parts of the Continent, as appears from feveral Inftances, particularly in *Skie*, and the oppofite Weftern Ifles, in which there are many Valleys, &c. capable of good improvement, and of which divers Experiments have been already made; and befides moft of thofe Places have the convenience of Frefh-Water Lakes and Rivers, as well as of the Sea near at hand, to furnifh the Inhabitants with Fifh of many forts, and *Alga Marina* for Manuring the Ground.

IN many Places the Soil is proper for Wheat, and that their Grafs is good, is evident from the great product of their Cattle; fo that if the

Y

the Natives were taught and encouraged to take pains to improve their Corn and Hay, to Plant, Inclose and Manure their Ground, drain Lakes, Sow Wheat and Pease, and Plant Orchards, and Kitchin-Gardens, *&c.* they might have as great plenty of all things for the sustenance of Mankind, as any other People in *Europe*.

I have known a hundred Families of four or five Persons apiece at least maintain'd there upon little Farms, for which they paid not above five shillings *Sterl.* one Sheep, and some Pecks of Corn *per Ann.* each; which is enough to shew that by a better Improvement that Country would maintain many more Inhabitants than live now in the Isles.

IF any Man be dispos'd to live a solitary retir'd Life, and to withdraw from the noise of the World, he may have a Place of retreat there in a small Island, or in the corner of a large one, where he may enjoy himself, and live at a very cheap rate.

IF any Family reduc'd to low Circumstances, had a mind to retire to any of these Isles, there is no part of the known World where they may have the products of Sea and Land cheaper, live more securely, or among a more tractable and mild People. And that the Countrey in general

general is Healthful, appears from the good state of health enjoy'd by the Inhabitants.

I shall not offer to assert that there are Mines of Gold or Silver in the Western Isles, from any resemblance they may bear to other Parts that afford Mines, but the Natives affirm that Gold Dust has been found at *Griminis* on the Western Coast of the Isle of *North Uist*, and at *Copveaul* in *Harries*; in which, as well as in other parts of the Isles, the Teeth of the Sheep which feed there, are died yellow.

THERE is a good Lead Mine, having a mixture of Silver in it, on the West end of the Isle of *Ila*, near Port *Escock*; and *Buchanan* and others say, that the Isle *Lismore* affords Lead, and *Slait*, and *Strath*, on the South West of *Skie*, are in Stone, Ground, Grass, *&c.* exactly the same with that part of *Ila*, where there's a Lead Mine. And if search were made in the Isles and Hills of the opposite Main, it is not improbable that some good Mines might be discover'd in some of them.

I was told by a Gentleman of *Lochaber*, that an English Man had found some Gold Dust in a Mountain near the River *Locby*, but could never find out the Place again after his return from *England*. That there have been Gold Mines in *Scotland*, is clear, from the Manuscripts

Y 2

nuſcripts mention'd by Dr. *Nicholſon*, now Biſhop of *Carliſle*, in his late *Scots Hiſt.* Library.

THE Situation of theſe Iſles for promoting Trade in general, appears advantageous enough, but more particularly for a Trade with *Denmark*, *Sweden*, *Hamburg*, *Holland*, *Britain*, and *Ireland*. *France* and *Spain* ſeem remote, yet they don't exceed a Weeks Sailing, with a favourable Wind.

THE General Opinion of the advantage that might be reap'd from the Improvement of the Fiſh Trade in thoſe Iſles, prevail'd among conſidering People in former times to attempt it.

THE firſt that I know of, was by King *Charles* the Firſt, in Conjunction with a Company of Merchants, but it miſcarried, becauſe of the Civil Wars, which unhappily broke out at that time.

THE next Attempt was by King *Charles* the Second, who alſo join'd with ſome Merchants, and this ſucceeded well for a time. I am aſſured by ſuch as ſaw the Fiſh catch'd by that Company, that they were reputed the beſt in *Europe* of their kind, and accordingly, gave a greater Price; but this Deſign was ruin'd thus. The King having occaſion for Money, was adviſ'd to withdraw that which

which was imploy'd in the Fiſhery; at which the Merchants being diſpleas'd, and diſagreeing likewiſe among themſelves, they alſo withdrew their Money, and the Attempt has never been renew'd ſince that time.

THE Setling a Fiſhery in thoſe Parts, would prove of great advantage to the Government, and be an effectual Means to advance the Revenue, by the Cuſtoms on Export, and Import, &c.

IT would alſo be a Nurſery of Stout and Able Seamen in a very ſhort time, to ſerve the Government on all Occaſions. The Inhabitants of the Iſles and oppoſite Main Land being very prolifick already, the Country would beyond all peradventure become very Populous in a little time, if a Fiſhery were once ſetled among them. The Inhabitants are not contemptible for their Number at preſent, nor are they to learn the uſe of the Oar, for all of them are generally very dextrous at it; ſo that thoſe Places need not to be Planted with a New Colony, but only Furniſh'd with proper Materials, and a few Expert Hands to join with the Natives, to ſet on foot and advance a Fiſhery.

THE People Inhabiting the Weſtern Iſles of *Scotland*, may be about forty thouſand, and many of 'em want Imployment; this is a great encou-

Y 3

342 A Deſcription *of the*

encouragement both for ſeting up other Manufactories, and the fiſhing Trade among 'em; beſides a greater Number of People may be expected, from the oppoſite Continent of the High-Lands, and *North*; which from a late Computation, by one who had an eſtimate of their Number, from ſeveral Miniſters in the Country, are reckon'd to exceed the Number of *Iſlanders*, above Ten to One; and tis too well known, that many of 'em alſo want Imployment. The Objection, that they ſpeak only *Iriſh* is nothing, many of 'em underſtand *Engliſh*; in all the Conſiderable Iſlands, which are ſufficient to direct the reſt in catching and cureing Fiſh and in a little time the Youth would learn *Engliſh*.

THE Commodiouſneſs and ſafety, of the numerous Bays and Harbours in thoſe Iſles, ſeem as if Nature had deſign'd them for promoting Trade, they are likewiſe furniſhed with plenty of Good Water, and Stones for building. The oppoſite Main Land affords Wood of divers ſorts, for that uſe. They have abundance of Turff and Peat for Fewel, and of this latter, there is ſuch plenty in many parts, as might furniſh Salt Pans with Fire all the Year round. The Sea forces its paſſage in ſeveral ſmall Channels, through the Land, ſo as it renders the deſign, more eaſie and practicable.

THE Coaſt of each Iſle affords many thouſand load of Sea-ware, which if preſerved, might be

Weſtern Iſlands *of* **Scotland**, *&c.* 343

be ſucceſsfully us'd for making Glaſs, and likewiſe *Kelp* for Soap.

THE generality of the Bays afford all ſorts of Shel-fiſh in great plenty, as Oyſters, Clams, Muſcles, Lobſters, Cockles, *&c.* which might be pickled, and exported in great Quantities. There are great and ſmall Whales of divers kinds to be had round the Iſles, and on the Shore of the oppoſite Continent; and are frequently ſeen in Narrow Bays, where they may be eaſily caught. The great Number of Rivers, both in the Iſles and oppoſite Main Land, afford abundance of Salmon, which if rightly managed, might turn to a Good Account.

THE Iſles afford likewiſe Great Quantities of Black Cattle, which might ſerve the Traders, both for Conſumption, and Export.

STRATH in *Skie*, abounds with Good Marble, which may be had at an eaſie rate, and near the Sea.

THERE is good Wooll, in moſt of the Iſles, and very cheap; ſome are at the charge of carrying it on Horſe-back, about ſeventy or eighty Miles, to the Shires of *Murray*, and *Aberdeen*.

THERE are ſeveral of the Iſles, that afford a great deal of very fine Clay; which if Improved, might

Y 4

might turn to a Good Account, for making Earthen Ware of all sorts.

THE most Centrical and Convenient Places for keeping Magazins of Cask, Salt, *&c.* are those mentioned in the respective Isles; as one at *Loch Maddy* Isles, in the Isle of *North Uist.* A second the Isle *Hermetra*, on the Coast of the Isle *Harries*; a third in Island *Glass*, on the Coast of *Harries*; and a fourth in *Stornvay*, in the Isle of *Lewis.*

BUT for setling a Magazin or Colony for Trade in general, and Fishing in particular, the Isle of *Skie* is absolutely the most Centrical, both with regard to the Isles and opposite Main Land; and the most proper Places in this Isle, are Island *Isa*, in *Lochfallart*, and *Lochuge*, both on the West side of *Skie*; *Loch-Portrie*, and *Scowsar* on the East side; and Island *Dierman* on the South side; these Places abound with all sorts of Fish, that are caught in those Seas; and they are proper Places for a considerable Number of Men to dwell in, and Convenient for setling Magazins in 'em.

THERE are many Bays and Harbours that are Convenient for building Towns in several of the other Isles if Trade were settled among them; and Cod and Ling, as well as Fish of lesser size, are to be had generally, on the Coast

Coast of the Lesser as well as of the larger Isles. I am not ignorant that Foreigners, sailing through the Western Isles, have been tempted from the Sight of so many Wild Hills, that seem to be covered all over with Heath, and fac'd with High Rocks, to imagine that the Inhabitants, as well as the Places of their residence are barbarous, and to this Opinion, their Habit, as well as their Language have contributed. The like is suppos'd by many that live in the South of *Scotland*, who know no more of the Western Isles, than the Natives of *Italy*; but the Lion is not so fierce as he is painted, neither are the People describ'd here, so barbarous as the World Imagines: It is not the Habit that makes a Monk, nor doth the Garb in Fashion qualifie him that wears it to be vertuous; the Inhabitants have Humanity, and use Strangers Hospitably, and Charitably. I could bring several Instances of Barbarity and Theft committed by Stranger Seamen in the Isles, but there is not one Instance of any injury offered by the *Islanders*, to any Seamen or Strangers. I had a particular Account of Seamen, who not many Years ago, stole Cattle and Sheep in several of the Isles; and when they were found on board their Vessels, the Inhabitants were satisfied to take their Value in Money or Goods, without any further Resentment; tho' many Seamen whose Lives were preserv'd by the Natives, have made 'em very ungrateful returns. For the Humanity and Hospitable

Hofpitable Temper of the Iflanders to Sailers: I fhall only give two Inftances. *Captain Jackfon* of *White Haven,* about fixteen Years ago, was oblig'd to leave his Ship, being Leacky in the Bay, within Ifland *Glafs*, alias *Scalpa*, in the Ifle of *Harries*, with two Men only to take care of her, tho' loaded with Goods; the Ship was not within three Miles of a Houfe, and feparated from the dwellingPlaces by Mountains, yet when the Captain return'd about ten or twelve Months after; he found his Men and the Veffel fafe.

CAPTAIN LOTCH loft the *Dromedary* of *London* of fix hundred Tun burden, with all her Rich Cargo from the *Indies*, of which he might have faved a great deal, had he embrac'd the affiftance which the Natives offered him to unlade her; but the Captain's fhinefs, and fear of being thought rude, hindred a Gentleman on the Place to employ about feventy Hands, which he had ready, to unlade her, and fo the Cargo was loft. The Captain and his Men were kindly entertain'd there, by Sir. *Normand Mac Leod*,and tho' among other ValuableGoods, they had fix Boxes of Gold duft, there was not the leaft thing taken from them, by the Inhabitants. There are fome Pedlars, from the Shire of *Murray*, and other parts, who of late have fixed their refidence in the Ifle of *Skie*, and travel through the remoteft Ifles without any Moleftation; tho' fome of thofe Pedlars fpeak no *Irifh*.

Irifh. Several Barks come yearly from *Orkney* to the Weftern Ifles, to Fifh for Cod and Ling; and many from *Enftruther* in the Shire of *Fife*, came formerly to *Barray* and other Ifles to fifh, before the Battle of *Kilfyth*, where moft of them being cut off, that Trade was afterwards neglected.

THE Magazines and fifhing Boats, left by Foreigners in the Ifles above mentioned, were reckon'd fecure enough,when one of the Natives only was left in charge with them till the next Seafon, and fo they might be ftill. So that if a Company of Strangers from any part fhould fettle to Fifh or Trade in thefe Ifles, there is no Place of greater fecurity in any part of *Europe*, for the Proprietors are always ready to affift and fupport all Strangers within their refpective Jurisdictions. A few *Dutch* Families fettled in *Stornvay*, in the Ifle of *Lewis*, after K. *Charles* the *Second*'s Reftoration, but fome cunning Merchants, found means by the Secretaries to prevail with the *King* to fend them away, tho' they brought the *Iflanders* a great deal of Money for theProducts of theirSea and Land Fowl; and taught them fomething of Art of Fifhing. Had they ftayed the, *Iflanders* muft certainly have made confiderable Progrefs in Trade by this time, for the fmall Idea of Fifhing they had from the *Dutch*, has had fo much effect, as to make the People of the little Village of *Stornvay*, to excell all thofe of the Neighbouring

Neighbouring Iſles and Continent in the Fiſhing Trade, ever ſince that time.

FOR the better Government of thoſe Iſles in caſe of ſetting up a Fiſhing Trade there, it may perhaps be found neceſſary to erect the Iſle of *Skie*, *Lewis*, *Harries*, South and North *Uiſt*, *&c.* into a Sherivalty, and to build a Royal Borough in *Skie* as the Center, becauſe of the Peoples great diſtance in remote Iſles, from the head Borough of the Shire of *Inverneſs*. This would ſeem much more neceſſary here than thoſe of *Boot*, and *Arran*, that lie much nearer to *Dunbarton*; tho' they be neceſſary enough in themſelves.

IT may likewiſe deſerve the Conſideration of the Government, Whether they ſhould not make the Iſle of *Skie* a Free Port, becauſe of the great Incouragement ſuch Immunities give to Trade, which always iſſues in the welfare of the Publick, and adds Strength and Reputation to the Government. Since theſe Iſles are capable of the Improvements above-mention'd, it is a great loſs to the Nation they ſhould be thus neglected. This is the general Opinion of Foreigners, as well as of our own Countrymen, who know them; but I leave the further Enquiry to ſuch as ſhall be diſpos'd to attempt a Trade there, with the Concurrence of the Government. *Scotland* has Men and Money enough to ſet up a Fiſhery, ſo

ſo that there ſeems to be nothing wanting towards it but the Encouragement of thoſe in Power, to excite the Inclination and Induſtry of the People.

IF the *Dutch* in their Publick Edicts call their Fiſhery a Golden Mine, and at the ſame time affirm that it yields them more profit than the *Indies* do to *Spain*, we have very great reaſon to begin to Work upon thoſe Rich Mines, not only in the Iſles, but on all our Coaſt in general. We have multitudes of Hands to be employ'd at a very eaſie rate; we have a healthful Climate, and our Fiſh, eſpecially the Herring, come to our Coaſt in *April*, or *May*, and into the Bays in prodigious Shoals in *July*, or *Auguſt*. I have ſeen Complaints from *Loch Eſſort* in *Skie*, that all the Ships there were loaded, and that the Barrel of Herring might be had there for Four Pence, but there were no Buyers.

I have known the Herring Fiſhing to continue in ſome Bays from *September*, 'till the end of *January*; and wherever they are, all other Fiſh follow 'em, and Whales and Seals in particular; for the larger Fiſh of all kinds feed upon Herring.

A Brief

Arinagour, Coll

Women using quem and waulking cloth, Talisker

Cottage interior, Islay

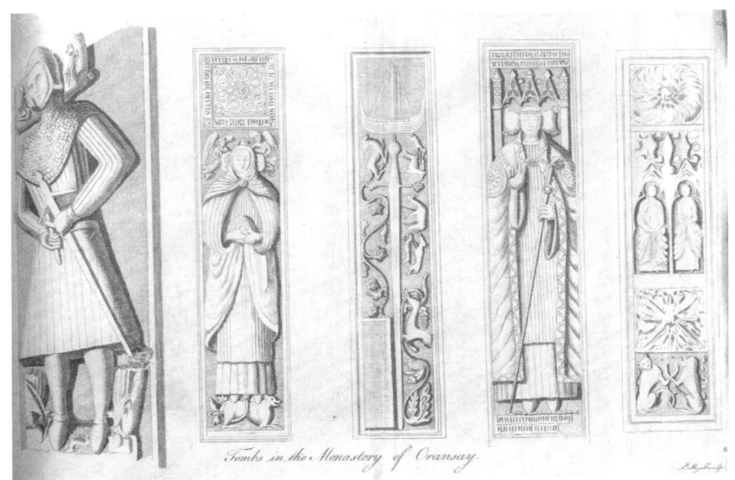

Illustrations of tombstones, Oronsay

An Account of the Second Sight

1.Martin's 'Taish' is the Gaelic 'Taibhse' or 'Taidhbhse', the second sight or sometimes a ghost.

Various works have followed up the subject. They include at different periods: J. Frazer: Deuteroscopia, or A Brief Discourse concerning Second-Sight, commonly so-called Edinburgh 1707; an article by Ada Goodrich-Freer in TGSI Vol. XXI (1896-97) pp.106-115, and another by Dugald MacEchern in TGSI Vol. XXIX (1914-19) pp.290-314; JG Campbell: Witchcraft and Second Sight in the Highlands and Islands of Scotland Glasgow 1902; N. Macrae (edit.): Highland Second-Sight with Prophecies of Coinneach Odhar and the Seer of Petty Dingwall [1908]; HE Davidson (edit.): The Seer in Celtic and Other Traditions Edinburgh 1989.

The most celebrated Scottish seer was of course Coinneach Odhar, generally known as 'The Brahan Seer', who was alive in the 1570s. Several editions of accumulated prophecies attributed to him have appeared since the 1890s. Of more interest is a mid-eighteenth century collection of second sight occasions, said to have been assembled by William MacLeod of Hammer under a pseudonym [Theophilus Insulanus: A Treatise on the Second Sight, Dreams and Apparitions etc. Edinburgh 1763. Reprinted in Miscellanea Scotica Glasgow 1820 Vol. III] Among the numerous instances in the book is one recorded in a letter of 27 December 1756 from 'Mr Donald Martin of Beallach in Trotternish', tacksman of the lands reputedly associated with the family of which Martin Martin is supposed to have been a member. It tells of an episode in 1733 when one of three boys travelling 'from the *North* of *Duntulm*, to the place of my residence at *Bellach*', cried out because he was apparently surrounded by 'some hundreds of men' [Treatise pp.116-118].

Further examples and descriptions of the second sight are given in 'An Accurate Account of Second-Sighted Men in Scotland: In Two Letters from a Learned Friend of Mine in Scotland' in Miscellanea Scotica Vol. III pp.207-225. And Armstrong's Gaelic Dictionary has a lengthy entry under 'Taibhse' quoting various authors including Martin.

2.The parish of St Mary's is more commonly known as Kilmuir parish (see Skye n.42).

3.'*Mogstot*', the name of a residence of Macdonald of Sleat after the abandonment of Duntulm Castle, appears in records also as 'Mungestot', 'Mougstot', 'Mugstot(e)', 'Mogustot', and on the OS maps became 'Monkstadt', a curiously German-looking transformation. It is in Kilmuir parish (see Skye n.23)

[Blaeu; MA MSS 4272/4, 4276/3; DP NLS MS 1389 f.184]

4.The word '*Taisk*', which Martin says 'is a way of foretelling Death by a Cry', is given in the dictionaries as meaning in English a pledge or a treasure, but also a 'reconnoitring' or 'spying'. As a verb it means to store or lay up. But it may be related to 'taisgealadh', prognosticating, or be a version of 'tannasg' (tannas), a spectre or ghost, possibly Martin's Lowland '*Wrath*' (wraith). [Armstrong pp.539, 541].

5. For Rigg see Skye n.4

6. For '*Loch-Skeriness*' cf. Skye n.21. The church of Snizort was nearby and probably the old church at the river Skeabost is the one meant here.

7. It seems that, as in the case of Roderick in St Kilda, Martin used the word 'impostor' to denote someone who imposed

upon people what he, Martin, or others considered false doctrine.

8. Since the exact seer lived in the parish of St Mary's (Kilmuir) and in 'the Village *Knockow*', the location of Knockow was certainly in the north of Trotternish. It would appear to have been a little north of Mugstot, and near the coast, where the Blaeu map of Skye has 'Knocko' and this finds confirmation in that 'Bornskittag' (Bornaskittaig) was later described by Martin as 'the next adjacent village' to Knockow.

9. 'Mr. *Sacheverel*' was William Sacheverell who was appointed Governor of the Isle of Man in 1692. In 1688, when probably in his early twenties, he had written of his 'Voyage to I-Columb-Kill' (Iona), and in 1702 he wrote his *Account of the Isle of Man*', which helps therefore to date this passage in Martin's book. Sacheverell was 'an enthusiastic promoter of local industry' and provided information, much like Martin, on air, soil, waters, flora and fauna, language, customs, habits and beliefs of the people, about all of which he too used the word 'remarkable curiosities'.

10. In 1718 a holding called 'Hoill' was partly tenanted by John Martine. The rental placed it next to 'Shadder' which is in Glen Conon at the back of Uig. This would suggest that it was indeed in Kilmuir and not to be confused with Holm which is not in that parish. (FEP NAS E656/2/2)

11. Mr Morison, minister of Stornoway in Martin's time, was apparently Mr Kenneth Morison. [Matheson (1970) Appendix C p.191].

12. Martin's opinion (p.315) of holy water here again illustrates his strongly protestant distaste for anything that sounds like a Catholic practice or ritual. (cf. Lewis n.43, St Kilda n.4)

13. For the detailed account of John Morison, of '*Bragir*', believed to have been the brother of Rev. Kenneth Morison (n.11 above), given by Matheson and for Martin's acquaintance with him see Lewis n.41.

14. If Martin visited Lewis in 1695, as is possible (see Introduction pp. xiii-xvi), this would mean that the haunting by the spirit continued in 1696 when the 'minister of the parish', Mr Morison, was possibly still Mr Donald Morison, as the parish was that of Barvas. However it is supposed that Donald Morison, old and infirm, died about 1696; and he was succeeded by his son Rev. Allan Morison who could have been the minister to whom Martin refers.

15. '*St. Maries* on the West side of the Isle of Skie' is Kilmuir near Dunvegan and in the parish of Duirinish, where in Martin's time the minister was Dugald Macpherson, son of Rev. Martin Macpherson his predecessor and mentioned by Martin again a little later by name (pp.318, 323).

[Fasti Vol. VII p.168]

16. For Bornaskittaig in Kilmuir parish and 'Kyle Raes' [Kyle Rhea] see no.8 above and Skye nn.20, 8, 50. The name Daniel is a frequent alternative for Donald.

17. Sir Norman MacLeod was Sir Norman of Bernera. Lachlan MacLean of Torloisk died in 1687. He is said to have been married to a daughter of Sir Donald Macdonald, first baronet of Sleat, but the family pedigree in *The Clan Donald* (Vol. III p.471) gives Lachlan's wife as Barbara, Sir Donald's granddaughter. Sir Donald's uncle, Donald Gorm Mor, was married first to a daughter of Norman MacLeod of Dunvegan.

[A.M. Sinclair: The Clan Gillean Charlottetown 1899 pp.218, 459; Macdonalds Vol. III]

18. The names '*John Mack Normand*' (John son of Norman) and '*Daniel Mack Ewin*' (Donald son of Ewen) are typical of subtenants and the use of them by Martin suggests either familiarity with the individuals, who seem to have been heading towards Kilmuir parish, or a wish to convey an impression of precise sources for an instance of second sight – or perhaps both. The exceptional burial of persons of distinction 'from another Parish' at Snizort may have taken place in the old and important graveyard at the Skeabost river.

19. James Beaton was of the Pennycross family in Mull and may have been briefly visiting the North Uist Beaton surgeons to the Macdonalds of Sleat, whose surgeons in Sleat were also Beatons.

[Bannerman pp.16-21, 24, 30-31, 53, 128]

20. Sir George Mackenzie of Tarbat, later Viscount Tarbat, became Secretary of State for Scotland in 1702 and in 1703 became Earl of Cromartie. He was one of the original members or 'Fellows' of the Royal Society, and it was in this capacity that he was in communication more than once with Martin.

[E Richards & M Clough pp.12-25; DP NLS MS 1389 f.84 (see introduction p.)]

21. Mr Daniel or Donald Nicholson was minister of the parish of St Mary's (Kilmuir) from 1663, but deserted his charge and was probably 'outed' in 1696. Though said to have died in 1697 he was still alive in 1698. In 1708 and again in 1711 there are records of Patrick Nicolsone, son to the late Mr Donald Nicolsone, and to 'Mr Malcom Nicleson', son and heir to the late Mr Donald 'somtymes minister of St Maries Kirk in Troterness'. An account of Mr Donald as 'the best known of the chiefs' of the Nicolsons of Scorrybreac is a useful biography.

[Fasti Vol. VII p. ; DC Section I 850/4 and 850/6; WDH Sellar & A Maclean pp.15-16]

22. Mr Daniel Martin living in '*Knockow*' (see n.8 above) was possibly Martin Martin's eldest brother, back from Uist. Three occurrences of the name appear in 1718 rentals of Trotternish but none of them are 'Mr': Donald Martin in Loanfern and his son Alexander, Donald Martin 'Frail' in Erisco, and Donald Martine in Graulin.

[FEP NAS E656/1&2]

23. '*Normand Mac Leod* of *Graban*' [Macleod (1934): Grabam] should be Norman of Groban in Waternish from whom Martin received his payment as governor to the young MacLeod in the 1680s. The discharges of payment on 29 July 1688 and thereafter were signed by Martin in Edinburgh.

[DC e.g. Section 3 13/2/1, 13/7, 8/92/2-4]

24. The Scots word Browny or Brownie was used in many parts of Scotland for a sort of supernatural creature. See Skye n.34.

A Brief Account of the Advantages the Isles afford

1. In addition to his search for 'curiosities' to send to the Royal Society Martin evidently had in mind, perhaps in response to some request, the economic potential of the Hebrides and the development of trade. At various stages of his book this concern is apparent, as for instance at the end of his account of Shetland where he notes 'the great number of Foreign Ships' visiting the area each year to fish, a fact which 'ought to excite the People of *Scotland*, to a speedy Improvement of that profitable Trade; which they may carry on with more Ease and Profit in their own Seas, than any Foreigners whatever.' Fisheries would bring greater rewards than agriculture in the

islands, but much could be done to improve agricultural knowledge and method.

2. Martin's comments on island resources include mention of gold dust and mines, and lead mines. Whatever speculation on gold there may have been in earlier years there does not seem to have been any known source in the Hebrides before and in Martin's day.

[R W Cochran-Patrick: Early Records relating to Mining in Scotland Edinburgh 1878]

3.The idea of 'Setling a Fishery' in the Hebrides and on the west coast of the mainland, and of seeing such an enterprise as also 'a Nursery of Stout and Able Seamen in a very short time' was repeated frequently over the next two centuries in relation to the islands.

4.The island '*Isa*' is Isay at the entrance to Loch Bay, Waternish, Skye. For this and other Skye placenames here see Skye nn.3,7,17 etc.

5.Martin's observations on the impressions of foreigners and 'South of *Scotland*' people remained relevant long after his own time. His comments on merchants in 'the little Village of *Stornvay*' and his suggestion that the Outer Hebrides, Skye and perhaps other islands should be made a distinct county or sheriffdom also find some reflection in developments and attitudes in more recent times, especially with regard to the difficulties arising when the administrative centre is far away from an area for which it is responsible.

A Brief Deſcription of the Iſles of Orkney, *and* Schetland, *&c.*

THE Iſles of *Orkney* lie to the North of *Scotland*, having the Main *Caledonian* Ocean, which contains the *Hebrides* on the Weſt, and the *German* Ocean on the Eaſt; and the Sea towards the North, ſeparates 'em from the Iſles of *Schetland*. *Pictland Firth* on the South, which is twelve Miles broad, reaches to *Dungisbie-Head*, the moſt Northern Point of the Main Land of *Scotland*.

AUTHORS differ as to the Origine of the Name, the *Engliſh* call it *Orkney*, from *Erick*, one of the firſt *Pictiſh* Princes that poſſeſs'd 'em; and it is obſerv'd, that *Pict* or *Pight* in the *Teutonik* Language ſignifies a Fighter. The *Iriſh* call 'em *Arkive*, from the firſt Planter, and Latine Authors call 'em *Orcades*. They lie in the Northern Temperate Zone, and 13th Climate; the Longitude is between 22 Degrees, and eleven Minutes, and Latitude 59 Degrees, 2 Minutes; the Compaſs varies here eight Degrees; the longeſt Day is about 18 hours. The Air is temperately cold, and the Night ſo clear, that in the middle of *June* one may ſee to read all Night long; and the Days in Winter are by conſequence very ſhort. Their Winters

Winters here, are commonly more ſubject to Rain, than Snow, for the Sea-air diſſolves the latter; the Winds are often very boiſtrous in this Country.

THE Sea Ebbs and Flows here as in other parts, except in a few Sounds, and about ſome Promontories, which alter the Courſe of the Tides, and make 'em very impetuous.

THE Iſles of *Orkney* are reckon'd twenty ſix in Number; the leſſer Iſles called *Holms*, are not Inhabited, but fit for Paſturage; moſt of their Names end in *a* or *ey*, that in the *Teutonick* Language ſignifies Water, with which they are all ſurrounded.

THE Main Land called by the Ancients *Pomona*, is about twenty four Miles long, and in the middle of it on the South ſide lies the only Town in *Orkney*, called *Kirkwall*, which is about three quarters of a Mile in length, the *Danes* called it *Cracoviaca*. There has been two fine Edifices in it, one of 'em called the King's Palace, which is ſuppos'd to have been built by one of the Biſhops of *Orkney*, becauſe in the Wall there's a Biſhop's Mitre, and Arms engraven, and the Biſhops anciently had their Reſidence in it.

THE Palace now called the Biſhops, was Built by *Patrick Stewart*, Earl of *Orkney*, *Anno* 1606. THERE

THERE is a Stately Church in this Town, having a Steeple erected on four large Pillars in the middle of it; there are fourteen Pillars on each fide the Church, it is called by the Name of St. *Magnus* his Church, being Founded as the Inhabitants fay, by *Magnus* King of *Norway*, whom they believe to be Interr'd there. The Seat of Juftice for thefe Ifles is kept here; the Steward, Sheriff, and Commiffary, do each of them keep their refpective Courts in this Place. It hath a Publick School for Teaching of Grammar Learning, Endow'd with a Competent Sallary.

THIS Town was Erected into a Royal Borough when the Danes poffefs'd it, and their Charter was afterwards confirm'd to them by King *James* the Third, *Anno* 1486. They have from that Charter a Power to hold Borough-Courts, to Imprifon, to Arreft, to make By-Laws, to choofe their own Magiftrates yearly, to have two Weekly Markets, and they have alfo Power of Life and Death, and of fending Commiffioners to Parliament, and all other Privileges Granted to Royal Boroughs. This Charter was Dated at *Edinburgh* the laft Day of *March*, 1486, and it was fince Ratified by King *James* the Fifth, and King *Charles* the Second. The Town is Govern'd by a Provoft, four Bayliffs, and a Common-Council.

ON

ON the Weft end of the Main is the King's Palace, formerly mention'd, Built by *Robert Stewart* Earl of *Orkney*, about the year 1574. Several Rooms in it have been curioufly Painted with Scripture Stories, as the Flood of *Noah*, Chrift's Riding to *Jerufalem*, &c. and each Figure has the Scripture by it, that it referrs to. Above the Arms within there is this lofty Infcription, *Sic fuit, eft, & erit*. This Ifland is Fruitful in Corn and Grafs, and has feveral good Harbours; one of 'em at *Kirk-Wall*, a fecond at the Bay of *Kairfton* Village, near the Weft end of the Ifle, well fecur'd againft Wind and Weather; the third is at *Deer-Sound*, and reckon'd a very good Harbour; the fourth is at *Grahamfhall*, towards the Eaft fide of the Ifle, but in Sailing to it from the Eaft fide, Seamen would do well to Sail betwixt *Lambholm*, and the Main Land, and not between *Lambholm* and *Burray*, which is fhallow.

ON the Eaft of the Main Land lies the fmall Ifle *Copinfha*, Fruitful in Corn and Grafs; it is diftinguifh'd by Sea-faring-Men for its Confpicuoufnefs at a great diftance. To the North end of it lies the *Holm*, called the Horfe of *Copinfha*. Over againft *Kerfton Bay*, lie the Ifles of *Hoy* and *Waes*, which make but one Ifle, about twelve Miles in length, and Mountainous,

Z

tainous. In this Iſland is the Hill of *Hoy*, which is reckoned the higheſt in *Orkney*.

THE Iſle of *South Ronalſhaw* lies to the Eaſt of *Waes*, it is five Miles in length, and Fruitful in Corn; *Burray* in the ſouth end, is the Ferry to *Duncanſbay* in *Kathneſs*. A little further to the ſouth lies *Swinna Iſle*, Remarkable only for a part of *Pightland-Firth* lying to the Weſt of it, called the Wells of *Swinna*. They are two Whirl-pools in the Sea, which run about with ſuch violence, that any Veſſel or Boat coming within their reach, go always round until they ſink. Theſe Wells are dangerous only when there is a dead Calm, for if a Boat be under ſail with any Wind, it is eaſie to go over them If any Boat be forced into theſe Wells by the violence of the Tide, the Boat-Men caſt a Barrel or an Oar into the Wells, and while it is ſwallowing it up, the Sea continues calm, and gives the Boat an opportunity to paſs over.

TO the North of the Main lies the Iſle of *Shapinſha*, five Miles in length, and has a Harbour at *Elwick* on the South. Further to the North lie the Iſles of *Stronſa*, five Miles in length, and *Eda* which is four Miles; *Ronſa* lies to the North Weſt, and is ſix Miles long. The Iſle *Sanda* lies North, twelve Miles in length, and is reckon'd the moſt Fruitful and Beautiful of all the *Orcades*.

THE

THE Iſles of *Orkney* in general are Fruitful in Corn and Cattle, and abound with ſtore of Rabbets.

THE Sheep are very Fruitful here, many of them have two, ſome three, and others four Lambs at a time; they often die with a Diſeaſe called the *Sheep-dead*, which is occaſion'd by little Animals about half an inch long, that are engendred in their Liver.

THE Horſes are of a very ſmall ſize, but hardy, and expos'd to the rigour of the Seaſon, during the Winter, and Spring; the Graſs being then ſcarce, they are fed with Sea-ware.

THE fields every where abound with variety of Plants and Roots, and the latter are generally very large, the Common people dreſs their Leather with the Roots of Tormentil inſtead of bark.

THE main Land is Furniſhed with abundance of good Marl, which is us'd ſucceſsfully by the Husband Man for Mannuring the Ground.

THE Inhabitants ſay there are Mines of Silver, Tinn and Lead in the Main Land, South *Ronalſha*, *Stronſa*, *Sanda* and *Hoy*. Some Veins of Marble are to be ſeen at *Buckquoy*,

Z 2 and

and *Swinna*. There are no Trees in thefe Ifles, except in Gardens, and thofe bear no Fruit. Their common Fuel is Peat and Turff, of which there is fuch Plenty, as to furnifh a Salt-pan with Fuel. A South-Eaft and North-Weft Moon caufe High Water here.

THE *Fin-Land* Fisher-men have been frequently feen on the Coaft of this Ifle, particularly in the year 1682. The People on the Coaft, faw one of them in his little Boat, and endeavour'd to take him, but could not come at him, he retir'd fo fpeedily. They fay the Fifh retire from the Coaft, when they fee thefe Men come to it.

ONE of their Boats fent from *Orkney* to *Edinburgh*, is to be feen in the *Phyficians-Hall*, with the Oar he makes ufe of, and the Dart with which he kills his Fifh.

THERE is no Venomous Creature in this Country. The Inhabitants fay there is a Snail there, which has a bright Stone growing in it. There is abundance of Shel-Fifh here, as Oyfters, Mufcles, Crabs, Cockles, &c. of this latter they make much fine Lime; the Rocks on the fhoar afford plenty of Sea-ware, as *Alga-Marina*, &c.

THE Sea abounds with variety of Fifh, but efpecially Herring, which are much neglected, fince

fince the Battle of *Kilfyth*, at which time, the Fifhermen from *Fife*, were almoft all killed there.

THERE are many fmall Whales round the Coaft of this Ifle, and the *Amphibia* here are Otters and Seals.

THE chief Product of *Orkney* that is yearly exported from thence; is Corn, Fifh, Hides, Tallow, Butter, Skins of Seals, Otter skins, Lamb skins, Rabbet-skins, Stuffs, white Salt, Wooll, Pens, Down, Feathers, Hams, &c.

SOME *Sperma Ceti*, and *Ambergreefe*, as alfo the *Os Serpier* are found on the fhoar of feveral of thofe Ifles.

THIS Country affords plenty of Sea and Land Fowl, as Geefe, Duks, Solan Geefe, Swans, Lyres, and Eagles, which are fo ftrong as to carry away Children. There is alfo the Cleck-Goofe, the fhels in which this Fowl is faid to be produced, are found in feveral Ifles fticking to Trees by the Bill; of this kind I have feen many, the Fowl was covered by a Shell, and the Head ftuck to the Tree by the Bill, but never faw any of them with life in them upon the Tree, but the Natives told me that they had obferv'd 'em to move with the heat of the Sun.

Z 3 THE

THE *Picts* are believ'd to have been the first Inhabitants of these Isles, and there are Houses of a round form in several parts of the Country, called by the name of *Picts* Houses; and for the same Reason the *Firth* is called *Pightland*, or *Pentland Firth*. Our Historians call these Isles the ancient Kingdom of the *Picts*; *Buchannan* gives an account of one *Belus* King of *Orkney*, who being defeated by King *Ewen* the second of *Scotland*, became desperate, and killed himself. The Effigies of this *Belus* is engraven on a stone in the Church of *Birsa* on the Main Land. *Boethius* makes mention of another of their Kings called *Bannus*, and by others *Gethus*, who being Vanquished by *Claudius Cesar*, was by him afterwards, together with his Wife and Family carried Captive to *Rome*, and there led in Triumph, *Anno Christi*, 43.

THE *Picts* Possessed *Orkney* until the Reign of *Kenneth* the second of *Scotland*, who subdued the Country, and annexed it to his Crown; from that time *Orkney* was peaceably possessed by the *Scots*, until about the year 1099, that *Donald Bane* intending to secure the Kingdom to himself, promised both those and the Western Isles to *Magnus* King of *Norway*, upon condition that he should support him with a competent Force, which he perform'd; and by this means became Master of these Isles, until the

the Reign of *Alexander* the Third, who by his Valour expelled the *Danes*. The Kings of *Denmark* did afterwards resign their Title for a sum of Money, and this Resignation was Ratified under the Great Seal of *Denmark*, at the Marriage of King *James* the sixth of *Scotland*, with *Anne* Princess of *Denmark*.

ORKNEY has been from time to time a Title of Honour to several Persons of great Quality; *Henry* and *William Sinclairs* were called Princes of *Orkney*, and *Rothuel Hepburn* was made Duke of *Orkney*; Lord *George Hamilton* (Brother to the present Duke of *Hamilton*) was by the late King *William* Created Earl of *Orkney*. The Earl of *Mortun* had a Mortgage of *Orkney* and *Zetland* from King *Charles* the First, which was since reduc'd by a Decree of the Lords of Session, obtain'd at the instance of the King's Advocate against the Earl; and this Decreet was afterward ratified by Act of Parliament, and the Earldom of *Orkney*, and Lordship of *Zetland*, have since that time been erected into a Stewartry. The reason on which the Decreet was founded, is said to have been, that the Earls Depury seiz'd upon some Chests of Gold found in the Rich *Amsterdam* Ship called the *Carlmelan*, that was lost in *Zetland*, 1664.

THERE are several Gentlemen of Estates in *Orkney*, but the Queen is the Principal Proprietor

Z 4

prietor, and one half of the whole belonging to the Crown, besides the late accession of the Bishop's Rents, which is about 9000 Merks *Scots per Ann.* There is a yearly Roup of *Orkney* Rents, and he that offers highest is preferr'd to be the King's Steward for the time, and as such, he is Principal Judge of the Country. But this precarious Lease is a Publick loss to the Inhabitants, especially the Poorer sort, who complain that they would be allowed to pay Money for their Corn and Meal in time of scarcity, but that the Stewards carried it off to other Parts, and neglected the interest of the Countrv. The interest of the Crown suffers likewise by this means, for much of the Crown Lands lie waste, whereas if there were a constant Steward, it might be much better managed, both for the Crown, and the Inhabitants.

THERE's a Tenure of Land in *Orkney*, differing from any other in the Kingdom, and this they call *Udal Right*, from *Ulaus* King of *Norway*, who after taking possession of those Islands, gave a Right to the Inhabitants, on condition of paying the third to himself; and this Right the Inhabitants had successively, without any Charter. All the Lands of *Orkney* are *Udal* Lands, Kings Lands, or Fewed Lands.

THEY

THEY differ in their Measures from other parts of *Scotland*, for they do not use the Peck or Firlet, but weigh their Corns in *Pismores*, or *Pundlers*; the least quantity they call a *Merk*, which is eighteen Ounces, and twenty four make a *Leispound*, or *Setten*, which is the same with the *Danes*, that a stone weight is with us.

The Ancient State of the Church of Orkney.

THE Churches of *Orkney* and *Zetland* Isles were formerly under the Government of a Bishop; the Cathedral Church was St. *Magnus* in *Kirkwall*; there are thirty one Churches, and about one hundred Chappels in the Countrey, and the whole make up about seventeen Parishes.

THIS Diocess had several great Dignities and Privileges for a long time, but by the Succession and Change of many Masters they were lessened. Dr. *Robert Keid* their Bishop, made an erection of seven Dignities, *viz.* a Provost, to whom under the Bishop the government of the Canons, *&c.* did belong; he had alotted to him the Prebendary of *Holy Trinity*, and the Vicarage

Vicarage of *South Kanalſhaw*. 2. An Arch-Deacon. 3. A Precentor, who had the Prebendary of *Ophir*, and Vicaridge of *Stennis*. 4. A Chancellor, who was to be learn'd in both Laws, to him was given the Prebendary of St. *Mary* in *Sanda*, and the Vicaridge of *Sanda*. 5. A Treaſurer who was to keep the Treaſure of the Church, and Sacred Veſtments, *&c.* he was Rector of St. *Nicholas* in *Stronſa*. 6. A Sub-Dean, who was Parſon of *Hoy*, *&c.* 7. A Sub-Chanter, who was bound to play on the Organs each Lords Day, and Feſtivals; he was Prebendary of St. *Colme*. He erected ſeven other Canonries, and Prebends, to which Dignities he aſſign'd, beſides their Churches, the Rents of the Parſonages of St. *Colme* in *Waes*, and *Holy-Croſs* in *Weſtra*, as alſo the Vicaridges of the Pariſh Churches of *Sand*, *Wick*, and *Stromneſs*. He erected beſides theſe, thirteen Chaplains, every one of which was to have 24 *Meils* of Corn, and ten Merks of Money for their yearly Sallary, beſides their daily diſtributions, which were to be rais'd from the Rents of the Vicaridge of the Cathedral Church, and from the Foundation of *Thomas* Biſhop of *Orkney*, and the 12 Pounds mortified by K. *James* the 3*d*, and *James* the 4th of *Scotland*. To theſe he added a *Sacriſt*, and ſix Boys to bear Tapers. The Charter of this Erection is dated at *Kirkwall*, *Octob.* 28, *Anno* 1544.

THIS

THIS was the State of the Church under Popery. Some time after the Reformation, Biſhop *Law* being made Biſhop of *Orkney*, and the Earldom united to the Crown (by the Forfeiture and Death of *Patrick Stewart* Earl of *Orkney*) he with the conſent of his Chapter, made a Contract with King *James* the Sixth, in which they reſign all their Eccleſiaſtical Lands to the Crown, and the King gives back to the Biſhop ſeveral Lands in *Orkney*, as in *Hom*, *Orphir*, &c. and his Majeſty gave alſo the *Comiſſariot* of *Orkney* to the Biſhop and his Succeſſors, and then a competent number of Perſons for a Chapter were agreed on. This Contract was made *Anno*, 1614.

The

The Ancient Monuments and Curiosities in these Islands are as follow.

IN the Isle of *Hoy*, there's the Dwarfie-stone between two Hills, it is about thirty four Foot long, and above 16 Foot broad; it is made hollow by Humane Industry; it has a small square Entry looking to the East, about two Foot high, and has a Stone proportionable at two Foot distance before the Entry; at one of the ends within this Stone there is cut out a Bed and Pillow, capable of two Persons to lie in: At the other opposite end, there is a void space cut out resembling a Bed, and above both these there is a large Hole, which is suppos'd was a vent for Smoak. The Common Tradition is, that a Giant and his Wife made this their Place of retreat.

ABOUT a Mile to the West of the Main Land at *Skeal-house*, there is in the top of high Rocks, many Stones disposed like a Street, about a quarter of a Mile in length, and between twenty and thirty Foot broad. They differ in Figure and Magnitude, are of a Red Colour, some resemble a Heart, some a Crown, Leg, Shoe, Last, Weavers Sickle, &c.

ON

ON the West and East side of *Loch Stennis*, on the Main Land, there is two Circles of large Stone erected in a Ditch; the larger which is round on the N.West side, is a hundred Paces Diameter, and some of the Stones are twenty foot high, and above four in breadth; they are not all of a height, nor placed at an equal distance, and many of them are fallen down on the Ground.

ABOUT a little distance further, there is a Semicircle of larger Stones than those mentioned above. There are two Green Mounts, at the East and West side of the Circle, which are supposed to be Artificial, and *Fibuler* of Silver were found in 'em some time ago, which one side resembled a Horse-shoe, more than any thing else.

THE Hills and Circles are believed to have been Places design'd to offer Sacrifice in time of *Pagan* Idolatry; and for this reason the People called them the Ancient Temples of the Gods, as we may find by *Boetheus* in the Life of *Manius*. Several of the Inhabitants have a Tradition, that the Sun was worshiped in the larger, and the Moon in the lesser Circle.

IN the Chappel of *Clet*, in the Isle of *Sanda*, there is a Grave of nineteen Foot in length; some who had the Curiosity to open it, found only

only a piece of a Man's Back-bone in it, bigger than that of a Horſe. The Miniſter of the Place, had the Curioſity to keep the Bone by him for ſome time. The Inhabitants have a Tradition of a Giant there, whoſe Statue was ſuch, that he could reach his Hand as high as the top of the Chappel. There have been large Bones found lately in *Weſtra*, and one of the Natives who died not long ago, was for his Stature diſtinguiſhed by the Title of the *Micle* or Great Man of *Waes*.

THERE are erected Stones in divers parts, both of the Main, and leſſer Iſles, which are believed to have been erected as Monuments of ſuch as diſtinguiſhed themſelves in Battle.

THERE have been ſeveral ſtrange Inſtances of the effects of Thunder here, as that of burning *Kirkwel* Steeple by Lightning, in the the Year 1670. *Atſtromneſs* a Gentleman, had twelve Kine, ſix of which in a Stall, was ſuddenly killed by Thunder, and the other ſix left alive; and it was remarkable that the Thunder did not kill them all as they ſtood, but kill'd one, and miſt'd another; this happen'd in 1680, and is atteſted by the Miniſter, and others of the Pariſh.

THERE is a ruinous Chappel in *Papa Weſtra*, called St. *Tredwels*, at the Door, of which there's a heap of Stones; which was the ſuperſtition of the Common People, who have ſuch a

a Veneration for this Chappel above any other, that they never fail at their coming to it, to throw a Stone as an offering before the Door; and this they reckon an indiſpenſible Duty enjoin'd by their Anceſtors.

LADY KIRK in South *Ronal-ſhaw*, tho ruinous, and without a Roof, is ſo much reverenc'd by the Natives, that they chooſe rather to repair this Old One, than to build a new Church in a more Convenient Place, and at a Cheaper rate: Such is the Power of Education, that theſe Men cannot be aſſured of theſe ſuperfluous fancies, tranſmitted to them by their ignorant Anceſtors.

WITHIN the Ancient Fabrick of *Lady-Church*, there is a Stone of four Foot in length, and two in breadth, tapering at both ends; this Stone has engraven on it the print of two Feet, concerning which the Inhabitants have the following Tradition; that St. *Magnus* wanting a Boat to carry him over *Pickland Frith* to the oppoſite Main Land of *Cathneſs*, made uſe of this Stone inſtead of a Boat, and afterwards carried it to this Church, where it continues ever ſince. But others have this more reaſonable Opinion, that it has been us'd in time of Popery; for Delinquents who were obliged to ſtand bare foot upon it by way of Pennance. Several of the Vulgar Inhabiting the leſſer Iſles, obſerve the Anniverſary of their reſpective Saints: There is one

one day in Harveſt on which the Vulgar abſtain from Work, becauſe of an Ancient and fooliſh Tradition, that if they do their Work, the ridges will bleed.

THEY have a Charm for ſtoping exceſſive bleeding, either in Man or Beaſt, whether the Cauſe be Internal or External; which is perform'd by ſending the Name of the Patient to the Charmer, he adds ſome more Words to it, and after repeating thoſe Words the Cure is perform'd, tho' the Charmer be ſeveral Miles diſtant from the Patient. They have likewiſe other Charms which they uſe frequently at a diſtance, and that alſo with ſucceſs.

THE Inhabitants are well proportioned, and ſeem to be more Sanguine than they are; the Poorer ſort live much upon Fiſh of various kinds, and ſometimes without any Bread. The Inhabitants in general are ſubject to the Scurvy, imputed to the Fiſh and Salt Meat, which is their daily Food; yet ſeveral of the Inhabitants arrive at a great Age; a Woman in *Evie* brought forth a Child in the 63 Year of her Age.

ONE living in *Kerſton* lately, was one hundred and twelve Years Old, and went to Sea at one hundred and ten. A Gentleman at *Stronſa*, about four Years ago, had a Son at 110 Years Old. One *William Muir* in *Weſtra* lived 140 Years, and died about eighteen Years ago.

ago. The Inhabitants ſpeak the *Engliſh* Tongue, ſeveral of the Vulgar ſpeak the *Daniſh* or *Norſe* Language; and many among them retain the Ancient *Daniſh* Names.

THOSE of *Deſtruction* are Hoſpitable and in Obliging, the Vulgar are generally Civil and Effable. Both of 'em wear the Habit in Faſhion in the Low Lands, and ſome wear a Sealskin for Shoes, which they do not ſow, but only tie them about their Feet with Strings, and ſometimes Thongs of Leather, they are generally able and ſtout Seamen.

THE Common People are very Laborious, and undergo great Fatigues, and no ſmall hazard in Fiſhing. The Iſles of *Orkney* were formerly liable to frequent Incurſions by the *Norwegians*, and thoſe inhabiting the weſtern Iſles of *Scotland*. To prevent which each Village was obliged to furniſh a large Boat well Man'd to oppoſe the Enemy, and upon their landing all the Inhabitants were to appear arm'd, and Beacons ſet on the top of the higheſt Hills and Rocks, to give a general warning on the ſight of an approaching Enemy.

ABOUT the Year 1634, Dr. *Graham* being then Biſhop of *Orkney*, a Young Boy called *William Garioch*, had ſome Acres of Land, and ſome

A a

ſome Cattle, &c. left him by his Father deceas'd, he being Young was kept by his Uncle, who had a great deſire to obtain the Lands, &c. belonging to his Nephew, who being kept ſhort ſtole a ſetten of Barley, which is about twenty eight Pound Weight, from his Uncle; for which he purſued the Youth, who was then eighteen Years of Age, before the Sheriff; the Theft being prov'd, the Young Man received Sentence of Death, but going up the Ladder to be hang'd, he prayed earneſtly that God would inflict ſome viſible Judgment on his Uncle, who out of Covetouſneſs had procur'd his Death. The Uncle happen'd after this to be walking in the Church-Yard of *Kirkwall*, and as he ſtood upon the Young Man's Grave, the Biſhop's Dog run at him all of a ſudden, and tore out his Throat, and ſo he became a Monument of God's Wrath againſt ſuch Covetous Wretches: This Account was given to Mr. *Wallace* Miniſter there, by ſeveral that were Witneſſes of the Fact.

ZETLAND.

ZETLAND.

ZETLAND lies North Eaſt from *Orkney*, between the 60 and 61 Degree of Latitude; the diſtance between the Head of *Sanda*, which is the moſt Northrerly part of *Orkney*, and *Swinburgh-head* the moſt Southerly Point of *Zetland* is commonly reckon'd to be twenty or twenty one Leagues, the Tides running betwixt are always Impetuous, and Swelling as well in a Calm as when a freſh Gale blows, and the greateſt Danger is near the fair Iſle, which lies nearer to *Zetland* than *Orkney* by four Leagues.

THE largeſt Iſle of *Zetland*, by the Natives called the main Land is ſixty Miles in length from South Weſt to the North Eaſt, and from ſixteen, to one Mile in breadth. Some call theſe Iſles *Hethland*, others *Hoghland*, which in the *Norſe* Tongue ſignifies *Highland*, *Zetland* in the ſame Language ſignifies *Sealand*.

THIS Iſle is for the moſt part Moſſie and more Cultivated on the ſhore than in any other part, it is Mountainous and covered with Heath, which renders it fitter for Paſturage than Tillage. The Inhabitants depend upon

A a 2 the

the *Orkney* Ifles for their Corn. The Ground is generally fo Boggy that it makes riding Impracticable, and travelling on Foot not very Pleafant, there being feveral parts into which People funk to the Endangering their Lives, of which there have been feveral late Inftances. About the Summer *Solftice*, they have fo much light all Night that they can fee to read by it: The Sun fets between ten and eleven, and rifes between one and two in the Morning, but then the Day is fo much the fhorter, and the Night longer in the Winter: This together with the Violence of the Tides and Tempeftuous Seas, deprives the Inhabitants of all foreign Correfpondence from *October* till *April*, and often till *May*, during which fpace they are altogether Strangers to the reft of Mankind, of whom they hear not the leaft News, a remarkable Inftance of this happen'd after the late Revolution, they had no account of the Prince of Orange's late landing in *England*, Coronation, &c. until a Fifherman happen'd to land in thefe Ifles in *May* following, and he was not believed, but indited for High Treafon, for fpreading fuch News.

THE Air of this Ifle is cold and piercing, notwithftanding which, many of the Inhabitants arrive at a great Age. Of which there are feveral remarkable Inftances, *Buchannon* in his Hift. lib. 1. gives an Account of one *Laurence* who lived

lived in his time, fome of whofe Offspring do ftill live in the Parifh of *Waes*, this Man after he arrived at one hundred Years of Age Married a Wife, went out a Fifhing when he was one hundred and forty Years Old, and upon his return, died rather of Old Age, than of any Diftemper.

THE Inhabitants give an Account of one *Tairville*, who arrived at the Age of one hundred and eighty, and never drank any Malt Drink, diftilled Waters, nor Wine. They fay that his Son liv'd longer than him, and that his Grandchildren liv'd to a Good Age, and feldom or never drank any ftronger Liquors than Milk, Water or Bland.

THE Difeafe that Afflicts the Inhabitants here moft is the Scurvy, which they fuppofe is occafion'd by their eating too much Salt Fifh: There is a Diftemper here call'd Baftard Scurvy, which difcovers its felf, by the falling of the Hair from the Peoples Eyebrows, and the falling in of their Nofes, &c. and as foon as the Symptoms appear, the Perfons are remov'd to the Fields where little Houfes are built for them on purpofe, to prevent Infection. The Principal caufe of this Diftemper is believed to be want of Bread, and feeding on Fifh, alone particularly the Liver, many poor Families are fometimes without Bread, for three, four, or

A a 3

or five Months together. They say likewise that their drinking of Bland which is their Universal Liquor, and preserved for the Winter as part of their Provisions, is another cause of this Distemper. This Drink is made of Buttermilk mix'd with Water, there be many of 'em who never taste Ale or Beer, for their scarcity of Bread is such, that they can spare no Corn for Drink, so that they have no other than Bland, but what they get from Foreign Vessels that resort thither every Summer to Fish.

THE Isles in general afford a great quantity of Scurvy-grass, which us'd discretely is found to be a good Remedy against this Disease. The Jaundice is commonly cured by drinking the Powder of Shell-snails among their Drink, in in the space of three or four days. They first dry, then Pulverize the Snails, and it is observable that tho' this Dust should be kept all the Year round, and grow into Vermine, that it may be dry'd again, and Pulveriz'd for that use.

THE Isles afford abundance of Sea-fowl, which serve the Inhabitants for part of their Food, during Summer and Harvest, and the Down and Feathers bring 'em Great Gain.

THE several Tribes of Fowl here build and hatch apart, and every Tribe keeps close together, as if it were by consent. Some of the lesser

lesser Isles are so crowded with variety of Sea-fowl, that they darken the Air when the flie in great Numbers, after their coming, which is commonly in *February*, they sit very close together for some time, till they recover the fatigue of their long flight from their remote Quarters; and after they have hatched their Young, and find they are able to flie, they go away together to some other unknown Place.

THE People Inhabiting the lesser Isles, have abundance of Eggs and Fowl, which contribute to maintain their Families during the Summer.

THE Common People are generally very dextrous in climing the Rocks, in quest of those Eggs and Fowl, but this exercise is attended with very great danger, and sometimes proves fatal to those that venture too far.

THE most remarkable Experiment of this sort, is at the Isle called the *Noss* of *Brassah*, and is as follows. The *Noss* being about sixteen Fathom distant from the side of the opposite Main. The higher and lower Rocks have two Stakes fasten'd in each of them, and to these there are Ropes tied, upon the Ropes there is an Engine hung which they called a Cradle, and in this a Man makes his Way over from the greater to the lesser Rocks, where he makes a considerable purchase of Eggs and Fowl,

A a 4

Fowl, but his return being by an aſcent,makes it the more dangerous, tho' thoſe on the great Rock have a Rope tied to the Cradle, by which they draw it and the Man ſave over for the moſt part.

THERE are ſome Rocks here, computed to be about three hundred Fathom high, and the way of climbing them, is to tie a Rope about a Mans middle, and let him down with a Basket, in which he brings up his Eggs, and Fowl. The Iſle of *Foula* is the moſt dangerous and fatal to the Climbers, for many of them periſh in the attempt.

THE Crows are very numerous in *Schetland*, and differ in their colour from thoſe on the main Land, for the head wings and tail of thoſe in *Schetland* are only black, and their back breaſt and tail of a grey colour. When black Crows are ſeen there at any time, the Inhabitants ſay it is a preſage of approaching Famine.

THERE are fine Hawks in theſe Iſles, and particularly thoſe of *Fair Iſle* are reputed among the beſt that are to be had any where; they are obſerv'd to go far for their Prey, and particularly for Moor-Fowl, as far as the Iſles of *Orkney*, which is about ſixteen Leagues from them.

THERE

THERE are likewiſe many Eagles in and about theſe Iſles, which are very deſtructive to the Sheep and Lambs.

THIS Country produces little Horſes, commonly called *Shelties*, and they are very ſprightly, tho' the leaſt of their kind to be ſeen any where; they are lower in ſtature than thoſe of *Orkney*, and it is common for a Man of ordinary ſtrength to lift a *Skeltie* from the ground, yet this little Creature is able to carry double. The Black are eſteem'd to be the moſt hardy, but the Pied ones ſeldom prove ſo good; they live many times 'till thirty years of age, and are fit for ſervice all the while. Theſe Horſes are never brought into a Houſe, but expos'd to the rigour of the Seaſon all the year round, and when they have no Graſs, feed upon Sea-ware, which is only to be had at the Tide of Ebb.

THE Iſles of *Zetland* produce many Sheep, which have two and three Lambs at a time; they would be much more numerous, did not the Eagles deſtroy them; they are likewiſe reduc'd to feed on Sea-ware, during the Froſt and Snow.

The

The Lesser Isles of SCHETLAND *are as follow.*

THE Isle *Trondra,* which lies opposite to *Scalloway* Town, on the West 3 Miles long, and two broad.

FURTHER to the North East lies the Isle of *Whalsey,* about three Miles in length, and as many in breadth, the Rats are very numerous here, and do abundance of mischief by destroying the Corn.

AT some further distance lie the small Isles called *Skerries,* there is a Church in one of them. These Isles and Rocks prove often Fatal to Seamen, but advantageous to the Inhabitants, by the Wrecks and Goods that the Wind and Tides drive ashoar, which often supplies them with Fuel, of which they are altogether destitute. It was here that the *Carmelan* of *Amsterdam* was cast away, as bound for the *East-Indies, Ann.* 1664. among the Rich Cargo she had several Chests of Coin'd Gold, the whole was valued at 3000000 Guilders, of all the Crew four only were saved. The Inhabitants of the small Isles, among other advantages they had by this Wreck, had the pleasure

pleasure of drinking liberally of the strong drink which was driven ashore in large Casks, for the space of three Weeks.

BETWEEN *Brassa Sound,* and the opposite Main, lies the *Unicorn,* a dangerous Rock, visible only at low Water; it is so called, ever since a Vessel of that Name perished upon it, Commanded by *William Kirkaldy* of *Gronge,* who was in eager pursuit of the Earl of *Bothwell,* and very near him when his Ship struck.

ON the East lies the Isle call'd *Fishholm*; to the North East lies little *Rue,* and on the West mickle *Rue*; the latter is eight Miles in length, and two in breadth, and has a good Harbour.

NEAR to *Esting* lie the Isles of *Vemantry,* which has several Harbours, *Orney,* little *Papa, Helisha,* &c.

TO the North West of the *Ness* lies St. *Ninian's Isle,* it has a Chappel and an Altar in it, upon which, some of the Inhabitants retain the ancient superstitious Custom of burning Candle.

PAPA-STOUR is two Miles in length, it excells any Isle of its extent for all the Conveniences of humane Life; it has four good Harbours

bours, one of which looks to the South, another to the Weft, and two to the North.

THE *Lyra-Skerries*, fo called from the Fowl of that Name that abound in them, lie near this Ifle.

ABOUT fix Leagues Weft of the Main, lies the Ifle *Foula*, about three Miles in length, it has a Rock remarkable for its heighth, which is feen from *Orkney* when the Weather is fair, it hath an Harbour on one fide.

THE Ifle of *Braffa* lies to the Eaft of *Tingwal*, it is five miles in length, and two in breadth; fome parts of the Coaft are arable ground, and there are two Churches in it.

FURTHER to the Eaft lies the fmall Ifle called the *Nofs* of *Braffa*.

THE Ifle of *Burray* is three Miles long, has good Pafturage, and abundance of Fifh on its Coaft; it has a large Church and Steeple in it. The Inhabitants fay that Mice do not live in this Ifle when brought to it; and that the Earth of it being brought to any other part where the Mice are, they will quickly abandon it.

HAVE-

HAVEROT-ISLE, which is a Mile and a half in length, lies to the South Eaft of *Burray*.

THE Ifle of *Tell* is fixteen Miles long; and from eight to one in breadth; it lies North Eaft from the Main, there are three Churches and feveral fmall Chappels in it.

THE Ifle of *Hakafhie* is two Miles long, *Samphrey* Ifle one Mile long, *Biggai* Ifle is a Mile and a half in length, all three lie round *Round-Tell*, and are reputed among the beft of the leffer Ifles.

THE Ifle of *Fetlor* lies to the North Eaft of *Tell*, and is five Miles in length, and four in breadth, it hath a Church, and fome of the *Picts* Houfes in it.

THE Ifle *Unft* is eight Miles long, and is the pleafanteft of the *Schetland* Ifles; it has three Churches, and as many Harbours; its is reckoned the moft Northern of all the *Britifh* Dominions. The Inhabitants of the Ifle *Vaila* fay, that no Cat will live in it, and if any Cat be brought to it, they will rather venture to Sea, than ftay in the Ifle. They fay, that a Cat was feen upon the Ifle about fifty years ago, but how it came there was unknown. They obferv'd obſerv'd about the ſame time, how the Proprietor was in great Torment, and as they ſuppoſe by Witchcraft, of which they ſay he then died. There is no account of any Cat to have been ſeen in the Iſle ever ſince that Gentlemans death, except when they were carried to it, for making the above-mentioned Experiment.

THE Inhabitants ſay, that if a Compaſs be plac'd at the Houſe of *Udſta*, on the Weſt ſide of the Iſle *Fetlor*, the Needle will be in perpetual diſorder, without fixing to any one Pole; and that being tried afterwards in the top of that Houſe, it had the ſame effect. They add further, that when a Veſſel Sails near that Houſe, the Needle of the Compaſs is diſorder'd in the ſame manner.

THERE is a yellow ſort of Mettle lately diſcover'd in the Iſle of *Uzia*, but the Inhabitants had not found a way to melt it, ſo that it is not yet turn'd to any account.

The

The Ancient Court of Juſtice.

IN theſe Iſlands was held in a *Holm* in the Pariſh of *Tingwall*, in the middle of the Main Land. This *Holm* is an Iſland in the middle of a Freſh water-Lake; it is to this day called the *Law Ting*, and the Pariſh in all probability hath its Name from it. The Entrance to this *Holm* is by ſome Stones laid in the water, and in the *Holm* there are four great Stones, upon which ſate the Judge, Clerk, and other Officers of the Court. The Inhabitants that had Law Suits, attended at ſome diſtance from the *Holm* on the other ſide the Lake, and when any of them was called by the Officer, he entred by the ſtepping Stones, and being diſmiſſed, he return'd the ſame way. This was the practice of the *Danes*. The Inhabitants have a Tradition among 'em, that after one had receiv'd Sentence of Death upon the *Holm*, he obtain'd a Remiſſion, provided he made his eſcape through the crowd of People on the Lake ſide, and touch'd *Tingwall* Steeple before any could lay hold on him. This Steeple in thoſe days was an *Aſylum* for Malefactors and Debtors to flee into. The Inhabitants of this Iſle are all Proteſtants, they generally ſpeak the *Engliſh* Tongue, and many among them retain the

ancient

ancient *Daniſh* Language, eſpecially in the more Northern Iſles. There are ſeveral who ſpeak *Engliſh*, *Norſe* and *Dutch*, the laſt of which is acquired by their Converſe with the *Hollanders*, that Fiſh yearly in thoſe Iſles.

THE People are generally reputed diſcreet, and Charitable to Strangers, and thoſe of the beſt Rank are faſhionable in their Apparel.

ZETLAND is much more populous now, than it was thirty years ago, which is owing to the Trade, and particularly that of their Fiſhery, ſo much followed every year by the *Hollanders*, *Hamburgers*, and others. The increaſe of People at *Lerwick* is conſiderable; for it had but three or four Families about thirty years ago, and is ſince increas'd to about three hundred Families; and it is obſervable that few of their Fathers were Natives of *Zetland*, but came from ſeveral Parts of *Scotland*, and eſpecially from the Northern and Eaſtern Coaſts.

THE Fiſhery in *Zetland* is the Foundation both of their Trade and Wealth, and tho' it be of late become leſs than before, yet the Inhabitants by their induſtry and application make a greater profit of it than formerly, when they had them nearer the Coaſt, both of the larger and leſſer Iſles; but now the Grey Fiſh of the largeſt

eſt ſize are not to be had in any quantity without going further into the *Ocean*, the Fiſh commonly brought by Strangers here, is Cod and Ling; the Inhabitants themſelves make only uſe of the ſmaller Fiſh and Herrings, which abound on the Coaſt of this Iſle in vaſt Shoals.

THE Fiſh call'd *Tuſk* abounds on the Coaſt of *Braſſa*, the time for Fiſhing is at the end of *May*. This Fiſh is as big as a Ling, of a Brown and Yellow Colour, has a broad Tail, it is better freſh than ſalted. They are commonly ſold at fifteen or ſixteen Shillings the hundred.

THE Inhabitants obſerve that the further they go to the Northward, the Fiſh are of a larger ſize, and in greater Quantities. They make great ſtore of Oyl, particularly of the large Gray Fiſh by them called *Seths*, and the Younger ſort *Sillucks*, they ſay that the Liver of one *Seth* affords a Pint of *Scots* Meaſure, being about four of *Engliſh* Meaſure: The way of making the Oyl, is firſt by boyling the Liver in a Pot half full of Water, and when it boils the Oyl goes to the top and is skim'd off, and put in Veſſels for uſe. The Fiſhers obſerve of late that the Livers of Fiſh are leſs in ſize than they have been formerly.

THE *Hamburgers*, *Bremers*, and others, come to this Country about the middle of *May*, ſet

B b up

up Shops in ſeveral parts, and ſell divers Commodities, as Linnen, Muſlin, and ſuch things as are moſt proper for the Inhabitants, but more eſpecially, Beer, Brandy and Bread, all which they barter for Fiſh, Stockings, Mutton, Hens, &c. and when the Inhabitants ask Money for their Goods, they receive it immediately.

IN the Month of *June*, the *Hollanders* come with their Fiſhing Buſſes in great Numbers, upon the Coaſt for Herring; and when they come into the ſound of *Braſſa*, where the Herring are commonly moſt plentiful and very near the Shoar; they diſpoſe their Nets, &c. in order, but never begin till the twenty fourth of *June*, for this is the time limited among themſelves, which is obſerved as a Law, that none will venture to Tranſgreſs. This Fiſhing Trade is very Beneficial to the Inhabitants, who have Proviſions and Neceſſaries imported to their Doors; and Imployment for all their People, who by their Fiſhing, and ſelling the various Products of the Country, bring in a conſiderable ſum of Money yearly. The Proprietors of the Ground are conſiderable Gainers alſo by letting their Houſes, which ſerve as Shops to the Seamen, during their reſidence here.

THERE have been two thouſand Buſhes and upwards, Fiſhing in this Sound in one Summer, but they are not always ſo Numerous; they generally go away in *Auguſt* or *September*.

THERE

THERE are two little Towns in the largeſt of the *Shetland* Iſles, the moſt Ancient of theſe is *Scalloway*, it lies on the Weſt ſide of the Iſle, which is the moſt Beautiful and Pleaſant part of it. It hath no Trade, and but few Inhabitants, the whole being about ninety in Number. On the South Eaſt end of the Town, ſtands the Caſtle of *Scalloway*, which is four Stories high, it hath ſeveral Conveniences and uſeful Houſes about it, and tis well furniſhed with Water. Several Rooms have been curiouſly Painted, tho' the better part be now worn off. This Ancient Houſe is almoſt ruinous, there being no care taken to repair it. It ſerved as a Gariſon for the *Engliſh* Souldiers that were ſent hither by *Cromwel*. This Houſe was Built by *Patrick Stewart* Earl of *Orkney*, *Anno* 1600. The Gate hath the following Inſcription on it. *Patricius Orchadiæ & Zelandiæ Comes.* And underneath the inſcription. *Cujus fundamen ſaxum eſt Domus illa manebit; Labilis è contra ſi ſit arena perit.* That Houſe whoſe Foundation is on a Rock ſhall ſtand; but if on the Sand it ſhall fall.

THE Inhabitants ſay, that this Houſe was Built upon the ſandy Foundation of Oppreſſion, in which they ſay the Earl exceeded; and for that and other Crimes was executed.

THERE is a high Stone erected between *Tingwal* and *Scalloway*, the Inhabitants have a

Bb 2 Tradition

Tradition that it was set up as a Monument of a Danish General, who was killed there by the Ancient Inhabitants, in a Battle against the *Danes* and *Norvegians*.

THE second and latest built Town is *Lerwick*, it stands on that side of the Sound where the Fishing is; the Ground on which it is built is a hard Rock, one side lies towards the Sea, and the other is surrounded with a Moss without any Arable Ground.

ON the North the Cittadel of *Lerwick*, which was built in the Year 1665, in time of the War with *Holland*; but never compleated. There is little more of it now left than the Walls. The Inhabitants about thirty Years ago, fished up three Iron Cannons out of a Ship that had been cast away near eighty Years before, and being all over rust, they made a great Fire of Peats round them to get off the rust, and the fire having heated the Cannon, all the three went off, to the great surprize of the Inhabitants, who say, they saw the Ball fall in the middle of *Brassa* Sound, but none of 'em had any damage by them.

THERE are many *Picts* Houses in this Country, and several of them entire to this day, the highest exceeds not twenty or thirty Foot in height, and are about twelve Foot broad in the middle

middle, they taper towards both ends, the Entry is lower than the Doors of Houses commonly are now, the Windows are long and very narrow, and the Stairs goes up between the Walls. The Houses were built for Watch Towers, to give notice of an approaching Enemy, there is not one of them but what is in view of some other, so that a Fire being made in the top of any one House, the Signal was communicated to all the rest, in a few Moments.

THE Inhabitants say, that these Houses were called *Burghs*, which in the *Saxon* Language signifies a Town or Castle fenc'd all round. The Names of fortified Places in the western Isles, are in several parts called *Borg*, and the Villages in which the Forts stand, are always with *Borg*.

THE Inhabitants of *Orkney* say, that several Burying Places among them are called *Burghs*, from the *Saxon* word Burying.

IT is generally acknowledged that the *Pights* were Originally *Germans*, and particularly from that part of it bordering upon the Baltick Sea. They were called *Phightian*, that is Fighters. The *Romans* called them *Picti*, some Writers call them *Pictavi*, either from that Name of *Phightian*, which they took to themselves, or from their Beauty, and accordingly *Boethius* in his Character of them, joins both these together.

ther. *Quod erant corporibus robuſtiſſimis candidiſq;* and *Verſtegan* ſays the ſame of them.

THE *Romans* called them *Picti*, becauſe they had their Shields painted of divers Colours. Some think the Name came from *Pichk*, which in the Ancient *Scots* Language ſignifies Pitch, that they colour'd their Faces with, to make them terrible to their Enemies in Battle, and other think the Name was taken from their painted Habit.

THIS Iſle makes part of the Shire of *Orkney*, there are twelve Pariſhes in it, and a greater Number of Churches and Chappels. *Shetland* pays not above one third to the Crown of what *Orkney* does.

THE Ground being for the moſt part Boggy and Mooriſh, is not ſo productive of Grain as the other Iſles and main Land of *Scotland*, and if it were not for the Sea-ware by which the Ground is enriched, it would yield but a very ſmall product.

THERE is lately diſcovered in divers parts, abundance of Lime-ſtone, but the Inhabitants are not ſufficiently Inſtructed in the uſe of it, for their Corn Land.

THERE is plenty of Good Peats, which ſerves as fewel for the Inhabitants, eſpecially on the Main. THE

THE *Amphibia* of theſe Iſles, are Seals and Otters in abundance; ſome of the latter are train'd to go a Fiſhing, and fetch ſeveral ſorts of Fiſh home to their Maſters.

THERE are no Trees in any of theſe Iſles, neither is there any Venomous Creature to be found here.

THERE have been ſeveral ſtrange Fiſh ſeen by the Inhabitants at Sea, ſome of the ſhape of Men as far as the middle, they are both troubleſome and very terrible to the Fiſhers, who call them Sea Devils.

IT is not long ſince, every Family of any conſiderable Subſtance in thoſe Iſlands were haunted by a Spirit they called *Browny*, which did ſeveral ſorts of Work, and this was the reaſon why they give them Offerings of the Various Products of the Place, thus ſome when they churn'd their Milk, or brewed, poured ſome Milk and Wort through the Hole of a Stone called *Brownies* Stone.

A Miniſter in this Country, had an Account from one of the Ancient Inhabitants who formerly Brewed Ale, and ſometimes read his Bible, that an Old Woman in the Family told him that *Browny* was much diſpleas'd at his reading in that

that Book, and if he did not ceaſe to read in it any more, *Browny* would not ſerve him as formerly. But the Man continued his reading notwithſtanding, and when he brewed refus'd to give any Sacrifice to *Browny* ; and ſo his firſt and ſecond Brewing miſcarried without any viſible Cauſe in the Malt, but the third Brewing proved Good, and *Browny* got no more Sacrifice from him after that.

THERE was another Inſtance of a Lady in *Unſt*, who refuſed to give Sacrifice to *Browny*, and loſt two Brewings, but the third proved good, and ſo *Browny* vaniſhed quite, and troubled them no more.

I ſhall add no more, but that the great number of Foreign Ships, which repair hither yearly upon the account of Fiſhing ; ought to excite the People of *Scotland*, to a ſpeedy Improvement of that profitable Trade, which they may carry on with more Eaſe and Profit in their own Seas, than any Foreigners whatever.

FINIS.

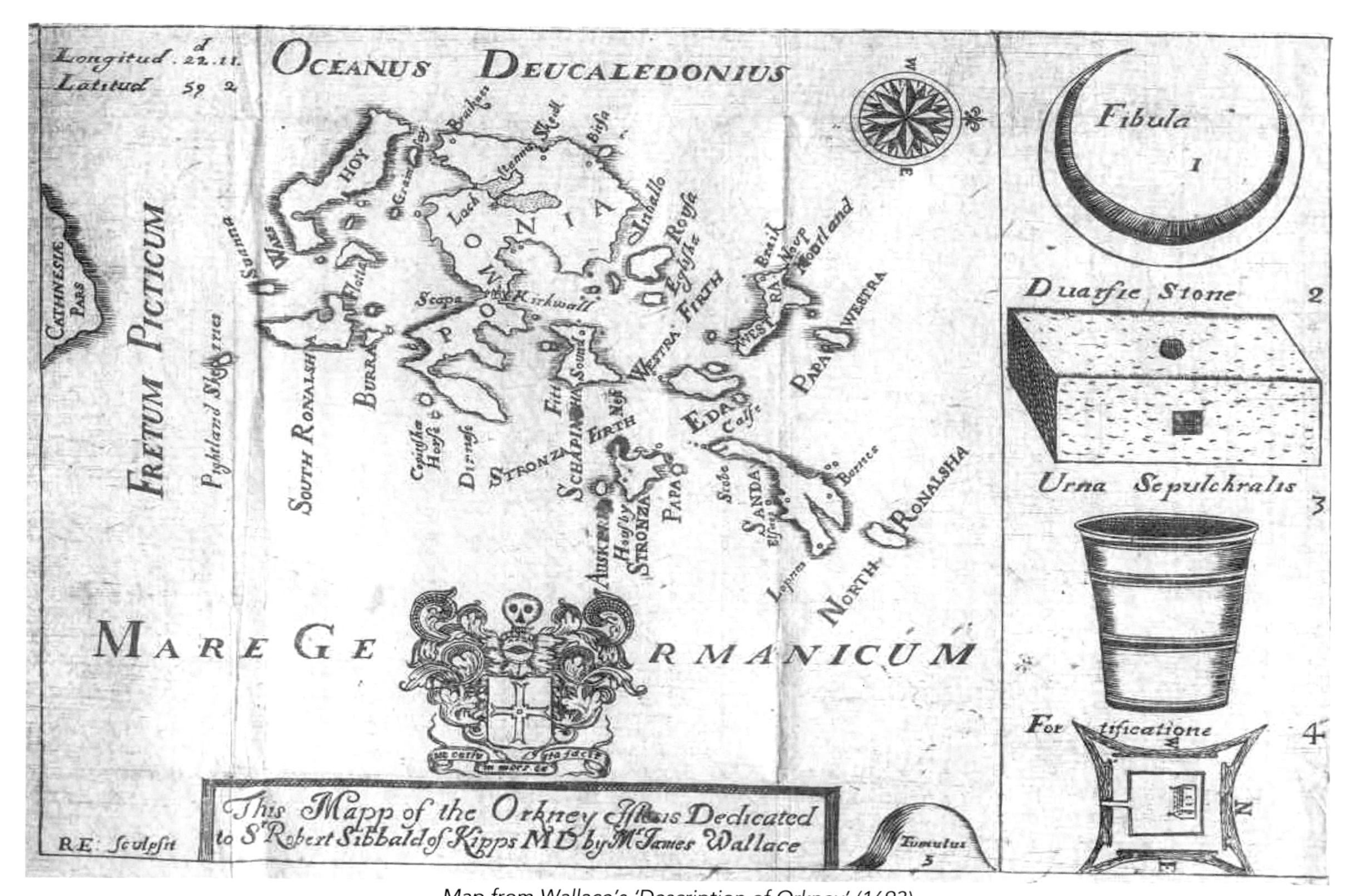

Map from Wallace's 'Description of Orkney' (1693)

Map from Sibbald's 'Description of Zetland' (1711)

of Orkney. 19

other small Lochs, which serve for no other use but to afford water to their milns & cattell. There be also some Lochs that have remarkeable properties: as St Tredwells Loch in papa westra, which they say is medicinall, & of which they say that it will appear like blood before anie disaster befall ye Royall familie. There is another Loch in Shapinsha, of which they say, that if anie wade in itt, itt will make his feet to brake out in blisters. The Loch of Swanna in the Main-land will have in some pairts a thick skume of Coper color upon itt; which makes some think yt there is some mine under itt. This Countrey is most Comodious for navigation there being everie where excellent Roads & Bays & Ports for shiping: of ye most remarkeable of which I have given and account in the first Chapter.

A South east & norwest moon causeth high water through= out all this Countrey.

Chapter 4e

The Ancient Monuments & Curiosities of this Countrey.

There is in Hoy, Lying betwixt two Hills, a ston called the Dwarfie-ston: thretie six foot Long, sixteen foot broad & nine foot thick, hollowed within by the hand of some meason (for the prints of the meason-irons are to be seen on itt to this verie hour) with a squaire hole of

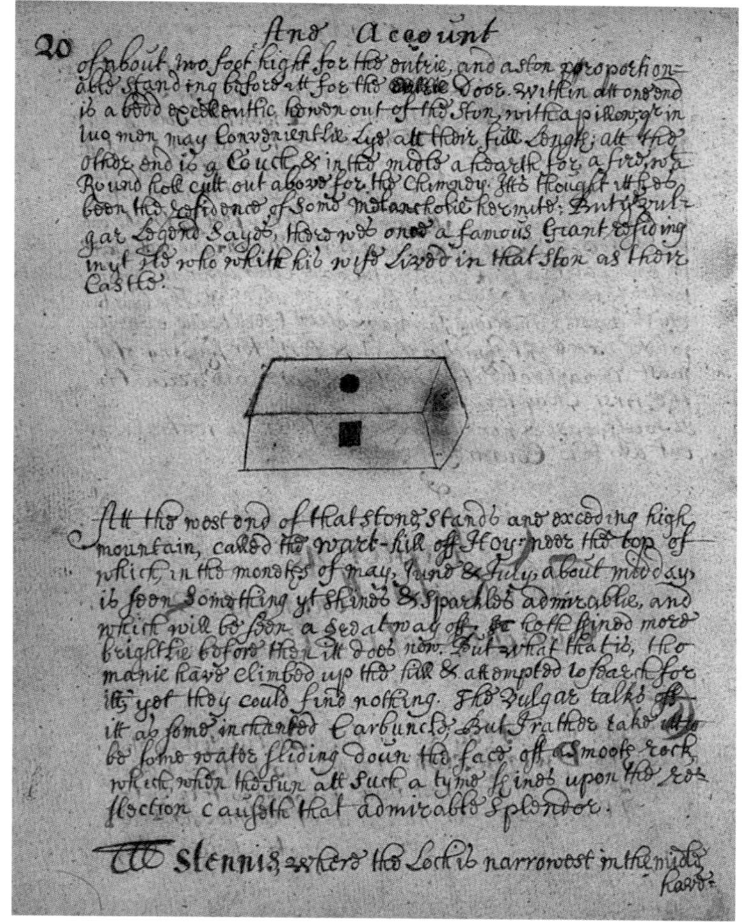

20 And Account

of about two foot hight for the entrie, and a ston proportionable standing before itt for the Doore. Within att one end is a bed excellentlie hewen out of the ston, with a pillow, qr in two men may convenientlie Lye att their full Length; att the other end is a Couch, & in the midle a hearth for a fire, wt a Round hole cutt out above for the Chimney. It's thought itt hes been the residence of some melancholic hermite: But ye vulgar Legend sayes, there was once a famous Giant residing in ye Ile who which his wife Lived in that ston as their Castle.

Att the west end of that stone stands and exceeding high mountain, called the wart-hill off Hoy: neer the top of which, in the moneths of may, June & July, about midday, is seen something yt shines & sparkles admirablie, and which will be seen a great way off. It hath shined more brightlie before then itt does now. But what that is, tho manie have climbed up the hill & attempted to search for itt, yet they could find nothing. The vulgar talks off it as some inchanted Carbuncle, But I rather take itt to be some water sliding doun the face off a smooth rock, which, when the sun att such a tyme shines upon, the reflection causeth that admirable splendour.

Att Stennis, where the Loch is narrowest in the midle, have

Pages from the manuscript of Wallace's 'Description of Orkney' (1693)

Noss-holm, Shetland.

Orkney and Shetland

Orkney

1. Martin's descriptions of Orkney and Shetland may seem out of place in a book on the 'Western Islands of Scotland', but they may have been expected of him if he made possibly a brief visit with John Adair. He seems to have drawn upon previous or contemporary accounts such as the Latin description of 1529 by 'Jo. Ben' (later translated into English), of which Sir Robert Sibbald had a copy, and *A short Relation of the most considerable things in the Orkney Islands by Mr. Matthew Mackaile Apothecarie at Aberdeen.* Mackaile perhaps wrote in the 1680s at which time he also sent letters (1683) to Sibbald. In 1693 the little book by Mr James Wallace, *A Description Of the Isles of Orkney*, was published, and issued again in 1700, so that both of these were available to Martin who drew extensively and in particular upon them. Sibbald wrote of the Orkney islands:

'what is remarkable in each of them is fully reported in the descriptions of these isles by the person [i.e.parson] of Kirkua Mr James Wallace, and his son the Doctor, in the descriptions they have published of them after diligent viewing of the Isles, and ane exact Inquiry, after what was observable in them, where also the Government of the isles, and the Historie of them and of the Planting of Religion here may be seene.'

Elsewhere Sibbald, in listing sources, noted that Rev. Wallace was 'a Learned and Ingenious Man'.

Sibbald himself wrote a brief kind of statistical account of 'The Stuartrie of Orkney' which drew upon Wallace and therefore bears some similarity to Martin's description.

[A Mitchell & J T Clark: Vol.III Preface pp.vi-xiii, pp.1-7,10-13,302-324; Sibbald Collections NLS Adv.Ms.15.1.5, Adv.Ms.33.3.16 p.29 (f.16r)]

2.The Gaelic or 'Irish' name for Orkney, given by Martin as 'Arkive' and by Wallace (p.1) as 'Arku', is still used today but normally in the spelling 'Arcaibh'.

[Dwelly (1949) p.1024]

3.The 'a or ey' ending to most island names is usually understood to be from the Norse and to signify 'island'.

4. What Martin calls 'the King's Palace' was probably the older part of the Bishop's Palace, while 'The palace now called the Bishop's' would seem to be the Earl's Palace and indeed built by Patrick Stewart around 1606.

[Inventory Vol.II pp.145-148, 142-145, nos. 402, 401]

5.The 'stately church', Sibbald's 'statelie Building', is St Magnus Cathedral.

[Inventory Vol.II pp.113-141 no.399]

6. The Charter of 1486 to Kirkwall created the town a royal burgh, and with the earlier Treaty of 1468 between Denmark and Scotland was described by John Mooney in his introduction to Charters and Other Records of the City and Royal Burgh of Kirkwall pp.xi-xiii

7. The Earl's Palace, Martin's 'King's palace', was described by Daniel Defoe in 1724 as having 'several rooms...curiously painted with Scripture stories'.

[Inventory Vol.II p.145 no.401]

8.The harbours are also in Sibbald's description (n.1 above). That at 'the bay of *Kairston* village' is south and east of Stromness. Thomson's map of Orkney had 'Korston Bow' on the coast east of Stromness and the island 'Gremsay' between Stromness and Hoy. Blaeu places 'Carestone' on Gremsay and 'Carestone holm' just to the north.

Blaeu's map shows 'Labholm' to the north of 'Burra'. Martin's advice to seamen suggests something picked up from John Adair, and that their ship sheltered off Grahamshall [Thomson: Gremshall] on the Mainland coast north of Lambholm, but in fact Wallace (p.9) gives the same directions.

9.The 'Hill of *Hoy*', otherwise known as Hoy Hill or the Ward Hill of Hoy, is indeed the highest in Orkney at 479m.

10. The Wells of Swinna are described by Wallace (p.78) in much the same way as by Martin.

12. Both Wallace (e.g. p.10 Sanda) and Martin remark on the great 'store' of rabbits in Orkney, or on the well-populated 'cuningars' (warrens).

[Wallace p.13]

13. The disease of '*Sheep-dead*' is probably now the liver-fluke, once called 'rot'.

[Wallace p.13]

14. Martin refers again to Wallace (p.17) for his information on mines of various sorts and on marble. A brief outline of Orkney's mineral resources is given in a more recent geological description [Miller p.24].

15. The '*Fin-land* Fisher-men', more usually called, as Wallace named them (p.28), 'Finnmen', appear to have no particular connection with Finland. They have been a subject of interest to various writers.

[J Brand: A New Description of Orkney, Zetland, Pightland – Firth and Caithness London 1703 pp.50-51; D. MacRitchie: The Testimony of Tradition London 1890 esp. Chapter I; D Fergus: 'Who were the Finnmen?' in Scots Magazine November 1991 pp.150-154]

16. For the snail with the bright stone see Wallace p.13 'There is a great Snail that hath a bright white stone growing in it'.

17. For '*Sperma Ceti*' and '*Ambergreese*' see: Harris n. 12.

18. The birds called 'lyres' are Manx shearwaters. Martin's bird list is largely derived from Wallace (p.16), including the 'Cleck-Goose' (Wallace: 'Claik-Goose').

19. Martin's 'Church of *Birsa*' appears to be the parish church of Birsay, where there is a window sill made of a portion of an inscribed lintel, the other portion being part of a window in a house nearby. The letters in the two pieces form the words Mons Bellus, which may have been one source for Martin's comments on '*Belus*', reputed to have been a king of Orkney. Another was probably Wallace (p.72).

[Inventory Vol.II pp.5-6 no.2]

20. '*Rothuel Hepburn*' should be 'Bothwell Hepburn', otherwise James Hepburn, Earl of Bothwell, who was created Duke of Orkney by Mary Queen of Scots.

21. Martin's references to 'the late King *William*', and soon afterwards to 'the Queen' as 'Principal Proprietor' in Orkney, indicates that he was writing at least this part of his Orkney

description in 1702 or afterwards, at most only a year before publication. He would therefore have been able to use the 'second' edition of Wallace's *Description* produced by the son, Dr James Wallace, in 1700. Another possible link with Martin is suggested by the fact that Dr Wallace was a member ('Fellow') of the Royal Society and that his father was in communication with Sir Robert Sibbald.

[Small p.viii; Wallace p.25]

22. Wallace (p.94) gave an explanation of 'Udall-lands' and 'Udaller'.

23. Martin seems to have drawn again on Wallace (p.34) for his remarks on weights and measures; the 'merk' is usually understood to be an amount of scots money (13s 4d).

24. Wallace (pp.43-52) was also Martin's source of 'The Ancient State of the Church of Orkney', in which a summary is given under Wallace's chapter heading.

25. The substance of Wallace's chapter (pp.21-28) on 'The Ancient Monuments and Curiosities of this Countrey' forms the basis of Martin's section. Most of the monuments and curiosities have been described in detail several times.

[Inventory Vol.II pp.110-112 no.385 (Dwarfie Stane), pp.299-314 nos.875-887 and possibly others, p.171 no.459 (Chapel of Cle[a]t), p.180 no.521 (St Tredwells chapel), p.282 nos. 811, 812, p.290 no.841]

26. The bleeding ridges are mentioned by Brand (1883 p.92), evidently Martin's source.

27. Raids on Orkney and on Shetland, by men from 'the western Isles' and elsewhere were the subject of traditions, and it seems probable that they did take place. After 1500 there is documentary evidence for them.

[Tudor p.59; Clouston pp.253-255]

28. Martin's reference to Dr Graham and the story of William Garioch is, in accordance with the concluding sentence, taken from Wallace (pp.37-38).

Shetland

1.It would seem that an important source of Martin's information on Shetland could have been a work published in a second edition the same year as his own Description i.e. J Brand: A New Description of Orkney, Zetland, Pightland-Firth and Caithness etc. London 1703. However it is not clear whether he had opportunity and time to see Brand's work. He may also have seen contributions from ministers resident in Shetland to the collections of information assembled by Sir Robert Sibbald as there are similarities between Martin's account and Sibbald's pages on Shetland, entitled

'Ane Description of Zetland and of the Isles thereto Belonging, full and exact done from the accounts, sent to me, by the Ministers their living, be order of their Bishop, the right reverend Doctor Mackenzie, the Bishop of Orkney at that time, and from the papers digested with this order by me.'

If Brand, a visiting minister, was one of the contributors then it might have been possible for Martin to have been shown his account by Sibbald. The latter's published account of Shetland did not appear until 1711 and was therefore too late to have been used as a source by Martin.

[Sibbald MSS NLS Adv. Ms. 15.1.5 ff.22-24; see n.8 below]

2. '*Swinburgh-head*' is clearly Sumburgh Head. Martin's version of the name is the same as that written by Brand (p.83) and by Sibbald ('Swinburgh Head'). Martin's '*Hethland*' is probably related to the 'Hjaltland' / 'Hetland' comments by Barnes. In Sibbald's account it is remarked of Shetland that 'in the Norse (the language of the old inhabitants) it is called YealtaLand'.

[M P Barnes: The Norn Language of Orkney and Shetland Lerwick 1998 p.15; Sibbald MSS as n.1 above]

3.The 'remarkable Instance' of isolation involving news of the landing in England of 'the Prince of Orange' is given by Brand (p.82). Laurence and Tairville appear in Sibbald's account (see n.1 above f.22r.)

4.On 'Bastard Scurvy' and 'a kind of Leprosy' cf. Brand (p.72), who also mentions the drinking of 'hot Bland (which is a kind of a Serum of Milk, of which more afterwards)'. The further comment follows on p.76. Sibbald (1711 p.13) gave the recipe for 'Bland or Blend'.

5.The '*Noss* of *Brassah*', its 'holm' or stack and 'cradle' were described by Brand. The 'cradle' became a famous feature as an exceptional method of reaching the holm.

[Brand pp.118-119]

6.Brand (pp.77-78) and Sibbald (See n.1 above f.23r.) both describe 'shelties'. Sibbald's account is fuller than Martin's:

'the Horses are of a small size generally, ane horse of 12 hands breadth, hight (is rare here), is esteemed very tall; but even those litle ones (which they call Shelties) are sharp and metall'd, above Beleefe, they will cary a Man with a Woman behind him 20 myles a day and live till they be 30 or 40 years of age, tho they be never stabled, summer or winter, and are not allowed shoos nor provender but fend for themselves in the open fields. Some of the Gentry have pretty big horses; for their sadle brought from Cathness or Orkney.

'the shelties g[o?] softly a naturall pace and are very sure footed in the most ragged and steep places, they are litle bigger than Asses, they are very durable. When they want food in the Hills and the fields they come doun to the coast when the sea Ebbs, (and so doe the sheep also) and eat the sea Ware. they serve the better that they be 4 years old or they be Backed, or putt to Work. these of a Black colour are esteemed most durable, and the pyot colour'd, often, prove not so good, the best of them are gott in Sanston and Eston, and they are good in Waes and Yell, these of the least size are in the Northern isles of Yell and Unste. they goe through the deep and Mossie places, wher others sink doun, and these litle ones Leap over ditches very nimbly, and mount Breas or Hillocks with heavy riders upon them. they will climb up Braes upon their knees which they could not ascend otherwise. so other big horses could not serve in this Country.'

7.The church in '*Skerries*' is dedicated to St Nicholas and is situated on Housay. The '*Carmelan*' is a common version of the 'Kennernerlandt'. The '*Unicorn*' rock is a reef off Hawks Ness between Deals and Laxfirth.

8.Fish Holm is a small island next to Linga and west of Lunna Ness at the south-eastern entrance to Yell Sound. At the mouth of Sullom Voe is the island of Little Roe, and in the inner part of St. Magnus Bay is Muckle Roe. Southward again are Vementry and Papa Little ('little *Papa*').

9. It is suggested that '*Orney*' and '*Helisha*' may be identified with Gruney and Linga.

10. '*St. Ninian's Isle*' is the striking peninsula, not an island, on the west coast of Dunrossness parish. As regards the burning of candles in the chapel, Sibbald (1711 p.36) noted of Northmaven parish that there was a ruinous chapel 'called the *Cross-kirk*, where the superstitious Commons of old used to frequent in the silence of the night, each carrying their Candles with them, and then feasted and sported until day, but this superstitious Custome is now banished'.

[Inventory Vol.III pp.44-45 nos.1185, 1186; R. Sibbald (1711) pp.15-16]

11. It is pleasant to think that Papa Stour 'excells any Isle of its extent for all the Conveniences of humane Life'. These seem to have most particularly included four harbours named, according to Sibbald, Hamna-voe, Housso-voe, Culle-voe, and possibly West Voe. The Lyra Skerries, which probably include Fogla Skerry, lie off the western tip of Papa, and take their name from the bird called the lyre – the Manx Shearwater.

[Sibbald (1711) p.32; see Orkney n.17; R Dunn pp.115-116]

12.The two churches on Bressay (Martin's '*Brassa*') are described by Sibbald (1711 p.29): 'It hath in it two Churches, the one in the North end, at Gunielstay named St. Olla's Church: the other in the East side at Cullensburgh, named St. Marie's Church, where the Minister hath his Manse.'

[Inventory Vol.III p.7 no 1103, pp.1-2 no 1083]

13. Sibbald (1711 p.26) also described the Burray church:

'Here is a Church, within a Mile to the Southmost end of the Island, standing near to the Sound side of Burray, called St Lawrence Church, (Built as it is reported, by the Mid-most of the three Norwegian Sisters, the eldest having built the Church of Tingwall, and the youngest sister the Church of Ireland) the steeple whereof, will be five or six Stories high, though a little Church, yet very fashionable, and its *Sanctum Sanctorum* (or Quire) yet remains.'

[Inventory Vol.III pp.74-75 no.1266]. The 'church of Ireland' was on St. Ninian's Isle.

14. Martin's '*HAVEROY ISLE*' is now South Havra, south of East and West Burra.

15. Sibbald (1711 p.34) wrote of Yell: 'it hath three Churches in it, in which there is Sermon, each near eight Miles distant from other...One of the Churches is named Refurd Church, which lyeth in the Southmost part of the Isle.' The Refurd Church was later known as a chapel at Reefirth, Mid Yell. There were also, according to Sibbald, 'about twentie Chapells' in the island; and the church of St Olaf is said to have served the parish of North Yell until 1750.

[Inventory Vol.III pp.158 no.1712, p.159 no.1713, p.166 nos.1733-1743 (sites of 11 out of the 20 chapels)]

17. The three islands of Hascosay ('*Hakashie*'), Samphrey and Bigga ('*Biggai*') lie off the east side and southern tip of Yell. Sibbald (1711 p.35) stated of Yell that 'to the East of it lyes *Hascosea*, two miles long; and to the South-west *Samphra* one Mile long; to the West, South-west Bigga, a Mile and a half long, all pleasant and well Grassed, and has much Fewel: all of them fit for Fishing.' Elsewhere he noted (p.12) that all were inhabited but possibly only half of Bigga belonged to Yell.

18. According to Sibbald (1711 p.35) 'there is one Church in it [Fetlar] for Sermons, and it hath ten or eleven Chapells.' When writing of Northmaven parish he mentioned (p.36) 'some old Ruinous Houses, built of dry stone, called *Picts houses* or

Broughs', and by his '*Picts* houses' in Fetlar Martin was probably referring to the remains of brochs ('Broughs').

19. Sibbald (1711 p.38) wrote that 'Unst hath three Parish Churches, one in the South part, call'd *Week*; another in the midle of it called *Balzistay*; and a third in the North part, called *Haralds-week*, and but one Minister'.

20. Udsta House is now more usually Oddsta.

21. Martin's 'Isle of *Uzia*' is the island called Uyea off the south coast of Unst.

22. The '*Holm*' in the Loch of Tingwall, once an island reached by a causeway, is now a small peninsula. '*Tingwall* Steeple' was demolished c.1790.

[Inventory Vol.III p.124 no.1522, Vol.I p.44; Sibbald (1711) p.42, where the Holm seems to be 'open fields']

23. With regard to 'the ancient *Danish* language' Sibbald (1711 p.4) uses different terms:

'The Natives are known from the Incommers by their want of surnames, having only Patronymic Names. Many of them, are descended from the *Norvegians,*and speak a *Norse* Tongue, corrupted, (they call *Norn*) amongst themselves, which is now much worn out. The Inclination of many of these of Norvegian Extract is base and Servile, Subtile and false, and Parasitick; they are wise to deceive, and if they be not restrained by severe Lawes, they are much given to Theft. They are, generally very Sharp, and consequently docile, and because of their Commerce with the *Hollanders*, they promptly speak Low Dutch.'

24. The fish called 'seth' may be what elsewhere and in the west is known as the 'saithe'.

25. For the Castle of Scalloway see Inventory Vol.III pp.118-120 no.1498.

26. The 'high Stone' between Tingwall and Scalloway is probably that standing near the south end of the Loch of Tingwall. It was measured in 1930, with a height of 6 feet 9 inches.

[Inventory Vol.II p.121 no.1505]

27. The 'Cittadel of *Lerwick*' became known as Fort Charlotte after it was repaired in 1781 and given the name of the Queen at that time.

[Inventory Vol.III pp.63-64 no.1244]

28. 'Picts' houses' were evidently brochs, as for instance that of Mousa [see n.18 above.]

29. Limestone occurs most notably at Tingwall and Whiteness, and there are veins elsewhere.

Notes and References: Bibliography

The following bibliography relates only to those collections, manuscripts and printed sources that have been found most useful for the purpose of this edition.

Abbreviations

Blaeu:	J Blaeu: Theatrum Orbis Terrarum sive Atlas Mours Pas Quinta Amsterdam 1654
DC:	Macleod Muniments, Dunvegan Castle, Isle of Skye
EUL:	Edinburgh University Library (Special Collections)
Fasti:	H Scott (edit): Fasti Ecclesiae Scoticanae 9 Vols. Edinburgh 1915-1961
FEP:	Forfeited Estates Papers
Inventory:	Reports and Inventories of the Royal Commission on Ancient and Historical Monuments of Scotland:- Ninth Report – The Outer Hebrides, Skye and the Small Isles 1928 Argyll – Vol. 1 Kintyre (Gigha) (1991); Vol. 3 Mull, Tiree, Coll & Northern Argyll (1980); Vol. 4 Iona (1982); Vol. 5 Islay, Jura, Colonsay & Oronsay (1984) Orkney and Shetland – Vols. I –III (1984)
Kirkwood:	Kirkwood Collection, New College Library, Edinburgh
MA:	Macdonald Papers, Clan Donald Centre, Armadale, Isle of Skye
MGC:	A Mitchell & JT Clark – Geographical Collections relating to Scotland made by Walter Macfarlane SHS 3 Vols Edinburgh 1906-1908
NAS:	National Archives of Scotland
NLS:	National Library of Scotland
NSA:	The New Statistical Account of Scotland – Argyleshire, Invernessshire, Ross and Cromarty
OPS:	Origines Parochiales Scotiae (edit. Cosmo Innes) Vol. II Pt. 1 Edinburgh 1854
OSA:	The Statistical Account of Scotland Reprint Vol. XX (Western Isles) Wakefield 1983
RMS:	The Register of the Great Seal

SHS: Scottish Historical Society
SND: Scottish National Dictionary
TGSI: Transactions of the Gaelic Society of Inverness
Thomson: J Thomson – Atlas of Scotland, or County Atlas Edinburgh 1931

Printed and Manuscript Sources

R. Armstrong: A Gaelic Dictionary London 1825
J A Balfour (edit.): The Book of Arran 2 vols. Glasgow 1910, 1914
J Bannerman: The Beatons – a medical kindred in the classical Gaelic Tradition Edinburgh 1986
J Bannerman: 'MacDuff in Fife' in A Grant and KJ Stringer: Medieval Scotland – Crown, Lordship and Community Edinburgh 1993
M P Barnes: The Norn Language of Orkney and Shetland Lerwick 1998
E Beveridge: Coll and Tiree – Their Prehistoric Forts and Ecclesiastical Antiquities Edinburgh 1903
E Beveridge: North Uist – Its Archaeology and Topography Edinburgh 1911
J Brand: A New Description of Orkney, Zetland, Pightland-Firth and Caithness London 1701. Second Edition 1703
J Brand: A Brief Description of Orkney, Zetland, Pightland-Firth and Caithness Reprint Edinburgh 1883
D Budge: Jura – An Island of Argyll Glasgow 1960
J B Caird: 'Early 19th Century Estate Plans' in F Macleod (edit.) Togail Tir Stornoway 1989
A Cameron: The History and Traditions of the Isle of Skye Inverness 1871
JG Campbell: Witchcraft and Second Sight in the Highlands and Islands of Scotland Glasgow 1902
J L Campbell (edit.): The Book of Barra London 1936
J L Campbell: Canna – The Story of a Hebridean Island Oxford 1984
J L Campbell and D Thomson: Edward Lhuyd in the Scottish Highlands 1699-1700 Oxford 1963
A Carmichael: 'Grazing and Agrestic Customs of the Outer Hebrides' in Report of the Royal Commissioners of Inquiry on the Condition of Crofters etc. Appendix A no.XCIX pp.451-482 Edinburgh 1884
A Carmichael: Carmina Gadelica 6 vols. Edinburgh 1900-1971

J S Clouston: A History of Orkney Kirkwall 1932

R W Cochran-Patrick: Early Records relating to Mining in Scotland Edinburgh 1878

Dictionarium Scoto-Celticum: A Dictionary of the Gaelic Language The Highland Society of Scotland 2 vols. Edinburgh 1828

R A Dodgshon: From Chiefs to Landlords – Social and Economic Change in the Western Highlands and Islands, c.1493-1820 Edinburgh 1998

R Dunn: The Ornithologist's Guide to the Islands of Orkney and Shetland London 1837

E Dwelly: The Illustrated Gaelic – English Dictionary Fifth Edition Glasgow 1949

EUL Colin Campbell Collection MS 3097.12 Letter from J Morison

D Fergus: 'Who were the Finnmen' in Scots Magazine November 1991

J Ferguson: 'The Place Names of Berneray' in TGSI Vol. LIII (1982-1984) Inverness

I Fisher: Early Medieval Sculpture in the West Highlands and Islands Edinburgh 2001

I A Fraser: The Place Names of Arran Glasgow 1999

S Gordon: The Charm of Skye – The Winged Isle London 1929

H D Graham: The Birds of Iona and Mull (edit. J A Harvie-Brown) Edinburgh 1890

I F Grant and H Cheape: Periods in Highland History London 1987

R Gray: The Birds of the West of Scotland including the Outer Hebrides Glasgow 1871

S Grieve: The Book of Colonsay and Oronsay 2 vols. Edinburgh 1923

M Harman: An Isle called Hirte Waternish 1997

J A Harvie-Brown and T E Buckley: A Vertebrate Fauna of the Outer Hebrides Edinburgh 1888

J A Harvie-Brown and T E Buckley: A Vertebrate Fauna of Argyll and the Inner Hebrides Edinburgh 1892

J K Hewison: The Isle of Bute in the Olden Time 2 vols. Edinburgh 1893-1895

D Lamont: Strath - in the Isle of Skye Glasgow 1913

R Lawson: Ailsa Craig – Its History and Natural History New edition Paisley 1895

W Lawson: Harris in History and Legend Edinburgh 2002

J Locke: Some Thoughts concerning Education London 1693

J de V Loder: Colonsay and Oronsay in the Isles of Argyll Edinburgh 1935

J Love: Rum – A Landscape without Figures Edinburgh 2001

K Macaulay: The History of St Kilda London 1764

A Macdonald: Gaelic Words and Expressions from South Uist and Eriskay (edit. J L Campbell) Dublin 1958

A & A Macdonald: The Clan Donald 3 vols. Inverness 1896-1904

D Macdonald: Lewis – A History of the Island Edinburgh 1978

A I Macinnes: Clanship, Commerce and the House of Stuart, 1603-1788 East Linton 1996

J MacInnes: 'The Panegyric Code in Gaelic Poetry and its Historical Background' in TGSI Vol. L (1976-1978) Inverness

I F Maciver: 'A 17th century "Prose Map"' in F Macleod (edit.) Togail Tir Stornoway 1989

M Mackay (edit.): The Rev. Dr John Walker's Report on the Hebrides of 1764 and 1771 Edinburgh 1980

H H Mackenzie: The Macleans of Boreray Inverness 1946

W Mackenzie: Skye – Iochdar-Trotternish and District Glasgow 1930

W C Mackenzie: History of the Outer Hebrides Paisley 1903

D MacKillop: 'Rocks, Skerries, Shoals and Islands in the Sounds of Harris and Uist and Around the Island of Berneray' in TGSI Vol. LVI (1988-1990) Inverness

J M Mackinlay: Ancient Church Dedications in Scotland (Non-Scriptural Dedications) Edinburgh 1914

A Maclean: 'Notes on South Uist Families' in TGSI Vol. LIII (1982-1984) Inverness

M MacLennan: A Pronouncing and Etymological Dictionary of the Gaelic Language Stornoway 1979

N Macleod: Raasay – The Island and its People Edinburgh 2002

P MacNab: The Isle of Mull Newton Abbot 1970

J R M MacPhail (edit.): Highland Papers SHS 4 vols. Edinburgh 1914-1934

D MacRitchie: The Testimony of Tradition London 1890

D C MacTavish (edit.): Minutes of the Synod of Argyll SHS 2 vols. Edinburgh 1943, 1944

J Marsden: Galloglas – Hebridean and West Highland Mercenary Warrior Kindreds in Medieval Ireland East Linton 2003

[Martin]: The Martins of Skye Glasgow ND

W Matheson (edit.): The Blind Harper Scottish Gaelic Texts Society Edinburgh 1970

W Matheson: 'The Morisons of Ness' in TGSI Vol. L (1976-1978) Inverness

W Matheson: 'Notes on North Uist Families' in TGSI Vol. LII (1980-1982) Inverness

J Mercer: Hebridean Islands – Colonsay, Gigha, Jura Glasgow 1974

R Miller: Orkney London 1976.

Minutes of the Synod Of Argyll NAS CH2/557

Morrison MS: The Morrison Manuscript (edit. N Macdonald) Stornoway 1975

T S Muir: Characteristics of Old Church Architecture Edinburgh 1861

T S Muir: Ecclesiological Notes on Some of the Islands of Scotland Edinburgh 1885

R W Munro: Monro's Western Isles of Scotland and Genealogies of the Clans 1549 Edinburgh 1961

A Nicolson: History of Skye – A Record of the Families, and the Social Conditions and the Literature of the Island (edit. A Maclean) Second Edition Portree 1994

A Nicolson: Sea Room – An Island Life London 2001

H Palsson: 'Aspects of Norse Place Names in the Western Isles' in Northern Studies Vol.31 Edinburgh 1996

T Pennant: A Tour in Scotland and Voyage to the Hebrides; 1772 Chester 1774

T Pennant: A Tour in Scotland 1772 Part II London 1776

F A Pottle and C H Bennett: *Boswell*'s Journal of a Tour to the Hebrides with Samuel Johnson, LL.D. 1773 London 1963

H H Read (edit.): Rutley's Elements of Mineralogy 24th Edition 1949

L Reed: The Soay of our Forefathers NP, ND

E Richards and M Clough: Cromartie: Highland Life 1650-1914 Aberdeen 1989

C M Robertson: 'Topography and Traditions of Eigg' in TGSI Vol.XXII (1897-1898) Inverness

M Robson: Rona – The Distant Island Stornoway 1991

M Robson: A Desert Place in the Sea – The Early Churches of Northern Lewis Ness 1997

M Robson: Cornelius Con – An Irish Priest in the Hebrides Port of Ness 2002

W D H Sellar and A Maclean: The Highland Clan MacNeacail (MacNicol) – A History of the Nicolsons of Scorrybreac (edit. CBH Nicholson) Waternish 1999

Sibbald Collection NLS Adv. MSS

R Sibbald: The Description of the Isles of Orkney and Zetland [Shetland] Edinburgh 1711

A M Sinclair: The Clan Gillean Charlottetown 1899

W F Skene: Celtic Scotland – A History of Ancient Alban 3 vols. Edinburgh 1876-1880

J Small (edit.): A Description of the Isles of Orkney by the Rev. James Wallace Edinburgh 1883

G G Smith: The Book of Islay Privately Printed 1895

K A Steer and J W M Bannerman: Late Medieval Monumental Sculpture in the West Highlands Edinburgh 1977

M Storrie: Islay – Biography of an Island Second edition Islay 1997

C Tolan-Smith: The Caves of Mid Argyll Edinburgh 2001

J Tudor: The Orkneys and Shetland; Their Past and Present State London 1883

D Viner: The Iona Marble Quarry Second edition Iona 1992

J Wallace: A Description of the Isles of Orkney Edinburgh 1693

J Wallace (Dr.): An Account of the Islands of Orkney London 1700

W J Watson: 'Classic Gaelic Poetry of Panegyric in Scotland' in TGSI Vol. XXIX (1914-1919) Inverness

W J Watson: The History of the Celtic Place-Names of Scotland Edinburgh 1926

P Youngson: Jura – Island of Deer Edinburgh 2001

Index

The items listed below are in many cases the versions appearing in Martin's book, with some modern equivalents, alternatives or explanations appearing alongside. The book often has different spellings for the same name or word, some of which are printing errors. Page numbers are those of the original book.